W9-BUC-217

Bread for Each Day

Bread for Each Day

365 DEVOTIONAL MEDITATIONS

by

M. R. DE HAAN, M.D.

and

HENRY G. BOSCH
Editor and Co-Author

ZONDERVAN
PUBLISHING HOUSE   OF THE ZONDERVAN CORPORATION
GRAND RAPIDS, MICHIGAN 49506

BREAD FOR EACH DAY
Copyright 1962 by Radio Bible Class
Grand Rapids, Michigan

Twentieth printing   1980
ISBN 0-310-23260-0

Printed in the United States of America

DEDICATION

*This volume is joyfully dedicated to that blessed spiritual
minority who still maintain daily devotions; and in particular to that select group of 414 men, women, and
children who in the past year have written to
tell us that through reading one or more
of these meditations they have been
led to receive Him who is the
"True Living Bread!"*

INTRODUCTION

For more than six years the Radio Bible Class has been publishing each month a 32-page booklet of daily meditations. Well over 2,000 churches, representing a wide diversity of denominational affiliation, receive quantities of these devotionals regularly for their constituency. Tens of thousands of interested individuals on our membership mailing list, along with hundreds who write in response to our broadcasts each week, also are sent copies. The messages in the *Our Daily Bread* booklets have been enthusiastically received by people in all walks of life, and the spiritual impact has been equally gratifying. Therefore, in answer to many requests, we have compiled some of the "cream selections" of these monthly editions in this second cloth-bound volume: *Bread for Each Day!*

We have carefully indexed all material both as to topic and Scriptural reference to facilitate its use by pastors and lay workers. We trust that its simplicity of presentation and wealth of illustrative material will commend it as well to the average Christian who is seeking practical and spiritual help in maintaining his daily devotions.

We send forth this book of Scriptural meditations with the hope and prayer that through it the blessing and comfort of God's Word may become more real to every reader for the glory of our Saviour!

The Editors
M. R. De Haan, M.D.
H. G. Bosch

Bread for Each Day

THOUGHTS ON THE NEW YEAR

READ PSALM 90

Remember me, O my God, for good. Nehemiah 13:31

Nehemiah's prayer might well be ours as we tread upon the threshold of another year. As we pause reflectively at the close of one segment of time, and hopefully look ahead to the unfolding promise of another, it is well that our thoughts turn to Him who holds our future in His loving hands. Trial, disappointment, yes, even death may face us in the coming months, but with His grace to keep us, and His rod and staff to comfort us, we need not fear. As we look trustingly to Him and ask the Saviour to remember and keep us, we may be sure that all things *will* work together *for our good* (Romans 8:28)!

> Thou standest and thou asketh,
> "What have the days in store?"
> He answereth thee, "Blessing!
> Yea, blessing more and more."
> What form that blessing taketh
> Thou mayest not yet know,
> But blessing upon blessing
> He waiteth to bestow.

It is comforting to know that each footfall into the new year ahead will lead us a step closer to the city of God! Yes, a shout, a trumpet voice, a cloud of glory, and we all may be gathered Home! If the One who *always remembers us* should suddenly appear, will He find that we too have *remembered His command* — *"occupy till I come"?*   — H.G.B.

> It may be the last of the years swiftly flying.
> It may be the year when the Master will come;
> When the land of the holy, for which we are sighing,
> Will burst into view—the Father's glad Home!
> It may be the last! when all mystery ending
> In radiant light from the sunshine of God!
> And, O, what a welcome, as we are ascending!
> 'Twill more than make up for the difficult road!
> —M. I. Reich

"God bless thy year—the rough, the smooth, the bright, the drear—
GOD BLESS THY YEAR!" — G. BROWN

DON'T JUST STAND THERE!

READ EPHESIANS 6:10-19

> *. . . speak unto the children of Israel, that they GO FORWARD.*   Exodus 14:15

Yes, go forward because you can't turn back. The year just gone cannot be recalled, its journey cannot be retraced, its mistakes cannot be undone, but we can *go forward.* This was the Lord's command to Israel soon after they left Egypt. They were saved, but it was not the end of the journey. Forward! March! That was the order. It took faith. To the right and left lay a howling wilderness, and behind them was the host of the Egyptians pressing upon them. Where else could they go but *forward?* But it must be in faith, because the way ahead was also blocked by the waters of the Red Sea. But orders were orders — and when they obeyed, the Lord divided the sea and they passed safely through while their pursuers perished in the waters.

This new year must be a year of going forward and not just standing still. I would direct my words to new converts to Jesus. For you a new spiritual year has begun, but your conversion was only the beginning, just as the birth of a baby is only the first step to maturity. The order now is *Forward! March!* You may be faced with impassable seas and unscalable mountains, but your Captain goes before. Set your aims high — don't be content with average progress. Make the most of your talents!

An Arabian prince received a new sword, and one of his friends found fault saying, "The sword is too short"; but he wisely replied, "To a brave man no sword is too short. If it be too short, take one step forward and it will be long enough." Forward, march, this year — *Don't just stand there — do something! Bon voyage!*   —M.R.D.

> Move forward! reaping as you move!
> Angels are watching from above
> Around are witnesses a host;
> Arouse ye now and save the lost —
> MOVE FORWARD!
>   — G. W. Crofts

"If you cannot do great things, you can at least do small things in a great way!"

"TAKE UP THY BED"

READ MARK 2:1-12

> . . . *Arise, and take up thy bed, and walk.* Mark 2:9

A man in great misery of soul, not knowing which way to turn, was wandering one evening along a country lane in England. He continued walking until at length, completely exhausted, he decided to rest for a few moments beside a nearby hedge. As he sat there, he heard two girls talking on the other side. They were speaking to one another about a sermon which they heard in a London church. One of them said of the pastor, "I heard him preach just once, but it gave me a big spiritual lift. I shall never forget one thing in particular that he said." The other girl asked what it was that the preacher had presented which had so greatly stirred her. The other replied that in speaking of the paralytic and his marvelous cure, as recorded in Mark 2, the minister had declared, "The world will always say, '*You made your bed, and you must lie on it*'; but One greater than the world has said, '*Take up thy bed and walk, thy sins are forgiven.*'"

The troubled and despairing man on the other side of the hedge heard these gracious words, and through it the Holy Spirit lifted the shadow from his soul.

To every burdened one who finds forgiveness through grace, Jesus in effect says the same today: "Take up your bed — take up your cross; and then bear your burden graciously as you walk in My strength!"

If you are troubled today, and much encumbered with a load of care, heed Jesus' gracious command and "*Take up thy bed and walk!*"   —H.G.B.

> "Rise and walk," the Master speaketh
> Words of cheer to comfort thee;
> "All thy sins are now forgiven —
> Take thy cross and follow Me!"
>   —G. W.

"The bed of your affliction can become the shining trophy of your new life in Christ if you will only bear it cheerfully before the world."

THE OLD RUGGED CROSS

READ MATTHEW 27:33-50

. . . he humbled himself, and became obedient unto death, even the death of the cross. Philippians 2:8

The cross was a symbol of shame, humiliation, and disgrace. It was reserved only for the worst criminals, who were guilty of the most dastardly crimes. It was a pagan instrument of torture and execution. The cross itself was a crude, unfinished piece of rough timber, hastily nailed together from almost any branch or piece of wood. It was a rugged cross, and symbolized entire disgrace and deepest humiliation. Few people think of the cross in that way; instead, they conceive it to be a beautiful ornament worn as a piece of jewelry about the neck, or as a stick pin, or as something to be worn on the lapel of one's coat.

Man has tried to remove the shame and horror of the cross by beautifying it, covering it with gold, plating it with silver, or setting it with precious stones. It is even covered with luminous substances, so that it glows in the dark. All these attempts to beautify the cross are totally foreign to Scripture. It was not a beautiful, gold-plated, luminous thing of beauty, but only a rough, unembellished piece of wood. It was indeed the "old rugged cross." But man seeks to avoid the "offence" of that kind of a cross and so he adorns it and makes it an inoffensive ornament. Even more unscriptural is the crucifix — a cross with a dead Christ upon it. We glory not in the crucifix with a dead Saviour upon it, but in the "empty cross" of One who is risen again from the tomb. Jesus told us to "bear His cross," but foolish man has changed it to "wear the cross." Just wearing a cross means nothing until we understand the real meaning of the crude, unadorned, unfinished, rugged cross on which Jesus died. We are never told to wear the cross — but to bear it. Then, and then only, will we know the meaning of "His" cross. The cross is the place of death. To bear His cross means to die to self and to live for Him. —M.R.D.

This the story of the Saviour,
  Through the cross He reached the Throne,
And like Him our path to glory,
  Ever leads through death alone!
        —A. B. Simpson

"The curse of the cross was changed by Christ into a blessing for us!"
        — H. D. LOES

KEEP YOUR EYES ON HIM

READ HEBREWS 12:1-3

Looking unto Jesus.   Hebrews 12:2

I have read of a great artist who made it a practice to keep a number of beautiful gems on his easel. The sparkling colors of these sapphires, emeralds, and rubies always caught the eye of his patrons. When asked the reason for keeping the jewels in such an odd place, he replied that there was a danger of his paints becoming faded by usage, and his eye getting toned down so that the tints on his canvases would lose their brilliance. Therefore he kept his eyes toned up by constantly referring to the original colors of these jewels which never fade.

There is a lesson for all of us in this story. We too are in danger of toning down our spiritual perception by looking at earthly things — things which fade. How important it is, therefore, to keep our eyes on Jesus. Let us gaze often into His face, for the brilliance of the crucified yet ever living Christ will tone up our spiritual vision and intoxicate our whole heart and life. This will help us to "walk even as He walked." Let us never tone down or allow our vision to grow dim. When we look at human fraility and earthly trial, it is so easy to "cast away our confidence," but if we "look to Jesus" our spiritual perception is heightened and our faith strengthened.

It is said that when Blondin, the great tight-rope walker, crossed the Niagara on a thin cable suspended high above the falls, he always had a star fixed on the opposite side to which he glued his eye. Had he looked down at the roaring cataract, fear might have crept into his heart, resulting in catastrophe; but by fixing his attention on the object at the end of the wire he found no difficulty in walking safely across the narrow cable. We too are not to look at circumstances but keep our eyes on Jesus. If we do, we will have no difficulty in walking the "narrow way."

—H.G.B.

Oh, look away to Jesus, when sorrow presses sore,
    And when temptations gather thick, keep looking all the more.
'Tis looking unto Jesus turns darkness into light,
    Looking unto Jesus makes it right, all right. —C. J. C.

"Look at self and you will have doubts; look at circumstances and you will be discouraged; but look to Jesus and you will always be safe, satisfied, and blessed!"

THE UNCHANGING CHRIST

READ DEUTERONOMY 8:10-20

Beware that thou forget not the LORD *. . . when . . . thy gold is multiplied.* Deuteronomy 8:11, 13

How few people can stand success and prosperity! What changes it produces in many people! There are very few people who can take success in a humble way without becoming proud and haughty. But there is One who never changes. "Jesus Christ the same yesterday, and today, and for ever" (Heb. 13:8).

An incident is related from the life of Abraham Lincoln. It was during the dark days of 1863, on the evening of a public reception given at the White House. The foreign legations were there gathered about the President. A young English nobleman was just being presented to the President. Inside the door, evidently overawed by the splendid assemblage, was an honest-faced old farmer who shrank from the passing crowd until he and the plainfaced old lady clinging to his arm were pressed back to the wall. The President, looking over the heads of the assembly, said to the English nobleman, "Excuse me, my lord, there's an old friend of mine." Passing backward to the door, Mr. Lincoln grasped the old farmer's hand and said, "Why, John, I'm so glad to see you. I haven't seen you since you and I made rails for old Mrs. ——— in Sangamon county in 1847. How are you?" The old man turned to his wife with quivering lips and, without replying to the President's salutation, said, "Mother, he's just the same old Abe!" So we say of Christ:

His *love* is the same, for it is "everlasting" (Jer. 31:3).
His *keeping* is the same, for it is constant (I Pet. 1:5).
His *power* is the same, for it is enduring (I Tim. 6:16).
His *ministry* is the same, for "he ever liveth" (Heb. 7:25).
His *pleasures* are the same, for they are lasting (Ps. 16:11).
His *promises* are the same, for they are sure (II Cor. 1:20).
He *Himself* is the same, for He is immutable (Mal. 3:6).

— M.R.D.

Yesterday, today, forever,
Jesus is the same,
All may change, but Jesus never!
Glory to His name.
—A. B. Simpson

"If wealth increases, cling more closely to Him who is ever the same, otherwise thy gold may well become thy god!"

PRACTICAL CHRISTIANITY

READ II CORINTHIANS 1:1-4

For as the body without the spirit is dead, so faith without works is dead also. James 2:26

Dorothy C. Haskin tells of a testimony meeting held in the south by a visiting Methodist minister. At this service a woman arose and began to relate how much comfort her "religion" gave her in times of trouble. "That's fine, sister," commented the visiting evangelist. "But how about the practical side? Does your 'religion' make you strive to prepare your husband a good dinner? Does it make you keep his socks darned?" Just then he felt a yank at his coattail; looking around he discovered it was the local pastor seeking to get his attention. There was a smile on his face as he whispered hoarsely, "Press dem questions, Doctor, press dem questions! Dat's my wife!"

Yes, we all need to "press dem questions" home to our own hearts. The grace of God should do more than make us happy and satisfied, it should energize us to service and good works. For instance, when God comforts us He does not do it just to make us comfortable, but rather to make us, in turn, *comforters* (see II Cor. 1:4).

It is easy to do big "showy" things for God, but it's in the little kindnesses, the humdrum details of life, that our true Christian character is most accurately mirrored.

Faith alone is like a *zero* in arithmetic: no matter how often it is repeated, it represents nothing; however, when there is added to it the *units* of our good works, then our faith becomes meaningful to others and has practical value.

Rev. J. A. Methuen once asked a simple Christian whether he thought it was possible for a child of God to live an ungodly life; he received the following answer: "Mr. Methuen, if I pour boiling water into a cup, it makes the outside hot as well as the inside. So, too, sir, when the Gospel once gets into a man's heart, the new life will soon show itself." — H.G.B.

Help me to walk so close to Thee
That those who know me best can see
I live as godly as I pray,
And Christ is real from day to day.
—B. C. Ryberg

"Faith is never so beautiful or obvious as when it has on its working clothes."

THE EYES OF GOD

READ PSALM 139:7-16

*The eyes of the Lord are in every place, beholding the
evil and the good.*   Proverbs 15:3

There is nothing hid from God. Hagar was all alone in the
desert but still could say, "Thou God seest me" (Gen. 16:13).
If we could only live in the realization that God sees all we do,
and hears all we say, and knows all our thoughts, it would keep
us from many a sin and mistake. Samuel said, "Man looketh on
the outward appearance, but the Lord looketh on the heart"
(I Sam. 16:7). God never sleeps. David says, "He that keepeth
thee will not slumber" (Ps. 121:3). This is both a comforting
and a disturbing thought. It is a comfort to the child of God
to know that a loving Father is watching constantly over him.
But it is also a disturbing thought for the sinner and for the
Christian who is not walking uprightly before Him.

The modern inventions of men have made it much easier to
understand the great truth that God sees all. For example, some
weeks ago there was flashed on the television screen a picture
of an actual operation on the heart of a man. You could see the
heart pulsating, watch the graph of the pulse beats, the fluctu-
ations in blood pressure and the rate of respiration. The operation was being performed 1500 miles away, yet by means of
television it could be seen in our homes as though we were
actually present. We marvel at this; but there is not a throb of
the human heart unknown to God. He sees it all. What a solem-
nizing thought to know that, today, our every act, word, and
thought is being noticed by Him. If He were standing right
behind me now as I write these words, looking over my shoulder,
He would not be any nearer than He actually is. In one of the
offices of the Class hangs a sign: *"You are being watched!"* O
Lord our God, help us today to do nothing which we would
hide from Thee whose "eyes behold, and eyelids try, the children
of men" (Ps. 11:4).   — M.R.D.

> There is an Eye that never sleeps
>   Beneath the wings of night;
> There is an ear that never shuts,
>   When sink the beams of light.
> Soul, guard thy ways and words today,
>   For thou art in His sight!
>   —Anon.

**"No man has absolute privacy; God and angels constantly behold
him." — G. W.**

A DISCOURAGING WAY

READ NUMBERS 21:1-5

*. . . and the soul of the people was much discouraged
because of the way.* Numbers 21:4

Because the hostile people and unfriendly land of Edom
barred the approaches to Canaan, the children of Israel had to
go on a long, roundabout march that was not at all pleasant.
Their passage was accompanied by much discomfort. For one
thing, their route was extremely stony, hot, and sandy; and for
another, the water was scarce. Yet they should have realized that
the Lord who had led them with a mighty hand out of Egypt
and provided them with daily manna from heaven would certainly guard and keep them as they traveled this new and
difficult way. Their faith, however, was weak, and soon they
fell to murmuring and complaining and were much discouraged.

Can we not see in this picture of the weary and fearful
Israelites our own silhouette in bold relief? Often the way to
Heaven too seems roundabout and long. In the wilderness of this
world we find dry, arid stretches, rough going, and many hostile
foes. Yet, if we look back to the greatness of our salvation and
ahead to the vastness of the glory which is our destiny, should
we not be ashamed of our discouragement? Our most trying
afflictions here are "light" and but "for a moment" when compared with the exceeding and eternal weight of glory that awaits
us at the end of the road (II Cor. 4:17). If God is leading and
our steps are of His ordering; if our very hairs are numbered,
and He has assured us that He will supply every need (Phil.
4:19), then we have no right to murmur or to be disheartened.
Let us lift up our eyes and, seeing the Shekinah glory going on
before, let us trustingly move forward and be of good courage.
In spite of the difficulties and roughness of the way, this is the
right road Home! — H.G.B.

I cannot always see the way
    That leads to heights above;
I sometimes quite forget He leads
    Me on with hand of love.
But yet I realize the path must lead
    Me to Emmanuel's Land,
And when I reach life's summit, I
    Shall know and understand.
—Anon.

"When faithfulness is most difficult, it is most necessary."

HE FIGHTS FOR US

READ ZECHARIAH 4:1-7

*. . . In returning and rest shall ye be saved; in quietness
and in confidence shall be your strength.* Isaiah 30:15

Israel was in trouble, and instead of turning to the Lord for
help, they tried to solve their own problems and turned to Egypt
for help. They are reminded that the battle is the Lord's if they
will but trust Him. "In quietness and in confidence shall be your
strength." We need to learn our own weakness before we can
appreciate His strength, and often the Lord lays us aside for
awhile to teach us this lesson.

How many of you, during your days of health, felt that you
were indispensable? You were convinced that if anything happened to you, everything would go wrong. You *had* to be there.
You rushed and fretted and hurried around and then the Lord,
probably to rebuke you, laid you aside, and you found out to
your surprise that they got along as well without you. God saw
you through experiences which you thought you could never
endure. You learned that God can undertake and do things far
beyond comprehension! Zechariah 4:6 says: "Not by might, nor
by power, but by my spirit, saith the Lord of hosts."

Are you one of God's shut-ins? Did you have to learn some
of these hard lessons? Ah, then your life has been enriched, and
I know that even now you can praise God for His wonderful
dealings.

A gardener planted a flower bush beside the wall of his
garden, cared for it, watered it, and nourished it, but — no
flowers. And then he noticed a flower peeping over the other
side of the wall and found the roots of his flower had penetrated
under the wall and were blooming luxuriantly on the other side.
Christian, your labor is not in vain. If you do not see it here —
you will find it blooming on the "other side."   — M.R.D.

Shall defeat, yea death cause us to grieve,
And make our courage faint or fall?
Nay, let us faith and hope receive;
The "rose" still grows beyond the wall.
Scattering fragrance far and wide,
Blest by God "on the other side."

—Anon.

"Blessed is the man who can use his stumbling blocks as paving
stones in the way of spiritual service."

ESTABLISHED BUT STUCK

READ GALATIANS 5:22-26

*But grow in grace, and in the knowledge of our Lord
and Saviour Jesus Christ.*   II Peter 3:18

God is not content to simply save men, He wants to continue working through this same power of grace to impart corresponding virtues and new blessings to them. Grace, therefore, stands connected with service and growth.

Rowland Hill, watching a child enjoying himself on a rocking-horse, once wittily remarked, "He reminds me of some Christians — there is plenty of motion, but no progress." Yes, some people are established in the faith but they never mature. Because they are spiritual babies, they cannot be helpful to others nor of much service to their Saviour.

An old farmer, in describing his Christian experience, frequently used the phrase, "Well, I'm not making much progress, but *I'm established!*" One springtime when this same farmer was getting out some logs, his wagon sank into the mud in a soft place in the road. Try as he would, he could not get it out. As he sat on top of the logs viewing the dismal situation, a neighbor, who had never appreciated the principle expressed in his oft-repeated testimony, came along and greeted him: "Well, brother Jones, I see you are not making much progress, but you must be quite content for *you are well-established!*" To be "stuck" on the road of sanctification is not a very satisfactory type of establishment, but it is not uncommon.

Do you ever have anything fresh to relate concerning what the Lord has done for you, or are you constantly digging up a few old experiences when you are asked to speak a word of testimony? How much have you grown since your conversion? If God's grace hasn't energized you to service, you are "established but stuck!"   — H.G.B.

Awake, my soul, stretch every nerve
And press with vigor on;
A heavenly race demands thy zeal
And an immortal crown.
                    — P. Doddridge

"Too many Christians who glibly quote Ephesians 2:8, 9 conveniently forget verse 10. Don't just be good; be good for something."—H.G.B.

CAMOUFLAGE

READ MATTHEW 23:1-12

> *. . . why feignest thou thyself to be another?*
>
> I Kings 14:6

The wife of the wicked Jeroboam was practicing the art of camouflage. Her son was sick and she desired help from the aging prophet of the Lord, Ahijah. But she did not want the prophet to know who she was, for fear the prophet would rebuke her for their wickedness and disobedience. So she pretended to be someone else (I Kings 14:6). She thought she could disguise herself and fool the blind prophet, but the Lord had warned the prophet of her coming, and before she could even practice her deception the prophet heard her footsteps and said, "Come in, thou wife of Jeroboam; why feignest thou thyself to be another?" Her cleverness was discovered and her disguise had failed.

The sinner is like this woman. He too tries to camouflage himself and pretends to be something else than what he really is. Adam started the practice of camouflage when he tried to conceal his nakedness with aprons of fig leaves. Jacob practiced it when at the suggestion of his mother he impersonated his brother with the skins of goats on his hands and neck.

Abraham Lincoln is credited with the saying, "You can fool some of the people all of the time, and all of the people some of the time, but you cannot fool all of the people all of the time." No one can deceive God *any of the time!* Camouflage is deception; it is hypocrisy.

A group of students in an eastern university sought to confuse their professor in biology. They took the body of a moth, put on it the legs of a grasshopper, the wings of a dragon fly, and the head of a locust. They took it to the professor and asked him what kind of a bug it was, firmly convinced that he would be baffled. Without a moment's hesitation, however, he replied, "This is a humbug." Are you pretending to be something you are not? Your fig leaves will not do. Today, be genuine, be true, be "clothed with humility." Don't be a humbug!   —M.R.D.

> Let me never from Thee stray,
>   Make me humble, Lord, I pray;
> Fill my soul with joy divine,
>   Keep me, Lord, forever Thine.
>
> —Anon.

"Hypocritical piety is double iniquity!"

SPIRITUAL CONTAMINATION

READ JAMES 4:4-8

> *. . . keep (yourselves) . . . unspotted from the world.*
> James 1:27

We hear much today about contamination. For instance, we are keenly aware of radioactivity and how it can adversely affect our physical being. We know too of disease germs and viruses that attack us when we come in contact with them; but are we equally conscious of the danger of spiritual contamination?

Recently the Audubon Society called attention to the senseless slaughter of thousands of Atlantic sea birds due to the needless dumping of oil and other like substances from the ocean-going ships. The smallest amount of this material on a bird's body mats its feathers. This interferes with their proper function in flight and in providing insulation. Tests prove that a spot of oil no larger than a twenty-five cent piece will work its way through the feathers of a sea bird to bring about slow but certain death from exposure and starvation. So too, a Christian may become spotted and contaminated by dabbling in the things of the world. Compromise with evil at first may appear trifling, but if left unchecked, worldliness will permeate the character to such an extent that the testimony of the individual will become wholly ineffective.

Noah sent out two birds from the ark. One was a raven — a ceremonially unclean creature; the other, a dove, was typical of the Spirit of God and holiness. The raven did not return to the ark, even though the waters were still upon the earth. No doubt it found a place to rest upon the floating body of some dead animal. The second bird, however — a ceremonially clean creature — returned to Noah, for she could find "no rest for the sole of her foot." The dove would not alight upon an unclean thing like a corpse! Someone has said, "In a world of sin we too have the choice of being a raven or a dove—unclean or clean—spotted or unspotted."

By the power of grace let us keep ourselves uncontaminated from the things of the world.   — H.G.B.

> Is your life a shining witness
> With a testimony true?
> Could the world be won to Jesus
> Just by what they see in you?
> —Georgia B. Adams

"While the Christian must live in the world, he should not let the world live in him."

BECAUSE

READ JOHN 3:1-16

. . . because the Lord loved you . . . . Deuteronomy 7:8

Do you know the best reason in the world for anything is "BECAUSE"? It is the end of all questions and argument. When I was a boy and asked mother for something I wanted, she would often say "No." This always called for a "Why" from me, and invariably ended in mother's answer "BECAUSE." That settled it! Mother said "Because." I was yet too young to understand, and so the only satisfactory answer was "BECAUSE." Someone has said that "because" is a woman's reason; and if it is, it is the best reason in the world. You can answer more questions in less time with a final, conclusive, unquestionable "BECAUSE," than with anything else. Of course we don't know why, it's just "BECAUSE." None of us can give a good reason why we do anything. We do it "BECAUSE."

Why did you fall in love with your wife? I challenge you to give a single good reason except "BECAUSE." Don't tell me it was because she is the most beautiful woman. I challenge that statement! I married the most beautiful one! And why? "BECAUSE." Why do you like to play golf, but detest mowing the lawn? No man can give a good reason for preferring ginger ale to root beer, or beef to mutton. It is just your opinion and a thousand others will disagree with you. Be honest — it's just "BECAUSE."

But God's reason for doing as He does is also just "BECAUSE." He does not have to give a reason. All we need do is believe it. There is a verse in Deuteronomy 7:7 which will illustrate the validity of the "BECAUSE." He says to Israel, "The LORD did not set his love upon you, nor choose you, because ye were more in number than any people but BECAUSE the LORD LOVED YOU." Why did God love you? Listen! He loved you BECAUSE He loved you. That's reason enough! Do you want a better reason? There is none. Why? BECAUSE!

— M.R.D.

Because He heard my voice, and answered me,
Because He listened, ah, so patiently,
And now through grace my soul is saved, restored;
Because of this, I love — I love the Lord.

—Anon.

"God saves us from ourselves BECAUSE He wants us for Himself."
—C. N. BARTLETT

PATIENT WAITING ON GOD

READ PSALM 27

Wait on the Lord: be of good courage.   Psalm 27:14

We are all so much in a hurry! We live in an impatient age. Yet the best things that God has for us often take time to mature, and we must patiently wait on God at such occasions and not run before Him. Someone has said, "Give God time, and even when the knife flashes in the air, the ram will be seen in the thicket. Give God time, and even when Pharaoh's host is on Israel's heels, a path through the waters will be suddenly opened. Give God time, and when the bed of the brook is dry, Elijah shall hear the Guiding Voice."

> God's delays are not denials;
> You will find Him true,
> Working through the hardest trials
> What is best for you.

We are told to "run with patience" the race which is set before us. George Matheson has a wise observation in regard to this. He said, "We commonly associate patience with lying down. We think of it as the angel that guards the couch of the invalid. Yet there is a patience which I believe to be harder — the patience which can run. To lie down in the time of grief, to be quiet under the stroke of adverse fortune, implies a great strength; but I know of something which implies a strength greater still: it is the power to work under a stroke; to have a great weight at your heart and still to run; to have a deep anguish in your spirit and still perform the daily tasks. It is a Christ-like thing! The hardest thing is that most of us are called to exercise our patience, *not in bed, but in the street.*" To wait is hard, to do it with "good courage" is harder!

Do not try to hasten the unfolding of God's bud of promise; you will only spoil the perfect flower. "In patience possess your soul."
— H.G.B.

> Wait on the Lord: in confidence,
> And expectation wait;
> His promises are ever sure;
> His mercies truly great.
> —F. S. Shepard

"The STOPS of a good man are ordered by the Lord as well as his STEPS!"
— G. MUELLER

THE NEED OF PRUNING

READ JOHN 15:1-14

. . . every branch that beareth fruit, he purgeth it.
John 15:2

I have several grapevines in my garden and each year I cut out loads and loads of long spindly vines, because I know that unless I remove these, they will take all the strength that should go into fruit. So also our precious Lord prunes His children. The knife is sharp and it hurts, but the Father knows best. No vine can be fully fruitful without "pruning."

The richest, the fullest, the most fruitful lives are those that have been in the crucible of testing, that have been broken upon the wheel of tribulation. We have no right to believe that God will do anything with our lives until He has broken us. There are in this world few entirely unbroken lives that are useful to God. There are few men and women who can fulfill their own hopes and plans without interruptions and disappointments all along the way. But man's disappointments are ever God's appointments; and what we believe are tragedies are only blessings in disguise, and the very opportunities through which God wishes to exhibit His love and grace.

There are some lives in which human plans are so completely thwarted that they seem pathetic as we look at them from a merely human standpoint. Yet if we but study these lives carefully, we see that the lives which have been afflicted are most effective. Are you, my friend, being broken today? Has the dearest in life been torn from you? Have all your dreams faded? Have all your hopes failed? Then remember that if you could see the purpose of these thorns in your life from the standpoint of God's wisdom and of eternity, if you could interpret these trials in this aggregate of life's blessings, you would be able to dry your tears and praise the Lord for them all. He will not withhold any good thing "from them that walk uprightly."

— M.R.D.

These cutting trials I oft employ
From self and pride to set thee free;
And break the schemes of earthly joy,
That thou may'st seek thy all in Me!
—John Newton

"God would have no furnaces if there were no gold to separate from the dross."

INEXHAUSTIBLE GRACE

READ JOHN 1:6-16

> . . . *the God of all grace . . . hath called us unto his*
> *eternal glory by Christ Jesus.*   I Peter 5:10

"The God of all grace." This is an exceeding beautiful title applied to our Father in Heaven. He has *justifying grace* for all believers, *illuminating grace* for every seeker, *comforting grace* for the bereaved, *strengthening grace* for the weak, *sanctifying grace* for the unholy, *living grace* for the pilgrim, and *dying grace* for the end of the journey. Bring hither the pitchers of your need — the grace of God will perfectly conform itself to each specially shaped sorrow and trial.

The ocean is known by several names according to the shores it washes, but all of it is actually just part of one great flood which makes up two-thirds of the surface of our globe. We speak of the "Seven Seas" but they actually flow into each other. So it is with the grace of God; though each one in distress discovers and admires its special adaptation to his need, it is all part of His boundless love! If there be any virtue, help, and sustenance, it is from Him; for He is truly the God of *all grace.*

On the Island of Trinidad there is a crater in an extinct volcano which is completely filled with pitch. This asphalt is hard enough for folk to walk upon, although here and there gas escapes in bubbles from its surface. Men dig great chunks from this tar-like lake and load train cars full of it to pave the roads of the world. It is said, however, that no matter how large a hole is made in this Pitch Lake, no cavity will remain after 72 hours, for it immediately fills up from down below. For over 63 years they have been taking shiploads of asphalt out of this crater, yet it never runs empty. They have gone down as far as 280 feet and still they have found this black, gumlike substance bubbling up. There seems to be an unlimited supply. So, too, with God's grace, no matter how great your need, it can't exhaust His love! Put Him to the test today. His grace is sufficient!

— H.G.B.

His love has no limits; His grace knows no measure,
  His power has no boundary known unto men;
For out of His infinite riches in Jesus
  He giveth, and giveth, and giveth again!
—A. J. Flint

"Grace is infinite love expressing itself in infinite goodness!"

A WONDERFUL NAME

READ LUKE 1:57-66

. . . thou shalt call his name John. Luke 1:13

Selecting a name for the new baby has become quite a problem in our modern homes. A generation ago a certain time-honored rule was followed by naming the baby after the parents or grandparents. And then in their order came the uncles and the aunts for their share of the honors. It was a serious breach of respect to deviate from this practice. But the present generation is a backslidden clan. We utterly ignore the respect due our elders, and choose names for our children without rhyme or reason.

As a result of this evident degeneration of respect for family names, the old custom of naming babies after famous Bible characters has disappeared. The names Adam, Abel, Noah, Ezra, Enoch, Abraham, and Jeremiah have been discarded, reflecting our waning respect for the Bible.

In the Bible the naming of the baby was often no problem at all, for the parents were told by God what to name it. God told Abraham to call his son "Isaac." Zacharias was ordered to call his son "John." But the outstanding example is "Jesus." But "Jesus" is only one of hundreds of names which He bears. And all these names — Saviour, Lord, Redeemer, Prince of Peace, Mighty God, Lamb of God, etc., etc. — are gathered up by Isaiah when he says, "His name shall be called *Wonderful.*" This is the name above every other name.

A saint of God lay dying, and in his last moments could speak of nothing but Jesus. Over and over he repeated the words, "Wonderful Jesus." Before he died, a paper was discovered which imperatively required his signature. The old saint took the pen — wrote one word, and fell back on his pillow — dead. And on the paper he had written — not his own name — but the only name he could remember — "*Wonderful.*" It was the only name that mattered. — M.R.D.

> Wonderful name He bears, wonderful crown He wears,
> Wonderful blessings His triumphs afford;
> Wonderful Calvary, wonderful grace for me,
> Wonderful love of my Wonderful Lord!
> —A. H. Ackley

"God spells 'Wonderful' with five letters — J-E-S-U-S!"—G.W.

GOD OUR SHIELD

READ PSALM 18:30-35

Our soul waiteth for the Lord: he is our help and our shield. Psalm 33:20

In himself man is weak and vulnerable; therefore, he often needs a shield to protect him. Today we hear of the special equipment which is necessary to preserve human life in atomic plants and in space travel. We're also told of a radar shield, consisting of many military bases encircling American territory, which is needed to warn us of approaching danger from enemy attack. Everywhere there is talk of the envelope of air that guards the earth and its inhabitants from deadly rays and meteors that bombard us from outer space. Spiritually, too, man is certain to fall before the onslaughts of the powers of evil unless he has a "hedge" built about him by the love and providence of God. When we are saved we may claim the promise of Christ's abiding presence and protection, and we may confidently say, "He is our help and *our shield.*" Nothing can touch us that is outside His perfect will.

There is a sweet story that illustrates what it means to have Christ between us and everything else. A lady in England tells of being awakened one morning by a very strange noise. It sounded like the pecking of a bird. When she got up she saw a butterfly flying back and forth inside the windowpane in great fright. Outside a sparrow was frantically pecking and trying to get in. The butterfly did not see the glass, and expected every moment to be caught; the sparrow did not see the window either and expected every minute to catch the butterfly. Yet all the while the butterfly was as safe as if it had been miles away, because of the glass which came between it and the sparrow. So it is with Christians who are abiding in Christ. His presence is between them and every danger. How blessed to be able to look into the future confidently and say with assurance, *"Thou art my hiding place and my shield"* (Ps. 119:114). — H.G.B.

Our hope is on Jehovah stayed,
In Him our hearts are joyful made,
Our help and shield is He;
Our trust is in His holy Name,
Thy mercy, Lord, in faith we claim,
As we have hoped in Thee.

—Anon.

"Faith hath no better bed to sleep upon than the shielding providence of God."

DOUBLE VISION

READ LUKE 11:33-38

> . . . *if therefore thine eye be single, thy whole body shall be full of light.*
>
> Matthew 6:22

To be "single-eyed" does not mean to see with only one eye, but it means that both eyes see the same thing. The normal eye is so constructed that the image of the thing looked at is transmitted to the brain in such a way that both images from both eyes are blended perfectly together and appear as one. In certain diseases this perfect balance is disturbed and the patient has "double vision." He sees two objects when there is really only one. It is a serious and dangerous thing, interfering with walking and picking up things. To walk safely the eye must be single. If we are to walk worthy of Christ we must see only Him. Walking with one eye on Him and another on the world will make us stumble and fall, for Jesus says, in explaining the single eye, "no man can serve two masters."

A friend of mine has a dog so trained that he can hold a piece of juicy steak right before the dog's eyes and within a few inches of his nose. He says, "Don't touch," and the hungry dog remains motionless, with the tempting aroma filling his nostrils. But the command, "No! Don't touch" is obeyed, and for minutes not a move toward the meat is made. Finally, I noticed the secret. The dog never once looked at the meat, but all the while looked straight into the face of the master. He had a "single" eye and overcame temptation by keeping his eye on his master.

Beware of the compromise of sin. If your eyes are on Him you will walk in the light. Don't put out the light by seeing double. A drunkard staggering home one night found a candle left burning for him by his wife. "Two candles," said the poor drunk, for his drunkenness made him see everything double, "I will blow out just one of the two," said he, and as he blew it out he found himself in total darkness. Sin and compromise will rob you of the "single eye." Today *keep your eyes on Him!*   — M.R.D.

I need Thee ev'ry hour, stay Thou near by;
Temptations lose their power when Thou art nigh.
—A. Hawks

"We will not stumble if we keep our eyes on Him, for where God leads us He will light us!"

HONESTY

READ ROMANS 12:12-17

Providing for things honest, not only in the sight of the Lord, but also in the sight of men. II Corinthians 8:21

Many years ago, when my father was still living, it was my privilege to work with him during the summer months. Each morning we stopped to pick up the early edition of a local newspaper which we would read at "coffee break." One morning when we got to work my father found that by mistake he had taken two newspapers instead of one, as the edition was extremely thin that day. He thought first of paying the man the extra price for the paper the following morning, but then, after a moment's consideration, he said, "No, I had better go back with this paper, for someone will no doubt lose out on their morning news, and also I do not want Mr. K——, who is not a Christian, to think that I am dishonest." He got into his car, rode back to the store, and returned the additional newspaper. About a week later a robbery occurred in this same grocery. When they figured back the time when it could have happened, only two people had been in the store during that period: my dad, and another man! The grocer immediately eliminated my father from consideration. He said, "That man is really honest. He came all the way back here just to return a newspaper he got by mistake. It must be the other customer who is the thief." The police apprehended the culprit, who soon made a full confession. Father's honesty and Christian character had borne fruit. He had made an impression upon the worldly storekeeper. His actions had also left an indelible mark upon my young and pliable mind.

The late Dr. Will Houghton used to tell of a soldier who became a Christian through watching a believer who was also a serviceman. The thing that impressed him was the fact that although the other men of the regiment made fun of this Christian, *they always left their money in his possession for safe keeping!* How important to provide things honest in the sight of all men! Say, does your Christian *walk* square with your Christian *talk?*   — H.G.B.

The cause of much gossip and hardship and ills,
Is the fair-talking fellow who won't pay his bills.
                                                        —Anon.

"Live innocently — God is watching!" — LINNAEUS

SELF-DENIAL

READ MATTHEW 16:24-27

> *. . . let him deny himself.*   Luke 9:23

There is a great difference between "denying self" and "self-denial." We usually think of self-denial as abstaining from certain things we would like to have or do. Many people try to reduce in weight by self-denial. A certain ladies' society in a modernistic church formed a "self-denial missionary club." One day each month they would practice "self-denial day" and would refrain from cocktails and dancing and the theater, and playing bridge for money, and then they would give the money so saved for the support of missionaries to the poor benighted heathen. They practiced self-denial but knew nothing about denying *self!* To deny self is to forget self entirely and think only of others and their welfare, no matter what the cost to self may be.

A certain man visiting a lighthouse said to the keeper, "Are you not afraid here? It is a dreadful place to remain in constantly." "No," replied the man, "I am not afraid. We never think of ourselves here." "Never think of yourselves! How is that?" The reply was a good one. "We know that we are perfectly safe, and only think of having our lamps burning brightly, and keeping the reflectors clear, so that those in danger may be saved." That is what Christians ought to do. They are safe in a house built on the Rock which cannot be moved by the wildest storm, and in a spirit of holy unselfishness they should let their light gleam across the dark waves of sin, that they who are in peril may be led into the harbor of eternal safety. Those who forget themselves in living for others, live for God.

If the letters which make up the word "self" are reversed and the letter "h" is added, the "flesh" is revealed. Self is always the flesh in some form.   — M.R.D.

> Higher than the highest heavens,
>   Deeper than the deepest sea,
> Lord, Thy love at last hath conquered;
>   Grant me now my spirit's longing —
> None of self, and all of Thee!
>   —P. D. Monod

"Self is the cork in the bottle of blessing which must be removed if one is to be filled with joy and spiritual power."—I. HONCY

WOMAN'S HIGHEST CALLING

READ PROVERBS 31:10-31

And Adam called his wife's name Eve; because she was the mother of all living. Genesis 3:20

Martin Luther once said, "When Eve was brought unto Adam, he became filled with the Holy Spirit, and gave her the most sanctified, the most glorious appellation. He called her Eve, that is to say, the *Mother* of all. He did not style her wife, but simply *mother*. . . . In this consists the glory and the most precious ornament of woman."

Oh, how many today have forgotten that the highest calling of womanhood is to become a saintly, Christian mother. Attend college, be accomplished in any other field however desirable; yet a young woman has not attained to the pinnacle of success nor ascended to the heights until she has attained to motherhood. The tremendous influence of a godly woman in the family circle cannot be overestimated.

I remember my father saying that one of the main things that led to his conversion was coming home unexpectedly and finding his mother on her knees audibly pouring out her heart to God for his salvation.

John Randolph, in speaking of the influence of his Christian mother, said: "I believe I should have been swept away by the flood of French infidelity if it had not been for one thing, the remembrance of the times when my sainted mother used to make me kneel by her side, take my little hands into hers, and cause me to repeat the Lord's Prayer."

I doubt not that many mothers will be going on before when the saints of God ascend the golden streets to the throne of glory!

If you have experienced the hallowing impress of a godly mother, you have been blessed with great spiritual riches.

— H.G.B.

How sweet and happy seem those days of which I dream,
When memory recalls them now and then!
And with that rapture sweet my weary heart would beat,
If I could hear my mother pray again.
She used to pray that I on Jesus would rely,
And always walk the shining gospel way:
So trusting still His love, I seek that Home above,
Where I shall meet my mother some glad day.
—J. Rowe

"An ounce of mother is worth a pound of clergy!"

THE CURE FOR SELFISHNESS

READ I CORINTHIANS 10:23-33

> *Let no man seek his own, but every man another's*
> *wealth.*   I Corinthians 10:24

The word "wealth" may also be properly translated "welfare." If you want to lose friends, insist on talking about yourself and your own interests. If you would win friends, show an interest in their problems and trials. Paul could say: "Not seeking mine own profit, but the profit of many" (I Cor. 10:33). In this, Jesus is our great example, "For even Christ pleased not himself" (Rom. 15:3).

There is a tradition connected with the site on which the Temple of Solomon was erected. It is said to have been occupied in common by two brothers, one of whom had a family, the other did not. On this spot was sown a field of wheat. On the evening succeeding the harvest, when the wheat had been gathered in separate shocks, the elder brother said to his wife, "My younger brother is unable to bear the burden and heat of the day. I will arise, take some of my shocks and place them in his field without his knowledge." The younger brother being actuated by the same benevolent motives, said within himself, "My elder brother has a family, and I have none. I will arise, take some of my shocks and place them with his." Imagine their mutual astonishment, when, on the following day, they found their respective shocks undiminished. This course of events transpired for several nights; then each resolved to stand guard and solve the mystery. They did so; and on the following night they met each other halfway between their respective shocks with their arms full. Upon ground hallowed by such associations as this was the Temple of Solomon erected — so spacious and magnificent that it became the wonder and admiration of the world! Alas! in these days how many would sooner steal their brother's whole shock than add to it a single sheaf!   — M.R.D.

> Others, Lord, yes others,
> Let this my motto be,
> Help me to live for others,
> That I may live like Thee!
>   —C. D. Meigs

"Giving should be based on principle, regulated by system, and beautified by self-sacrifice."

HONORING MOTHER

READ PROVERBS 1:1-8

Honour . . . thy mother.   Deuteronomy 5:16

The first ten years of the life of a child lie in the heart of its mother. All the remaining years will be colored by the touches of those "mother-years." How fitting it is then that we should follow the spiritual admonition to "honor our mothers" not only one day of the year, but at all times. One can hardly over-estimate their influence.

When the mother of John Phillips Brooks died, that great preacher of a former generation, together with his brothers, erected a grave marker in grateful testimony to her saintly character. On the tombstone they inscribed these precious words spoken by Christ to a Syrophoenician mother: "Oh woman, great is thy faith, be it unto thee even as thou wilt." Indeed many men who attain true greatness trace much of their success back to the hallowing influence of such a parent. Think of Augustine, John Newton, and the zealous Wesleys whose names would otherwise probably never have lighted the pages of history. Abraham Lincoln said, "God bless my mother; all I am or hope to be I owe to her."

Think too of some of the great men of the Bible like Moses, Samuel, and Timothy — where would they have been had it not been for their praying, Spirit-led mothers?

Most of us will recall that the simple prayers our infant lips first fashioned were but the echoes from her heart. Can we fail to honor her then as we remember her night vigils, her seasons of intercession, her well-marked Bible, and her soulful words of Christian admonition? Indeed the law of self-sacrifice and devotion with which she governed her home spoke eloquently of Him who taught us of the greater love of God! What tragedy if we fail to honor Christian mothers! What eternal consequences if we forget mother's God!   — H.G.B.

> My deepest love, my mother dear,
>   And fondest thoughts go out to you,
> Not only on your natal day,
>   But on each day the whole year through.
> And now I pray that God will crown
>   Your life with joy and happiness —
> With richest blessings from above,
>   Oh, may His smile your life caress!
>   —B. P. Vander Ark

"The best monument that a child can raise to a mother's memory is that of a clean, upright life, such as she would have rejoiced to see him live."

AN OPEN DOOR

READ I CORINTHIANS 15:51-58

> *. . . I have set before thee an open door, and no man can shut it.* Revelation 3:8

The book of the Revelation has much to say about doors — both open and closed. In Revelation 3:20 Jesus stands outside a closed door knocking for admittance. In Revelation 4:1 a door is opened in Heaven and John is caught away (a picture of the rapture). In Revelation 19:11 Heaven is opened again and Jesus comes as conqueror riding upon a white horse. Today the doors are being closed upon the earth. Men's hearts are becoming harder and harder. Thousands of churches have no room for Jesus as the Son of God, Saviour, and Lord. There are thousands of churches where a sinner could go year after year and never learn how to be saved. And after a man is truly born again, he would have a hard time getting into one of these "religious social centers."

A poor simple laborer was wonderfully saved, and soon after felt that he must seek fellowship and identify himself with a church. There was only one church nearby, a beautiful and impressive building and the "nicest" people. The minister was a great orator, the choir the finest in the land, the organist of national renown. The poor man, knowing not the difference, as a babe in Christ, sought membership in this church, but when they saw his threadbare suit, they ignored him. He tried again and again, only to be ignored. And then one day (so the legend goes) he met Jesus and told Him of his difficulty. The Lord gently replied, "My child, don't let it trouble you; I Myself have tried to get into that church for years, without success." It is just a story, but a pointed one. How much more important to come through Him who said, "I am the door: by me if any man enter in, he shall be saved, and shall go in and out, and find pasture" (John 10:9). — M.R.D.

> Thou art the Way, the Truth, the Life:
> Grant us that Way to know,
> That Truth to keep, that Life to win,
> Whose joys eternal flow.
> —Anon.

"The key that unlocks Heaven doesn't fit every church door."

THE HEDGE

READ JOB 1:1-20

Hast not thou made an hedge about him?   Job 1:10

Job was a "perfect and upright" man — a real saint — and as such he was providentially protected by a "hedge" of angels (Ps. 34:7 and Heb. 1:14), and the sheltering love of God. Yet no true servant of the Lord escapes the eye of the adversary. Satan and his hosts are constantly seeking to trap us and hinder us as we walk the pilgrim pathway to the City of God. Nothing, however, can harm us or come inside the hedge unless God allows it. We are guarded on all sides by His presence, for He is *before* us (Isa. 48:17); *behind* us (Isa. 30:21); to the *right* of us (Ps. 16:8); to the *left* of us (Job 23:9); *above* us (Ps. 36:7); *underneath* us (Deut. 33:27); and — in this dispensation — even *within* us (I Cor. 3:16). When things which seem adverse happen to us, we must recognize immediately that they come to us with divine permission and definite purpose.

Austin Dibb, a pastor and true child of God, was once extremely ill. In his weakened condition, he was severely attacked by the evil one. "I have had a terrible conflict with the enemy today," he said in his quaint way. "The Devil said, 'Thou hast been my enemy all thy life, Austin, and now I have thee fast, and now I shall have my revenge on thee on the deathbed.' " "And what did you say to him then, Austin?" said a friend who had called to comfort him. The old man raised himself upon one elbow and with a loud and vigorous voice exclaimed, "I said, 'Devil, the Lord hath put a hedge about me, and thou canst not touch me.' " "What did the evil one say to that?" asked his friend. "Nothing!" replied the venerable old gentleman. "The old serpent just fled, and I fell into a peaceful sleep!" From that moment Austin Dibb had no further doubts, for he recognized his divine security and protection.

In God's care we too can be at peace, for He keeps "the hedge."   — H.G.B.

Our God hath given promise —
And His grace for this hath planned:
His child shall rest securely
In the hollow of his hand.
—Wm. M. Runyan

"When God allows extraordinary trials, He also prepares for His people extraordinary comfort."

POWDER AND PAINT

READ I PETER 3:1-6

. . . the ornament of a meek and quiet spirit, which is in the sight of God of great price.   I Peter 3:4

Good morning, ladies! I do hope you had a good beauty sleep and are ready to be witnesses for Jesus today. I suppose you spent considerable time in the "powder room" before the mirror; and wasn't it a problem to decide what you were to wear today? Will it be this dress or that one? My suede shoes or those open-toed red ones? Now sit down a moment and let me ask you: How much time did you take to make yourself attractive to the people you expect to meet today? But have you taken time to make yourself attractive and acceptable in God's sight? Peter warns against the extremes of dress and jewelry and cosmetics. There is no wrong in being well-dressed and clean. God does not want us to be "sloppy" and "tacky." But it must be modest. Are the clothes you wear today such as become a child of God, or the fashions of the world? Peter says, "Whose adorning let it not be that outward adorning of plaiting the hair, and of wearing of gold, or of putting on of apparel." Peter is warning against the danger of extremes and living only for the outward. Dare to be different! With all your make-up, will people suspect you are a child of God?

Little Tommy looked at some movies and saw a tribe of Indians painting their faces, and asked his mother the significance of this. "Indians," his mother answered, "always paint their faces before going on the warpath — before scalping, and tomahawking, and murdering."

The next evening after dinner, as the mother entertained her daughter's young man in the parlor, Tommy rushed downstairs, wide-eyed with fright. "Come on, Mother!" he cried. "Let's get out quick! Sister is going on the warpath!"

The fashion of this world passeth away.   — M.R.D.

Be humble, be modest, and don't paint your face;
Let all your adorning be seasoned with grace.
Remember, you're mortal — a vessel of clay;
And you — like earth's fashions — will soon "pass away!"
—G. W.

"Like meekness and modesty, PAINT and PRIDE often go hand-in-hand!" — I. HONCY

PHARISEES OR PUBLICANS?

READ LUKE 18:9-14

*Two men went up into the temple to pray; the one a
Pharisee and the other a publican.*   Luke 18:10

Whether we like to admit it or not, all of us are to some degree "Pharisees." It is interesting to note that the prayer life of an individual is quite indicative of his spiritual stature. If we are not humble in the presence of God Himself, then there is little hope that we will exhibit humility before men.

You remember that the Pharisee said in his prayer, "*I* fast, *I* pray, *I* give tithes." Those with humble and contrite hearts do not address God in that manner. Recognizing their innate depravity, true saints give God first place, and put themselves in the background.

A poor Hottentot in South Africa visited with a Hollander who always had daily, family devotions. On this occasion the Dutchman selected the story of the Pharisee and the publican. The poor savage, whose heart was already awakened, looked earnestly at the reader as he intoned, "God, I thank Thee that I am not as other men." "No, I am not; but I am worse," whispered the poor savage. The man read on, "I fast twice in the week, I give tithes of all that I possess." "I don't do that; I don't pray in that manner. What shall I do?" whispered the distressed Hottentot. Finally they came to the part of the publican who "would not lift up so much as his eyes unto heaven." "That's me!" said the dark-skinned hearer. "Standing afar off," read the other. "That's where I am," said the native. "But smote upon his breast, saying, God be merciful to me a sinner." "That's me; that's my prayer!" cried the poor creature, and beating on his breast, he repeated the prayer, "God be merciful to *me a sinner.*" Like the publican, he too went down to his own house that day a saved and happy man.

How much of the Pharisee is still left in you and me? How much of the publican?   — H.G.B.

God, be merciful to me,
  On Thy grace I rest my plea;
Wash me, make me pure within,
  Cleanse, oh, cleanse me from my sin.
                              —Anon.

"The beginning of greatness is to be little, the increase of greatness is to be less, and the perfection of greatness is to be nothing."
                              — D. L. MOODY

THE FOOLISH WISE MAN

Read II Samuel 17:1-23

And when Ahithophel saw that his counsel was not followed, he saddled his ass, and arose, and gat him home to his house, to his city, and put his household in order, and hanged himself, and died. II Samuel 17:23

Ahithophel was one of the counselors of the traitor Absalom, son of King David. The great King David was in dire straits and Absalom was ready to administer the decisive blow. So he called in his counselors and asked their advice. First, he called Ahithophel who gave his advice on how to capture David without destroying his army (II Samuel 17:1-4). But before accepting this advice, another counselor (Hushai) was called in. His advice was accepted and the counsel of Ahithophel was rejected. This decision was such a blow to the pride of Ahithophel that he decided to commit suicide.

Ahithophel was a wise man, for he had found a place within the inner circle of the counselors of Absalom. He was also a good businessman. Before he committed suicide he was careful to leave his business affairs in good order. He went home to "set his house in order," which, of course, implies that all his business affairs were in proper order. Moreover this man was methodical, punctual, and deliberate in all his actions. Having decided to commit suicide he would do it only in a perfectly proper and honorable (?) way. Instead of killing himself on the spot, he considers first every detail. He saddles his ass, he arises, he goes home, he goes to the bank and his attorney and takes care of all his business matters, and then goes and hangs himself.

What is the lesson? The wisest man on earth is still a fool unless he is on the side of the Lord Jesus. Ahithophel with all his fine points was on the side of Absalom instead of David. Until a man has received Jesus Christ as Lord, he is still a fool and a spiritual suicide, no matter how wise, successful, respected, and prosperous he may be in material things. Your first business today is to renew your allegiance to your King, lest tragedy overtake you.   — M.R.D.

> If with wrecks of early promise
> Many a path is strawed,
> 'Tis because some ardent dreamer
> Would not walk with God!
> —A. B. Simpson

"Knowledge is folly unless grace guides it."

THE THOUGHT-LIFE

READ PSALM 94:3-11

For as he (a man) thinketh in his heart, so is he.
Proverbs 23:7

How would you like to have your every thought for the past six months flashed upon a screen for all your acquaintances, neighbors, and church friends to see? If such a thing were possible, and you knew the showing was to be tomorrow night, I suppose you would take the first train out of town! If there is one thing which reveals the presence of the old carnal nature, it is the evil imaginations of the heart. You may fool your preacher, and even your loved ones, but God sees the inner man. The composite of the thoughts you entertain in your mind make up your true, spiritual portrait! How guilty and shamefaced we all stand before His holy scrutiny. Yet, praise God, the Holy Spirit is ever ready to help us bring "into captivity every thought to the obedience of Christ" (II Cor. 10:5).

In Mammoth Cave of Kentucky one can see enormous pillars which have been formed by the steady dropping of water from the roof of the cavern. This artistry in rock, made by the slow and silent processes of nature, is truly marvelous. It is said that a single drop of water finds its way from the surface down through the roof of the cavern to deposit its minute sediment on the floor of the cave. Another drop follows it, and still another, until the "icicle of stone" begins to grow. Ultimately it forms a tremendous pillar of massive rock. So, too, a similar process is going on in each of our hearts. Every thought which sinks into the soul makes its contribution, and the total produces the pillars of our character. Subtly and inescapably the ideas you hold in your mind help to form the facets of the personality and make up the real "you."

Take a red pencil and circle Philippians 4:8 in your Bible. It is God's recipe for your "thought-life." — H.G.B.

The foolish thoughts of sinful men,
How vain they are the Lord doth know;
He tries the hearts and judges right,
From Him all truth and knowledge flow.
—Anon.

"There is nothing so fatal to true Christian character as the constant entertaining of evil and impure thoughts!"

LOOKING IN ALL DIRECTIONS

READ PSALM 139:1-13

> *But Jonah rose up to flee . . . from the presence of the Lord.*
> Jonah 1:3

What fools men become when they disobey the commandments of the Lord. Surely Jonah knew better than to imagine that he could escape from the Lord by hiding himself in the hold of a ship. Yet how many there are who live as though God were stoneblind and cannot see what they do, and stonedeaf so that He does not hear what they say. Yet these too must know better, for the Bible says that "the eyes of the Lord run to and fro throughout the whole earth" (II Chron. 16:9). David says in Psalm 139: "O Lord, thou hast searched me, and known me. Thou knowest my downsitting and mine uprising, thou understandest my thought afar off, and art acquainted with all my ways. For there is not a word in my tongue, but thou knowest it altogether."

Why do we try to hide things from people? Why do men practice things in secret which would make them ashamed if others knew of it? Why do people think they are "getting away" with something because others are not aware of it? Do we forget that there is ONE who sees and hears all we do and say? If we don't want people to know, how is it that we are so unconcerned about the fact that God knows? *Do we really believe that God sees all?* Read again Psalm 139.

A father and little son were riding in the country and saw a watermelon patch a little way off the highway. The father said to the lad, "You watch here, while I go get a melon." He entered the patch, lifted a choice melon from the vine, and called to the boy. "Is anyone coming — look both ways." The little fellow replied, "But daddy, *shouldn't we look UP too?*" Yes, that is the most important place to look. How do you behave when no one is looking but God? Test yourself by this rule.   — M.R.D.

> You cannot hide from God, tho' mountains cover you,
>   His eye our secret thoughts behold,
> His mercies all our lives enfold,
>   He knows our purposes untold,
> You cannot hide from God!
> —A. H. Ackley

"The real character of a man may be measured by what he does WHEN NO ONE IS LOOKING."

GETTING IN SHAPE

READ PSALM 71:15-20

*For which cause we faint not; . . . though our outward
man perish.*　　　　　　　　　　II Corinthians 4:16

A well-known evangelist is quoted in an English publication
as having told the following true story in one of his campaigns.
He said: "I have a friend who during the depression lost a job,
a fortune, a wife, and a home, but tenaciously held to his faith
— the only thing he had left. One day he stopped to watch some
men doing stone work on a huge church. One of them was
chiseling a triangular piece of rock. 'What are you going to do
with that?' asked my friend. The workman said, 'Do you see that
little opening way up there near the spire? Well, *I am shaping
this down here so that it will fit in up there.*' Tears filled his
eyes as he walked away, for it seemed that God had spoken
through the workman to explain the ordeal through which he
was passing." Some of you who are reading this devotional are
also going through difficult times. Perhaps you are experiencing
a great deal of pain and physical disability. The outward man
seems to be "perishing." Yet if you are a child of God you should
not despair nor "faint"; for all these things are from the loving
hand of your Heavenly Father who is "shaping you down here
so you will fit in up there."

All of us live in houses of clay which will soon return to dust;
yet it is blessed to know that as God works upon the pliable
putty of our human frailty, it can result for us in "an eternal
weight of glory" if, through the process, our inward man is renewed and shaped more perfectly according to His divine will.
The chisel of trial may hurt, but remember, it is *"shaping you
down here so you will fit in up there!"*　　　　　　— H.G.B.

> Be this the purpose of my soul,
> 　My solemn, my determined choice,
> To yield to Thy supreme control,
> 　And in my every trial rejoice.
> 　　　　　　—Anon.

**"The wounded oyster mends his shell with a pearl; so too, God uses
our earthly trials to form jewels for His crown."**

BY FAITH WE UNDERSTAND

READ HEBREWS 11:8-14

Through faith we understand.   Hebrews 11:3

Faith begins where reason ends! As long as we can understand a thing, see it, taste it, handle it, we do not need faith to believe it. Psychologists and psychiatrists deal only in the realm of the physical and the psychical, but stop short of the spiritual. Beyond the physical and mental realm lies the infinity of faith. When we have reached the limit of logic, reason, and understanding, it is then we can rise up on the wings of faith and find that faith is the *substance* of things hoped for and the evidence of things not seen.

A certain learned psychiatrist, an avowed infidel, went to a gospel meeting with the intention of ridiculing the preacher. After the preacher had asserted his faith in Christ, the doctor challenged him and said to him, "How do you know there is, or ever was, a Christ? Have you ever seen Him?" "No!" "Have you ever tasted Him?" "No!" "Have you ever smelled Him?" "No!" He then asked, "Have you ever felt Him?" and the answer was "Yes." To the question: "What does He feel like?" the answer was, "Only those who have felt Him could understand." "Aha," said the doctor, "four of the five senses: taste, smell, hearing, and sight, tell you nothing and the fifth, feeling, you can't explain." But the simple preacher had an answer. He said, "You are a doctor and deal with pain. Did you ever see a pain?" "No!" "Taste a pain?" "No!" "Smell a pain?" "No!" "Did you ever hear a pain?" "No!" "Feel one?" "Yes, I have!" "What does it feel like?" "Well, ah, ah, it, it, well you've got to experience it to understand it." "Yes, and so it is with salvation. To all others it is foolishness!"   — M.R.D.

Skeptics all may doubt He liveth,
Yet, in me, He deigns to dwell.
In my heart I feel His presence
'Tis a joy no tongue can tell.
—G.W.

"Bible critics should be called 'Crickets,' for they do all their chirping in the dark."

THE BOLL WEEVILS OF PROVIDENCE

READ PSALM 32:7-11

I will instruct thee and teach thee in the way which thou shalt go . . . .   Psalm 32:8

In the center of the busy main street in Enterprise, Alabama, there stands one of the strangest monuments in the world. *It is a memorial in honor of an insect.* Handsomely carved in stone is the likeness of a boll weevil! Charley McCaull relates the following interesting story concerning the strange leading of Providence which led to its erection. He says, "From early plantation days all the farmers of the community struggled to raise cotton — it was their main crop. When it failed, they failed. As seasons unfolded, a serious pestilence was brought forth. A little beetle began to damage the boll of the plant. In time it became almost impossible to 'make' a crop. George Washington Carver, the Negro scientist, along with others, became desperate and began research. Peanuts were the answer. They found that this underground vegetable could be planted and harvested in the area with very little loss. Soon peanut-oil mills took the place of cotton gins, and the region became known as 'The Peanut Center of the World.' Moreover, they found their new profits far exceeded those of their former efforts. Many became wealthy due to the changeover. And the insect — however destructive — that brought such a boon of prosperity was not forgotten. The statue stands as a memorial to its work."

Is there a lesson here for us? Maybe God lets "weevils" work havoc in our lives for a purpose. *Maybe we are trying to grow cotton when we should be planting "peanuts!"*

We need to learn that delays and disappointments are often the "boll weevils of Providence" sent by a gracious God to make us plant a more profitable crop of His choosing!   — H.G.B.

Could we read the final chapter
Of our life, then we would see
Great advantages and blessings
Come from our adversity.
—M. C. Turk

"Difficulties are God's errands; when sent upon them we should recognize their necessity as the proof of His love for us, and their end as ever being our good."

PRAYING BIG

READ PSALM 62

> *. . . my expectation is from him.*   Psalm 62:5

> *Call unto me, and I will answer thee, and shew thee great and mighty things, which thou knowest not.*
>
> Jeremiah 33:3

Someone has said, "Blessed is the man who expects nothing; he shall never be disappointed." Whoever invented that gloomy beatitude (?) certainly did not know his Bible, for no one who has looked to Christ in expectation has ever been disappointed. The reason we are so impoverished is because we expect so little. We ask God for things and then we are surprised when God answers our prayers. A lady, all excited, said to me, "How wonderful! How wonderful! The Lord has answered my prayer!" But what was so wonderful about that? Was she surprised at God's answer? We should be surprised if He *did not* answer. We receive so little because we expect so little. "Call unto me, and I will answer thee, and show thee great and mighty things which thou knowest not."

A minister was visiting a poor old woman when a storm arose. Suddenly there was a flash and a mighty clap of thunder. The old lady fell to her knees and cried out, "Oh God, save me, save my house, save my cow, save the minister, my children, the people in this village . . . in every village." The minister was surprised and said, "You have covered just about everybody, Mary." After the storm was over she explained. She said she always prayed BIG because she did not want to miss anything. She had heard of a man working in a field when thunder began, who had put his head into a hole in the wall and prayed, "Lord, save what's out of me." But he should have prayed for all of him, for suddenly the wall fell and hit his head. If he had only prayed big for all of him, this judgment (as she was told) would not have come. How big are your prayers? How much of it is for *you* and *yours*, and how much for others? Ask for, and expect, big things. James says, "Ye have not, because ye ask not."

— M.R.D.

> Lord, teach me how to pray —
> Unselfish my request;
> And help me then to know
> Thou sendest what is best!
> —G.W.

"Prayer is not conquering God's reluctance, but laying hold of His willingness."

BROTHERLY LOVE

READ I PETER 1:18-22

But as touching brotherly love . . . we beseech you,
brethren, that ye increase more and more.
I Thessalonians 4:9, 10

Scripture gives five names to Christians: 1) Saints — for their holiness in Christ; 2) Believers — for their faith; 3) Witnesses — for their testimony; 4) Disciples — for their knowledge; and 5) Brethren — for their *love.*

Sometimes the latter grace is not much in evidence. Extreme sectarianism has led to much hatred, backbiting and dissension, which has caused the world to sneer and ask, "Where is the holiness and brotherly love you talk about but practice so little?" Denominations, which are man-made, should never make us so biased and spiritually unbalanced as to disregard the God-made unity of all those who are under the cleansing blood (see I John 1:7). It is well for us to remember that all Christians, no matter what church they attend, are part of the mystical Body of Christ which embraces all believers.

John Wesley was much troubled at one time in regard to the various sects and denominations. He wondered much about whether their members would finally still be accepted by God, or whether they would face eternal punishment. One night in a dream he seemed to be transported to the gates of Hell. Seizing the opportunity Wesley asked, "Are there any Roman Catholics here?" "Yes," was the reply. "Any Presbyterians?" "Yes," was again the answer. "Any Congregationalists?" "Yes." He hesitated a moment and then said, "Not any Methodists, I hope!" To his great indignation the answer was, "Yes." Suddenly his dream changed and he stood at the gate of Heaven. Once again he inquired, "Are there any Roman Catholics here?" "No," was the reply. And so down through the list he went until finally he came to the question which most interested him, "Are there any Methodists in Heaven?" He was shocked to receive the same stern reply, "No!" "Well, then," he asked, lost in wonder and surprise, "pray who are they inside?" "*Christians!*" was the jubilant answer. Let us remember to love ALL the brethren! — H.G.B.

Blest be the tie that binds
Our hearts in Christian love;
The fellowship of kindred minds
Is like to that above.
—J. Fawcett

"Some men preserve their orthodoxy in vinegar."

HOW IS YOUR SON?

READ II TIMOTHY 1:1-11

. . . is it well with the child?   II Kings 4:26

This devotional is for Christian parents. Before you go to work — this question — "Is it well with your family?" If disaster should strike today — would there be any regrets? Job prayed daily and sacrificed in advance lest his children should sin against God. What kind of a father or mother have you been?

Today a generation is growing up whose chief memory of father will be a man who came home to eat and sleep, whose sole interest was to make money, who was so busy with social and business obligations he had no time for his family. The only memory many children will have of a mother will be the vision of a giddy, painted, card-playing, highball-sipping, cigarette-smoking woman called mother, who gave them birth into this world but neglected to prepare them for the world to come.

A professing Christian businessman spent an evening at a club drinking and playing cards for large stakes. Elated over his winnings, he went home planning to tell his pampered, spoiled, indulged son he was going to buy him the coveted convertible he had wanted so long. But the son was not at home. Soon the telephone rang and a voice informed him his son was in the hospital severely injured in an accident while on a spree with the boys. The father, conscience-smitten at the thought of his son dying and being eternally lost, hurried to the hospital to find him near death. "Oh, God, save my boy," he cried as he began to pray. But the boy stopped him and gaspingly said, "No use, dad; it's too late now. You sent me to dancing school instead of Sunday school; you took me to the races and the theaters instead of to church; you never taught me the Bible, but filled the house with popular magazines. And now I'm dying, lost forever." And with that word he made the leap into eternity. The father prayed but his prayer was too late.

Father! Mother! Is it well with the child?   — M.R.D.

> Are all your children safely in?
>   What have you done their souls to win?
> If you have failed, oh now begin,
>   Tell them of Christ, and bring them in!
> — H.G.B.

"If a parent takes one step into the world, his children will take two."
— CECIL

WHO'S ON THE THRONE?

READ GALATIANS 2:16-21

> *. . . I live; yet not I, but Christ liveth in me.*
>
> Galatians 2:20

Every man's heart is a throne. Before one is saved, self reigns there supreme in arrogance and pride. Only the grace of God can dethrone the ego and let Christ have His rightful place. But even in the Christian, self is the last enemy to be destroyed. It will make any concessions if it only will be allowed to live. Self will permit the believer to *do* anything, *sacrifice* anything, *suffer* anything, *be* anything, *go* anywhere, *take any liberties, bear any crosses, afflict soul or body to any degree* . . . ANYTHING if it can only be allowed to live. Yes, it will even permit a rival if it can just have first place. *Self Dies Hard!* Yet, self must die if Christ is to reign supreme.

A famous violinist was making his way through a great American forest one day when he came to a hut in which dwelt a hermit who had left his home in the city in bitterness of heart. An old violin helped him to pass away the tedious hours. At night he took down the instrument and played some very simple airs. The master violinist said, "Do you think I might play a bit?" "I hardly think it possible; it took me years to learn, but you may try if you like." The great master took the instrument, drew his bow across the strings, and instantly the room was filled with harmony. Then he played, "Home Sweet Home," "Nearer, My God, To Thee," and other simple songs until the old hermit sobbed like a child. What a difference between the violin in the hands of the hermit and in the hands of the master! Oh, that we might let God take the bow and play upon the violin of our life the melody of His will. Say, who is sitting in the throne room of your heart — Christ, or self?   — H.G.B.

> I knelt in tears at the feet of Christ,
>   In the hush of the twilight dim,
> And all that I was or hoped or sought,
>   I surrendered unto Him.
> Crowned, not crucified! My heart shall know
>   No king but Christ, who loves me so.
>
>   —Anon.

"The first lesson in the school of Christ is self-denial."

IT'S ME, O LORD, IT'S ME!

READ JOSHUA 7:16-26

> . . . *man by man.*   Joshua 7:18

A great sin had been committed in Israel by one man, but no one knew who he was except he himself. Achan had taken some spoils in the conquest of Jericho, which had been strictly forbidden. To find the man, eleven tribes were first eliminated, and the tribe of Judah was taken. Then all the families of Judah were eliminated except one family. Then this family was examined *man by man.* One by one the members of the family were examined till they found the guilty man — Achan. After establishing his guilt, he was justly executed. Achan was found out because they were examined *one by one.* It was *man by man.* Before God we cannot hide in the crowd. We can go to Hell with the crowd, but we go to Heaven man by man — one by one. Salvation comes only when we learn to say, "It's me, O Lord, it's me." It is not enough to say, "We are all sinners," but we must confess I . . . I . . . *I, am the guilty one!* It is *man by man,* and so it will be at the judgment. Have you ever come personally as a lost sinner to Christ?

A colored Christian told a preacher, "I was saved in your meeting last winter. It was a stormy day and I was the only one in your audience. Whenever you said something hard about sinners, I looked around to see who you meant. But there wasn't anybody else, so I figured you must mean me. When you said, 'You must be born again,' I looked around to see who you meant, but there wasn't anyone else, so I said, 'Zeke, he must mean you,' and that did it, and your whole audience got saved that day." Yes, it's *man by man.* You can't be saved with the crowd.

— M.R.D.

> I need Jesus, I need Him to the end;
>   No one like Him, He is the sinner's Friend;
> I need Jesus, no other friend will do;
>   So constant, kind, so strong and true,
> Yes, I NEED JESUS!
>
> —G. O. Webster

"Salvation pushed aside is Christ denied; salvation received is Christ believed!" — G. W.

NEGLECTED OPPORTUNITIES

READ ECCLESIASTES 11:1-6

Preach the word; be instant in season, out of season.
II Timothy 4:2

Spiritual Christians should ever be good witnesses. How often we excuse ourselves, however, for not giving a word of testimony by saying, "It was not an opportune moment!" And yet the words of our text tell us to scatter the living seed both when conditions are favorable, and when they seem to give little promise of success. It is true that we must be "wise as serpents and harmless as doves," but this applies to the *method* of our approach rather than to the *season* of our sowing.

R. A. Torrey tells how one day when he and Mr. Alexander were in Brighton, England, one of the workers went out before the meeting to get a meal in a restaurant. His attention was drawn toward the man who waited upon him, and there came to his heart a strong impression that he should speak to that waiter about his soul. However, it seemed to him such an unusual thing to do that he kept putting it off. When the meal was ended and the bill paid, he stepped out of the restaurant, but still had such a feeling that he should speak to that waiter that he decided to remain outside until the man came out of work. In a little while the proprietor saw him and asked him why he was standing there. He replied that he wanted to speak to the man who had served him at the table. A very solemn look came over the proprietor's face. "You will never speak to that man again. After waiting on you, he went to his room and shot himself!"

How many similar opportunities have we disregarded?

We may testify for our Lord "in season," but how are we in scattering the seed of the Word "out of season"? — H.G.B.

> Sowing in the sunshine, sowing in the shadows,
>   Fearing neither clouds nor winter's chilling breeze;
> By and by the harvest, and the labor ended,
>   We shall come rejoicing, bringing in the sheaves.
> —K. Shaw

"The seed is the Word; the sowing time is always; and the reward is sure!"

BACK TO THE ALTAR

READ GENESIS 12:10—13:4

Unto the place of the altar, which he (Abram) had made there at the first.   Genesis 13:4

Abram had built an altar on a mountain between Bethel and Hai (Gen. 12:8); here he had worshiped and was happy. Then a famine came and Abram, unwilling to trust God, went into Egypt (type of the world) and got himself into a peck of trouble. (Did you read the Scripture at the beginning? Well! Stop! and do it now!)

After his narrow escape in Egypt he returned to the altar called "The place of the beginning," and was restored to fellowship. Are you, my friend, out of fellowship, away from the altar where you started? Remember how happy you were when you first met Jesus? What has happened? You have forgotten where you began — at the cross. Don't forget where Jesus found you — retrace your steps, confess your drifting, and begin anew at "the place of beginning."

An ancient legend tells us that the little dwarf, Zacchaeus, lived in Jericho to a ripe old age. Every morning at sunrise he would go out for a walk, and when he returned he was always beaming with joy as he began his day's work. His wife became curious to learn his holy secret and one day followed him. He went to the old sycomore tree he had climbed when Jesus saw him (Luke 19:4, 5), took a pail and proceeded to pour water on its roots all around. Then he pulled the weeds, and with folded hands, he stood reverently looking up into its branches for a few moments and said, "Thank you, Lord, thank you!" and smilingly went about his task for the day. If each day you go back to the place of the beginning and say, "Thank you, Lord!" it will keep you happy. Take time each morning — no matter how busy — for a word from Him (in the Book), and a word with Him (in prayer). Try it! It works!   — M.R.D.

Take time to be holy, the world rushes on;
  Spend much time in secret with Jesus alone,
By looking to Jesus, like Him thou shalt be;
  Thy friends in thy conduct His likeness shall see.
                                              —W. D. Longstaff

"Gratitude to God should be as habitual as the reception of His mercies is constant." — SENECA

THREE KEYS TO HAPPINESS

READ PSALM 121

> *. . . happy is that people, whose God is the Lord.*
> Psalm 144:15

An old man when asked what had robbed him most of joy, promptly replied, "Things that never happened!" All of us, I think, can look back at many needless burdens that we also put upon our shoulders, which the Lord actually never laid upon us, and which by His grace we did not have to bear. The frown of discontentment often seen upon the brow of Christians is out of place, for it is the "brand" of the "demon worry" which should have been "cast out" long ago by the sanctifying power of trust and perfect love (see I John 4:18).

Someone has said that the three keys to Christian happiness are: fret not, faint not, and fear not.

1. *Fret Not* — He loves thee — (See John 13:1).
2. *Faint Not* — He holds thee — (See Ps. 139:10).
3. *Fear Not* — He keeps thee — (See Ps. 121:5).

"When just a small child," says W. B. Davidson, "I accompanied my father on a short trip to see Grandmother, who lived three miles from our home. We remained longer than we should have, and night overtook us. Between our home and Grandmother's house was a swamp. That night the frogs' croaking and the crickets' chirping, together with the darkness and the shadows of the trees, frightened me. I inquired of my father if there was any danger of 'something catching us' but he assured me that there was nothing to dread. And so, taking me by the hand, he said, 'I will not allow anything to harm you.' Immediately my fears passed away and I was ready to face the world, for my father had me by the hand." As we rest in the love and keeping power of Christ and recognize that God holds our hand, we too shall be happy and unafraid.

Use the "three keys to happiness" to open your prison of worry and discouragement, and step out into the full joy and liberty of the sons of God!　　　　　　　　　　　　　　　　　— H.G.B.

> When the way is dim, and I cannot see
> 　Through the mist of His wise design,
> How my glad heart yearns and my faith returns
> 　By the touch of His hand on mine.
> 　　　　　　　　　　—J. B. Pounds

"Trust in God is the perfect antidote for fear."

THE POINSETTIA

READ II CORINTHIANS 6:11-18

Judge not according to the appearance.   John 7:24

For years I had admired the beautiful poinsettias in the South when we were permitted to spend a little time in Florida. They were gorgeous in their gaudy garments of purple, red, and pink. One day I remarked to a native, "What beautiful flowers on that poinsettia." The man shocked me by replying, "Those are not flowers, they are just leaves. Poinsettias are hypocrites, parading as flowers, but they lie." Then he took me over to examine one closely, and to my surprise I found that the flower itself was a little, insignificant, unattractive thing, while what I had mistaken for flower petals were only the highly colored leaves which surrounded the flower. Yes, the poinsettia is beautiful, but the flower I am told contains no nectar and it bears no useful fruit. It is a sham, a fraud, and a hypocrite. I don't like poinsettias any more. They don't even smell good.

Many men are like the poinsettia. They cultivate their outward virtues and graces and put on a great public show, but the heart is still corrupt and is hidden by the beautiful leaves. Jesus cursed the barren fig tree, not because it had leaves, but because it had leaves *without fruit!* To profess to be a Christian when there is no fruit is a mockery, and when the leaves fall there is nothing left. Adam used leaves to cover his nakedness but it could not take away his sin. The Pharisees made the most show of their religion, but in their hearts were a "generation of vipers." What a difference between the showy poinsettias and the modest sweet clover. Sweet clover has a tiny white flower and very small leaves, but it fills the air with fragrance. The bees prefer it above all others as a source of honey. It bears abundant seed and sows the whole countryside with its offspring. Religion is like a poinsettia — salvation is like sweet clover. "Judge not according to appearance."

— M.R.D.

Nothing but leaves for the Master?
Oh, how His loving heart grieves,
When instead of the fruit He is seeking,
We offer Him nothing but leaves.
—Mrs. H. S. Lehman

"Leaves are outward testimony—fruit is inward grace!" — M.R.D.

CORN OR CHAFF?

READ PSALM 1

The ungodly are . . . like the chaff which the wind driveth away.   Psalm 1:4

Chaff is a mere shadow of its former self; it is a shell, a husk — the best of it is gone. And so it is with man. As someone has said, "Man, once good wheat, has lost the kernel of all goodness — God."

Chaff is easily driven to and fro by the elements. So too the ungodly are unstable in all their ways and quickly yield to the winds of adversity and temptation.

Threshing floors in ancient times were generally situated on top of hills, or at least on high mounds of earth, so that the winds could freely do their work. When beaten with a rod and exposed to the wind, the chaff would soon be blown away, but the true grain would remain at the feet of the flailer, ready for his use. All this, in parabolic form, presents both the reactions of the wicked and of the saved in the presence of affliction. The unconsecrated soul in rebellion flies up in the face of God when it feels the sting of the rod; while the true corn falls at His feet in loving, trustful submission — ready for more acceptable service when the chastening is over.

The end of the whole matter is seen in Luke 3:17: "He will throughly purge his floor, and will gather *the wheat into his garner;* but the *chaff he will burn with fire unquenchable.*"

Friend, when the rod of affliction is laid upon you, do you fly up in God's face like the chaff — agitated and completely ruffled; or do you react as the more solid kernel of value, so full of faith and deep settled peace that you fall resignedly at His feet in humble worship — ready to be used as He sees fit? When the winds of adversity blow about you, it will soon be made manifest whether you are true "corn" or valueless "chaff"!   — H.G.B.

> The holiness for which I long,
>   Is often reached through pain,
> I know the sheaves must needs be threshed
>   To yield the golden grain.
> —Grace Troy

"When the flail of affliction is upon me, let me not be the chaff that flies in Thy face, but the corn which lies at Thy feet."

MEMORIES

READ PSALM 77:1-12

I remember the days of old.   Psalm 143:5

David was given to much meditation and reminiscing. Again and again we hear him saying, "I remember" (Ps. 42:4; 63:6; 77:10; 137:6). Memory may be either a great comfort or a great torture. The memory of our sins can haunt us to distraction. The memory of God's faithfulness is a source of infinite strength. Memory can take away fear or it can lead to despair. When David says, "I remember the days of old," he must have been thinking of his childhood days when he was just an obscure shepherd lad. Now he was a great king, and prone to become proud and haughty. Remembering how God in grace had called him, he bows humbly before Him and says, "Who remembered us in our low estate: for his mercy endureth for ever" (Ps. 136:23).

Paul says, "Wherefore remember, that ye being in time past Gentiles . . . without Christ . . . aliens . . . having no hope, and without God in the world" (Eph. 2:11, 12).

There is a story of a Persian King who was elevated from a poverty-stricken home to the glory of a royal throne. When he became king he sent his servants to the old shack where he was reared, with orders to gather every relic of those days. They brought fragments of his home; many broken toys, his patched pantaloons, an old torn and tattered shirt, a crude wooden bowl from which he ate, and numerous worthless mementos of his childhood. All these he arranged in a special room of his palace, and each day he spent one whole hour sitting among the memories of his humble past. On the wall hung a prayer: "Lest I forget." Let us keep such a chamber of memory, and daily praise Him who brought us up also out of an horrible pit, out of the miry clay, and set our feet upon a rock. Lord make me humble! Remember!

— M.R.D.

> Recalling former days
>   And all Thy wondrous deeds,
> The memory of Thy ways,
>   To hope and comfort leads.
>   —Anon.

"O memory thou bitter-sweet; thou art both a joy and a scourge."
—M. DE STAEL

THE PREACHER'S BLACK BOOK

READ GALATIANS 6:1-4

Let us not therefore judge one another any more . . . .
Romans 14:13

One of the greatest sins among believers is the error of "judging others." Only God is able to judge righteously, for He alone knows all the circumstances of our lives. Dr. DeWitt Talmadge pointedly remarked one time, "I lay this down as a rule without any exception, that those people who have the most faults themselves are the most merciless in their watching of others. From the scalp of head to soles of foot, they are full of jealousies and hyper-criticisms. They spend their life hunting for muskrats and mud turtles, instead of hunting for Rocky Mountain creatures and soaring eagles. They are always looking for something mean instead of something grand."

A noted preacher had a shrewd way of handling critics in his congregation. He had in his desk a special black book labeled *"Complaints of Members Against One Another."* When one of his people called to tell him about the faults of another he would say, "Well, here is my complaint book. I will write down what you say, and you can sign it. Then when I have time I will take up the matter officially concerning this brother." The sight of the open book and the ready pen had its effect. "Oh, no, I couldn't sign anything like that!" they would say. The result of it all was that in forty years this preacher opened his black book a thousand times but never got anyone to write a line in it.

How much better to try to *restore* those who are overtaken in a fault, and *let God be the judge* of their mistakes.   — H.G.B.

> I used to censure everyone,
>   I was a Pharisee;
> Until, quite unexpectedly,
>   I got a glimpse of me.
> —Anon.

"Where love is thin, faults are thick!"

SHEEP AND PIGS

READ JOHN 10:22-30

My sheep . . . follow me.   John 10:27

Some time ago I saw a picture of trained pigs who had been taught by the owner to follow his commands. The acts were very simple. Any dog, even a mutt, could be taught these things, and no one would think them unusual. Then why the oh's and ah's and thunderous applause from the gallery when a pig stood on its hind legs to reach an ear of corn? Simply because these were not normal pigs. They did not act like pigs. Ordinary pigs cannot be led — they must be driven to the slaughter. How different a sheep — it follows the shepherd. The shepherd "leadeth them out" (John 10:3), and "he goeth before them" (John 10:4).

A sheep not only follows the shepherd but looks up into the shepherd's face. You have all seen the beautiful painting of a shepherd holding a lamb in his arms, while the mother sheep with lifted head looks up at the lamb and the shepherd's face. But how different is the pig; it has no neck — so cannot lift its head. Its eyes are set so they look toward the ground. While a sheep grazes and browses, a pig only roots and grubs. The only way a pig can be made to look up is to turn him on his back. I visited a sick friend and told him this comparison of pigs and sheep. "Yes," he said, "I'm learning my lesson on my back in bed. I have been so busy with material things — my business, my civic duties — that I haven't been looking up as I should. And now on my back, the only way I can look is *up*. I've been so piggish, but thank God, He is turning me over." Are you on your back today, and wondering why? Maybe He is trying to teach you to look *up*, and not be so busy with earthly cares that you neglect *spiritual things!*   — M.R.D.

    Shut in?
        O hearken to thy Lord,
        And in His presence sweet abide;
        He always has some special thought
        For those whom He has called aside.
        It may be that He wants your will
        More fully yielded to His own;
        So for a while He takes your strength,
        That you may lean on Him alone.
                    —Anon.

"Keep looking up; remember there is only mud under your feet."

THE RAINBOW

READ GENESIS 9:1-17

*I do set my bow in the cloud, and it shall be for a token
of a covenant between me and the earth.*   Genesis 9:13

The rainbow springs out of the conflict between light and
darkness — it is a child of the storm. It is caused by the sun of
heaven shining upon the fast-dripping tears of earth. After the
flood it became the gracious pledge to man and every living
creature that God would never again use water to destroy the
earth.

Typically, the rainbow seen upon the billows of justice, spoke
of grace. It looked ahead to the cross where God's wrath against
sin would once-for-all be visited upon the believer's substitute,
Jesus Christ. When the *Light* of the world and the storm *clouds*
of judgment met at Calvary, a beautiful bow of promise and
forgiveness came into view. Its soft beauty and gracious promise
of eternal life ever delights the spiritual eye. It is the token that
we shall someday live with God in fellowship with all the saints
around His rainbow-circled throne (Rev. 4:1-3).

The rainbow too is a parable. It tells one and all that nothing
beautiful ever comes to pass in this life except there first be
clouds, and storms, and sorrow. Yet trial alone cannot give birth
to this beautiful spectrum of grace, for it needs not only the fast-
falling tears of distress below, but — even more important — the
sunshine and glory from Heaven above! Unless the light of God
floods our sorrow, there can be no beautiful rainbow of hope, no
glow of promise, no beauty in the darkness. In human character
there is hardly anything useful or attractive, but it has had suffering for a necessary condition — *suffering lighted up by love!*

Are you experiencing the clouds of trouble? If so, allow God's
light to fall upon them. His comfort in sorrow is assured, for
He has said: "When I bring a cloud . . . the bow shall be in (it)
. . . and *I will remember!"*   — H.G.B.

> Through gloom and shadow look we
> On beyond the years —
> The soul would have no rainbow
> Had the eyes no tears.
>
> —Anon.

"In the tears of His saints God sees a rainbow."

I AM ON MY WAY

READ II KINGS 5:20-27

> . . . *Whither goest thou?*   Zechariah 2:2

"Do you know where you are going?" I asked the driver of a car in which I was riding. I was in a strange city, and to get to my destination, the driver took all the shortcuts through alleys and back streets, and on and off the main highway with its choked lanes of cars. I was completely confused and the only direction I was sure of was "straight up." The driver assured me he knew where he was going, and I felt much better. Usually when men start on a journey they have a definite objective in view. If it is a long trip into unknown regions, they obtain all the information they can, procure road maps, and carefully choose the clothing and provisions for the journey. Yet how foolish the natural man is concerning his eternal destiny. He knows he is going somewhere at any moment—into a future land. But where? Where are you going? If I knew I might be called any day to leave suddenly for Africa, I would be a fool if I did not inquire about transportation, passport, and visa. I would inquire about the country, its climate and geography so I would be ready. Man knows he may be called to go at any moment, yet makes no inquiry as to the way to get there or the climate when he arrives. The way is in the "road map," the Bible, and all the information you need is in the Word of God. Better find out where you are going.

A certain speaker at a great convention was late for the meeting. He rushed from the train, jumped in the first cab, and said to the driver, "Drive me as fast as you can — I am in a hurry." Off they went, bouncing and bumping, for the driver was a veritable Jehu. After several minutes the speaker shouted, "Are we almost there?" "Where?" said the cabby. "All you told me was to *drive fast!*" Some people drive fast but, where are they going? Have you settled it? Receive Christ; He will lead you to glory!

— M.R.D.

> Soon, borne on time's most rapid wing,
>   Shall death command you to the grave, —
> Come sinner, haste; your sins now bring
>   While God yet waits to hear and save.
>   — T. Dwight, alt.

"Procrastination has never landed one soul in Heaven, but it has doomed many to an eternal Hell."

NEVER IRRITATED!

READ I CORINTHIANS 13:4-13

[Love] ... is not easily provoked.   I Corinthians 13:5

We are told that this verse is not accurately translated. Actually the word "easily" appears nowhere in the original. Literally the passage reads, "(Love) ... is not touchy, or fretful, or resentful." In other words; the love of God in our heart should keep us from becoming "exasperated." Christians should be able to ignore the pinpricks of life and keep from irritableness and temper tantrums even in the presence of rudeness, insult, and injustice. When we look at our own lives, however, we see how far we fall short of this ideal and how "touchy" we are. In fact, we often dramatize to ourselves "personal grievances," and consequently hold grudges against those who slight us, or hurt us with snide remarks. Yet if we truly have the love of Jesus in our heart and have died to "self," we should be able to gain the victory over "irritableness."

D. L. Moody's son in his biography informs us that a man once grossly and deliberately insulted his father. Mr. Moody momentarily flared up in anger at the unjust attack. Coming to the pulpit a bit later, however, he made this humble admission: "Friends, before beginning tonight, I want to confess that out in the hall I yielded just now to my temper. I have done wrong. I want to confess my error before you all, and if that man is present here whom I thrust from me in anger, I want to ask his forgiveness and God's. Let us pray." Moody's sincere apology reflected not a hint of excuse or self-vindication for the insult he had suffered. It is said that the meeting which followed was a scene of unusual blessing because of his straight-forward, Christian confession of having been "exasperated and angry."

Oh, for the sweet, unruffled composure of true discipleship, for a love that is not soon provoked. Resolve by God's grace not to be "irritated" today!   — H.C.B.

> When I have talked in anger,
>   And my cheeks were flaming red,
> I have always uttered something
>   Which I wish I had not said.
>   —Anon.

"Don't permit your feelings to be hurt, for basically that is only a form of egotism."

WHAT DO YOU REMEMBER?

READ GENESIS 41:9-32

> *. . . I do remember my faults this day.* Genesis 41:9

This is the statement of the butler whose dream had been interpreted by Joseph while they were in the prison in Egypt. Joseph requested that he (the butler) would remember him and mention him to Pharaoh upon his release (Gen. 40:14). But the butler soon forgot (Gen. 40:23). And now, when Pharaoh was unable to find an interpreter for his dream, the butler suddenly remembered what Joseph had done for him, and exclaims, "I do remember my faults this day." What base ingratitude — to forget so soon his benefactor. He gave no excuses but confessed it was his fault. Probably the hardest thing in all the world to do is admit our faults. Instead we defend, deny, or excuse them. The three hardest words to say are, "I was wrong." It is not so hard to say, "You were right," as to turn the point to ourselves, "I was wrong." How easy to see another's faults — how difficult our own.

A Christian heard that one of his brethren had been talking against him. Instead of trying to "get even," he went to his brother and said, "I understand you have been talking against me and told about my faults. I want you to tell me to my face what you see wrong in me, for I want to know so I can confess them and get rid of them." The brother agreed to frankly tell him. "But first," said the first man, "we will get down and pray about it. I want you to pray for me, that I may accept your criticism, see my faults, and be delivered from them. Pray for me, brother." The rebuke found its mark and the man dropped to his knees and cried out to God to forgive him his own sin of gossiping and slander. Arising to his feet he said, "If I had prayed first, instead of now, this would never have happened. Forgive me, brother." Before you talk to others about your brother, first talk to Father about it. Will you do that? Then, like the butler, you will remember your own faults — not others.

— M.R.D.

Go talk to God of others' faults,
  Don't criticize your brothers;
We've all so much we should improve —
  Just show Christ's love to others.

—Anon.

"The best way to forget the faults of others is to concentrate on your own."

THE CHRISTIAN HOME

READ I TIMOTHY 5:1-4

> *. . . let them learn first to show piety at home . . . for that is good and acceptable before God.*   I Timothy 5:4

When I was a boy we used to have a motto hanging over our doorway which said, "Christ is the Head of this home." I do not see many such plaques today. I wonder sometimes if we have assigned our Christianity to one day of the week (when we go to church), and forgotten to exhibit true piety at home. Did you ever consider the fact that where two or three Christians are gathered together — there Jesus is present in a special way?

A Japanese girl who studied at an American college spent her Christmas vacation in the home of one of her classmates. She had enjoyed much in America, but one thing she longed for most of all to see was the inside of a true Christian home, as this one was reported to be. She was treated royally and had a delightful time, but as she was about to leave, the mother of the Christian family said, "How do you like the way we Americans live?" "Oh," said the girl, "I love it! Your home is truly beautiful; yet, there is one thing I miss." A faraway look came into her eyes as she continued, "It all seems very queer to me. I have been with you to your church, and have seen you worship there, but *I have missed God in your home!* You know, in 'heathen' Japan we have a '*god-shelf*' in every home, so we can worship right there in the house. Excuse me, but do not you Americans worship God in your home?" Her host was shamefaced, for it was true that they had not established a "family altar" of any kind. They had not learned to show "piety at home."

Christ is the unseen Guest at every family gathering of believers; do we properly recognize Him? Do we consistently have a family altar?   — H.G.B.

> Rear you an altar which will last forever,
>   Longer than any shafts or marble dome;
> Erect it there beside your own hearth-fire —
>   The chaste, white family altar in the home.
>   —Anon.

"A family altar would alter many a family."

PRESCRIBING A PLACEBO

READ II CORINTHIANS 12:10-18

> *. . . nevertheless, being crafty, I caught you with guile.*
> II Corinthians 12:16

When Mrs. ———— came to me for treatment of a very exciting and exceedingly rare illness, I prescribed a *placebo*. Do you know what a "placebo" is? You probably have taken some and they helped you. But if you had known it was a placebo you would have been very angry at your doctor. So the doctor didn't tell you what he was giving you. But we must get back to Mrs. ————. She enjoyed very poor health. She was never so miserable as when she couldn't find anything wrong with herself. One day she read about a sickness she had never had. She liked it and promptly developed all the symptoms: headache, nausea, constipation, palpitation of the heart, blurring eyes, etc., etc., etc., etc., and she called me to come immediately as she thought she was dying. Upon examination I found nothing wrong with her. She was as healthy as a carp in muddy water. What to do for her? That was the problem. If I told her she was not sick she would have been furious and discharged me for another doctor. So I told her she was very ill (she was — in her head), but I would soon relieve her. So I gave her a placebo — a whole box full of pretty pink pills — made of sugar — nothing but a few grains of milk sugar. Take one every 15 minutes (keep her so busy taking pills she would forget her illness). The recovery was spectacular. Did I deceive her? Yes, but it cured her. That is the doctor's business — to cure people — and if sugar does it — why not?

Paul says he had taken the Corinthians by "craft" and "guile." The word guile is *dolos*, and means "bait." He had baited his hook to catch them for Jesus. His conduct and love for them had won them for Jesus.

Is your gospel hook "baited" for those you will meet on life's ocean? Will you attract any souls to Christ today?　　— M.R.D.

> Fishers of men must crafty be
> Yet harmless as a dove,
> Baiting their hooks with thought and care
> To reach men with Christ's love.
> —G. W.

"Get IN TUNE WITH CHRIST and His compassion and you will not find it hard to KEEP IN TOUCH WITH HUMANITY and its needs."

CHRISTIAN SELF-CONTROL

READ PROVERBS 25:25-28

*He that is slow to anger is better than the mighty; and
he that ruleth his spirit than he that taketh a city.*
                                                Proverbs 16:32

Unless you can control yourself, you will never be able to properly control and influence others! The secret of quietness, gentleness, and sober self-control is found in always keeping nearer to God than to anything or anyone else. A Christian can endure with composure almost any circumstance if he has properly yielded himself to the Spirit of God.

Many years ago the *Gospel Herald* carried the story of Samuel Stokes, an American missionary who walked through the villages in the darkest part of India, carrying only a water-bottle and a blanket. This dear man of God trusted wholly to native hospitality and the providence of God for his food and lodging. In one village he was given a very hostile reception. The head men of the town sat in chairs in a circle smoking and eating, leaving him to recline on the dirty floor. When he asked if he might nurse their sick and teach them of Christ, they hurled horrible insults at him; but by the grace of God he controlled his tongue and made no reply. Finally they gave him some food — just a few stale crusts in a filthy bowl. He thanked them courteously and, in order to win them to Christ, ate what had been set before him. For two days they treated him thus. On the third day, the head man laid his turban at Mr. Stokes' feet as a token of his respect. He explained that they had heard that Jesus' disciples were commanded to love their enemies and they could not believe the truth of this statement. They had decided, therefore, to put him to the test when he came to their town. The result had amazed them. Now they brought him their choicest food and were eager to hear his teaching. He realized then that if he had lost his temper, he would have missed his chance to witness to this benighted group of heathen. Let us also pray for grace to be meek and in full control of our own spirit.   — H.G.B.

Who govern their passions with absolute sway,
Grow wiser and better as life wears away.
                                                —Watts

"Self-control is promoted by humility." — SIGOURNEY

SIMPLE REMEDIES ARE BEST

READ II KINGS 5:9-14

. . . He will surely come out to me, and stand, and call on the name of the Lord his God, and strike his hand over the place, and recover the leper. II Kings 5:11

Naaman the Syrian was a leper. He heard about a prophet in Samaria, of whom a little captive Jewish girl had told his wife. When he came to Elisha, the prophet simply told him to go wash in Jordan seven times. This seemed so childishly simple that it made Naaman very angry and he started back home. He expected a great display of occult mumblings and grotesque movements on the part of the healer. He wanted a dramatic spectacle of acting, but the prophet said, "Just take a bath!"

The same superstition still prevails in the world today. People reject the Gospel because salvation is too simple. They too expect noises, visions, lights, and feelings before they will believe. But the Bible says, "Only believe." It just seems too simple. The Gospel needs no embellishment. That is the pagan way. They go through all sorts of contortions, cooking strange brews and mumbling unintelligible phrases. It is all a "cover up" for their deception. The Gospel needs no "props," jazz music, foreign costumes, tricks, or juggling acts. Paul told Timothy, "Preach the word."

The world is full of quacks and nostrums. They recommend a remedy because of its strange ingredients. "Only Poo-Poo Powders contain CKLZ." "Four out of five doctors recommend the ingredients in this Sucker Syrup." "Dumb-Clux Dope" contains not *one* ingredient but *five* — and so on, and so on. And the more mysterious it is, the more it deceives. This is true of much religious excitement; people are sold another gospel which is "not another." Beloved, let us not be led astray by the pageantry and display of much "modern evangelism." The pure gospel message has not lost its power — it only needs to be set free from the fleshly methods of the world. "Preach the Word!"

— M.R.D.

How firm a foundation, ye saints of the Lord,
Is laid for your faith in His excellent Word!
What more can He say than to you He hath said,
To you, who for refuge to Jesus have fled?
—G. Keith

"He who wrests the Scriptures never finds true rest in them."

PURIFIED BY FIRE

READ I PETER 4:12-19

And he shall sit as a refiner and purifier of silver: and he shall purify the sons of Levi, and purge them as gold and silver.   Malachi 3:3

A Christian is not to think it strange if he is called upon to suffer great trials and difficulties in this life. For the "refiner's fire" is sent to make faith stronger and purer by its heat. For every sanctified tear shed here in the furnace of affliction, there will be a jewel over there in the glory world (see Rom. 8:18). The rewards of Heaven will more than compensate for the "fiery trials."

The refiner of old *sat* at his work, for it was of such a delicate and skilled nature that it was necessary for him to be close to his crucible so that he might intently watch the process. Neither too little nor too much heat must be applied. The dross had to be removed at the precise moment when it could best be done without hurting or losing any of the precious metal. So, too, every Christian must endure some suffering according to the will of God if the dross of sin and self is to be purged away. These experiences are not pleasant to the flesh, but we may be assured that God loves us too much to give us a bit more pain than is actually needed. He sits close by so that He may direct every minute detail of our spiritual cleansing.

The alchemist of old knew when his gold was pure by the fact that he could see his image mirrored in it. In the same manner, only when Christ is formed in us by grace, and we reflect His glory, may the furnace of affliction be left behind.

May our prayer be, "O refining fire, go through my life and purge it of all that would hinder a perfect reflection of my Saviour!"   — H.G.B.

> Burn in me, fire of God,
>   Burn till my heart is pure.
> Burn till I love God fervently,
>   Burn till my faith is sure.
>   —Anon.

"God had one Son on earth without sin, but never one without suffering." — AUGUSTINE

THE HARD-BOILED MISSIONARY

READ PSALM 21

> . . . *all things work together for good to them that love*
> *God.* Romans 8:28

A lady who had been suffering for a long time was visited by many friends seeking to comfort her with verses of Scripture. One verse which was used most frequently was Romans 8:28. Instead of being encouraged, she began to resent the verse repeated so monotonously by those who were well and healthy. They little realized that it is easy to quote these verses glibly and loosely, when not in the same situation. It is not always easy to understand that our sufferings and trials and pain are for a purpose. It takes great faith to appropriate it. Let us be careful not to thoughtlessly quote Scriptures, for sometimes we cannot see God's purpose until later when the testing is past.

Yet it is true, whether we realize it or not, that everything God permits to come into our lives must have a reason. Whatever God sends upon us is necessary and for some good purpose which we shall understand afterward.

A missionary was captured by cannibals. "I suppose you intend to eat me?" said the missionary, and the chief grunted his affirmation. "Try a sample first, and see if you like it," said the missionary as he took his knife and cut a slab from the calf of his leg and handed it to him. "Try this and see." The chief took one bite and choked. The missionary had a cork leg. The chief wanted no more of it and the missionary was spared. Years before, he had thought it a great misfortune to lose his leg and to wear an artificial one, but *afterward* it saved his life. It worked out "for good." — M.R.D.

> Lord, I would clasp Thy hand in mine,
> Nor ever murmur nor repine,
> Content, whatever lot I see,
> Since, 'tis my God that leadeth me!
> —J. H. Gilmore

"Those who leave everything in God's hand will eventually see God's hand in everything."

SORROW: GOD'S TOOL

READ PSALM 142

When my spirit was overwhelmed within me, then thou
knewest my path. Psalm 142:3

> I walked a mile with Pleasure,
> She chatted all the way,
> But left me none the wiser,
> For all she had to say.
> I walked a mile with Sorrow,
> And ne'er a word said she;
> But, oh, the things I learned from her
> When Sorrow walked with me!

Our greatest difficulties usually turn out to be our greatest opportunities! Suffering and glory, testing and usefulness are always associated in the Scripture. Henry Ward Beecher points out discerningly that "The steel that has suffered most is the best. It has been in the furnace again and again; it has been on the anvil; it has been tight in the jaws of the vise; it has felt the teeth of the rasp; it has been ground by emery; it has been heated and hammered and filed until it does not know itself, but finally it comes out *a splendid knife!* If men only knew it, what are called their 'misfortunes' are God's best blessings, for they are the molding influences which give them shapeliness and edge, and durability and power."

Are you almost overwhelmed? Is your spirit gravely troubled? Do not despair; God knows all about it, and is in this trial. The path, though dark to you, is plain to Him. Take courage, trust His good leading, and you will "be enlarged in distress."

— H.G.B.

> Teach me to yield my will to Thine, dear Lord.
> And yielding, trusting, just lie still and rest;
> Show me a loving Father knows, dear Lord,
> For His beloved child just what is best.
> —Annie Moore

"When God is going to do something wonderful, He begins with a difficulty; when He is going to do something spectacular, He begins with an impossibility!"

WHICH WAS FIRST?

READ JOB 38:24-41

Where wast thou when I laid the foundations of the earth? declare, if thou hast understanding. Job 38:4

There are 40 question marks in the 38th chapter of Job. There are 19 question marks in chapter 39 and 20 in chapter 41. They are questions propounded by Jehovah to Job to show him how little he knew and how ignorant he was. With all man's wisdom. he still knows *nothing* as compared with God's omniscience. How foolish of men to refuse to believe what they cannot understand. If this be true, then we cannot believe anything. A little boy asked me, "What is it we eat *before* it is born and *after* it is dead?" After admitting I did not know, he said wisely, "A chicken." Even that I cannot understand: how from an egg with white and yolk can come, in 21 days, a fully developed chick with all the genetic characteristics of its ancestors!

At the dinner table of a Christian lady, a skeptic began railing on the Bible story of creation. She interrupted him by saying, "The Bible explains one thing you cannot answer." She picked up an egg and asked, "Where did this egg come from?" "Why, from a hen, of course." The lady asked, "And where did the hen come from?" He was forced to reply. "From an egg." "And where did that egg come from?" "From the hen." And so on — the egg — the hen; the hen — the egg; etc., etc., etc. "Which then was first — the hen or the egg?" The reply was, "The hen, of course." "Then a hen existed before an egg? Where did the hen come from?" Frustrated, the infidel admitted his folly.

Push back egg to hen, hen to egg, to its beginning and you come to God who made the hen that laid the egg from which all other hens and eggs have come. Understand it? If you do, you are wiser than I am. The Bible says the hen was created by God — and the hen laid the egg. The argument is settled in Genesis 1:20.

— M.R.D.

All things bright and beautiful,
All things great and small,
God our Heavenly Father
In wisdom made them all.
—Author Unknown

"Note the inconsistency of atheism: The thing formed says nothing formed it; and that which is made — IS, while that which made it — IS NOT! The folly is infinite!"

"NO RETREAT"

READ LUKE 9:57-62

No man, having put his hand to the plough, and looking back, is fit for the kingdom of God. Luke 9:62

Unstable Christians are poor witnesses. You cannot be an effective soul winner or a true disciple unless you are willing to go straight on for God regardless of what it costs you personally. No wavering or looking back to the ways of the world and the "unfruitful works of darkness" can be permitted. The life of victory demands unreserved consecration, unremitting diligence, and enduring perseverance.

During the Revolutionary War, Washington came with his army to Brandywine Creek. After they had crossed the bridge spanning the stream, one of the soldiers asked him, "General, shall we burn the bridge, or leave it? After all, the enemy might drive us back, and then we would need it *to make good our retreat!*" Washington gave a memorable reply: "Burn the bridge! It is victory or death!"

When Napoleon was engaged in the great and momentous battle of Waterloo, among those taken prisoner was a Highland piper. Napoleon, impressed by the man's strange mountain garb and determined air, struck up a conversation with the captured but unvanquished foe. Seeing that he had his instrument with him, Napoleon asked him to play a tune. The highlander obliged. "Now play a march," said Napoleon. Once again, the Scotchman did as he was told. Finally the Emperor said, "Play a retreat." "Nay, nay," said the highlander, "that I cannot do. I never learned to play one."

The saints of God too should never learn to "play a retreat." Bridges of compromise must ever be burned behind us so that we leave no way back into the world. We must make a complete break with our old sinful life.

The furrows of our testimony will only be straight as we keep our eyes fixed on Jesus. Follow Him no matter what the cost, Christian. Never look back! *Never retreat!* —H.G.B.

We know not where the path may lead,
As yet by us untrod;
We "look not back" but sweetly trust
The providence of God!
—H.G.B.

"For victory in the Christian life, don't look back, don't look within, don't look around at others; just keep your eye on Jesus!"

NO SHOES

READ ROMANS 10:12-17

> *. . . How beautiful are the feet of them that preach the gospel.*   Romans 10:15

Have you ever noticed your pastor's feet? If he is a God-sent minister you should take a good look at his feet. People notice the pastor's features, his suit, or tie, or haircut, but if you have overlooked his feet you have missed something important. No matter how homely or unattractive the preacher may be — God says his feet are beautiful. He says it three times (Isa. 52:7; Nahum 1:15; Rom. 10:15). God wants people to see the preacher's feet.

When Jesus sent forth His disciples He said, *"Take no shoes,"* (Matt. 10:10). Instead they were to wear *"sandals"* (Mark 6:9). Why sandals instead of shoes? There are several reasons.

1. Shoes "hide" the feet. Sandals reveal the feet, for they consist of little more than a sole held to the foot by a strap. The preacher must be known as a man who uses his feet as well as his mouth.

2. Sandals were for servants. The noblemen wore ornate shoes — the slaves went barefooted — but *servants* wore sandals. The preacher is God's servant.

3. Sandals can be quickly removed. In the presence of God, we must come barefooted as unworthy slaves. Moses was commanded to take off his shoes (Ex. 3:5). See also Joshua 5:15 and Ruth 4:7, 8. It was an acknowledgment of unworthiness.

4. Sandals can be slipped on in a moment. They need no buttoning or lacing. They speak of readiness to obey immediately God's command. Ready to take off the sandals for *revelation* alone with God — Ready for the *road,* to carry the revelation to others? Ready for either — *take no shoes — be shod with sandals.*

Today take a good look at your pastor's feet. He may not be all you want him to be — *but look at his beautiful feet.*   —M.R.D.

> "How beautiful the feet of them"
> Who seek their Master to obey,
> Ready to humbly kneel or serve
> As He directs their chosen way!
> — H.G.B.

"God can accomplish little through a DE-FEETED messenger!"

"MAN, DO YOU PRAY?"

READ PSALM 4

*I will both lay me down in peace, and sleep; for thou,
Lord, only makest me dwell in safety.*   Psalm 4:8

This verse has been called David's "Now I Lay Me," because
there is little doubt but that this was an "evening prayer."
Americans take over six tons of aspirins and sleeping pills each
night in an attempt to get some rest. Yet, how much better not
only to sleep, but to do so *"peacefully"* because we know our
Heavenly Father is watching over us and tenderly guarding
our soul!

Many years ago Robert Morrison, the famous missionary, was
anticipating leaving for China. While still in New York, however,
he was taken seriously ill and could not take passage. A good
friend invited him to his home so that he might take care of him.
He decided to let the missionary rest in his own bed. In the
same room was a little child sound asleep in her own seven-year
crib. He decided to leave her there and not awaken her. Not
long after Missionary Morrison had crawled under the sheets,
the little girl across the room opened her eyes. She looked at
the bed where she expected to see her father, but he was not
there. She was alarmed to see a strange man in his place. Who
was he? Where was her father? In a frightened little voice she
asked, *"Man, do you pray to God?"* Mr. Morrison was touched
and calmly answered, "Yes, my dear, I pray to God every day.
He is my best Friend." That answer took the fear out of the
child. She smiled and in a few moments was again sound asleep.
After his recovery from the serious illness the missionary went
on to China where he preached the unsearchable riches of Christ.
There, however, he was often in great danger, but no matter
how great the difficulties and hardships, he was always able to
lie down at night and sleep peacefully. Secure in the care of his
Lord, he often thought of the experience he had had in the home
of his friend in New York. He never forgot the lesson the child
had taught him. What is your answer to the little girl's question:
"Man, do you pray?"   — H.G.B.

'Tis sweet to keep my hand in His,
    While all is dim,
To close my weary, aching eyes,
    And trust in Him.
                                            —Anon.

"We LIE to God in prayer if we do not RELY on Him after prayer."
                                            — DAVID LIVINGSTONE

NEW BROOMS

READ LUKE 19:11-27

. . . here is thy pound, which I have kept laid up in a napkin.   Luke 19:20

This unfaithful servant had certainly been "faithful (?)" in watching over his pound. He had carefully wrapped the precious gift in a clean cloth and placed it in a safe place. But the pound had been given to him to invest and make additional pounds for the donor. It was not to be merely preserved, but used as well. The pound represents the gift of salvation, and is given to us to use, not to hide. Yet, how many prize their salvation for themselves, but never use it to help others. Our salvation must be utilized, our faith must work. We must not spare it but set it to work. It reminds one of the silly proverb, "A new broom sweeps clean." But this is utterly ridiculous, for a new broom never sweeps at all. How then can they sweep clean? The moment you sweep with a broom it is not new any more — it is secondhand. You will never get your house clean by putting a plastic bag over it and then setting it in a corner.

May I compare your conversion experience with a broom. God did not save you just to save *you.* He saved you to be used in His service and to share your experience. God gave you your mouth, your hands, your feet, to bring the precious gift to others. Keeping it to yourself will stunt you and deprive others of the blessing. You can be so enamored with a new tool that you hesitate to use it. A woman may be so pleased with her new dress she hesitates to wear it for fear of damaging it. The Bible says, "Whosoever will save his life, shall lose it." What does this mean? To be concerned with your own comfort and ease is to lose the very essence of life — *service to others.*

NO! A new broom does not sweep clean — it will even get dirty by standing in the corner. What gifts has God given you? Use them, brother and sister! Use them today — *or lose them!*

— M.R.D.

Use me today to scatter the seed,
  Bringing the blessing someone may need.
Whether I toil or quietly pray,
  Blessed Lord Jesus, use me today.
—G. R. Dugan

"Christians are either walking Bibles or living libels."

EBENEZER COMFORT

READ I SAMUEL 7:7-13

Then Samuel took a stone, and set it between Mizpeh and Shen, and called the name of it Ebenezer, saying, Hitherto hath the Lord helped us. 1 Samuel 7:12

The stone which Samuel erected and which he called "Ebenezer" was a memorial to God's help and faithfulness. We too as Christians must not fail to remember God's benefits, for there is blessed comfort in taking spiritual inventory. As we look back over our lives, we recognize that God always came to our rescue no matter how serious the crisis we faced. It is true that often we did not understand His leading at the time, but in the end we found His way was best. What comfort and assurance this gives us for the future!

The late Dr. James M. Gray often related how when he was convalescing from a long illness it was suggested to him that he should plan a visit to the British provinces. This his doctors thought might bring the change of scenery and relaxation which he sorely needed. The arrangements were all laboriously made when suddenly, quite unexpectedly, another malady struck him and once again confined him to his bed. Dr. Gray was greatly disappointed and wondered what God could want of him by continually confining him to a sickroom. Soon he received a wonderful answer to his doubtful questioning. Some mornings later, upon picking up the newspaper, he read an account which related the tragic news that *the steamer on which he would have sailed had struck a reef upon entering St. John's harbor, and had sunk almost instantly!* The Lord who had helped him in the past had once again perfectly directed his way and protected him from death.

Christian, as you look back upon God's gracious leading in the past, you too should face the future confidently; for the God who cared for you then is still your divine Protector today. This is your "Ebenezer comfort." — H.G.B.

> "Hitherto the Lord hath helped us"
> When our way was rough and steep;
> Safely led us o'er the mountains,
> Sometimes through the water deep;
> Yet He gave us strength for weakness,
> Thus with confidence we say,
> Let us raise our "Ebenezer,"
> He has led us all the way.
> — H. Western

"Be sure if God sends you on stony paths, He will provide you with strong shoes."

TASTE AND SEE

O taste and see that the Lord is good.   Psalm 34:8

An old proverb goes: "The proof of the pudding is in the eating thereof." This is in perfect harmony with the teaching of the Scripture. Only those who have personally experienced the new birth and have received Jesus Christ as personal Lord and Saviour can talk with any authority about the reality of redemption. To all others the Gospel and the preaching of the cross is foolishness (I Cor. 1:18).

The natural man receiveth not the things of the Spirit of God, neither can he receive them until spiritually enlightened. Most of the critics of the Bible have never read the Bible once, and yet they set themselves up as judges of things about which they know nothing.

An infidel was lecturing one day on the unreasonableness of salvation just by believing on Jesus. He then invited anyone with a question to come to the platform. Immediately a man, who before his conversion had been a notorious drunkard in the town, stepped up. Without asking a question he coolly and quietly peeled an orange and slowly began to eat it. The exasperated infidel lecturer thundered out, "Man, stop your acting foolish and tell me your question!" The man finished his orange and looking him straight in the eye said, "Tell me, was this orange sweet or sour?" "How should I know?" said the infidel. "I never tasted it." "Then stop criticizing the Gospel until you too have tasted it. I have tasted it and know that it is the power of God which is able to transform a Hell-bound drunkard into a saint." And pointing to his town's folk he concluded, "And those can testify what it has done for me. Don't find fault with something you never tasted. Meeting adjourned!"   — M.R.D.

> O taste and see that God is good
>   To all that seek His face;
> Yea, blest the man that trusts in Him,
>   Confiding in His grace.

"An infidel cannot find God for the same reason that a thief cannot find a policeman!"

THE "HEALING" WORD

He sent his word, and healed them . . . .   Psalm 107:20

A Christian in the line of duty was once called upon to visit a man in an asylum who had severe mental hallucinations. Recalling the story in I Samuel 16, how David calmed Saul in his demented moments by singing one of his precious, inspired songs to him, and conscious too of the power of the Bible upon his own soul, he decided to read from the Psalms to this one who was mentally tormented. He found that the Word of God had a soothing and "healing" effect upon the poor fellow. He therefore returned many times to the asylum to perform this spiritual labor of love — almost invariably with happy results. One day the superintendent, an unconverted man, said, "Your treatment may be good, but it does not always succeed." "What makes you say that?" asked the Christian. "Well," said the other, "in desperation last night I tried to calm the patient by your method, when he was in one of his perturbed and frantic moods, and my efforts failed completely." The Christian was surprised. "What portion did you read to him?" he asked . "Oh, I just began at the front — *all about a most high and mighty prince named James . . . !"* Apparently in his ignorance the attendant had read the *preface to the King James Bible,* which of course was not inspired. No wonder it had no effect! Only the life-giving Word of God has attached to it the immutable promise: "It shall not return unto me void, but it shall accomplish that which I please" (Isa. 55:11). No one can read the Scripture and remain unmoved! The Bible's influence cannot be shaken off. Every time it comes in contact with us it either increases our doom or draws us graciously toward Heaven!

What effect does the Bible have upon you?   —H.G.B.

> Thy Word is chart and compass
> That o'er life's surging sea,
> 'Mid mist and rocks and darkness
> Still guides, O Christ, to thee.
>   —W. W. How

"The Bible is the only Book that always finds me!" — COLERIDGE

ADMONITION TO PREACHERS

READ JOSHUA 24:1-15

> *Take heed therefore unto yourselves, and to all the flock, over the which the Holy Ghost hath made you overseers, to feed the church of God, which he hath purchased with his own blood.*   Acts 20:28

The Scripture makes it clear that the work of the teaching elders, or pastors, is first to keep themselves in the love of Christ as examples of holiness, and secondly, to be sure to feed the flock of God with the food of the Word. Those who do not follow this Scriptural pattern in their work as "bishops" hinder the cause of Christ.

There are many dear men of God who are fine Christians and indeed know how to expound the Word, but who never seem to drive home the urgency of the gospel invitation by *"preaching to a decision!"* In this connection a story is told of a layman who visited a great city church some years ago while on a business trip. After the service, he congratulated the minister on his delivery and sermon. "But," said the manufacturer, "if you were my salesman, I would discharge you. You got my attention by your appearance, voice, and manner; and your prayer, reading, and logical discourse aroused my interest. In fact you warmed my heart with a desire for what you preached from the Word; and then — *and then you stopped without asking me to do something about it!* In business the important thing is to get folks to sign on the dotted line." Ah, that's where some preachers, and many others who bear Christian witness, often fail; they do not press for a decision for Christ. Oh, that with a forthrightness of a Joshua they might say to their hearers, *"Choose you this day whom ye will serve!"* (Josh. 24:15).   — H.G.B.

> I do not ask that crowds may throng the temple,
> That standing room be priced;
>   I only ask that as I voice the message
> Men may see Christ!
> I do not ask that men may sound my praises,
> Or headlines spread my name abroad;
>   I only pray that as I voice my message
> Hearts may find God!
> —Ralph C. Cushman

"There was a time when they used to chain the Bible to the pulpit; today I sometimes think it would be wise if they would chain the preachers to the Bible!" — REV. E. VANDERJAGT

HE MAY COME TODAY!

READ LUKE 12:35-40

Be ye therefore ready also.   Luke 12:40

The surest thing in all the world is the return of Jesus Christ to take His own unto Himself. The time of His coming is not made known so that we may be constantly looking for Him. The consciousness of His "any moment return" is the greatest incentive for holiness, evangelism, revival and soul-winning. If you knew Jesus would come today — what would you do? *He may come today! He is coming some day!*

A gentleman visiting a certain school gave out the information that he would give a prize to the pupil whose desk he found in the best order when he returned. "But when will you return?" some of them asked. "That I cannot tell," was the answer. A little girl, who had been noted for her disorderly habits, announced that she meant to win the prize. "You!" her schoolmates jeered; "why your desk is always out of order." "Oh! but I mean to clean it the first of every week?" "But suppose he should come at the end of the week?" someone asked. "Then I will clean it every morning." "But he may come at the end of the day." For a moment the little girl was silent. "I know what I'll do," she said decidedly; "I'll just keep it clean." So it must be with the Lord's servants who would be ready to receive the prize of His coming. It may be at midnight, at cock-crowing, or in the morning. The exhortation is not "Get ye ready," but *"BE ye ready!"*
— M.R.D.

Watch and pray, nor leave our post of duty,
   Till we hear the Bridegroom's voice;
Then, with Him the marriage feast partaking,
   We shall evermore rejoice.
Watch and pray — the Lord commandeth;
   Watch and pray — 'twill not be long;
Soon He'll gather home His loved ones
   To the happy vale of song!
—F. J. Crosby

"I never begin my work without thinking that perhaps He may interrupt that work and begin His own. His word to all believing souls is: 'Til I come." — G. CAMPBELL MORGAN

TIME OUT FOR GOD

READ MATTHEW 14:1-13

> *. . . And he took them, and went aside privately into a*
> *desert place. . . .*   Luke 9:10

Throughout Jesus' ministry we find periods when He took time out for meditation and prayer and silent communion with the Father. In this He set us an example. The quiet hours spent before the Lord are the filling stations of grace which prepare us for the emergencies and difficulties of life.

We have heard of one man, with more than his share of difficulties, who regularly finds blessed relief by locking himself in his room, away from his family and the telephone, that he may there have quiet, sweet communion with Heaven. He feels that it is necessary to first get his body and mind into a proper attitude, so he lies down on a couch until his muscles are completely relaxed and his mental tension begins to subside. Then, after prayer and some Bible study, he picks up the old book of gospel hymns, which he always has handy, and reads the comforting lyrics until the blessing of it all stirs his soul to joy and singing. By the time their messages of faith and hope are absorbed, he says his troubles no longer seem insurmountable. The mountains of difficulty are laid low and the "rough places" are made "plain."

The hours of the soul's communion with God are the truly precious times in life. They are fountains in the desert where the fainting traveler can revive his strength.

Henry Martin, the great preacher, once confessed, "Want of private devotional reading and shortness of prayer, through incessant sermon making, has produced much strangeness between God and my soul." If a preacher preparing sermons must make such a confession, *how much more should those of us who let the things of this world keep us from quiet communion with the Saviour?*

How long since you have sought out a quiet spot and had a "little talk with Jesus"?   — H.G.B.

> We come now to the quiet place,
> The sanctuary of the heart,
> Where silent and alone we may
> A new strength to our souls impart.

"If you want God's best, quietly tarry at a promise until the Lord meets you there."

PRACTICE MAKES PERFECT

READ MATTHEW 6:1-17

> *. . . when thou prayest, enter into thy closet, and when*
> *thou hast shut thy door, pray.*   Matthew 6:6

After the disciples had witnessed the prayer life of Jesus, they came to Him and said, "Lord, teach us to pray, as John also taught his disciples" (Luke 11:1). They did not say, "Teach us to preach," or "Teach us to sing." We all admit that instruction and training and practice are essential in making good preachers and singers. But who ever heard of "training" people to pray? We have schools of music and courses which offer instruction in song leading and singing. We have seminaries to teach young men how to become preachers and missionaries. They offer courses in Greek and Hebrew, homiletics and church history, etc. But did you ever hear of a course in Bible school or seminary devoted exclusively to teach men *how to pray?*

Before the minister delivers his sermon or the soloist sings, he has practiced and practiced for hours. How much do you practice effectual praying?

A British soldier one night was caught creeping stealthily back to his quarters from a nearby woods. He was immediately hauled before his commanding officer for an explanation. The man pleaded that he had gone into the woods to pray; that was his only defense. "Have you been in the habit of spending hours in private prayer?" growled the officer. "Yes, sir." "Then down on your knees and pray now!" he roared. "You never needed it so much." Expecting immediate death, the soldier knelt and poured out his soul in prayer that for eloquence could have been inspired only by the power of the Holy Spirit. "You may go," said the officer when he had finished. "I believe your story. If you hadn't drilled often you couldn't have done so well at review." — M.R.D.

> Teach me to pray, Lord, teach me to pray;
> This is my heart-cry, day unto day;
> I long to know Thy will and Thy way;
> Teach me to pray, Lord, teach me to pray.
> —A. S. Reitz

"The prayer closet is the indispensable school for Christian workers."

"MY CUP RUNNETH OVER"

READ PSALM 84

> *. . . thou anointest my head with oil; my cup runneth*
> *over.* Psalm 23:5

To fully appreciate the expression, "My cup runneth over," one must understand the oriental way of showing hospitality. When a generous host poured for his guests, he spared nothing. No dainty, polite "half measures" would do. He lavishly filled each vessel to overflowing to demonstrate his hearty friendship. It is the Good Shepherd's unstinting love for us that is emphasized by the "flooded cup" of blessing.

Sometimes the wells where shepherds brought their sheep were very deep. The water then had to be brought to the surface by a rope with a leather bucket at the end. This was let down and drawn up hand over hand, by a slow, laborious process, and the water poured into large stone cups beside the well. If the man had a hundred sheep, he might have to draw for two hours if he allowed the flock to drink all they wanted. Here is where the hireling shepherd displayed his heartlessness. As soon as a poor sheep had taken just a few mouthfuls of water he would push it aside in order to save himself work. But the good shepherd has no such disposition. He would draw and draw and fill the watering cups to overflowing until all his thirsty sheep were completely satisfied. So, too, God's giving to us, His children, has always been "good measure, pressed down, and running over."

It is interesting to note that the overflowing cup was not provided until the sheep had first been anointed and refreshed with oil. This is true also in the Christian's life. There is never a constant stream of overflowing joy until the heart has been surrendered to Christ and anointed by the "oil" of the Holy Spirit.

God does not make our cup run over simply to give us the selfish joy of superabundance, but more particularly that through us the blessing might overflow to others round about us. Is your cup running over? It can, you know! — H.G.B.

> In the midst of affliction my table is spread;
> With blessings unmeasured my cup runneth o'er;
> With perfume and oil thou anointest my head;
> Oh, what shall I ask of Thy providence more?
> —J. Montgomery

"A pint of true overflowing spirituality is worth a barrel of pumped-up religious piety " — G.W.

THE GOSPEL IN ACTION

READ JAMES 2:20-25

. . . I will shew thee my faith by my works. James 2:18

Only God can see "faith" in the heart of man. People see our faith only by our works. Faith is like a seed planted in the ground. It is hidden from view but if it is a living seed it will soon manifest itself by pushing its stalk up through the soil for all to see. We may talk about our "faith" from morning till night without results, but when that faith *works,* men must recognize it.

Out of the war comes a story of faith in action. A godly chaplain in the army found a dying soldier on the battlefield, and being anxious about his salvation he took out his Bible and said, "Shall I read a portion of Scripture to you?" But the soldier replied, "No sir, I am thirsty and need a drink of water." At the risk of his own life, amid bursting shells, the chaplain went in search of water and having found some, gave it to the wounded man. Then he asked again, "Shall I read some Scripture to you?" But the man replied, "No thank you, I am so cold, I am almost freezing." The chaplain removed his own coat and wrapped it about him, and once more asked with shivering body and chattering teeth, "Now may I read to you?" Again the reply was "No sir, I am too uncomfortable on this rough ground." The chaplain gently lifted him up and placed him across his knees with his head in his arms and once more asked the same question. "Yes sir," he replied, "for if what you are going to read can make a man willing to risk his life like this to ease a dying stranger, I want to hear about it!" And there on the battlefield he was told about Jesus *who died that we might live.*

This is the Gospel in action. It is what the world is waiting for today! Amid the clamor of religious cant the world is looking for a cup of cold water in the Master's name. Faith without works is dead. —M.R.D.

How sad to save our lives for self
And lose them for alway!
What joy to lose them for our Lord
And find them, in that day!
—Sarah C. Lewis

"Count that day lost in which your faith has not been translated into action."

CONQUERED BY CHRIST

READ GENESIS 32:9-32

> *And Jacob was left alone; and there wrestled a man with him until the breaking of the day. And when he saw that he prevailed not against him, he touched the hollow of his thigh; and the hollow of Jacob's thigh was out of joint, as he wrestled with him.* Genesis 32:24, 25

Jacob's night of wrestling, as recorded in Genesis 32, was a turning point in his life. If we read the context we see that he is literally at "wit's-end corner." Up until that time, by scheming and conniving he had craftily tried to direct his own future, but now he has finally come to the end of human devices. God is seeking by these adverse events to take full control in his life. The Man who wrestled with Jacob (no doubt, the Lord Jesus Christ Himself) makes him realize what a poor, feeble creature he is by throwing his hip out of joint. Jacob surrenders, seeks a blessing, and God takes over.

J. H. McConkey once said to a physician friend of his, "Doctor, what is the exact significance of God's touching Jacob upon the sinew of his thigh?" The doctor replied, "The sinew of the thigh is the strongest in the human body. A horse could scarcely tear it apart." "Ah, I see," said McConkey. "God has to break us down at the strongest part of our self-life before He can have His own way of blessing with us."

God is not looking for brilliant men; He is not dependent upon eloquent men; He is not even shut up to the use of talented men in sending His Gospel out to the world. As the late Dr. Ironside has remarked, "God is looking for broken men, for men who have judged themselves in the light of the cross of Christ. When He wants anything done, He takes up men who have come to an end of themselves and whose trust and confidence is not in themselves but in God." If you will let God touch the strongest part of your "self-life" — the thing that is holding back His full blessing — you too will become a "prince" and a power with God.

— H.G.B.

Christ alone the victory giveth,
  Oh! How sweet by faith to cry —
"Surely my Redeemer liveth,
  He hath conquered, and not I."
—R. K. Carter

"There is victory in surrender when we are conquered by Christ."
—G.W.

GOD'S PART AND MAN'S PART

READ EXODUS 11

> *. . . take . . . a lamb.*
> *. . . And ye . . . shall kill it.*
> *And they shall take of the blood.*
> *. . . strike the lintel and the two side posts.*
>
> Exodus 12:3, 6, 7, 22

What a flurry of sudden activity among the slaves of Egypt! Nine plagues or judgments had fallen upon the Egyptians. Water into blood, frogs, lice, swarms of flies, pestilence among cattle, boils on men and beasts, hail and fire, locusts, and three days darkness. In all this Israel was safe, though they did *nothing* to prevent the judgment from touching them. They just sat still — God did it all for them. It was not because they were better than the Egyptians, but it was all God's sovereign grace. It was simply because God had chosen them and put a difference between the Egyptians and the children of Israel.

Now notice the change in the last and final judgment — the death of the firstborn! Here it was not a matter of sitting still and letting God do it all. *Now they must do something.* Take a lamb — kill it — take the blood — sprinkle it on the doorposts — stay inside — eat the lamb — and be ready to go. The first nine judgments speak of sovereign *grace.* The last one emphasizes Israel's part — *faith.* It all comes down to a matter of *faith.* If they did not believe Moses, they would not act, but just sit still as before. God's grace was their protection, but it must be received by faith. You can go to Hell by hiding behind the sovereignty of God. You *must believe* and act. We often hear it said, you do nothing to be saved. The truth is you do nothing to be lost! You are already lost — you do nothing to be lost. But you must do something about it to be saved. Not work, but believe. Listen to Paul in answer to the question: What must I do to be saved? *"Believe on the Lord Jesus Christ!"*

—M.R.D.

> Come to Jesus, hear His pleading,
> Come, there's rest and peace for thee;
> "Whosoever" is His promise,
> Come, and thou shalt be made free.
> —A. H. Heinz

"God doesn't do for us what He has given us power to do for ourselves!"

UNION AND COMMUNION

READ COLOSSIANS 1:1-10

. . . this grace wherein we stand. Romans 5:2

. . . walk worthy of the Lord unto all pleasing.
Colossians 1:10

Standing and walking. These two words describe the ideal relationship of the believer with His Lord. Every believer has a permanent "standing" in Christ, never to be lost. Positionally by grace, he is complete in Him (Col. 2:10). This settles our salvation and guarantees our security forever in Him. But after we have received our standing we are to begin walking. Our "standing" justifies us in God's sight because it is all of grace and does not depend upon the slightest merit or worth or works of our own. It establishes our *union* with Christ.

But those who "stand" in Christ are admonished to walk (Rom. 4:12, I Cor. 7:17, Eph. 5:15, I John 2:6). Walking means going forward — growth in grace and the knowledge of Christ. We are told to walk *honestly,* walk *in love,* walk *in the Spirit.* This walking determines our fellowship, assurance, fruitfulness, joy, and reward.

Some Christians have been saved 20 to 30 years but are no farther along than they were when they started. By faith we stand justified in His sight; this is *union.* But our *communion* and fellowship depends on our walk. Our union is once for all and cannot be broken (John 10:28), but our communion can be broken by carelessness and sin, and must be restored by confession and repentance. Christ left us two ordinances: Baptism and the Lord's Supper. The baptism speaks of *union* once for all, never to be repeated. But *communion* is to be observed often — "as often as ye eat this bread" (I Cor. 11:26). Union is God's free gift; communion is our responsibility. "If we walk in the light as He is in the light, (then) we have fellowship (communion) one with another" (I John 1:7). "Walk in the Spirit, and ye shall not fulfil the lust of the flesh" (Gal. 5:16). Brother, sister, watch your step today as you walk the pathway of sanctification.   — M.R.D.

Trying to walk in the steps of the Saviour,
Trying to follow our Saviour and King;
Shaping our lives by His blessed example,
Happy, how happy, the songs that we bring.
—E. E. Hewitt

"No one can possibly enjoy communion with God and go where God does not go."

HE DIED FOR ME!

READ I THESSALONIANS 5:1-10

For God hath not appointed us to wrath, but to obtain salvation by our Lord Jesus Christ. Who died for us. . . .
                                        I Thessalonians 5:9, 10

Oliver Cromwell once ordered that a soldier should be shot for his crimes at the ringing of the evening curfew bell. For some reason that night the bell did not toll. The incident has been immortalized in poetry and song. It seems that the girl whom the condemned soldier was to marry had climbed up into the belfry and clung to the great clapper of the bell to prevent it from striking. When she was called by Cromwell to give an account of herself, she only wept and showed him her bruised and bleeding hands. Cromwell's heart was touched and he said, "Your lover shall live because of your sacrifice. *Curfew shall not ring tonight!*" So too all of us are rebels against God and under a sentence of death. Another, Christ, has intervened in our behalf. We too are saved, but only at the expense of His blessed Person. When skeptics questioned the truth of substitutionary atonement after His resurrection from the dead, Christ showed them His hands — *His bruised, nail-pierced hands!* If you claim Him as the Lover of your soul, the curfew of eternal death will never toll for you!

A converted Japanese woman was once trapped by a prairie fire. Seeing that it was going to catch up with her and the child she carried on her back, she laid the little one down, desperately scooped a hole in the earth with her hands, and with trembling haste laid the child in it, covering its body with her own. Later they found the two. The poor woman was dead, but the child was saved. A Christian Japanese who discovered them said with tears, "So too Jesus died that I might live. He put His blessed body between me and the everlasting fire." He had caught the truth of I Thessalonians 5:10.

Can you say with a confidence born of faith in Christ and His Word: "He died for me"?   —H.G.B.

> It was for crimes that I had done,
>   He groaned upon the tree!
> Amazing pity! Grace unknown!
>   And love beyond degree.
>   —Isaac Watts

"Christ died among sinners that we might live among saints."

CAN YOU ANSWER THIS?

READ ISAIAH 28:9-13

For precept must be upon precept, precept upon precept; line upon line, line upon line; here a little, and there a little. Isaiah 28:10

A man held in his hand two coins, a total of just 55 cents, but one of them was *not* a nickel. How was he able to do it? You will be able to give the answer if you will read the riddle slowly, carefully, and if need be, repeatedly. Few people get a message the first time they hear it, and for this reason things must be repeated over and over again before they really "get" it. Modern business recognizes the impact and power of "repetition," and in their advertising repeat and repeat some striking phrase about their product until it makes an indelible impression. The slogan: "Say it briefly and say it often" is sound promotion. In our school days we soon found out that in our memory work the secret lay in repeating a thing over and over again. This, too, is the meaning of the text, "Precept upon precept, line upon line, here a little and there a little." Over and over again the Lord had warned Israel, and even then they did not learn their lesson (see verse 13).

One of the most important rules of Bible study is this rule of "repetition." The first time we read a passage we may miss the meaning entirely. We may have to go over it again and again before the truth dawns upon us. Read your Bible *slowly* and *repeatedly.* It is not how *much* you read, but how *well* you read. Reading just a little with understanding is better than reading an entire book just out of duty or habit. Let me ask Philip's question to the Eunuch, "Understandest thou what thou readest?" If not — read it again!

Now back to our riddle: "I have two coins totaling 55 cents, but one is *not a nickel.*" You don't know how I do it? Then read it again. *One* of the two coins was *not* a nickel — It was a fifty cent piece! Of course, *the other was a nickel!* It's all in *how* you read it. How do you read your Bible? Have you studied it today *with profit?* —M.R.D.

Oh, may I love Thy precious Word
May I explore the mine,
May I its fragrant flowers glean,
May light upon me shine.
—E. Hodder

"Study the Bible to be wise; believe it to be safe; practice it to be holy!"

THE WONDROUS POWER OF PRAYER

READ JAMES 5:11-20

> *. . . The effectual fervent prayer of a righteous man availeth much.*
> James 5:16

When we come to the end of all human devices there is ever a great untapped reservoir of power available to us — it is the power of prayer! The wonders that have been wrought by God through the intercession of His saints would fill so many volumes that the libraries of the world would scarcely be able to contain them all. Here is just one such authentic incident:

While crossing the Atlantic many years ago, Dr. F. B. Meyer was asked to address the passengers. At the captain's request he spoke on "Answered Prayer." An agnostic who was present at the service was asked by his friends, "What did you think of Dr. Meyer's sermon?" He answered, "I didn't believe a word of it." That afternoon Dr. Meyer went to speak to the steerage passengers. Many of the listeners at his morning address went along, including the agnostic, who claimed he just wanted to hear "what the babbler had to say." Before starting for the service, the agnostic put two oranges in his pocket. On his way he passed an elderly woman sitting in her deck chair fast asleep. Her hands were open. In the spirit of fun, the agnostic put the two oranges in her out-stretched palms. After the meeting, he saw the old lady happily munching one of the pieces of fruit. "You seem to be enjoying that orange," he remarked with a smile. "Yes, sir," she replied, "My Father is very good to me." "Your father! Surely your father can't be still alive?" "Praise God," she replied, "He is very much alive." "What do you mean?" pressed the agnostic. She explained, "I'll tell you, sir. I have been seasick for days. I was asking God some-how to send me an orange. I suppose I fell asleep while I was praying. When I awoke, I found He had not only sent me one, *He had sent me two oranges!*" The astonished agnostic came under conviction, and was later led to Christ. He had received an unex-pected confirmation of Dr. Meyer's morning discourses on "An-swered Prayer."

Yes, prayer changes things!   —H.G.B.

> Sweet as breath of spices burning,
>   Keep our hearts like incense rare —
> All our being Heavenward turning
>   In a cloud of ceaseless prayer!
> —Anon.

"Where prayer focuses, power falls!"

THE CALL OF GOD

Moreover, whom he did predestinate, them he also called.
Romans 8:30

A Christian is a person who has answered the call of God. The word for "church" in the Greek is *ekklesia,* and is a compound word. The first syllable is *ek* which means "out from." The last part of the word comes from the Greek word *kaleo,* which means "to call." The church is, therefore, a company of people "called out from the world." The Bible mentions at least five things to which the believer is called. He is called "out," but also "into" something. Notice the five calls:

1. *Out* of darkness (conversion) I Peter 2:9;
2. *Unto* fellowship (communion) I Corinthians 1:9;
3. *To* holiness (consecration) I Peter 1:15;
4. *For* blessing (compensation) I Peter 3:9;
5. *Unto* glory (coronation) I Peter 5:10.

The Christian's calling begins with the call of the Gospel to his heart, and which, by the working of the Holy Spirit, results in his conversion by faith. This settles our salvation forever. It is the work of God's grace and can never be rescinded. But this is only the beginning. If we are called *out* of darkness it means we are also called *into* light. This results in communion and fellowship for "if we walk in the light as He is in the light we have fellowship." Then follows separation and holiness, "Because it is written, Be ye holy; for I am holy" (I Peter 1:16). And this path of fellowship, separation, and holiness results in blessing, "knowing that ye are thereunto *called,* that ye should inherit a blessing" (I Peter 3:9). This is our present compensation. And then comes the final call to coronation when the Lord shouts from the air and we shall finally be free from all the limitations of our sinful nature. How far have you gone in the path of "calling"? One of these days will be the crowning day! See then that today you "walk worthy of God, who hath called you unto his kingdom and glory" (I Thess. 2:12).

—M.R.D.

Sweetly, Lord, we have heard Thee calling,
Come follow me!
And we see where Thy footprints falling
Lead us to Thee!
—M. B. Slade

"The Christian life is not so much TALK as WALK!" — G. W.

DO YOU KNOW GRACE?

READ EPHESIANS 2:8-13

For by grace are ye saved.   Ephesians 2:8

Dwight L. Moody once took his concordance and studied every passage in the New Testament on the subject of "the grace of God." He became so enraptured that he immediately wanted to tell others of God's marvelous mercy. He therefore ran outside and accosted the first man he met with the enthusiastic question, "Sir, do you know grace?" Startled, the man replied, "Grace — *Grace who?*"

No, grace is not a person — but its blessings come to us *through a Person;* for grace is simply defined in Ephesians 2:7 as God's "kindness toward us *through Christ Jesus.*" Yes, the only way God's overflowing love and mercy can reach us is through the once crucified, but now ever living, Saviour!

There are various stages of grace; there is:

1. The *initial grace* by which we are *saved* (Eph. 2:8).

2. *The riches of His grace* after we are saved, wherein God abounds toward us in all wisdom, making known unto us the mystery of His will — the grace by which we are *sanctified* (Eph. 1:7-9).

3. Finally, there is *the exceeding riches of His grace* which will only be revealed to us in the eternal ages when we are completely *glorified* (Eph. 2:7).

A man in Ireland, deeply convicted of his sin, was on the point of believing when the Devil raised his oft-repeated objection, "If you do believe, you cannot keep on being a Christian. What about tomorrow?" The worker who was dealing with him pointed to a water mill nearby. "What turns the wheel today?" "The stream." "What will turn the wheel tomorrow?" "The stream," was the reply. "And the day after?" "The stream!" The anxious one was led to see that there was abundant grace to save, keep, and meet all needs. Yes, there is *grace* for today, *riches of grace* for tomorrow, and *exceeding riches of grace* for the future. "Wherefore he is able also to save them *to the uttermost* that come unto God by him" (Heb. 7:25).   — H.G.B.

> Marvelous, infinite, matchless grace,
>   Freely bestowed on all who believe;
> You that are longing to see His face,
>   Will you this moment His grace receive?
>   — J. H. Johnston

**"Simply defined, grace is:
God's Riches At Christ's Expense."**

THE APPLE OF HIS EYE

READ DEUTERONOMY 32:1-10

Keep me as the apple of the eye.   Psalm 17:8

None of the five senses is as precious as the sense of sight. Blindness is one of the greatest misfortunes of life. For this reason the Creator of the eye has protected it in a most careful and unusual way. The eyes are placed deep into sockets, surrounded by a wall of hard bone. In addition they are protected by eyelids, which completely cover the eye when danger approaches. On these eyelids are the hairy eyelashes to catch dust and other fine objects, and then, most wonderful of all, there is a system of perpetual irrigation or "washing." The tear glands secrete a soothing, salty solution which keeps the eye moist and clean at all times. To keep the eyes from blurring and the tears from running over, there are provided little channels or "tear ducts" which drain the cleansing fluid into the nose. All this illustrates how precious is the eye, and how the Creator has provided for its protection.

The Bible compares us to the eyes of God. Concerning Israel it says, "He kept him as the apple of his eye" (Deut. 32:10). In Zechariah 2:8 God says concerning His people, " . . . he that toucheth you toucheth the apple of his (the Lord's) eye." David prays in our text, "Keep me as the apple of the eye" (Psa. 17:8). The word "apple" in the Hebrew means literally the "little man." We can thus read: "I will keep you as the 'little man' of my eye." God's eye is on the "little man." No matter how obscure and forgotten you may be as a humble believer, the Lord watches over you every moment. Someone has observed that coal miners, after a whole day underground, come out with their entire faces black with dust; but there are two spots on their faces just as clean as when they went in in the morning — their eyes. Amid all the dirt and filth of this old world the Lord can keep us as clean as the "apple of the eye." Read and consider our memory verse for today. "He that planted the ear, shall he not hear? he that formed the eye, shall he not see?" (Psa. 94:9).   — M.R.D.

> Precious promise God hath given
> To the weary passerby,
> On the way from earth to Heaven,
> "I will guide thee with Mine eye."
> —N. Niles

"There is no risk in abandoning ourselves to God."

"FEEDING" THE DEAD!

READ EPHESIANS 2:1-7

And you hath he quickened, who were dead in trespasses and sins.   Ephesians 2:1

In China many still believe that the dead eat as well as the living! Besides the memorial rites which have to be held during the "seventh moon" of each year for the departed, the ancestors must also be provided with feasts two or three days before the most important national festivals. Especially before the new year this is deemed important, for it is thought that then the dead return seeking earthly food. Consequently, a banquet, including much food and wine, is dutifully supplied and made ready by the eldest son for the refreshment of "honorable ancestors." We shake our heads sadly at such an absurd practice; and yet, with equal folly, we often try to feed the "spiritually dead" and then express surprise when there is no growth and little reaction.

It is necessary to see to it that our children receive doctrinal training, and attend Sunday school regularly; in fact, it is highly commendable, but let us never suppose that this is in any way a substitute for earnestly and personally seeking to bring them to the foot of the cross for salvation. The implanting of the new life is a pre-requisite for their true growth in grace.

You too may attend church faithfully, go through a great deal of religious ritualism, and even read your Bible regularly, but unless you have experienced the "new birth," you are just trying to nourish a dead corpse!

Moody used to say, "We hear nowadays so much about 'culture.' Culture is all right when you have something to cultivate. If I should plant a watch, I shouldn't get any little watches, should I? Why? Because the seed of life is not there. But let me plant some peas or potatoes, and I will get a crop. Don't let any man or woman rest short of his being born of the Spirit of God. Don't cultivate a dead and corrupt thing. *First, make sure you have the divine nature, then cultivate it.*" Yes, one has to be born into the family of God before he can "grow in grace."   — H.G.B.

> Come thou soul-transforming Spirit,
>   Bless the sower and the seed;
> Let each heart Thy grace inherit;
>   And, oh, then the hungry feed.
> — J. Evans

"The reason so many do not truly hunger for the things of God is that they are still spiritually dead!"

"GOD'S CANDID CAMERA"

READ ROMANS 3:10-18

> *All the ways of a man are clean in his own eyes; but the*
> *Lord weigheth the spirits.* Proverbs 16:2

Salvation consists of accepting God's estimate concerning your wicked heart. It does not depend on how satisfied you are with your own goodness, but is God, who knows you far better than you do yourself, satisfied with you? It makes no difference how highly your neighbors and friends think of you; the vital question is, "What does God think of you?" Your only hope lies in acceptance of what God says about your depraved, hopeless, lost condition. God says about the heart of the unregenerate, no matter how moral or religious, that it is "deceitful above all things and desperately wicked" (Jer. 17:9). The very first requirement for salvation is to accept this verdict of God. Have you read our Scripture for today? That passage in Romans 3:10-18 together with Psalm 14 is God's photograph of the natural human heart. And God's "photographs" are not "touched up" to please the subject. The blemishes and wrinkles are all there. Once we see ourselves in God's mirror, all pride and conceit must disappear. Don't make the mistake of thinking you are as nice as you look to yourself. A young girl came to her pastor and said, "I am afraid I am guilty of the sin of vanity; for every time I look in the mirror I cannot help but admire my great beauty." The old pastor replied, "That's more than a sin — it is also a mistake."

A young photographer who specialized in "close-ups" was sent to China. He was unsaved, and in the course of his business called on a leading Chinese photographer. After talking business for awhile the Chinese photographer said, "You specialize in close-ups of people, but have you ever taken a close-up of your own heart?" Surprised, he asked, "What do you mean?" whereupon the native pulled out a copy of the New Testament and read to him Romans 3:10-18. For the first time he was brought face to face with God's own "close-up" of his unregenerate heart and was ultimately saved. —M.R.D.

> From righteousness all men depart,
>   Corrupt are they, and vile in heart;
> Yea, every man has evil done;
>   Not one does good, not even one.
> —Anon.

"If we give soft names to sin, we depreciate the value of the blood which was shed to deliver us from it."

"PRAISE THE LORD!"

READ PSALM 40:1-4, 14-17

> . . . *let such as love thy salvation say continually, The Lord be magnified.*   Psalm 40:16

We need more happy, shouting, praising Christians! Haven't we much for which to exalt and bless His Name? Few people who are just "religious" are ever heard to say "hallelujah," or "praise the Lord," but this should not be true of born-again believers. The children of God in Old Testament times did a lot of shouting in connection with their deep spiritual experiences and Heaven-sent victories. Indeed, at one time the rejoicing in Israel reached such a pitch of enthusiasm "that the earth rent with the sound of them" (I Kings 1:40).

Rowland Hill was once walking along a hillside in Gloucestershire when he saw a landslide at a gravel pit bury three laborers. He shouted so lustily for help that his voice was heard in the town below — *a mile distant!* No one blamed him for his earnestness, yet many people denounced him as a fanatic when he used this same heavy voice to warn sinners to "flee from the wrath to come," or when he shouted his "hallelujahs" of praise and adoration to the Saviour.

Christians who will "holler themselves hoarse" at a football game never seem to find enough joy in their Saviour, or sufficient enthusiasm concerning the blessings of grace, to say an "Amen" above a whisper. I recognize that some may go to extremes in these matters and disturb the assembly of the saints at times by their incessant shouting and mumbling; yet the coldness and lack of fervor exhibited by the majority of Christians should be of even greater concern to us. With the psalmist we would exclaim: "*. . . let all the people say, Amen. Praise ye the Lord*" (Psa. 106:48)!

Christian, you have something to be happy about. Don't be afraid to express yourself. Yea, "be glad in the Lord, and rejoice, ye righteous: and *shout for joy, all ye that are upright in heart*" (Psa. 32:11)!

                                                                 —H.G.B.

> Set us afire, Lord, stir us we pray,
>   While the world perishes, we go our way;
> Purposeless, passionless, day after day,
>   Set us afire, Lord, stir us, we pray.
>   —Anon.

"Some folks carry their religion on their shoulder like a burden, instead of in their hearts like a song." — DR. W. EVANS

ARE YOU GOD'S PRESERVE?

READ GALATIANS 5:1-15

. . . preserved in Jesus Christ.   Jude 1:1

Do you remember the preserves your mother used to make? I can still see the big pot on the stove boiling away, until after several testings the "preserves" were just concentrated enough and were poured into glasses or jars. There were strawberry preserves, raspberry preserves, currant preserves, peach and plum and apple. Why were they called "preserves"? Because they were preserved against spoiling. Fruits in the raw or untreated state soon deteriorate, decay, and perish. But "preserved" fruits lasted indefinitely because they were impregnated with "sugar." Sugar was the secret. The fruits were preserved in a sweet sugar syrup. To make good jam, advertises a certain cookbook, "A cup of sugar to a cup of fruit." Our text in Jude 1 says that we are "preserved in Jesus Christ." Could anything be sweeter than that? All true Christians ought to be sweet at all times if they are preserved "in Christ." Impregnated with Christ, filled with Him. The word "preserved" is *tereo* in the original and means "to guard against loss or spoiling." The Christian is watched over by the Lord and He guards and protects us.

The more we submit ourselves to Him, the more we meditate upon Him and seek His fellowship, the more we shall become saturated with His sweetness. It is an interesting thing to find that the word "reserved" in I Peter 1:4 is the same word *tereo* in the Greek. Peter says that we have an "inheritance incorruptible . . . reserved in heaven."

We are "preserved" in Christ Jesus, and our inheritance is "reserved" in Heaven for us. What security! We are preserved; our salvation is reserved; and both words mean "to guard against loss or spoiling." All this should make us sweet like the One in whom we are "preserved."   —M.R.D.

> Sweet is the tender love Jesus hath shown,
>   Sweeter far than any love mortals have known;
> Kind to the erring one, faithful is He;
>   He the great Example is, and pattern for me.
>   —W. A. Ogden

"When the sweetness of Christ completely permeates your being, your life will have a delightful, spiritual flavor!"

"KEEP PLODDING ON"

READ JOSHUA 6:1-20

And ye shall . . . go round about the city once. Thus shalt thou do six days . . . and the seventh day ye shall compass the city seven times . . . and the wall of the city shall fall down flat.   Joshua 6:3-5

The story of the fall of Jericho through the power of God is a thrilling one, rich with lessons for all of us. The monotonous and apparently useless marching assignment given to Joshua made little sense, but the eye of faith was strong; therefore the Word of the Lord was conscientiously followed, and the miracle occurred. Success in the Christian life too demands that we keep marching faithfully ahead, even though at times we see no results and find little use in going on. Even when our pathway leads in tiring circles and the walls of difficulty keep standing despite our most earnest prayers and efforts, yet there is no room for standing still when God says: "Go ye!" The continuous, roundabout march of Joshua is a good example of the fact that God accomplishes His purposes in mysterious ways. *Seldom does He lead in obvious paths those for whom He intends to perform the greatest miracle!*

God is ever looking for men and women who will bravely do His bidding with unchanging trust in His good purpose and design. By such the deriding voices on the "Jericho wall of the world" will be disregarded. Trial will not discourage such individuals, nor lack of success daunt them.

Often before the walls of our difficulty God puts into our hands a trumpet when we think it should be a sword, and still more often He sends us on a long circuitous march when we think He should retain us for a direct assault; yet by faith He wants us to go on in the way that He has planned, trustingly saying, *"One step enough for me!"*

"Keep plodding on for God," one dear old pastor used to say, "and you may be certain that the walls of your Jericho will eventually fall when the dear Lord deems it is time for you to enter the Promised Land!"   —H.G.B.

> Keep thou my feet; I do not ask to see
> The distant scene, one step enough for me!
> —J. H. Newman

"Although we cannot always see the promised LAND; yet we must trust the guidance of the promised HAND!"

FRAGRANT CHRISTIANS

READ LEVITICUS 1:9-13

> *But he shall wash the inwards and the legs with water:*
> *and . . . burn it upon the altar: it is a . . . sweet savour unto*
> *the Lord.* Leviticus 1:13

> *Christ . . . hath given himself . . . a sacrifice to God for a*
> *sweetsmelling savour.* Ephesians 5:2

Everything has some distinctive, identifying odor all its own. We may not be able to detect it with our limited sense of smell but it is there just the same. A dog can detect the scent of a rabbit or a bird where we notice nothing. Bees can detect intruders or bees from another hive right next to them by their different odor and immediately put them to death. Ants will follow the trail of other ants for long distances merely by the scent. The Christian, too, has a scent all his own. The spiritual Christian "smells like Jesus." Christ is the perfectly fragrant One, and contact with Him determines our fragrance. In the offering in the first chapter of Leviticus, the inwards and the bowels were to be burnt. Inwards contain the "offal," the corruption and waste matter of the body. It is offensive, putrid, and nauseating, to be carefully disposed of in private and never to be touched (Deut. 23:13). It represents our sin and defilement. It must be burned up and destroyed.

The burnt offering is Jesus. He became sin for us. That loathsome, abominable thing — He took upon Himself and consumed it on the cross. His sacrifice for our putrid, nauseating offal of sin becomes acceptable to God and a "sweet smelling savour." Jesus is the fragrant One — all His garments "smell of myrrh" (Psa. 45:8). To be much with Him is to "smell like Him."

A servant girl was sent into the fields by her mistress to gather myrtle of which she was very fond. This "bog myrtle" was very fragrant, and after she had delivered it to her mistress she exclaimed, "And didn't I smell lovely myself when I was done?" The more we gather the flowers of Christ in the field of His Word, the more folks will detect *His* fragrance in our lives. —M.R.D.

> Let the beauty of Jesus be seen in me,
> All His wonderful passion and purity;
> O Thou Spirit divine, all my nature refine,
> Till the beauty of Jesus be seen in me.
> —A. Osborn

"The perfume of holiness is distilled in the soul only by intimate communion with the Rose of Sharon." — H.G.B.

RESISTING TEMPTATION

READ I CORINTHIANS 10:6-13

> *And lead us not into temptation, but deliver us from*
> *evil ....*   Matthew 6:13

A pastor was once requested to speak to a young man who had gotten deep into sin. The youth was from a lovely Christian home and had received fine training. However, without his parent's consent or knowledge he began frequenting nightclubs. This soon led to drinking and other complications. His family then became aware of his backslidden condition and asked their pastor to counsel with him. The preacher told the young prodigal kindly that he could not continue to yield to the allurements of the world and still maintain a Christian testimony. In the course of the conversation he made these pointed remarks: "Young man, when you are enticed to go in doubtful paths, or when you are tempted to go into questionable places, you should simply stop where you are and say, 'Lord Jesus, here I am, *You lead me in.*' Do you think you would go into many of the establishments you have been frequenting if you did that?" The young man's reply was immediate, "No, pastor, I do not think I would." "Of course you wouldn't! Whenever temptation comes to you, breathe a prayer for guidance. You may be sure that the Lord Jesus will turn you around and send you the other way as fast as you can go. He will not direct you into the way of temptation!" It is said that the faltering Christian was reclaimed by the minister's good advice.

In our own strength we may often fail, but in the power of Christ we can conquer temptation and live on the victory side! "But God is faithful, who will not suffer you to be tempted above that ye are able; but will with the temptation also make a way to escape, that ye may be able to bear it" (I Cor. 10:13). Yea, "Blessed is the man that endureth temptation: for when he is tried, he shall receive the crown of life" (James 1:12)!   —H.G.B.

> When temptation's paths allure
>   With blossoms-bordered charm,
> Or peaks of pride and disbelief
>   Entice our steps toward harm,
> Give us the wisdom to reject
>   All but the highway trod
> By pilgrims on the upward road
>   Which leads them straight to God.
> — G. B. Burket

"Watch out for temptation — the more you see of it the better it looks!"

PERFECTLY CONTENTED

READ I TIMOTHY 6:1-12

. . . be content with such things as ye have. Hebrews 13:5

A certain evaporated milk has for its slogan, "From contented cows," and illustrates it with a beautiful picture of a herd of cattle, lying in a luxurious pasture contentedly chewing their cud. These are contented cows because they are satisfied. They wish for nothing more. This morning as I sat in my study I saw another picture of contentment. It is a dreary, dark day and it is raining. I watched a fat robin pull three worms from the grass, and then fly up to the telephone wire just outside my window. And there, ten feet from me, I imagined he gave me a knowing wink and began to sing. For a full half-hour I sat and enjoyed the robin's rendition of "Praise ye the Lord." He was content. He was satisfied with what the Heavenly Father had provided, and did not worry about tomorrow. He was singing in the rain!

The robin did not complain about the color or size of the worms, but was satisfied with what he found. Have you ever heard a robin grumble? Of course not! Then why do we? A little girl whose father was a chronic grumbler said to her mother, "I know what everybody likes in this family. Johnny likes hamburgers, Janie likes ice cream, Willie likes bananas, and mommy likes chicken." Irked because he had not been included in the list, the father grumblingly asked, "And what about me, what do I like?" The innocent little one replied, "You like everything we haven't got!" Paul could say, "I have learned in whatsoever state I am therewith to be content." Read the rest of Hebrews 13:5 — *"For He hath said, I will never leave thee, nor forsake thee."* Isn't that enough to satisfy anyone?

—M.R.D.

Said the Robin to the Sparrow, "I should really like to know
  Why these anxious human beings rush about and worry so!"
Said the Sparrow to the Robin, "Friend, I think that it must be
  That they have no Heavenly Father such as cares for you and me!"
            — E. Cheney

"Thankfulness is the soil in which joy thrives."

FORGIVING YOUR ENEMIES

READ LUKE 23:27-34

*And he kneeled down, and cried with a loud voice, Lord,
lay not this sin to their charge. And when he had said
this, he fell asleep.*   Acts 7:60

Stephen, the first martyr, following in the footsteps of his Lord,
forgave and prayed for his enemies.

Many years ago in the course of a pulpit debate, George Hol-
yoake sneeringly asked Dr. Parker, "What did God do for the
martyr Stephen when he was being stoned to death?" Dr. Parker
was embarrassed for a moment; then he gave a reply which he always believed was given to him in his moment of crisis by the
Lord Himself. He said, "I believe the Almighty did far more for
Stephen than first appears. True, He did not send an angel to
deliver him in his hour of agony; but God did enable Stephen to
say, 'Lord, lay not this sin to their charge.' I therefore believe that
when we see all the facts in the light of eternity, we shall recognize
that in *working this miracle of forgiveness in the heart of Stephen,
God did more than if He had sent a legion of angels to deliver
him.*"

It is human to hold a grudge, but it is Christ-like to forgive. Can
you find it in your heart to pardon and pray for those who have
"trespassed against you"?

In a local home for the aged in Grand Rapids, two Christian
men had been quarreling for many years. One was finally upon
what he believed to be his deathbed, so he called the other and
said, "John, I forgive you for what you have said and done against
me over the years, and I want you to do the same for me." The
other with tears said that he would. For a moment a faraway look
came into the eyes of the man lying in the bed, and then he said
with some spirit, "But John, *if I get better, this doesn't count!*"
That wasn't the spirit of true forgiveness at all!

Let the Holy Spirit root all hatred and bitterness out of your
heart. Heed the words of the Saviour who said, "*Love* your enemies,
do good to them which hate you, *Bless them* that curse you, and
pray for them which despitefully use you" (Luke 6:27, 28).

—H.G.B.

How oft shalt thou forgive thy brother? That depends:
How often has thy Lord forgiven thee?
Thy debt was great; it could not greater be,
And yet thou art forgiven and set free!

—Anon.

"When you 'bury the hatchet' don't leave the handle sticking out!"

I MET AN ANGEL

READ PSALM 53

The angel of the LORD encampeth round about them that fear him, and delivereth them.　　　Psalm 34:7

I met an angel some time ago while returning from a trip through Georgia. I was ill and very uncomfortable. On a turnpike south of Atlanta I stopped at an emergency turnout to rest for a moment. When I tried to start the motor of my car, it failed to respond. There we were, miles from a service station. I know nothing about automobiles except to steer when they run. The cars whizzed by at 65 miles per hour. And then, after only a few minutes, a station wagon slowed up, a man got out and asked, "Can I help you?" I replied that I couldn't start the car and was hoping for a state police car to come by. How happy I was when he said, "I am a highway patrolman in the employ of the trucking industry." After a brief consultation and another try to start the motor he suggested pushing it to make it start. It worked. I had merely "flooded" the carburetor. I stopped the car and offered to pay him but he refused. He asked my name, and when he heard it he stuck out his big hand and exclaimed, "You mean you are Dr. DeHaan of the Radio Bible Class? I listen to you every Sunday evening over an Atlanta station." He was a member of the Bible Class. Just a few sweet moments of fellowship on the highway and I got in my car and was on my way. I had met an angel to deliver me.

Coincidence you say? Oh no! Oh no! It was providence! It was the fulfillment of Psalm 34:7. Do you thank God for the "little" deliverances? When He delivers us in some crisis, a severe illness, a serious accident, a great trial, then we praise Him; but how about the "little" deliverances? Today, try and see how often He helps you in the minor, seemingly unimportant problems. Recognition of God in *everything* reveals a growth in grace. Learn to recognize the angel of the Lord. Yes, I met an angel on the highway!　　　　　　　　　　　　　　　— M.R.D.

Just when I need Him, Jesus is near,
　Just when I falter, just when I fear;
Ready to help me, ready to cheer,
　Just when I need Him most.
　　　　　　　　—Rev. W. Poole

"The wide-awake believer sees God not only in the forest — but in each individual tree!"

"KNEE MEDICINE !"

READ PSALM 5

Hearken unto the voice of my cry, my King, and my God: for unto thee will I pray. Psalm 5:2

When a Chinese convert was asked by a missionary what remedy he found most effective in overcoming the Opium habit he replied quaintly, "Knee Medicine." We live in an age of energy and force, but what Christians really need today is more "knee power!"

Peter MacKenzie, the famous Methodist preacher, was once speaking to a member of his congregation who complained bitterly, "My most earnest prayer has not been answered!" "Oh," replied Rev. MacKenzie, "that is very understandable, and it should not cause you to despair. Remember, many of our petitions are like promissory notes that guarantee payment *at some future date. You have just presented yours before it was due!* Do not cease to pray—God will honor *in His own good time!"*

Moses cried to God, and at the very moment when defeat seemed certain, the sea was divided. Hannah prayed for a son and in God's good time Samuel was born. The early Church prayed most fervently for Peter and at the proper moment the angel delivered him from prison. Indeed, "Men ought always to pray and not to faint!" God's delays are not denials — He is merely preparing a greater blessing. Some ask for strength that they might achieve, but God makes them weak that they might obey. Some ask for health that they might do great things, but God sends infirmity that they might do better things. Some ask for riches that they might be happy, but our Lord often gives poverty in order that they might be wise. Some ask for power, but are given weakness that they might feel more keenly the need of God. Yet all are more richly blessed than if they had been granted their blind request.

Remember, God always answers our prayers by giving us what we ask, or *what we would have requested if we could see as He sees!* — H.G.B.

At the blessed hour of prayer, trusting Him we believe
That the blessing we're needing, we'll surely receive;
In the fullness of this trust we may lose every care;
What a balm for the weary! Oh how sweet to be there!
— F. J. Crosby

"The Lord's answers to our prayers are infinitely perfect and eternity will show that often when we were asking for a STONE that looked like BREAD, He was giving us BREAD that looked like STONE."
— J. P. SOUTHEY

SHINING FOR JESUS

READ II CORINTHIANS 4:1-6

. . . among whom ye shine as lights in the world.
Philippians 2:15

"Shine, sir?" These words fell on my ear amid the roar of street traffic as I walked back from the restaurant to the hotel. I looked around and saw a shining black face, and he said again as he looked at my shoes, "Shine, sir?" Something told me to have my shoes shined and the little fellow went to work with a happy, slappy rhythm on my shoes. And while he worked he whistled a familiar tune which I immediately recognized. He was gaily whistling, "Jesus bids us shine with a clear pure light, like a little candle burning in the night," etc. I waited a moment and said, "Lad, do you know who you are shining for?" He looked me over and replied, "No, sah, ah don't recollect ah done ever see you befo.' " "But what was that tune you were whistling?" With a broad smile he said, "That was 'Shining for Jesus,' sir, ah done learn that in Sunday school." "But do you know this Jesus?" Without hesitation he said, "Ah sure do and I love Him." "Well then, who are you shining for, with your happy whistle?" He thought a moment and then — "For Jesus." "Yes, my boy, you are shining for Jesus with your whistle."

I did a lot of thinking after that. Here was a lad "in the midst of a crooked and perverse generation" (Phil. 2:15) among whom he shone as a light in the world. In the midst of the darkness of the great city — a little light, *shining for Jesus!* I like to think that in Heaven folks will seek out this colored lad and say, "I was led to Jesus through your whistle, for that little tune renewed thoughts of my Sunday school days, and mother's prayers, and awakened in me the memories of those tender years." Keep on whistling, Joe. You don't have to be a preacher or a specially trained person to witness for Jesus. Will you do anything today which will point people to Jesus? Try whistling!　　— M.R.D.

> Shine, shine, just where you are,
> Shine, shine, just where you are;
> Send forth the light, into the night;
> Shine for the Lord where you are!
> 　　　　—A. R. Habershon

"Don't expect God to use you as a lighthouse somewhere else, if He can't use you as a candle where you are!" — G.W.

OLD AGE

READ PSALM 71:1-18

Cast me not off in the time of old age; forsake me not when my strength faileth.   Psalm 71:9

An old Chinese Grandpa, too feeble to work, was considered by the family an unwanted burden — just another mouth to consume the meager supply of rice. Therefore the father of the home decided to put the old man on a wheelbarrow and take him up to the mountains to die. The little eight-year-old grandson went along, full of curiosity and questions. The father explained that the grandfather was old and helpless, and that there was nothing else to be done with him. Then the little chap had a happy thought: "I'm glad I came along, Daddy," said the youngster, "because *when you get old I'll know where to take you!*" The daddy stopped dead in his tracks, thought better of the whole situation, and brought the old gentleman back home.

Old age is beset with many such fears of being unwanted and cast off when youthful strength has departed. David too was not immune to such thoughts, and therefore he cries out to God to remember him in his declining years. God's answer to David comes ringing from the portals of Heaven through the mouth of the Prophet Isaiah: "Even to your old age I am he; and even to hoar hairs will I carry you: I have made, and I will bear; even I will carry, and will deliver you (Isa. 46:4)!

G. W. Aleen comments most wisely, "As we grow older in years and in our Christian experience, Satan is less able to tempt us to the sins more prevalent among youth, but it is then that he often succeeds in souring our spirit, making us critical, and at times outright mean . . . It has been my constant prayer that, if the Lord permits me to grow old, I may be a kindly old man, sweet in mind and spirit wherever I may be."

How beautiful a sight it is to see elderly Christians still looking to the future, still happily trusting God and clinging to His promises!   — H.G.B.

Thou who hast made my home of life so pleasant,
Leave not its tenant when its walls decay;
O Love divine, O Helper ever present,
Be Thou my strength and stay!
                    —Whittier

"An aged Christian with the snow of time upon his head reminds us that THOSE POINTS OF EARTH ARE THE WHITEST WHICH ARE NEAREST TO HEAVEN!"

SPIRITS OF CAMPHOR

READ ROMANS 5:1-11

> *. . . his hands full of sweet incense beaten small . . . .*
> *And he shall put the incense upon the fire.*
> Leviticus 16:12, 13

On the day of atonement, the High Priest was to take sweet incense, ground to powder, and cast a handful of it upon the fire of the altar. The original word for incense means "to produce fragrance by burning." A certain herb, odorless until crushed, was beaten small and cast into the fire on the altar, releasing its aromatic fumes in a pungent, fragrant cloud which filled the whole house. This was a sweet-smelling savor unto the Lord.

Notice two things: 1) It must be "beaten small," and 2) it must pass through the fire. So, too, the fragrance of our lives for Christ must be beaten small by the hammer of His Word and pass through the fiery trials of God's chastening to bring out the true fragrance. (Read again Rom. 5:3-5.) I have found the maximum of tender submissive fragrance in those lives which have been beaten in the fire.

Last winter I was introduced to a new tree in Florida. It was a stately, spreading tree with shiny, leathery leaves. Upon inquiry I was told it was a "camphor tree." "Smell the leaves," said my friend. I did — and smelled *nothing.* Then — "Crush those leaves between your palms," and as I did so the whole car was filled with an intensely invigorating fragrance of camphor. It only needed crushing to release its clean odor. I was told the tree was "disease free." No bugs, thrips, beetles, or worms would touch it. Birds and animals left it alone. Oh, to be a camphor tree for God, repelling and rebuking all the bugs and grubs of selfishness, greed, pride, envy, and defilement. Oh, to be beaten small by the hammer of the Word and to be purified by God's loving hand. That is how God makes "spirits of camphor" to revive fainting souls and to stimulate the heart of the faltering. — M.R.D.

> When I fear my faith will fail,
>   Christ will hold me fast;
> When the tempter would prevail,
>   He can hold me fast.
> —A. R. Habershon

"God first humbles us by 'beating us fine' with trial, and then exalts us by using us as a 'sweet-smelling savor' to shed forth the fragrance of His grace!" — G.W.

SEND ME!

READ ISAIAH 6:1-8

*Also I heard the voice of the Lord, saying, Whom shall
I send, and who will go for us? Then said I, Here am
I; send me.*   Isaiah 6:8

A deacon was once leading in prayer at a missionary meeting.
One of his stereotyped phrases was this: "Oh Lord, touch the
unsaved with Thy finger." After he intoned these words, he
suddenly stopped short. Other members came to his side and
asked him if he were ill. "No," he replied, "but something seems
to be saying to me, *'Thou art the finger.'*" How many of us have
prayed that God would "save the heathen," but have never
seriously considered our own personal responsibility to "go . . .
into all the world and preach the gospel"?

An elderly Christian worker upon encouraging a young man
to follow the call of the Lord was given an excuse that had a
familiar ring, "But I have never felt any compelling call to give
my life in that way." *"But, are you sure you are within calling
distance?"* was the somewhat disquieting reply.

Two brothers, both well established on their own farms, one
day investigated the possibility of giving their all in Christian
service. One finally determined to give up his opportunities for
wealth and material gain by becoming a missionary. Eventually,
therefore, he and his family invested their lives in South
America for Jesus Christ. The older brother, weighing his material opportunities, felt that they were too heavy to be sacrificed
in such a cause. Besides, life in the United States was too inviting and the hazards of the mission field too great. He therefore decided to disregard the call of Christ. A year or two later,
he died accidentally in a fire on the farm that he thought was so
safe! In trying to save his life, he had lost it! His brother on
the "dangerous foreign field" still lives today, and continues to
lay up much treasure in Heaven.

Have you heard God's call to service? Are you hesitating because the world seemingly offers so much? Oh that you might
say with Isaiah, "Here am I; *send me!*"   — H.G.B.

> Let none hear you idly saying,
> "There is nothing I can do,"
> For the souls of men are dying
> And the Master calls for *you!*
>
> —Anon.

**"Every heart without Jesus Christ is a mission field; every heart with
Jesus Christ should be a missionary!"** — BUD SCHAEFFER

MIRACLES OF RESURRECTION

READ ACTS 2:25-36

For I know that my redeemer liveth.   Job 19:25

Last fall we planted some choice narcissus bulbs, kindly sent to us by some dear friends in Oak Harbor, Washington. They were dry and hard and gave no signs of life at all. All winter long they lay in darkness, incarcerated in a tomb of hard, frozen earth. But today, five months later, I gaze out of my study window upon a scene of exquisite beauty – a gorgeous row of beautiful blooms, nodding smilingly at me through the window. Springtime is resurrection time.

Last fall the boys gathered cocoons in the swamp. These were dry, unattractive, and motionless. They were hung up in a cool place for the winter. Not long ago, however, they were moved to a place in the warm sun. Today there emerged from the tomb of the cocoon a gorgeous creature – a luna moth, gracefully unfolding its drying wings in readiness to take its flight into the sky. Indescribable are its colors, unspeakably graceful its unhurried stretching and folding of its airplane-like wings. Yes, springtime is resurrection time. But the blooming of the narcissus and the birth of the moth are not a resurrection from death but a metamorphosis of life. It is a change in form because of its inner life. The resurrection of Jesus Christ was *life from the dead.* But it is also a "metamorphosis," a change in form. It is the same creature in an infinitely more beautiful form. So shall our resurrection be also for the word, "fashioned," in Philippians 3:21 is *summorphos,* meaning to change form or "metamorphose." Our bodies will be changed and fashioned like the glorious body of our Lord Jesus. And all this is because *He arose.* "O death, where is thy sting? O grave, where is thy victory?" (I Cor. 15:55).   —M.R.D.

Light dawns in darkness, and comfort in sadness;
Death shall no longer our spirits dismay;
Tears turn to praise, and griefs change to gladness.
Jesus is risen, is risen today!

—T. C. Pease

"Christ's empty tomb is the gateway to Heaven."

SAVED BY GRACE

READ ACTS 15:5-11

*But we believe that through the grace of the Lord Jesus
Christ we shall be saved.*   Acts 15:11

Paul and Barnabas had been preaching the marvelous doctrine
of salvation by grace, when certain men came down from Judaea
to Antioch to spy out their liberty. These legalists said, "Except
ye be circumcised after the manner of Moses, ye cannot be
saved." It was an attempt to add law to grace, and it caused a
tremendous stir and division. The missionary work had to be
stopped and the whole matter threshed out at a special council
in Jerusalem, where Paul and Barnabas were completely exon-
erated of any false teaching.

Today there are still such legalists who are ever expounding
their own erroneous doctrines. They feel they are doing God
a service, but actually they are a serious impediment to the work
of the Gospel. Nothing delights Satan more than to confuse men
concerning the simple plan of salvation; for once the poor sinner
realizes that Heaven and forgiveness are by grace *plus nothing,*
his burdened soul soon finds rest in Christ.

Dr. Ironside frequently told the story concerning the conversion of Evangelist A. Stewart because it so well illustrated the
delusion under which unsaved individuals labor in their efforts
to find peace with God. Stewart, under deep conviction of sin,
was told to simply believe on the Lord Jesus Christ, but he mis-
takenly thought that this was far too easy, so he went about
according to his own ideas. He joined a church, sang in the
choir, and became quite a worker. He hoped in all these things
to gain salvation, but there was no inner satisfaction, no peace.
One day, as he was reading the parable of the sower, he came
to the words, "Then cometh the devil and taketh away the word
out of their hearts *lest they should believe and be saved.*" Stewart
threw down his Bible and said, "Well, will you look at that! Even
the devil knows that a man will be saved if he just believes!"
That day he settled it and turned to Christ, trusting Him as
Saviour.

Yes, God saves men by grace, *apart from the works of the law!*

— H.G.B.

> Free from the law, oh happy condition,
> Jesus hath bled and there is remission;
> Cursed by the law, and bruised by the fall,
> Grace hath redeemed us once for all.
> —P. P. Bliss

"Salvation is given — not gained!" — G.W.

WE WERE EXPECTING YOU!

READ II CORINTHIANS 5:1-9

Friend, wherefore art thou come?   Matthew 26:50

The Greek word translated friend in this verse is *hetaire,* and means a "comrade" or, as we might say, a "pal." There is probably no more touching, tender sentence in the entire Bible, nor one more easily overlooked. The speaker was Jesus in the garden. The person addressed was none other than *Judas,* the betrayer of Jesus. And Jesus, knowing the purpose for which Judas came, said to him, "Comrade, why did you come?" Friend, Comrade! Pal! *We've worked together for three years, and now this.* It is difficult to fathom the pathos and tenderness of our Lord. He calls him, "Friend."

The question our Lord asked Judas suggests surprise at his coming. Now of course Jesus knew Judas was coming, for He had predicted the betrayal (Matt. 26:23), and yet there is a note of surprise in Jesus' words. Certainly the disciples must have been surprised and disappointed, for they never expected this of Judas. Would people also be surprised if they could look through your outward piety into your *real heart?*

There is another surprise mentioned in the Bible. Peter was in prison, and the disciples called a prayer meeting for his release (Acts 12:5). When he was free and came to the prayer meeting, they were surprised and wouldn't believe it was he. They were not expecting him. What do people expect of you? Don't disappoint them. Don't be a hypocrite!

A certain woman was recovering from the anesthetic after an operation. Her eyelids fluttered and, dazed and half-conscious, she murmured, "Where am I? Where am I?" And then she said, "Is this Heaven — am I in Heaven?" At that moment her eyes fell on her husband George who was at her bedside. She murmured, "Heaven, Heaven, no it can't be. I see George." Are they expecting you in heaven?

— M.R.D.

> I dreamed I searched Heaven for you,
>   Searched vainly through Heaven for you;
> Friend, won't you prepare to meet me up there?
>   Lest I should search Heaven for you?
> —M. E. Wiess

"If people could really see your heart, would they be happily surprised or dismally disappointed?" — M.R.D.

KEEP LOOKING UP!

READ LUKE 21:25-28

. . . I . . . will look up.   Psalm 5:3

Robert C. McQuilkin used to tell of a young Christian who lacked assurance of salvation even though she had trusted Christ and said she had "surrendered and believed a thousand times." Hopeless and in darkness about it all, she told an older Christian woman of her difficulty. "Well," said this elderly saint, "just stop doing or trying to do anything, *and trust the Lord to do it all.*" "I have done that a hundred times," was the discouraged answer. The defeated one seemed to have no will to do anything, and yet she was hungry for victory and peace. The older woman tried again. "If you do nothing else, just lift your heart to Christ." "I can't even do that — my heart is too heavy to lift up," said the troubled one. "Well, one thing you can do, for it is just a physical act. *You can lift up your eyes.* Will you do that?" The younger woman promised that she would, and on the way home she kept them directed upward as unto Him. Not much later she gave the following testimony with a radiant face: "I lifted up my eyes, and *my heart went up with them!* Today I am rejoicing in the Lord!" Brother McQuilkin appended this application: "The victorious life is just as gloriously simple as that — just looking up — unto Jesus — and then *keep on looking!*"

As you climb the steep ascent of life, looking down will only make you dizzy and despairing. Put your hand into the nail-scarred palm of the One who said, "Him that cometh to me I will in no wise cast out" (John 6:37); *Look up,* and you won't lose your spiritual balance!   — H.G.B.

> When sins and fears prevailing rise,
> And fainting hope almost expires,
> Jesus, to Thee I lift mine eyes —
> To Thee I breathe my soul's desires.
> —A. Steele

"When the outlook is bad — try the uplook!"

WOUNDED FOR ME

READ ISAIAH 53:4-12

> *But he was wounded for our transgressions, he was bruised for our iniquities: the chastisement of our peace was upon him; and with his stripes we are healed.*
>
> Isaiah 53:5

In a painting of the crucifixion by the famous Dutch artist, Rembrandt, attention is first drawn to the cross and to Him who died there. Then, as you look at the crowd that gathers around the foot of the accursed tree, you are impressed by the various attitudes and actions of the people involved in the awful crime of crucifying the Son of God. Finally, your eyes drift to the edge of the picture and catch sight of another figure — almost hidden in the shadows. This, they tell us, was a representation of the artist himself; for Rembrandt recognized that *by his sins* he helped nail Jesus there! When we think of the cross it is so easy to consider it as merely a historical event; but actually we were all *participants* in the crucifixion!

Someone has aptly said, "It is a simple thing to say that Christ died for *the sin of the world.* It is quite another thing to say that Christ died for *my sin!* It may be an interesting pastime to point fingers at those who crucified Jesus, but it is a shocking thought that I can be as indifferent as Pilate, as scheming as Caiaphas, as calloused as the soldiers, as ruthless as the mob, or as cowardly as the disciples. It isn't just what they did — 'twas I that shed the sacred blood; I nailed Him to the tree; I crucified the Christ of God; I joined the mockery!"

Look again at the painting of the Dutch artist — if the Holy Spirit enlightens your eyes, you will see that in the shadows with Rembrandt you too are standing with blood-red hands, for He was wounded for *your transgressions!*   — H.G.B.

> Three crosses stood grimly side by side
>   On the hill of Calvary;
> On each a suffering man had died;
>   Two for THEIR crimes, the Other FOR ME!
> "If Thou art the Christ," they taunting said,
>   "Come down from the cursed tree";
> He heeded no jeering word they said,
>   But, bowing His head, HE DIED FOR ME!
>
> —Anon.

"The cross of Christ reveals the love of God at its best, and the sin of man at its worst." — C. N. BARTLETT

THE RESURRECTION – INCREDIBLE?

READ ACTS 26:1-8

Why should it be thought a thing incredible with you,
that God should raise the dead?   Acts 26:8

How is it possible that men should doubt the resurrection from the dead? It is far more incredible that there should be no resurrection. The surprised question of Paul to King Agrippa was, "Why should it be thought a thing incredible with you, that God should raise the dead?" If there be no resurrection, then life loses all its meaning; it becomes a hollow mockery. Then God who created us is a God of caprice and sadism. Is this life all? Just a few years of alternate crying and laughing – mostly crying – and then darkness? Then with Paul we can say, "If in this life only we have hope in Christ, we are of all men most miserable." But it should not be incredible, for things all around us remind us of resurrection. The buds on the trees, the flowers in the garden, the emerging life after a long winter of inactivity – all proclaim the resurrection.

In an ancient tomb in France, buried under tons of debris, archaeologists found flower seeds which had been there for *two thousand years!* The explorer took the seeds and planted them and they grew. Egyptian garden peas which had been buried for *three thousand years* were brought out and planted on the fourth of June, 1844. Within a few days they had germinated and broken the ground. Buried 3000 years – then resurrected. Why then should it be thought a thing incredible that God should raise the dead? If God could cause a lump of clay to become alive at the creation of man, why then think it incredible for this same God to bring a resurrection from the dead? Yes, it would be most incredible that after the life He lived Jesus should remain in death. Hallelujah! Christ arose!   – M.R.D.

> Up from the grave He arose
>   With a mighty triumph o'er His foes;
> He arose a Victor from the dark domain,
>   And He lives forever with His saints to reign;
> He arose! He arose! Hallelujah! Christ arose!
>   —R. Lowry

"Our Lord has written the promise of the resurrection, not only in . . . the Bible . . . but in every leaf of springtime."—M. LUTHER

THE LORD IS RISEN INDEED!

The Lord is risen indeed.   Luke 24:34

Surprise! The Lord is risen indeed! Thus did the disciples greet the two travelers from Emmaus, who had just entertained the risen Saviour in their home (Luke 24:29). What a shame that the news of Jesus' resurrection should be a *surprise.* This was inexcusable for He had told them repeatedly that He would arise after *three days* (see Matt. 26:61; Mark 8:31; and John 2:19). They had no excuse for being surprised. He had told them again and again, "I will arise!" Oh, the blindness of unbelief. And Jesus rebuked them severely for their little faith (see Mark 16:7, 14; and Luke 24:25, 26). For three days these disciples were plunged in gloom and despair. Whereas they could have been joyously and expectantly waiting for Him to arise.

Resurrection Day is a day of joy and victory; but on that first resurrection day there was gloom and sadness. Mark tells us the disciples "mourned and wept" when they should have been rejoicing. The death of Christ alone is of no comfort to us. The death of Christ alone leaves us in gloom and despair. It is the resurrection which gives meaning to the Cross. It is the capstone of the Gospel. The death of Christ alone is *bad news,* but followed by the resurrection it is *good news.* And why? Because the resurrection is the *proof* that *sin is put away.* Had one single sin remained unatoned for, Christ could not have arisen. Remember the wages of *sin (one sin)* is death. Jesus took our sins to Calvary. Had He atoned for all *but one,* He would still be in the tomb. His resurrection is the assurance that the work is *finished.* God was satisfied, and demonstrated it by raising Him from the dead (Acts 13:32, 33). Hallelujah! Yes, the Lord is risen indeed!   — M.R.D.

> Christ the Lord is ris'n today, Alleluia!
> Sons of men and angels say, Alleluia!
> Raise your joys and triumphs high, Alleluia!
> Sing, ye heav'ns and earth reply, Alleluia!
> —C. Wesley

"Live as if Christ died yesterday, arose this morning, and is coming back tomorrow!"

"IT CAME TO PASS"

*. . . the world passeth away, and the lust thereof: but he
that doeth the will of God abideth for ever.* I John 2:17

There are certain abiding elements in the Christian's life that
are always real and unchanging. Circumstances alter; loved ones
are snatched from our side by death, and the outward form of
this present world swiftly passes away (I Cor. 7:31), but the
truth of God's promises abides. As we build upon the rock foundation of the faithful Word, as we go forward by grace in the
will of God, we may face the changing world with confidence
and with peace in our soul. For us, the present is bearable because the future is so secure and glorious!

An ancient king once charged his wise men to create a sentence
which could ever be in view and be appropriated at all times
and in all situations. They finally presented him with a motto on
which were inscribed these words: "AND THIS TOO SHALL PASS
AWAY!" How true a slogan for those who live in this unstable
world. Joy is followed by sorrow, and sorrow by hope, but nothing abides.

It is said that some years ago a trolley car in Atlanta, Georgia,
bumped into the lamppost of the so-called *"eternal flame of the
Confederacy,"* and *the "eternal flame" went out!* A giant candle
was built in a town in New York to be lit once each year for two
thousand years, to symbolize friendship among the United
Nations; but shortly after this huge candle was created, it was
accidentally set afire and was consumed in *ten minutes!* Hitler
said that his "Third Reich" would last one thousand *years;* yet it
continued less than one thousand *days!* Yes, the world passeth
away and the lusts thereof, but praise His name, *"He that doeth
the will of God abideth for ever!"* In this confidence go forward
in faith. Life comes — to pass; but the best is yet to be! — H.G.B.

Soon the conflict will be done,
Soon the battle will be won,
Soon shall wave the victor's palm,
Soon shall ring the eternal song!
— A. B. Simpson

"Earth changes, but thy soul and God stand sure."—BROWNING

ADMIT YOUR IGNORANCE

READ I CORINTHIANS 1:18-31

> *. . . they . . . became vain in their imaginations, and their foolish heart was darkened. Professing themselves to be wise, they became fools.*   Romans 1:21, 22

The Apostle Paul says in Romans 12:16: "Be not wise in your own conceits." A conceited man is one who is very smart in his own estimation. He needs a good looking-glass so he can see how he looks to others. Conceit is a natural trait of the human heart. Man likes to strut and give the impression of being wise. A milder form of conceit is its negative aspect, refusing to admit your ignorance. A patient went to a young doctor with a skin rash all over his body. The doctor had never had a case like it before, and was deeply puzzled. He excused himself and went to his library to look up this malady, but could find nothing to help him. However, unwilling to admit his ignorance he asked the man; "Did you ever have this before?" "Yes," said the man, "twice before." "Ah yes, I thought so," said the sage, young M.D. "Well, you've got the same thing again!"

When I first began preaching I could answer every question in the book (such answers)! The older I become, the more often (and I mean "often") I must admit, "I don't know." May God deliver us from putting up a false front of wisdom, and teach us instead to say, "I don't know!" I am compelled again and again to resort to Deuteronomy 29:29 when people come to me with their questions.

Paul's charge against mankind was: "Professing themselves to be wise they became fools." The man who is truly wise is the man who finds out that he is a fool without Christ, utterly deceived by the Devil into thinking he can by his own goodness and wisdom be saved. As long as a man rejects Christ, he is a fool.

The wisest man is he who, in complete abandonment of self, bows before the Lord. Christ then becomes unto him "wisdom, and righteousness, and sanctification, and redemption" (I Cor. 1:30).

— M.R.D.

Perverse and foolish oft I strayed,
But yet in love He sought me,
And on His shoulder gently laid,
And home, rejoicing, brought me.
—F. W. Faber

"The biggest fool is he who fools himself!"

GIVE HIM YOUR BEST

READ DEUTERONOMY 12:5-11

All the best of the oil, and all the best of the wine, and of the wheat, the firstfruits of them . . . they shall offer unto the Lord . . . . Numbers 18:12

We have nothing that we have not received from the hand of the Lord. Therefore, once we are saved, duty and true gratitude demand that we place our all unreservedly at His disposal. We are to love God fully with all our mind, will, strength, and talents. We are not to expect the Saviour to be satisfied with a few beggarly tokens of our affection now and then.

Some years ago I read an article which told how Queen Mary used to make an annual visit to Scotland. So beloved was this sovereign that she could move freely among the people and needed no protective escort. One afternoon, while walking with some children, she went out rather far. Dark clouds came up unexpectedly, so she stopped at a nearby house of a commoner to borrow an umbrella. "If you will lend it to me, I will send it back to you tomorrow," she promised. The lady who answered the door was reluctant to give the stranger her best one, and so got an old castoff umbrella out of the attic. One of the ribs was broken, and there were several holes in the fabric. Apologizing, the lady turned it over to the Queen, whom she did not recognize. The next day there was another knock at the door. When she opened it, she saw a man in gold braid, evidently one of the royal guards, holding in his hand her old, tattered umbrella. "The Queen sent me," he said. "She asked me to thank you for loaning her this." For a moment the poor woman was stunned; then she burst into tears. "Oh, what an opportunity I missed when I did not give her my very best!" she cried. How many of us will someday say the same when we meet our King!

Christian, what is your *best talent* or your *choicest asset?* Have you given your all cheerfully and heartily to the Saviour? By this gauge, test your professed love for Jesus. — H.G.B.

I will not serve my Saviour in a poor and selfish way,
Nor with a life of idleness His tender love repay.
I want to do the utmost for His glory while I may—
I want to do my very best for Jesus.
— W. C. Martin

"Give God your best today; remember, delayed obedience is a brother of disobedience."

GOD'S PANACEA

READ PSALM 103

> *Bless the Lord, O my soul . . . who healeth all thy diseases.*   Psalm 103:2, 3

The promise of God to heal all our diseases has been grossly misunderstood and misinterpreted. It can be viewed as applying to the disease of sin as well as to actual physical illness. There are those who use this verse to prove that anyone can be cured of bodily illness by faith, or being anointed with oil, laying hands on a radio, or sending for a handkerchief. If this were true then *everyone* who did this would be healed, for the Scripture says, ". . . who healeth all thy diseases." There is no room for failures in this sense. The word *all* excludes any exception. It is of course true that in every case of recovery it is because God has so willed it. But there comes a time in everyone's life (*everyone*) when their physical sickness *is not* healed — and they die. Only when Jesus comes will this verse be fulfilled — He healeth *all* thy diseases. Until then all will continue to die, in spite of the foolish claims of men.

But the reference here is to the disease of sin, as the context will show. Sin is compared to sickness. Isaiah says of Israel, ". . . the whole head is sick, and the whole heart faint. From the sole of the foot even unto the head there is no soundness in it; but wounds, and bruises, and putrifying sores" (Isa. 1:5, 6). Before seeking physical healing we should seek spiritual health. All physical cures are temporary — ending in death — but spiritual healing results in eternal life!

I am often asked by doctors, "Aren't you sometimes sorry you left the practice of medicine and the healing of men's bodies — left a noble profession to become a despised preacher?" My answer is always *no!* All the patients I used to treat died sooner or later, but the people who take the medicine I now offer them (the Gospel) never die. The cure is permanent, and gives *eternal life*. The Gospel is God's panacea!   — M.R.D.

> There is healing at the fountain,
>   Come, behold the crimsom tide,
> Flowing down from Calvary's mountain,
>   Where the Prince of Glory died.
>   — F. J. Crosby

"Spiritual health is much more important than physical healing."

LIFE'S CHALLENGE

READ PSALM 16

Thou wilt show me the path of life....   Psalm 16:11

The sheep of God's pasture need guidance as they travel the road of life, for often it is rough and circumstances along the way are trying. But the Good Shepherd will show us the paths of peace and blessing if we do not willfully choose our own way.

It is said in some trackless lands, as a traveler passes through a forest, he breaks a twig here and there as he goes, that those who come after him may see the traces of his having been there and may know that they are not off the road. So too as we journey through the dark woods of affliction and sorrow, it is something to find here and there a broken spray, or a leaf-stem bent down with the tread of our Shepherd's foot and the brush of His hand as He passed by. For we may be sure that the path which He has trod before is a hallowed one that leads to the bright "pleasures" of the "forevermore."

How comforting are the words of the unknown poet who sings:

> I must go forth upon a pilgrim's journey
>   Along a strange and dimly lighted road;
> I cannot see what joy or care is waiting
>   Nor can I tell its length or test my load.
> But this I know, that faith will light my journey,
>   And mercy share the burden I must bring;
> That love divine will tread the road before me,
>   And lead the pilgrim to the palace of the King.

Make your life tell for Jesus today. Let Him direct your steps along the upward way of faith and service, and all your paths will be peace.   —H.G.B.

> My life shall touch a dozen lives before this day is done,
>   Leave countless marks for good or ill
>   ere sets the evening sun,
> This is the wish I always wish, the prayer I always pray:
> "Lord, may my life help other lives it touches by the way."
>   —Anon.

"The greatest use of life is to spend it for something that will outlast it." — W. JAMES

DO YOU TALK TO YOURSELF?

And when he came to himself, he said, ... Luke 15:17

Sitting in my car at the curb, waiting for the good spouse to purchase a pair of stockings, I entertained myself by watching the faces of people walking by, to observe the various emotions written on their faces. When people think nobody is looking, they will usually reveal their inmost thoughts by the expression on their faces. As the various ones passed by, I saw registered upon their faces happiness, sorrow, anxiety, fear, anticipation, determination, etc., etc. But one man in particular drew my attention, for he was deeply engrossed in talking to himself. He was so absorbed in his conversation that he bumped into another pedestrian. As he neared our car I could hear him mumbling. What he said I don't know, but it surely was a serious discussion. He was both a good conversationalist and a good listener. He reminded me of "Mose," who, being asked why he always talked to himself, replied, "I have two reasons: firstly, I like to hear a smart man talk, and secondly, I like to talk to a smart man!"

What do people talk about to themselves? It is either good or bad. The rich man in Luke 12:16-21 (or didn't you read the Scripture?) talked to himself about his riches and God called him a *fool*. The prodigal son in Luke 15 was talking to himself about his poverty, and resolved to seek the *better riches* of his father's house.

When you talk to yourself you are simply thinking out loud. Your private conversation reveals what is in your heart. A man is what he thinks! If his thoughts are evil, he will be evil. If his thoughts are pure, his life will be pure.

"Whatsoever things are true, honest, just, pure, lovely, of good report, if there be any virtue, and if there be any praise, *think on these things*" (Phil. 4:8). — M.R.D.

Thus come and go these thoughts of ours,
  Some, perfume-laden as the flowers,
While others sear our lives with blight,
  And bring no pleasure or delight.
Our thinking lifts us to the stars,
  Or seals our hearts with prison bars;
Confers on us both joy and strife,
  For as we think we fashion life.
—D. M. Robins

" 'As a man thinketh in his heart, so is he' — what do you talk to yourself about?" — M.R.D.

GIVING TILL IT COSTS!

READ MATTHEW 19:16-25

. . . give . . . and thou shalt have treasure in heaven.
Matthew 19:21

The only true way to give is to give until it costs! Someone has rightly said: "From the beginning, Christianity costs — it cost Christ His life — it should cost us something too (after we are saved) in terms of a surrendered life, good works, and sacrificial giving."

Some years ago the *Evangelical Christian* told the true story of Mrs. Inez Uptegrove, a dear child of God who testified, "I used to say, 'Oh Lord, if only I had something to give to Thee!' One night in a meeting I repeated that sad refrain, and a still small voice seemed to whisper to me, *'What hast thou in thy hand?'* I said, 'Only a nickel, Lord.' It was my carfare home, five miles away. The Lord said, 'Give that!' And I did. At the close of the service a member asked me to ride with her, which took me part of the way home. To my surprise, when I got out of the car, an old friend of the family emerged from a drugstore nearby and offered to take me the rest of the way. How I praised God for this 'two car' service because I had obeyed Him in a small way."

This experience of Mrs. Uptegrove led her to continue to prove God with increased courage and faith. She came to have a wonderful testimony concerning the Lord's faithfulness and abounding sufficiency to those who have implicit faith in His sure provision. In the course of time she was able to support several missionaries and adopt whole families in needy parts of the world and supply them with clothing and food. Many fields of service opened to her which had been hidden entirely until "the meager five-cent fare home had been sacrificed in love to the Saviour."

You may not have much of value down here, but you can have great treasure in Heaven if you will just do a little *sacrificial* giving. Perhaps our Christian lives are dull and uninspiring because we have not learned to take the "risk" with God of being "without a ride home!" How long since you actually *sacrificed* anything for Christ's cause? — H.G.B.

It's not what you'd do with a million
If riches should e'er be your lot,
But what you are doing at present
With the dollar and quarter you've got.
—Anon.

"Love is never afraid of giving too much."

MY NEW HOME

READ JOHN 14:1-6

> *. . . a man's life consisteth not in the abundance of the
> things which he possesseth.*　　　　　　Luke 12:15

The secret of contentment is to be satisfied where we are and with the things which we have. Wealth alone never brings true happiness. James said that God hath "chosen the poor of this world rich in faith, and heirs of the kingdom" (James 2:5). Paul was a happy man because he had learned to be content in whatsoever state he was (Phil. 4:11). He further says, " . . . godliness with contentment is great gain (wealth)" (I Tim. 6:6). He did not need much, for he could say, " . . . having food and raiment, let us be therewith content" (I Tim. 6:8). Hebrews 13:5 reads, " . . . be content with such things as ye have."

Sometime ago I was slowly driving through the colored section of a southern village. On a sand trail in the "sticks," I passed an isolated cabin of a Negro couple. It was only a shack of one room, furnished with a few pieces of homemade furniture. There were no panes or screens on the two windows and the door was off its hinges. On the stoop sat an elderly Negro reading his Bible. I stopped the car, got out, and asked, "What are you reading?" He answered, "The Good Book." Asked what he was reading in the "Good Book," his face lit up, his eyes sparkled as he replied, "I'se readin' about my new house they is buildin' for me in Heaven. The Lord am preparin' for me a mansion in the great City of the New Jerusalem." Placing his hand upon his well-worn Bible, soiled and grimy by much use, he looked at me and said, "Sir, it's going to be wonderful!" A faraway look in his eyes seemed to say, "I don't mind a few years in this shack, for they're building a mansion for me over There." What a sermon on contentment! I gave him a copy of *"Our Daily Bread"* and some tracts and went away ashamed and humbled — envying that old toothless colored man on the stoop in Mt. Dora, Florida. I never listened to a more impressive sermon. See you in Heaven, Joe! God bless you!　　　　　　　　　　　　　　— M.R.D.

> Where the charming roses bloom forever,
> And where separations come no more,
> If we never meet again this side of Heaven,
> I will meet you on that beautiful shore!
> —A. E. Brumley

"Man NEEDS so little here below; the trouble is he WANTS so much."

STOP YOUR COMPLAINING

READ NUMBERS 14:1-11, 22-24

Do all things without murmurings and disputings.
                                      Philippians 2:14

The children of Israel were constantly murmuring and complaining when they should have been trusting and praising. Many of them, therefore, never reached the Canaan of spiritual victory and blessing because the Lord could not tolerate such lack of resignation to His perfect guidance and leading. Still today, grumblers and complainers are never victorious Christians.

Too often people who watch the average churchgoer are offended by the conduct of those who claim to be children of God, for many are constantly unhappy, irritable, quarrelsome, and faultfinding.

No matter how disagreeable and unpleasant a task may be, Paul says it is to be done cheerfully as unto the Lord *"without murmurings and disputings."* I am sure we would all be surprised if we could hear a tape recording of our conversation for a single day. We would be amazed at just how much we complain, object, and murmur. Children fret about doing their homework or washing the dishes. Mother complains about the stack of mending and having to spend half her time "picking up" after the baby. Father comes home and makes bitter remarks about his "inconsiderate boss" and the difficulties of the day's work. And so it goes the whole day through. Often we complain so much that the joy of our Christian testimony evaporates in the fog of criticism and unhappiness. Hudson Taylor used to say, "If your father and mother, your sister and brother, yes, even the very cat and dog in your house, are not happier for your being a Christian, it is a question whether you really are one or not."

Instead of murmuring and complaining, let us follow the delightful admonition in Ephesians 5:19: "Speaking to yourselves in psalms and hymns and spiritual songs, singing and making melody in your heart to the Lord."   — H.G.B.

> Let us learn to walk with a smile or a song,
>   No matter if things do sometimes go wrong,
> And then be our station high or humble,
>   We'll never belong to the family of "Grumble!"
>   —Anon.

"It is usually not the greatness of our trouble but rather the littleness of our spirit that makes us complain."

FOR FOLKS OVER SIXTY

READ PSALM 37:18-25

I have been young, and now am old; yet have I not seen the righteous forsaken, nor his seed begging bread.

Psalm 37:25

This article is for folks old enough to be on Social Security. You are becoming vaguely conscious that you are not as strong and keen as you once were. God help us to recognize the frailties of age, for old age is a dangerous period. No wonder David prays as he does in Psalm 71, verses 9 and 18.

While visiting in a home in Jacksonville, Florida, I found the following by an anonymous author in a church bulletin:

A PRAYER AS I GROW OLDER

O Lord, Thou knowest I am growing older! I realize it also. Keep me from closing my eyes to the fact. Keep me from becoming a pest, a self-appointed sage with the fatal habit of thinking I must say something on every subject and on every occasion. Keep me from the temptation of trying to straighten out everybody's affairs. Make me thoughtful — but not moody, helpful but not bossy. With my vast store of wisdom it seems a pity not to use it all — but Lord, Thou knowest I don't want to lose all my friends by boring them with the past.

Keep my mind free from the recital and repetition of past experiences and endless details. Seal my lips about my rheumatism and gout. My aches and pains are unceasing, and rehearsing them is becoming sweeter day by day. I do not ask for improved memory, but for less cocksureness about the memory of others. Teach me to admit that sometimes I am mistaken. Keep me reasonably sweet; I do not care to be a saint (some of them are so hard to get along with). Make me sweeter and mellower as my age progresses. Let me never grow old — only older. May it be said of me, "Though our outward man perish, the inward man is renewed day by day" (II Cor. 4:16). — M.R.D.

> O keep me sweet, and let me look
>   Beyond the frets that life must hold,
> To see the glad eternal joys;
>   Yes, keep me sweet, in growing old!
>   —Mrs. J. O. Hazard

"A sour old person is the crowning work of the Devil."

HE IS MINE

READ JOHN 10:24-29

My beloved is mine, and I am his . . . .

Song of Solomon 2:16

When King George VI and his Queen visited Washington D.C. in 1939, there was present at the celebration an Indian chief named Whitefeather. He had been asked to appear on the program to sing the British national anthem. After he had done so, he surprised everyone by rendering the gospel song that begins with the words, "I'd rather have Jesus than silver or gold." After finishing the hymn he addressed the Queen and sought her permission to ask a question. With a smile she consented. Then Chief Whitefeather asked, "Your Majesty, do you believe in Jesus?" The Queen replied, "Yes. Some people know something *about* God, and some know something *about* Jesus Christ, but *He is the possessor of my heart and that of my husband also."* The King raised his head and added, smiling, "I'd rather have Jesus than silver or gold!"

It is a joyous and wondrous experience to know beyond a shadow of a doubt that you have passed from death into life. This delightful assurance is not attained by introspection — for the human heart is "deceitful above all things" and cannot be trusted. No, such certainty can be experienced only by those who rest on the unchanging Word of God which tells us that whosoever believeth on the Son *"hath* everlasting life" (John 6:47). Oh, that Christians would be wise enough to stop analyzing their *feelings* to see if they are saved, and instead rest their assurance upon the unwavering testimony of Scripture.

Have you come to Jesus in simple faith asking Him for His forgiveness, favor, and blessing? Then stop your doubting and say with a confidence born of a certain trust in His unfailing promises: *"My beloved is mine, and I am his!"*   — H.G.B.

Jesus left Heaven my Saviour to be, and He is mine;
  Tho' I am not worthy He dwells in my heart, and He is mine,
From Him I'll never, no never depart, for He is mine.
  He is mine — He is mine!
Though it is wonderful, yet it is true, that He is mine!
                                        —C. A. Miles

" 'It is finished' — PROVISION enough; 'It is written' — PROOF enough!"

SELF-MADE MEN

READ I CORINTHIANS 4:6-14

*For who maketh thee to differ from another? and what
hast thou that thou didst not receive?*

I Corinthians 4:7

The Apostle Paul, the greatest of the apostles, and who "labored
more abundantly than they all" (I Cor. 15:10), said in this same
verse, "But by the grace of God I am what I am." Paul did not
claim any credit for his success, but admits that it was "grace
bestowed" upon him.

A certain man once said to a friend, "I am a self-made man."
His friend replied, "That certainly relieves God of an embarrassing responsibility." If you are a self-made man, you must have
had some material to begin with. You are a success in business,
but you could not have been if God had not endowed you with
a mind. You had no choice in the matter of your birth. You
did not choose your parents, your environment. You could have
been born an idiot. You have excelled in athletics, but who gave
you that strong body? You could have been a paralytic. You are
successful as an orator, but who gave you your voice? No one
asked you about it, but you were born with that great blessing.
Maybe you are a preacher who has had great apparent success.
But who called you to be a preacher? Who ordered the circumstances of your life — praying parents, faithful ministers? Who
influenced you to be saved and to dedicate your life to Christ?
You cannot even claim credit for believing in Him, for even
saving faith is the gift of God (Eph. 2:8). "Where is boasting
then? It is excluded. By what law? Of works? Nay but by the
law of faith" (Rom. 3:27).

A proud Christian is an immature Christian. He is an anomaly.
Christian growth is expressed in John the Baptist's confession,
"He must increase but I must decrease" (John 3:30). Are you a
self-made man? Then you make of yourself a god. Oh, for true
humility! Stop making a "snow man" which will not endure the
Sun of Righteousness.

—M.R.D.

Bought with Thy holy, precious blood,
I am no longer mine.
Then take my life, blest Son of God,
As Thine and only Thine.

— A. Hoppe

"A man may have too much money or too much honor — but he cannot have too much GRACE."

THE REWARDS OF GRACE

READ I CORINTHIANS 4:1-5

*. . . the Lord . . . will make manifest the counsels of
the hearts: and then shall every man have praise of
God.* I Corinthians 4:5

Among the clippings I have in my scrapbook is one from the
pen of Velma B. McConnell, in which she tells the story of a
small child with whom she was personally acquainted. This little
one had a deep love for her mother and a constant desire to
show her affection. One day, while the child's mother was visiting a neighbor, little Frances, tired of looking at her story book,
spied a linen handkerchief her parent had been embroidering.
She picked it up and laboriously hemmed it. The mother, returning later with the neighbor, saw the work of her little girl.
As she gazed upon the crude results she beheld not the awk-
ward, uneven stitches, but the deep affection that had prompted
her child to "finish" the handkerchief. Her eyes filled with tears.
To her the work was beautiful. Says Velma McConnell, "How
often, with hearts filled with love and eagerness to please, we
too attempt to do something for our Heavenly Father. Though
our work is bungled or poorly done, yet He sees the heart and
the motive behind it." God who can read our innermost thoughts
will reward us for every good motive and each faithful endeavor.

A converted girl of thirteen lay dying. A lady visitor asked,
"Are you afraid, my child?" "Oh, no!" she replied; "but what
shall I say to Jesus when I meet Him, for I seem to have never
done anything for Him. You see, Mother died when I was eight.
I tried to do as she had done and took care of the four little ones,
kept the house tidy, and then—I was too tired to do more!" Taking the rough little hand into her own, the visitor, with eyes full
of tears, said tenderly, "I would not say anything, dear, but *just
show Him your hands!*"

Do what you can for Jesus today, no matter how small or
insignificant the deed may appear. You will reap the rewards of
grace when "every man shall have praise of God." — H.G.B.

> When you have given the best of your service,
> Telling the world that the Saviour has come;
> Be not dismayed when men don't believe you,
> He'll understand; He'll say, "Well done!"
> —L. E. Campbell

"If you praise God here, He will praise you hereafter." — G.W.

YOUR BROTHER'S KEEPER

READ I CORINTHIANS 8:6-13

*. . . take heed lest by any means this liberty of yours
become a stumbling block to them that are weak.*

I Corinthians 8:9

"I don't see any harm in what I am doing, and therefore it is
nobody's business but my own!" Have you ever heard anyone
say that—or probably said it yourself? You indulge some habit
which you feel is harmless in itself, but forget what effect it
may have on someone else. A man was entertaining some children by lighting a match and then, by placing the burning end
in his mouth, extinguishing it. The father of the children saw
it and said, "I wish you would not do that; it is dangerous." The
man replied, "I am not hurting myself." The reply was quick.
"But it may hurt someone else." Then he pointed at his little
son with a dressing on his upper lip. He said, "Yesterday my
little Jimmie saw you do this trick and he thought it was all
right for him to try it. See the result? He not only burned his
lip but set fire to the tablecloth, and we barely kept the flames
from spreading. You may not hurt *yourself*, but you have caused
someone else to get hurt by your example."

Sometimes Christians are equally thoughtless. "Do thyself no
harm," was Paul's wise word to the jailor (Acts 16:28), and it
was good advice; but Romans 13:10 says, "Love worketh *no ill
to his neighbour.*" The believer should consider others before
himself. The question should be: What effect has my liberty
upon my neighbor? The believer is to deny himself (Luke 9:23);
love his brother (I John 3:14); look on things of others (Phil.
2:4); minister to others' needs (Gal. 6:10); sympathize with sor-
rowing ones (Rom. 12:15); prefer others before himself (Rom.
12:10); and above all seek to please the Lord (Heb. 13:21).

To deny one's *self* is quite a different thing than self-denial.
We may deny ourselves some things because they are harmful
to us, but to deny one's *self* is to make the sacrifice because it
may harm others!

— M.R.D.

Let self be crucified and slain
And buried deep. And all in vain
May efforts be to rise again
Except to live for others!

—C. D. Meigs

**"None goes his way alone; all that we send into the lives of others,
comes back into our own!" — MARKHAM**

THE TRAGEDY OF "ALMOST"

READ ACTS 26:22-29

*The harvest is past, the summer is ended, and we are
not saved.*   Jeremiah 8:20

The harvest in Israel usually was limited to the two months
of April and May; later came the "ingathering of summer fruits."
Jeremiah in our text speaks to the people of what will happen
when the times of reaping are past and there is no longer opportunity to obtain the Living Bread that nourishes to eternal life.
What a tragedy when the springtime and harvest of life is over
and one has not reaped the fruits of grace and obtained the
salvation needed to enter heaven's sinless portals.

Has it ever occurred to you how near a sinner can come to
the Lord Jesus Christ and yet pass by the opportunity to receive
eternal life? The Bible contains many a solemn warning to show
us that individuals can almost come to the point of being saved,
and yet be lost forever. Think of the rich young ruler, held by
the Devil in a "grip of gold," or of procrastinating King Agrippa
who perished in his indecision. Call to mind the thief on the
cross who was so near to the Saviour that he could hear Him
pray, "Father, forgive them," and who yet went down to Hell an
unforgiven sinner, when he might have heard the joyous words
along with the other malefactor: "Today thou shalt be with me
in Paradise."

Judas is another illustration of how near a man can come to
Christ and yet remain unrepentant. Christ called him His "own
familiar friend." For years he moved in the very presence of the
Son of God Himself, heard His gracious words, listened to His
repeated invitations, and even His last soulful, personal appeal
to him at the Passover supper, and yet Judas went out into the
"night" of unbelief and everlasting perdition.

Jesus said, "Remember Lot's wife!" Why should we remember
her? Because she was *almost saved, but still lost!* She had heard
the Word of Life, and she had started to obey it, but she looked
back and perished. She is now with those who say: "The harvest
is past, the summer is ended, and we are not saved." *Lest her
fate be yours, accept Christ today!*   — H.G.B.

> To lose your wealth is much,
> To lose your health is more,
> To lose your soul is such a loss
> That nothing can restore!
> —Anon.

"Procrastination is the Devil's chloroform!"

STRIVING ABOUT WORDS

READ I TIMOTHY 4:7-16

> *. . . doting about questions and strifes of words, where-*
> *of cometh envy, strife, railings, evil surmisings.*
> I Timothy 6:4

We at the Radio Bible Class receive hundreds of letters from "hair-splitters." We never hear a word from them until they have some criticism to offer or fault to find. Many of these letters are not deserving of an answer, for they are written in a bitter, condemnatory spirit and are only designed to draw us into an argument by mail on some insignificant, unimportant matter of personal opinion. Of course, we do not have time to carry on a debate by mail which is to no profit. We try to conscientiously and sincerely help all who write us for advice, counsel, and comfort; we will not, however, be drawn into prolonged arguments over non-essentials with all the cranks who write to us.

It is said that the ancient philosophers spent days and weeks arguing about the question: "How many angels can dance on the point of a needle at one and the same time?" Indeed, one fool can ask more questions than ten wise men can answer!

The Bible warns us against wasting our time over things like that. Paul charges Timothy "that they strive not about words to no profit" (II Tim. 2:14). To Titus he writes, "But avoid foolish questions, and genealogies, and contentions, and strivings about the law; for they are unprofitable and vain" (Titus 3:9). Again in II Timothy 2:23 we read, "But foolish and unlearned questions avoid, knowing that they do gender strifes." We are to "shun profane and vain babblings" (II Tim. 2:16). Don't waste your time arguing when you ought to be working. Be practical; if a thing produces fruit—the rest is unimportant.

Two professors were arguing the grammatical correctness of saying "The hen was *sitting*—or the hen was *setting.*" Unable to agree, they asked Farmer Jones, who replied, "The question of sitting and setting I cannot answer, nor do I care. What I want to know is—when that hen cackles, is she *laying or lying!*"—M.R.D.

> I more than half think that many a kink
>   Would be smoother in life's tangled thread,
> If half that we say in a single day
>   Were left forever unsaid.
> —Anon.

"Take a tip from nature — man's ears weren't made to shut — his mouth was."

TROUBLED HEARTS AND TEAR-WASHED EYES

READ PSALM 25:14-22

*The troubles of my heart are enlarged: O bring thou
me out of my distresses.*　　　　　　　Psalm 25:17

Often a tear-washed eye and a troubled heart is designed by
God to tune our lives to some new symphony of grace and
blessing which He has prepared for us. Indeed "the road to the
Mount of Ascension invariably passes through the shadowed
Garden of Gethsemane, and over the steep ascent of Calvary,
and even down into the Garden of the Grave."

A blacksmith, about eight years after he had given his heart
to the Lord, was approached by an unbeliever with this question: "Why is it that you have so much trouble? Since you joined
the church and changed your way of living you have had twice
as many accidents and trials as you had before. I thought that
when a man gave himself to God his troubles were over." With
a thoughtful but glowing face the blacksmith replied: "Do you
see this piece of steel? It is for the springs of a carriage. But it
needs to be tempered. In order to do this, I heat it red hot and
then cool it with water. If I find it will take a temper I heat it
again; then I hammer it, and bend it, and shape it so it will be
suitable for the carriage. Often I find the steel too brittle and it
cannot be used. *If so, I throw it on the scrap pile.* Those scraps
are worth less than 1c a pound; but this carriage spring is valuable." He paused and then continued: "God saves us for something more than to have a good time. We have joy all right, for
the smile of God means heaven; but He wants us for service,
just as I want this piece of steel, and He puts the 'temper' of
Christ in us by testing and trials. Ever since I saw this I have
been saying to Him, '*Test me in any way You choose, Lord, only
don't throw me on the scrap pile.*'"

Earthly troubles are God's invitation to spiritual triumphs!

— H.G.B.

He washed my eyes with tears that I might see
　The broken heart I had was good for me;
He swept away the things that made me blind,
　And then I saw the clouds were silver-lined.
And now I understand 'twas best for me,
He washed my eyes with tears that I might see!
　　　　　　　　　　—I. Stanphill

**"Some of the Bible's most precious treasures are discerned only with
tear-filled eyes." — H.G.B.**

WHAT DOES IT DO?

READ ISAIAH 1:10-18

> . . . *we have been in pain, we have as it were brought*
> *forth wind.* Isaiah 26:18

This is the figure Isaiah uses to describe Israel's vain attempts to please Jehovah and work for their own redemption. They are represented as making this confession in the latter days of their conversion, "Like as a woman with child, that draweth near the time of her delivery, is in pain . . . we have been in pain, we have as it were brought forth wind" (Isa. 26:17, 18). Nothing to show for all her labor! How much labor there is which produces nothing. Like the folks in Jeremiah 51:58, the people "labor in vain."

Some months ago an inventor exhibited a wonderful machine. It had 5,626 wheels and gears, shafts and axles, eccentric wheels, chains and belts, together with too many bolts and nuts and screws, and cotter pins, to mention. The machine was about six feet high and at least five feet long. It ran perfectly. When he plugged it in, it began to hum and whirl and its thousands of wheels and gears began to spin. Then he was asked, "What does the machine do?" The answer was, "Absolutely *nothing!* It's just a bunch of wheels I put together for my amusement in my spare time. It produces *nothing!*"

How much Christian activity is a whir and a hum and a roar and a clanging of machinery but *nothing comes out!* It is organization, committees, boards, programs, and meetings, but no souls are saved, no missonaries are sent out, no hearts are stirred to service for Christ. Many churches have become just big social centers—places of entertainment amid a religious atmosphere. What have all the activities of your church program to do with saving souls and sanctifying saints? Must we say with Israel, "We . . . have brought forth wind"? It is not how busy we are, but what we produce that counts. Jesus said that He has ordained us to *"bring forth fruit!"* — M.R.D.

> Joyfully, joyfully laying aside
> All that may hinder to follow our Guide;
> Faithfully serving, glad workers are we,
> Swiftly obeying, His own we would be.
> —L. DeArmand

"You cannot fruitfully follow Jesus unless you are willing to leave the world behind." — C. H. CHURCHILL

TRUE RICHES

READ JAMES 5:1-8

But God said unto him, Thou fool . . . So is he that layeth up treasure for himself, and is not rich toward God.   Luke 12:20, 21

The rich man in Luke's gospel, although intelligent and successful, was called by God a "fool." Why? First, he tried to satisfy his soul with *things* such as "goods," "ease," "eating, drinking, and making merry!" Secondly, this poor "rich man" had deceived himself into believing that he *owned* his houses, barns, and money, and had forgotten that they were *only lent to him,* and that he would someday have to give an account of his stewardship concerning them. Finally, this man whom God holds up as a terrible example of folly was lost because with all his ability to provide for the future in this fleeting world, *he had not made adequate provision for eternity!* He had never sought salvation nor turned to Him who alone could prepare for him a "mansion" in Heaven.

A tax assessor came one day to a poor minister of the Gospel to determine the amount of taxes he would have to pay. "What do you possess?" he questioned. "Oh, I am very wealthy," replied the minister. "List your possessions, please," the assessor instructed. The man of God replied: "First, I have everlasting life —John 3:16. Secondly, I have a mansion in Heaven—John 14:2. Thirdly, I have peace that passeth understanding—Philippians 4:7. Fourth, I have joy unspeakable—I Peter 1:8. Fifth, I have divine love that never faileth—I Corinthians 13:8. Sixth, I have a faithful, pious wife—Proverbs 31:10. Seventh, I have healthy, happy, obedient children—Exodus 20:12. Eighth, I have true, loyal friends—Proverbs 18:24. Ninth, I have songs in the night— Psalm 42:8. Tenth, I have a crown of life awaiting—James 1:12." The tax collector closed his book and said, *"Truly, you are a very rich man, but your property is not subject to taxation!"*
Are *you* "rich toward God" (Luke 12:21)?   — H.G.B.

You may lay up vast riches of silver and gold,
  Of jewels most precious, and treasures untold,
Yet, when you come finally death's river to ford,
  Your wealth will be what you have given to the Lord!
                                                —Anon.

"The poorest man is he whose only wealth is money!"

WOMEN ARE FUNNY

READ LUKE 10:38-42, JOHN 12:1, 2

But Martha was cumbered about much serving.
Luke 10:40

There they made him a supper; and Martha served.
John 12:2

I do not understand women. I doubt if there lives a man who really does. Jesus was the only Man who ever lived who understood and fully sympathized with women. In Luke 10 Martha was rebuked by Jesus — *not* because she took so much pains to entertain Jesus with a sumptuous meal, but because she neglected a more important thing. She was more occupied with making a perfect meal — than she was with Him. I am sure that after she had learned her lesson and spent some time at Jesus' feet she went right back to the kitchen, baking the biscuits, garnishing the steak, decorating the table and arranging the forks and knives and napkins in perfect position. Somebody had to do it. In John 12 we find her serving again — but now she was not rebuked.

Most women are cumbered with many things. For example, I shall never understand Mrs. DeHaan. This vase must stand exactly here, and that figurine must be there — not an inch either way. The salad must sleep on a bed of rabbit food — "lettuce," "water cress" — or some other cattle feed. The meat must be decorated with parsley. The cherry on the dessert must rest right on top the pudding. Yes, women are different, and how glad I am. What a drab world it would be if they had no more sense of beauty, adornment, and artistic arrangement than we men. And so while we don't understand them — we appreciate them. I am sure Jesus commented warmly on the splendid, tastily prepared meal Martha had made. He probably remarked about the beautiful bouquet and the hand-embroidered linen. God help us to appreciate the fact that women are not like men.

Do you ever comment on your wife's good cooking and her artistic sense of beauty? It will brighten the whole day for her. Try it today! — M.R.D.

> The men of earth build houses,
> Halls and chambers, roofs and domes;
> But the women of earth — God knows —
> The women build the homes!
> —Anon.

"Without women this country would be — STAG-nation."

FAITH

READ EXODUS 14:13-31

> *And the children of Israel went into the midst of the sea upon the dry ground.* Exodus 14:22

The Bible is a Book of miracles! If you refuse to believe in the supernatural, you will soon lay the Scriptures aside.

One young man to whom I witnessed said, "I cannot accept Christ, for I have never seen Him. With me *'seeing is believing!'* " Of course, he had not been enlightened by the Holy Spirit and so my well-intended testimony beat helplessly against the iron doors of his unbelief. Yet he did not realize with all of his intelligence (for he was an excellent scholar), that the statement he made was in itself sheer nonsense. Seeing is not believing at all. Seeing is *knowing!* You don't have to "believe" that which you can *prove.* Faith, on the other hand, is *simply taking God at His Word* even though you cannot verify what He says with your feeble, human senses.

The crossing of the Red Sea by Israel is one of the many miracles recorded in the Bible which has to be received by faith. A ten-year-old with a vivid imagination who had heard the story at Sunday school was asked what he had learned that day at church. "Well," he said, "our teacher told us about when God sent Moses behind the enemy lines to rescue the Israelites. When they came to the Red Sea, Moses called for the engineers to build a pontoon bridge. After they had all crossed they looked back and saw the Egyptian tanks coming. Moses radioed headquarters to send bombers to blow up the bridge and save the Israelites." "Bobby," exclaimed his startled Mother, *"is that really the way your teacher told that story?"* "Well, not exactly — but if I told it her way, you'd *never* believe it!" Yes, *unbelief* which is the *root of all sin,* stumbles at the miraculous, even as it stumbles at the offer of salvation vicariously provided by a virgin-born Mediator. Oh, for faith to simply take God at His Word!

— H.G.B.

> Doubt sees the obstacles — Faith sees the way!
> Doubt sees the darkest night — Faith sees the day!
> Doubt dreads to take a step — Faith soars on high,
> Doubt questions, "Who believes?"—Faith answers, "I!"
> —Anon.

"Faith is a simple confidence that God is, and that He will faithfully do what He has promised." — L. S. CHAFER

I AM SUCH A GREAT SINNER!

READ COLOSSIANS 2:18-23

>   ... *be clothed with humility.*   I Peter 5:5

I don't want to be a "hair-splitter," for they are usually chronic critics who overlook all the flowers in a beautiful bouquet and pick on the one faded petal. But I may seem to be dealing in petty faultfinding when I object to the way some people begin or end their prayers. So often it begins, "We humbly come," or ends, "This we humbly ask." I know folks mean well, but really "humble" folks never mention it. In fact, no person is humble who admits or thinks he is. Paul refers to a "show of humility" in Colossians 2:23. The worst kind of pride is *humble pride,* which really is *proud humility.* A truly humble person will never suspect that he is humble but will be like Moses when he came down from the mountains. "Moses wist not that the skin of his face shone" (Ex. 34:29).

How can we recognize proud humility in ourselves? Do you like to talk about your own achievements and spiritual knowledge? Are you one who humbly(?) tells how much time you spend in prayer and studying the Bible? We hear folks tell us how much time they spend studying the Word, and when they get up to preach — well, we wonder. You don't need to advertise how early you get up to pray. If you really spend much time in prayer, people will soon know it without your telling them.

There is another form of humility we may call *false humility.* It consists of constantly depreciating ourselves to others, telling how bad we are and what a failure we've been; but secretly we want them to disagree with us and tell us how great we are.

A certain preacher became tired of hearing one of the ladies in the congregation constantly testify as to what a great sinner she was and what a wicked woman she was. One day she said again, "Pastor, I am such a wicked woman," and the pastor replied, "Yes, so I've been told." At this she became indignant and screamed at him, "Who told you I was a wicked woman?" He answered, "*You* did!"   — M.R.D.

>   Oh, to be saved from myself, dear Lord,
>   Oh, to be lost in Thee,
>   Oh, that it might be no more I,
>   But Christ, that lives in me.
>   — A. B. Simpson

"The smaller we become, the more room God has to work."

GRANDPA'S LAST HYMN

READ MATTHEW 26:26-32

And when they had sung an hymn, they went out.
                                        Matthew 26:30

Grandpa Bosch was a dear saint of God. I remember well my father telling of his final moments. It was shortly after the turn of the century, when the healing arts were not nearly so well advanced as they are today, that my grandfather became afflicted with a serious heart condition. The disease progressed until medical science could do no more for him. If he would sit, or lie down, his heart would not get sufficient blood and he would lapse into unconsciousness. He spent the last three days and nights of his life standing. His sons took turns helping to hold him up but at last his utter fatigue was so great that he realized he would soon have to sit down, and life here would end. He spoke lovingly to each one of his many children, and then said, "Come, let us sing a parting hymn." His voice quivered a bit on the first verse of "My Hope Is Built On Nothing Less Than Jesus' Blood and Righteousness," but he gathered strength for his favorite third stanza. "His oath, His covenant, His blood, support me in the whelming flood; *when all around my soul gives way, He then is all my hope and stay.* On Christ the solid rock I stand; all other ground is sinking sand." The others joined in on the chorus with streaming eyes. There was a last tender word of spiritual admonition and then grandfather's parting hymn was drowned out by the voice of the many harpers by the throne of God.

It is worthy of note that our Lord in the night on which He was betrayed concluded the first Communion service with *the singing of a hymn!* In so doing He set us an example as to how we should face death. Since then many martyrs and heroes of the faith have gone forth to meet the final enemy, glorifying God in song. Oh, for spiritual strength to walk the pathway of duty today singing the hymns of praise. Oh, for the faith to meet the future triumphantly in the assurance of grace!

If you were to face death tonight, would you be able to sing Grandpa's parting hymn?   — H.G.B.

> When darkness veils His lovely face,
> I rest on His unchanging grace;
> In every high and stormy gale,
> My anchor holds within the vale.
>   —E. Mote

"Death for the Christian is the golden key which opens the palace of eternity."

TOUCHING BOTTOM

READ PSALM 20

> *. . . your goodness is as a morning cloud, and as the early dew it goeth away.*   Hosea 6:4

Jehovah's charge against Ephraim was their fickleness. When in trouble, they cried unto the Lord and made great promises, only to forget them when the trouble disappeared. Man is still like that. How we can pray and cry to God when in distress and danger, and how soon we can forget the resolutions and promises we made!

Two men in a boat were caught in a sudden squall. The one took to earnest praying, while the other frantically rowed to reach shore. Soon the latter touched bottom with the oar, and turning to his praying comrade said, "There's no need to pray any more, for I can touch bottom now." Yes indeed, what is the use of praying "when you can touch bottom"? Don't smile at the story, for you may be smiling at yourself. There are thousands who think this man foolish, who by their conduct say the same thing. How many have cried to God in times of trial and sickness and made solemn promises to God, only to forget them when they recovered and could "touch bottom." How often in a time of peril and testing you have resolved it would never happen again, only to be forgotten when you could "touch bottom."

A miser, desperately ill and fearing death, called the minister to pray to God for his recovery and said, "I want to give $1000.00 to the church which I have so long neglected." (He couldn't touch bottom and so asked for prayer.) He recovered, but failed to keep his promise. He gave the great expense of doctor and hospital bills as his excuse for not keeping his promise of $1000.00. Have you kept your resolves and promises paid up? Have you covenanted with God, and made any resolutions and promises, and then failed to keep them? Then you, too, have said in your heart, "I can still touch bottom, why worry?"

Pay your vows; don't be fickle and hypocritical!   — M.R.D.

> His goodness bids me join the throng
> Where saints His praise proclaim,
> And there will I fulfill my vows
> 'Mid those who fear His name!
>
> —Anon.

"It is a sad religion that is never strong except when its owner is sick!"

COME AS YOU ARE

READ JOHN 6:28-37

For by grace are ye saved through faith . . . Not of works, lest any man should boast. Ephesians 2:8, 9

It was the year 1836 — a young girl was preparing to attend a dance. On her way to her dressmaker to have a fine gown made for the occasion, she met her pastor. Upon learning the purpose of her errand, he pleaded with her not to go, and spoke to her about receiving Christ. She became very angry at this and said, "I wish you would mind your own business!"

When the ball was held, this young lady was among the gaiest of all those who attended. She was flattered by her admirers, and danced until the wee hours of the morning. However, when she lay her weary head on her pillow she found no rest, for she was far from being happy. The sweet words of admonition by her preacher had pricked her conscience, and deep conviction made her extremely wretched. For three days she struggled with her load of sin until life itself seemed to become intolerable. Finally she went to her pastor and asked his forgiveness, which he readily gave. Then she cried, "Now I want to be a Christian; what must I do?" "My child, give yourself to the Lamb of God, *just as you are.*" "Just as I am?" she asked. "I am one of the worst sinners in the world. How can God accept me *just as I am?*" The preacher assured her that it was "not by works of righteousness" but by faith in the One who said "it is finished," that she could ever hope to find peace. She went home, knelt down, and after a struggle gave her heart to Christ, guilty and sinful as it was, for cleansing in His precious blood. Peace and joy filled her soul to overflowing. Grasping a pen she wrote her now immortal hymn: "Just As I Am Without One Plea." Charlotte Elliot little dreamed of the fame or immortality the words she had written would attain. She had but transcribed the truth of the Gospel in the language of her own heart — a heart which had experienced Ephesians 2:8, 9 in all its fullness!

Oh sinner, today stop trying, and *try trusting!* — H.G.B.

'Tis not doing, 'tis not praying,
  'Tis not weeping saves the soul;
God is now His grace displaying;
  Jesus died to make thee whole!
—Anon.

"Christ is not the sinner's Helper, He is the sinner's Saviour!"

FOLLOWING JESUS

READ MARK 1:14-20

> . . . *Come ye after me, and I will make you to become fishers of men.* Mark 1:17

There is a great difference between coming *to* Jesus and coming *after* Jesus. Coming *to* Jesus results in salvation (Matt. 11:28); coming *after* Jesus means following Him, bearing a cross, and carrying a yoke of service (Matt. 11:29). Following Jesus means separation from the world, walking the path of rejection and reproach. Following Jesus is no child's play, and before responding to a consecration service and coming forward to the strains of "Where He Leads Me I Will Follow," it is well that we first count the cost. Following Christ we shall: be obedient to God's will (John 12:24-26); enter the wilderness (Matt. 4:1); be rejected by our own (Luke 4:28, 29); be misunderstood (Luke 7:39); go with Him to Gethsemane (Luke 22:39); be falsely accused (Mark 14:56) and go with Him up the hill of Calvary (Gal. 2:20); *but* we shall also share in the victory of the resurrection (Phil. 3:11). Yes, following Jesus means going "without the camp, bearing his reproach" (Heb. 13:13).

An old Chinese woman brought her ancestral tablet to the missionary who had been the means of her conversion, and requested that it might be burned. The missionary responded to the request. A further request was made regarding the utensil in which the ashes of the ancestors were preserved, that it might be destroyed. The missionary suggested that the pot might do service to keep a plant in. "No," said the woman after thinking for a few minutes, "it belongs to the Devil, and all that's connected with him must be destroyed." Whereupon she picked it up, and going outside the missionary's house dashed it against the wall and began to sing in a cracked voice: "Follow, follow, I will follow Jesus, Anywhere everywhere, I will follow on."

Have you ever come to Jesus for salvation? If not, do it now. If you have come to Him, are you willing now to follow Him in complete dedication? Today where will your steps lead you?

— M.R.D.

> Jesus calls me, I must follow, Follow ev'ry hour,
> Know the blessing of His presence, Fullness of His pow'r.
> —M. W. Brown

"Full blessing is dependent upon our walk; as F. B. Meyer once said, 'Christians are either Bibles or libels.' "

ONE TALENT

READ MATTHEW 25:14-30

> *And unto one he gave five talents, to another two, and to another one; to every man according to his several ability.*   Matthew 25:15

A prominent businessman in America once wrote concerning the then obscure evangelist Dwight L. Moody: "The first time I ever saw him was in a little shanty that had been abandoned by a saloon keeper. He had managed to get possession of the place in order to hold a meeting that night. I was a little late and had never met Mr. Moody, but when I came in, the first thing I saw was a heavy-set man standing up holding a small Negro boy in his arms. By the light of a few tallow candles he was trying to read to him the story of the Prodigal Son. A great many of the words he could not make out and so he had to skip them. I thought, *if the Lord can ever use such an instrument as that for His honor and glory, it will certainly astonish me!* After the meeting was over, the man, who turned out to be Mr. Moody, said to me, 'Mr. Reynolds, I have only *one talent;* I have no education, but *I love the Lord Jesus Christ.* I want to do something for Him. Pray for me.'" Mr. Reynolds said that from that day on he never ceased to remember before the Throne of Grace that devoted soldier of the cross who said he had only one talent: "a deep love for the Lord Jesus Christ."

At a mission hall in London a lady who was quite deaf met an evangelist who was to speak that evening. Her cordiality and Christian character impressed him. "And what part do you take in this noble work?" he asked. "Oh," she answered, "*I smile them in, and I smile them out again.*" Soon afterward the preacher had opportunity to see the good results of her sympathy as a large crowd of working men entered the hall, apparently delighted to get a warm smile of Christian welcome from her. She too had the "one talent" which she put to a good use. There's no Christian, no matter how few his gifts, who cannot put this "*one talent of love*" to work for the Saviour.   — H.G.B.

> O Master, let me walk with Thee,
> IN LOWLY PATHS OF SERVICE FREE;
> Tell me Thy secret; help me bear,
> The strain of toil, the fret of care.
> —W. Gladden

"It is the greatest of all mistakes to do nothing because you can only do a little; do what you can!" — S. SMITH

A MOTHER'S LOVE

READ EXODUS 2:1-10

*As one whom his mother comforteth, so will I comfort
you.*   Isaiah 66:13

At this season of the year especially, our thoughts turn to her
who gave us birth. Like so many modern customs and practices,
"Mother's Day," which is celebrated the second Sunday in May,
dates back to a festival derived from the custom of mother worship in ancient Greece. With the coming of Christianity it soon
became a worship of the mother church as a religious, holy day
during Lent, when children brought special gifts to their mothers.
In the United States, official recognition of Mother's Day was
given by Congress on May 8, 1914. The white carnation, signify-
ing sweetness, purity, and endurance, was adopted as the
emblem.

Mother's Day is here and though we attach no spiritual significance to it, it is well that we be reminded of the blessings of
godly motherhood. Is your mother alive? How long has it been
since you found time to visit her? Today pay a visit to mother
— or if the distance is too great, give her a call on the phone. The
cheapest thing one can do is just sending a card written by
others. Why not write a personal letter to her today? Think of
all the sacrifices she has made for you—doing without that you
might have!

A teacher asked little Katie a question in fractions. She said,
"If your mother made a pie and there were ten at the table:
father, mother, and eight children, how much of the pie would
you get?" She replied, "One-ninth, teacher." "Don't you mean
one-tenth, Katie? Don't you know your fractions?" "Yes, said she,
"I know my fractions—but you don't know my mother. She would
say, I'll do without—I don't care for any tonight."   — M.R.D.

No one knows the work it makes
    To keep the home together;
Nobody knows the steps it takes,
    Nobody knows but mother.
Nobody knows the lessons taught
    Of loving one another;
Nobody knows the patience sought,
    Nobody knows — but MOTHER!
                                    —Anon.

**"There is nothing human so dependable, so irresistible, so unselfish
as true mother love."**

DO WHAT YOU CAN

READ MARK 14:1-9

She hath done what she could.   Mark 14:8

Mary of Bethany had just shown her love for Jesus by anointing Him with precious ointment. Some objected to her actions, but Jesus commends her and sets her up as an example for us to follow. Each must give in his own way *the best he has!* Someone has rightly said, "I am only one, but *I am one,* I cannot do everything, but *I can do something.* That which I can do, I ought to do, and by the grace of God *I will do!"*

To every Christian, God has given some task whereby he may glorify the Saviour. D. L. Moody tells a story that illustrates this truth: A passenger crossing the Atlantic was sent to his bunk during a storm because he was terribly distressed by seasickness. A cry of "man overboard" was heard. "May God help the poor fellow, but there is nothing I can do the way I feel," said the sick passenger. Then he thought to himself, "Wait, there *is* something I can do; I can at least put my lantern in the porthole." He struggled to his feet and hung the light so it shone out into the darkness. The man who was drowning was rescued, and in recounting the story the next day said, "I was going down for the last time when someone put a light in a porthole. *It shone on my hand, and a sailor in a lifeboat grabbed it and pulled me in!"*

Everyone holding forth his own light, or using his one talent, no matter how small, will help accomplish God's purpose on this earth, and will thus glorify the Saviour. What a joy it will be when the Master looks into our eyes in that future day and with a loving smile of approval says, "Good and faithful servant, *you did what you could*—enter now into the joy of thy Lord!" —H.G.B.

> Somebody gave the Gospel true
>   To a soul borne down with despair;
> The message gripped, the Spirit worked,
>   The Word had power — and we beheld
> A life released from Satan's snare!
>   WAS THAT SOMEBODY YOU?
>
>   —A.L.N.

"Our lives are God's gift to us; what we do with them is our gift to God."

SHORT-WEIGHT SCALES

READ DEUTERONOMY 25:13-16

*Divers weights are an abomination unto the Lord; and
a false balance is not good.*   Proverbs 20:23

Cheating is sin and is severely condemned in the Scriptures. So common is the practice of "snitching" a little here and a little there, that the government maintains a large force of men to inspect the scales of merchants and shopkeepers, to see that they conform to the requirements of the U.S. Department of Standard Weights and Measures.

Many a man would not think of robbing a bank or stealing a dollar outright, but will think nothing of being a "sharper" in business and driving a hard bargain or being guilty of short weight or measure. It costs the government millions of dollars to keep an eye on the "chiselers." In the eyes of God stealing is stealing, no matter what form it takes. Honesty is one of the surest tests of character.

A certain grocer said to one of his former customers before a group of friends, "Mary, I don't believe you are saved and I am going to ask these people to pray for your salvation. I am greatly burdened for you." Mary was shocked and asked why the grocer thought she was not saved. He replied, "If you were, you would not try to cheat me on the butter you sell me. For several weeks now I have detected that every pound of your butter is two ounces short." Mary thought for a minute and then said, "Oh, I know why that is. Several weeks ago I lost my pound weight — and I have been using for a weight instead, a one-pound bag of sugar which I purchased from you!" Deep silence — and a red-faced grocer!

Can all your business dealings stand inspection? Jesus said, "He that is unjust in that which is least is unjust also in much."
                                                                — M.R.D.

Ever be honest, good, and sincere;
    Dare to be upright, never know fear;
Stand firm for justice, hold to the true
    God then will bless you, all the way through!
                                                — Anon.

**"Only by being on the level with men can we climb to the heights
with God!"**

PROPER PRAYER

READ MARK 11:22-26

> . . . *if we ask any thing according to his will, he heareth us.*
> I John 5:14

The Holy Spirit is the mainspring of all spiritual life and communion with God. He helps us to pray acceptably. To receive answers to our petitions *we must ever pray according to God's will.* The problem is "we know not what we should pray for as we ought" (Rom. 8:26); therefore the Spirit must frequently change our poor prayers completely in order to make them conform to God's Word and will. As a result, we are often amazed at the answers we get, for they do not correspond to our petitions, but to His.

We must be on praying ground if we expect our intercession to be effective. *We cannot dwell in sin and then expect to have God's blessing* (see I John 3:22 and Isa. 59:2). Also, *we must "pray in faith, nothing wavering"* (James 1:6); that is, we must not secretly disbelieve God, nor faithlessly anticipate that there will be "no results" anyway. Doubt kills prayer like water douses fire!

Because prayer is such a powerful force, Satan does his utmost to snatch that weapon of our warfare from us, or otherwise hinder us in its proper use.

A little boy saying his nightly prayers was heard to plead: "Please, God, make Boulder the capital of Colorado." His mother was quite surprised, and questioned with amazement, "Why do you ask that?" "Because," the lad explained, *"that's what I put down on my examination paper today!"* We smile at the ridiculous prayer of this youngster, but as adults we often are just as guilty when we selfishly request unscriptural things to cover our own negligence. Prayer is not a "magic wand" to be waved indiscriminately, but a sacred privilege to be exercised within the bounds of the Word.

Today, with the disciples of old, let us make request, "Lord, *teach us to pray!*"
— H.G.B.

> There's never a year nor a season
> That prayer may not bless every hour;
> And never a prayer need be helpless
> When linked with God's infinite power.
> — Anon.

"Seven days without prayer makes one weak!"

CAN YOU TAKE CRITICISM?

READ MATTHEW 5:3-12

*Blessed are ye, when men shall revile you, and perse-
cute you, and shall say all manner of evil against you
falsely, for my sake. Rejoice, and be exceeding glad;
for great is your reward in heaven.*　　Matthew 5:11, 12

How are you at making enemies? No, I did not ask, How are
you at making friends? That is easy. Just be a good Joe, an
easy spender, a tolerant sort of fellow who never offends anyone.
Solomon wisely says, " . . . the rich hath many friends" (Prov.
14:20). And again he says, "Wealth maketh many friends, but
the poor is separated from his neighbor" (Prov. 19:4). Yes, you
can have lots of friends if you are willing to *pay* them for it.
And again we read, "A man's gift maketh room for him, and
bringeth him before great men" (Prov. 18:16). Yes, there are
many ways of making friends.

But how good are you at making enemies? If you are a child
of God and you can move among wicked, ungodly, cursing men
and women today, and not be different enough to incur their
disfavor or even reviling, you certainly are not much of a testimony. Do you just silently endure cursing and taking the Lord's
name in vain for fear of the jeering? Do you indulge in a little
"game" or take "just a nip" because you fear ridicule? Do you
dread criticism for your faith in Christ? Are you ashamed of
Him for fear of losing friends? I would rather make enemies
for Jesus' sake than make friends for my own comfort's sake.

In the thousands of letters we receive each week we have both
letters of appreciation from our listeners, and also *many* of criticism and condemnation. I can honestly say that I appreciate
the "critical" letters (some of them unprintable) as much as any
others, for it confirms the Gospel I preach — that it's a *two-edged
sword* cutting both ways: a savor of life — and a savor of death
(II Cor. 2:16).　　　　　　　　　　　　　　　　　— M.R.D.

> Jesus, and shall it ever be,
> 　A mortal man ashamed of Thee?
> Ashamed of Thee, whom angels praise,
> 　Whose glories shine through endless days?
> 　　　　　　　　— J. Grigg

**"One sign of growth in grace is the ability to take criticism for Jesus'
sake."**

ABOVE THE STORM!

READ EPHESIANS 2:1-7

*But God, who is rich in mercy . . . hath raised us up
together, and made us sit . . . in heavenly places.*
Ephesians 2:4, 6

The believer is already seated in heaven — in Christ. As members of His Body (Eph. 5:30), we have been crucified with Christ, (Gal. 2:20), quickened with Christ (Eph. 2:5), and positionally in Christ are already seated in the heavenlies. As such the believer is safe from condemnation (Rom. 8:1) and has eternal life (John 5:24); and this we have in Christ. In our walk we are still imperfect, but in Christ, God sees us as already in heaven. We are therefore lifted above the judgment of condemnation forever.

Recently on a flight to Boston we passed over a severe thunderstorm. Riding at an altitude of about 20,000 feet, we had a wonderful view of the great rolling thunderclouds towering in the sky. Below us was a sea of clouds — we could see the jagged streaks of lightning leaping from cloud to cloud or from cloud to earth. It was an awesome sight. I found myself wondering what would happen if that lightning struck the plane. Then I remembered that lightning always strikes *down — not up,* and we were above the storm. We were riding in the sunlight, above the storm, in perfect safety from the crashing, flashing thunderbolts. Only those below the storm were in danger.

So it is with the believer in Christ. He is not under judgment, but above condemnation. He lives above the storm of God's wrath, in the sunshine of God's promise in John 10:28, 29. I must confess I was at first a bit fearful as I saw the storm so close by, until I remembered lightning is dangerous to those under the cloud, but harmless to those above it. Our Pilot has taken us through — and *safely!* This is our blessed assurance!   — M.R.D.

In the heavenlies I'm resting,
Blessed and sheltered, I abide;
There no foes nor storms molest me,
For in Christ I safely hide.
—M. D. James, alt.

"Don't look down at your troubles, Christian, remember your position and look up, for 'It is the lifted face that feels the shining of the Sun.'"

WRONG NUMBER, PLEASE!

READ ACTS 2:32-42

> *. . . ye shall be witnesses unto me . . . .*   Acts 1:8

Spurgeon says, "In order to learn how to discharge your duty as a witness for Christ, look at His example. He is always witnessing: by the well of Samaria, in the Temple at Jerusalem, by the well of Gennesaret, or on the mountain's brow." Yes, every Christian is saved to serve! Yet, many who should be bearing testimony each day have not a word to say for their Lord and Saviour. Why? Probably because their power has seeped out through worldliness. If they proceed without the Spirit and without love, they become mere "clanging cymbals" — fruitless and ineffective.

Many also excuse themselves on the basis of "lack of opportunity," but if one really loves the Lord, opportunities can be "made." I remember one dear lady in our church who was confined to her home by illness, yet she prayed most earnestly for some way to be of service. Soon afterward, the phone rang. Someone had called her number by mistake, but she took advantage of the opportunity and said, "No, friend, actually you haven't got the wrong number, for I have been praying that someone would contact me today in order that I might witness to them concerning my wonderful Saviour." She then gave a stirring word of testimony and the unbeliever was under deep conviction before the conversation ended. From then on she prayed most earnestly that many others would inadvertently dial her number; and God answered her petition. Time and again the phone would ring, and as often as it did, she would give a good witness. Folks spread the word about her ministry and before long she was counseling many, praying for others, and leading souls to the Saviour by means of her telephone.

Do you really want to be a soul winner? Pray about it and God will provide the opportunity, *even if it must be through a wrong number!*   — H.G.B.

> Make me a channel of blessing today,
>   Make me a channel of blessing, I pray;
> My life possessing, my service blessing,
>   Make me a channel of blessing today.
> —H. G. Smyth

"We don't need to be STARS in order to shine for Jesus; it was by the ministry of a mere CANDLE that a woman recovered her lost piece of silver." — DR. J. H. JOWETT

GETTING BY GIVING

READ PROVERBS 11:1-8

There is that scattereth, and yet increaseth.
Proverbs 11:24

If you want to *get,* you must first learn to *give.* To hoard up precious seed corn in the granary will never result in an increase. Money hidden in the mattress will earn no interest. The talent that is not put to use is lost.

Science tells us the mole has eyes but because he does not use them, he has lost the use of them. This is also true of the bat. Immobilize an arm or leg and it will atrophy and waste away. Only exercise can keep it strong. Very few people begin the day with the question, "How much can I *give* today?" The most common question is, "How much can I *get* today?" How often, when asking someone for help or aid in a worthy project, we are met with the remark, "What is there in it for me?" My friend, you will get "out of it" in direct proportion to what you put "into it." One miser, being asked for a donation to a charitable cause said, "It is my money and I got it by not giving it away." His friend then asked, "How much did you begin with? When you came into the world, you came with *nothing,* and someday you will leave it with *nothing.* It is not yours at all, it is only a loan for which you will be called into account." Christian, take notice. God will call you into account not only for how you spent your time, your talents, but how you spent your money. More than that, we shall be judged for our *lies,* when we sing, but do not practice,

"Take my silver and my gold,
Not a mite would I withhold."

How inconsistent the sight of a man in church with a $500.00 diamond on his finger, singing lustily, "Were the whole realm of nature mine, that were a present far too small," while all the time he is fumbling through a handful of dollars, halves, and quarters to find a nickel for the collection!　　　　— M.R.D.

Give your best some hearts to gladden,
As through life they weary plod;
Place your bank account in Heaven
And grow richer toward your God.
—Anon.

"It is a law of nature that we either USE or LOSE."

ALONE WITH GOD

READ I KINGS 19:1-13

And he took him aside . . . .   Mark 7:33

When Jesus came one day to the seacoast of Galilee, they brought unto Him one that was deaf and had an impediment in his speech, beseeching our Lord to heal him. Jesus did as they requested, but not until He had taken the man aside from the multitude. There He touched first his ears, and then his tongue.

Many are the lessons for us in this brief account. Often before the Lord can work His miracle He has to call us aside from the hurry and restless activity of the work-a-day world. *First He would touch our ears* that we might hear His loving voice of guidance and assurance, for He knows that *only then can our tongue be properly loosed* to speak His praises, and plainly tell others of His grace. Do not be restless therefore when the Lord isolates you for awhile through sickness or circumstance; just be certain He is seeking to bestow a rich blessing upon your soul by thus setting you aside.

Years ago a man who operated an icehouse lost a good watch in the sawdust on the floor. He offered a reward, and although many went through the wood-sawings with rakes, they were unable to find the lost treasure. When they left the building for lunch, a small boy entered and came out a few moments later with the treasured timepiece. They asked him how he had found it and he replied, "I just lay down in the sawdust and quietly waited *until I heard the watch ticking!*" Many of us have lost much more than a watch. If we will just be still and listen quietly, the Lord will speak to us and show us where we lost our power and testimony.

Let us "study to be quiet" when God takes us aside, for only thus will we know the miracle of His grace, and the peace of His blessing. Listen like Elijah for the "still small voice."

— H.G.B.

Taken aside by the Master to feel the touch of His hand,
    To rest for a while in the shadow
        Of the Rock in a weary land.
Taken aside by the Master in the loneliness dark and drear
    Where no other comfort may reach you
        Than the sound of His voice so dear.

—Anon.

"As Isaac met his bride in the fields at eventide, so do true souls find their joy and consolation in the loneliness of solitude, and at the sunset of their earthly pleasures."

SUCKERS!

READ ROMANS 8:5-13

Mortify therefore your members which are upon the
earth.   Colossians 3:5

Stop! Don't read the rest of this until you have read our Scripture: Romans 8:5-13.

What do you know about "suckers"? I am not speaking of fish, or of certain gullible folks who fall for every new scheme. I am speaking of suckers on a fruit tree which must be constantly pruned off if there is to be fruit. A few years ago I planted a pear tree. It was really two pear trees, for the root and lower stem was from a "seedling" which grew wild. The nursery man cut off the wild branches, and a branch from a tame tree was grafted or budded in. On this branch would grow good fruit, if we would only keep the "suckers" down. Suckers are sprouts or branches which grow *below* the graft, out of the old wild root, and have the wild nature. Failure to prune off the wild suckers prevents the strength of the tree from going into the tame, fruit-bearing branches. If there is to be fruit, the "suckers" must be constantly discouraged by cutting them off. Thus the same tree may bring forth two kinds of fruit, wild and tame, but the more the tree produces of one kind, the less there will be of the other.

We too are trees. By nature we are wild, due to our birth from father Adam. We begin with a natural, sinful nature. When we are born of the Spirit, a bud-graft of the divine life is introduced within us, enabling us to bring forth the fruit of the Spirit (Gal. 5:22, 23). But the old nature is still there, and if left without pruning will stunt the new growth and render it fruitless. This is the reason for the battle in the Christian life. The secret of victory is getting rid of the suckers — the works of the flesh (Gal. 5:19-21). Watch the suckers today, brother, and "put off . . . the old man, which is corrupt . . . and put on the new man . . . created in . . . true holiness" (Eph. 4:22, 24). Crucify *self!*
WATCH THOSE SUCKERS!   — M.R.D.

Lord, save me from my evil self,
  To Thee for help I flee;
Teach me Thy perfect way to know
  That I may live for Thee.
                                    —Anon.

"The verdure of the self-life may make a wonderful display, but God desires the 'fruit of the Spirit.' "

PRAISE THE LORD!

READ PSALM 150

Let every thing that hath breath praise the Lord. Praise ye the Lord.   Psalm 150:6

The book of Psalms presents truth not abstractly "but in terms of human experience." It opens with a well-blessed and happy man whose delight is in the Word and will of God, and concludes on a glorious pinnacle of joy in Psalm 150 with thirteen peals of glory on the silver trumpet of praise! In this final doxology we find nothing of man himself left in the picture. Even the author of the Psalm is not mentioned. How symbolic this is of the pathway of sanctification. At the end there is nothing but glory and praise to God. In Heaven, faith turns to sight and prayer to fulfillment, but praise never dies; it goes singing on into eternity. How important it is for us to tune our life, therefore, to that good and noble end for which we were created: namely, to adore and magnify our Creator.

It is said that when the farmers of Scotland walk out early in the morning they often flush the larks from the deep grass. As the birds rise they sing, and as they sing they circle. Higher and higher they ascend until their melody dies out in the distance. But so sweet and ethereal is their tender strain that it always rejoices the hearts of those who hear it. So, too, as we lift our hearts and voices in praise, the world will stop to listen to our joyous adoration.

In certain parts of the Alps a beautiful and touching custom prevails. Just as the sun leaves the valley and the last rays touch the snowcapped summit, the shepherd whose hut is farthest up the peak takes his alpenhorn and with trumpet voice cries: "Praise the Lord!" Instantly each shepherd, standing at the threshold of his cabin, repeats in turn the same appeal until the echo is heard far and wide. Like a sea of glory it rolls from one jagged peak to another until finally all the mountain resounds with the hearty — "Praise the Lord!"

You may think yourself small and hidden away, yet the mountain of your environment should also re-echo with your joyous hallelujahs of gratitude.   — H.G.B.

> O for a thousand tongues to sing
> My great Redeemer's praise,
> The glories of my God and King,
> The triumphs of His grace.
> —C. Wesley

"God listens for thy praise, and all the music of His great universe is richer and sweeter when thou givest thanks."

STORM WARNING – GET READY!

READ ISAIAH 38:1-6

> . . . *Set thine house in order: for thou shalt die, and not*
> *live.*   Isaiah 38:1

I love fishing for recreation. Somehow my friends will never tell me where I can really catch a big one. That is – with one exception. One summer a good friend invited me to go with him into Canada and "talked me into it (?)" by his tales about the big ones. A diminutive, bowlegged Indian guide took us to his "secret" fishing hole. He was a remarkable Indian. With a pack-sack weighing sixty pounds and a big canoe on top of that, he fairly flew up the hill on the narrow rocky trail, a hill so steep my partner and I had to stop every few feet to rest. Finally we were drifting quietly on a beautiful lake. Loons screamed their disapproval of our intrusion; a big black bear ambled out of the brush to the shore. And then, an owl broke the silence with a long solemn, "Whoo, whoo, whooooo, who-who." The Indian stopped his canoe paddle and said, "Did you hear that? An owl hooting in the daytime. Do you know what he said? The owl say, 'Indian! Drop everything and set up camp. Secure your tepee, gather dry wood, and get ready for a storm.' That's what the owl say to Indian. Whenever an owl hoots in the daytime, it means rain before next day." And sure enough, that night it began to rain. Immediately my mind turned to our text. "Set thine house in order . . . Prepare to meet thy God" (Amos 4:12). Man heeds the warning signs of nature and neglects the warning of God.

All around us are the warnings of the coming storm. There is an eternity ahead, and without the shelter of Christ's redeeming blood it will mean disaster. "Indian – stop what you are doing – set up camp – gather dry wood – a storm is coming."

Have you made provision for that inevitable day by trusting Christ and taking shelter under His wings? If not, *stop every-thing* and "set your house in order," for death is coming!

P.S. Oh yes – the fishing? The old, old story – "You should have been here yesterday!"   – M.R.D.

> Say, are you ready? Oh, are you ready?
> If the death angel should call;
> Say, are you ready? OH, ARE YOU READY?
> Mercy stands waiting for all!
>   —Anon.

"Procrastination is the Devil's toboggan slide to Hell."

GOD'S WATCHCARE

READ GENESIS 16:6-13

> *. . . Thou God seest me.*   Genesis 16:13

The biographer of Bishop Watts relates that when this man of God was still a child he was one day in the house of a very old woman who asked him to read a motto she had upon the wall. It contained the words of Hagar: "Thou God seest me." The old woman said, "When you are older, my boy, people will tell you that God is always watching to see when you do wrong, in order to punish you. I do not want you to think of it in that way, but I want you to take the text home, and to remember all your life that *God loves you so much that He cannot take his eyes off of you!*" These words became for Bishop Watts the basis of a living creed, an incentive to a useful and beautiful life.

The knowledge that God is watching us should also preserve us from unhallowed thoughts, selfish motives, and insincerity in word and action. Despondency and loneliness fade into oblivion in the light of this truth.

Richard Klick tells the following incident from his own childhood: "As a little tyke I had been invited to a very auspicious birthday party of a school chum. But the heavy blizzard had made our little village streets impassable; therefore, I had been forbidden to leave the house. 'Other parents love their children enough to allow them to go!' I shouted angrily. Father was manifestly stung by my bitter words. Presently, he turned to me, replying softly, 'You may go.' Nonplused but overjoyed, I donned my hardiest wardrobe and plunged into the raging storm. The snows made vision impossible. The drifts almost covered me. The howling winds tossed me down repeatedly. Only by a sheer miracle did I arrive at the birthday house a few blocks away all of half an hour later. As I rang the bell, I turned to look out into the storm. Just then I caught the shadow of a retreating figure. It was my father! He had been following my every step in the storm. How tremendously he really loved me!" God's precious watchcare is the same. He is always sympathetically concerned, yes, even when we press impatiently along our self-willed ways, for "He abideth faithful."   — H.G.B.

> We cannot see before us, but our all-seeing Friend
> Is always watching o'er us, and loves us to the end.
>   —F. R. Havergal

"Never be afraid to entrust an unknown future to a known God!"

THE SIN OF LAZINESS

READ II THESSALONIANS 3:6-15

Not slothful in business; fervent in spirit; serving the Lord. Romans 12:11

Laziness is sin. The Bible strongly condemns laziness and slothfulness. Lazy Christians are "disorderly" brethren, and we are to shame them by refusing them fellowship (II Thess. 3:6).

Someone has defined laziness as "being afraid of work," but someone else has said, "He isn't afraid of work — he can go to sleep right in the middle of it." The Bible says we should not be lazy in: (1) business, (2) spirit, or (3) in our service. If God has given you a good head for business and the ability to make money, you are to use it. If you don't, you are as much a shirker as a man who is called to preach and fails to do so, or a person called to the mission field but who prefers to stay at home.

We are living in an age of laziness. When I was a boy my father worked from 7 A.M. to 6 P.M., six days a week, and from 7 P.M. to 9:30 P.M. on Tuesday and Saturday nights. For this he received $9.00 per week, and I never heard him complain. Today men work for five days, eight hours a day or less, and now they are clamoring for a four-day week or a thirty-hour week. And even with this abbreviated work week, there is more clock-watching and feather-bedding than ever before. On the other hand the workers complain of high prices and the shrinking dollar. But *the reason a dollar will not do as much for people as it once did, is because people won't do as much for the dollar as they once did!*

Work becomes play if we appreciate the health to work and the opportunity of earning a living. A Christian employer should give his men what they are worth, and the employee (if a Christian) should give the employer his money's worth — result: *No strikes.*

A man applied for a job, and in discussing wages, the employer said, "We will pay you what you are worth." "No thank you," said the applicant. "I'm getting more than that where I am now!"

Make your work a testimony of your Christian profession. Try it today. — M.R.D.

Only this hour is mine, Lord;
May it be used for Thee;
May ev'ry passing moment
Count for eternity.
— A. B. Christiansen

"The lazy man aims at nothing and generally hits it!"

I BELONG THERE!

READ MARK 15:22-39

For Christ also hath once suffered for sins, the just for the unjust, that he might bring us to God. I Peter 3:18

A missionary in Africa was telling the heathen the precious story of the life and ministry of our Lord. The natives gathered in a special clearing which had been made in the forest, while the servant of God told them in vivid language of the wonderful miracles and the sacrificial offering of Christ on the cross. Seated in the front row was the chief of the tribe who listened intently to all the missionary had to say. As the story came to its climax, and the chief heard how Christ was cruelly nailed to Calvary's tree, he could contain himself no longer, but jumped to his feet crying, "Stop! Take Him down from the cross; *I belong there, not Him!*" He had truly grasped the meaning of the Gospel, for he understood that he was a sinner, and that Christ was the sinless One.

Yes, Jesus took *our place* and died in *our stead.* In that He bore our sins, the just for the unjust, He has brought us back into fellowship with the Father.

J. G. Mantle in his wonderful book entitled, *Beyond Humiliation* says: "To see what your sin really means, bring it into the light of the cross, and say as you gaze upon that marred visage and those pierced hands and feet: 'It was *my* pride, *my* lust, *my* unbelief, *my* selfishness, that pointed the nails and fixed the thorns.'"

As once again you recall that scene of the Son of God hanging there in "agony and blood," will you say from your heart, "*I belonged there!*" Then go one step further and receive Him as your Saviour, so that you can say with Paul, "I am crucified with Christ, nevertheless *I live.*" If you will identify yourself with His sacrifice, God will identify you with Christ's righteousness.

— H.G.B.

'Twas I that shed the sacred blood,
  I nailed Him to the tree,
I crucified the Christ of God,
  I joined the mockery.
Yet nonetheless that blood avails
  To cleanse away my sin,
And not the less that cross prevails,
  To give me peace within.
—Anon.

"The cross is the key that unlocks the gate of Heaven!"

THE OLD SWIMMING HOLE

READ NUMBERS 11:1-6

They feared the Lord, and served their own gods.
II Kings 17:33

Do you remember the old swimmin' hole of your boyhood days? What fun it was to splash about in the muddy pond. Now we have beautiful swimming pools like the one right outside the door of the motel where Mrs. DeHaan and I are spending the night. But little as the *modern* swimming pool resembles the old swimming "hole," I notice the people are still the same. There are sitters, dippers, waders, puddlers, and *divers*. Watch them! One of them just sits on the side looking on. Another has just dipped his toes in and "Brrr," he cries out as he shivers, "Oh, it's so cold!" Another has gone in up to his ankles, and he also declares it is awfully chilly. But see, another takes a header from the bank, and rises all in a glow; all his blood is circulating, and he cries, "Delicious! What a fine morning. The water is splendid!"

It is a picture of Christians in any church. There are the sitters — just getting a tan (they should be given a tanning). There are the splashers, the puddlers, and the divers. The divers are the "all-outers" for God. The others are "half-baked," half-hearted, half-surrendered Christians. Like the people in our text, they "feared the Lord — but served their own gods." One foot in the water — one on the ground; one foot in the world — one foot in the church. You, Christian people, who are paddling about in the shallow of religion, and just dipping your toes into it, you stand shivering in the cold air of the world which you are afraid to leave. Oh, that you would plunge into the river of life, how it would brace you; what tone it would give you! Be a Christian out-and-out. Give yourself wholly to Him who bought you with His blood, and you will find the "more abundant life!" — M.R.D.

Oh, this is life: oh, this is joy,
My God, to find Thee so;
Thy face to see, Thy voice to hear,
And all Thy love to know.

—Anon.

"Beware of floating in the ocean of God's truth when you should be out swimming."

A SOFT ANSWER

A soft answer turneth away wrath: but grievous words stir up anger. Proverbs 15:1

Two little girls were playing together. The older one had a beautiful new doll in her arms, which she was tenderly caressing. The younger one crept up softly behind her, and gave her a sharp slap on her cheek. A visitor, unobserved, was sitting in an adjoining room and saw it all. She expected to hear another slap, a harder one, in retaliation. But, no; the victim's face flushed and her eyes had a momentary flash of indignation. She rubbed her hurt cheek with one hand, while she held the doll closer with the other. Then, in a tone of gentle reproof, she said, "Oh, Sallie, I didn't think you'd do that!" Sallie looked ashamed, as well she might, but made no reply. "Here, Sallie," continued the elder girl, "sit here in sister's chair. I'll let you hold dolly a-while if you'll be very careful." Sallie's face looked just then as if there were some "coals of fire" somewhere around, but she sat down with the doll on her lap, giving her sister a glance of real appreciation, mingled with shame. The hidden onlooker was deeply touched by the scene. It was unusual, she thought, to see a mere child show such calm dignity and forgiveness under persecution. Presently she called the child and questioned her. "How can you be so patient with Sallie, my dear?" "Oh," was the laughing reply, "I guess it is because I love Sallie so much. You see, Sallie's a dear sister," she said excusingly, "but she's got an awful temper, and — Sallie forgets herself sometimes. Mamma said if Sallie should do any angry thing to me, and I should do angry things to her, we'd have a dreadful time, and I think we would. Mamma said I should learn to give the 'soft answer,' and I'm trying to." The lady took her in her arms and kissed her. "My dear," she said firmly and earnestly, "I think you have already learned the lesson."

"He that is slow to anger is better than the mighty; and he that ruleth his spirit than he that taketh a city" (Prov. 16:32). —H.G.B.

Help me guard my lips, O Saviour —
Keep me sweet when sorely tried;
Answers "soft" to others giving,
Meekly "swallowing my pride."
—Anon.

"Unless you can control yourself, you will never be able to control others."

THE SOURCE OF TRUE HAPPINESS

READ I JOHN 5:9-13

*He that believeth on the Son of God hath the witness
in himself . . . .*   I John 5:10

What is the "witness of the Spirit?" This question is inces-
santly asked, and many of the answers are most confusing, although the Bible is perfectly clear on it. The witness of the
Spirit is the inspired Word of God. *The Bible is the Spirit's
testimony!* Believing the promises of the Word is God's witness
to our hearts. Emotions may follow — but emotions are not the
witness. Happiness may result — but joy is not the witness. Feelings may accompany our experience, but our emotion, happiness,
and joy — are because God's promises are true. Emotions vary;
happiness depends too often on circumstances. Feelings change
from day to day, but the *promises of God are ever the same!* We
are saved because we believe what God says is true; namely,
that "whosoever shall call upon the name of the Lord shall be
saved" (Rom. 10:13). If I believe that — then joy follows, feelings and emotions are stirred — but these are not the "witness of
the Spirit," rather they are the result of relying on the *promises*
of God. Are you trusting your emotions (which change) or are
you resting on the abiding Word of God?

"Oh, Doctor De Haan," said a dear old lady, "we had such a
gude time in our shurch last night. Everybody was so heppy
we was all cryink. My what a gude time we had. We shouted
and sang and even yumped up and down. Oh what a gude time
we had." Finally I asked her, "What were you all crying about?"
Her answer was, "I don't know why, but it was a wonderful
feeling — we had a gude time."

Beloved, I have no objection to your having a good time, singing, crying, laughing, even "yumping," but be sure your joy flows
from a *fact* — the solid promises of the Word of God. When the
"yumping" stops, you need something more to *stand on.* — M.R.D.

> My hope is built on nothing less
>   Than Jesus' blood and righteousness;
> I dare not trust the sweetest frame,
>   But wholly lean on Jesus' name.
> On Christ the solid Rock I stand;
>   All other ground is sinking sand.
> —E. Mote

**"Even when I feel bad — I feel good to know that John 3:16 has not
been affected by my feeling."**

A DAY TO REMEMBER

READ EXODUS 12:1-14

. . . it is appointed unto men once to die. Hebrews 9:27
And this day shall be unto you for a memorial.
Exodus 12:14

Today is Memorial Day when we pause to honor the cherished memory of our loved ones gone before. If there is anything that this day underscores, it is the truth that all men take one common path to the grave. Rich and poor, great and small, young and old — all have a final appointment to keep with death (unless the Lord Jesus suddenly returns). Indeed, "our hearts like muffled drums are beating funeral marches to the grave."

The Nation of Israel had a Memorial Day, too, but what a contrast it offered to the one we celebrate. We remember the *dead*, but they commemorated *deliverance from death* through the blood! God, as you may recall, had commanded Israel to take the blood of the paschal lamb and strike it upon the upper part of the two sideposts of the doors of their homes. When the destroying Angel of Death came to slay the Egyptians, he saw the sign of grace and "passed over" those protected by the crimson stain. This all looked forward in type to the blessed "Lamb of God" who would someday actually take away "the sin of the world" through His sacrificial death upon the cross.

Unsaved friend, this can truly be a "memorable day" for you if by faith in the Saviour you find a similar deliverance through the atoning blood of the Perfect Sacrifice. Only thus can you be ready to meet your final and inevitable appointment with God!

As we view the decorated graves today, may we remember the precious promise of the Redeemer who said: "And this is the will of him that sent me, that *every one which seeth the Son, and believeth on him, may have everlasting life: and I will raise him up at the last day*" (John 6:40). This bright hope of life and Heaven makes our "final appointment" a time of victory and glory. What a comfort to know that our redemption will be crowned with a "memorable" resurrection day!   — H.G.B.

We sorrow not as others do,
Whose hopes fade like the flow'rs;
There is a hope that's born of God,
And such a hope is ours!
—E. McNeil

"That death might happy be, TO LIVE LEARNED I; that life might happy be, I LEARNED TO DIE." — OLD EPITAPH

THAT BLESSED HOPE

READ JOHN 11:20-29

Thy brother shall rise again.   John 11:23

This was the blessed comfort which Jesus gave to Martha in answer to her cry of sorrow, "Lord, if thou hadst been here, my brother had not died." There was in her plaint, a hint of blaming the Lord for the delay in His coming when He first heard the news of Lazarus' illness (John 11:6). But Jesus ignores the suggestion and answers, "Thy brother shall live again." Look ahead, Martha, not to the past. Look ahead, for the past is gone and holds only memories. Surely there are precious memories, but they are made real in the hope of meeting again. Memory does have comfort for those whose loved ones have passed on. Yet memory is not an unmixed comfort. There are thorns among its flowers: "For sorrow's crown of sorrow is remembering happier things."

True joy and settled peace cannot exist on memories alone; for that we look to the future. Hope of the future relieves the pang of the past. It tells of the reunion, the partingless meeting. It leaps over the years of waiting, the valleys of loneliness, and drives the shadows of today away by the light of the promise of hope. Have you recently lost loved ones? Is your heart sad? Are you prone to be morbid and confused as you engage only in memories? Then listen! Don't seek the living among the dead. Remember Jesus' words. He shall live again.

Don't be like the wife who spent hours each day in a seat by the grave of her husband weeping and sobbing over memories. It is well to show our affection and love, but to that wife we would say, "Why seek ye the living among the dead?" Rather, be like the dear old widowed lady who looked up from her Bible and smiling brightly said, "I was just reading and rejoicing in His promise, that those who sleep in Jesus will God bring with him; for my John will be there. Oh happy day!"

— M.R.D.

> Oh, then what raptured greetings
> On Canaan's happy shore!
> What knitting severed friendships up,
> Where partings are no more!
> —H. Alford

"There is a very good reason why God did not put eyes in the back of our head. He wants us to look AHEAD." — M.R.D.

CHRISTIAN SYMPATHY

> *. . . weep with them that weep.*   Romans 12:15

Christ was at the wedding in Cana and added to the joy of the occasion; but He also went to be with the sisters of Lazarus and wept at the grave of His friend. Jesus did this because He was full of compassion. As His followers, we too should lovingly participate in both the joy and the distress of others. If we truly love the Lord we cannot help but sympathize with those who are in the agonies of sorrow. It is a consolation to those who weep to see the sympathetic tear in the eye of a friend and to feel his warm handclasp. Love does not need many words to express its feelings. When one member of the Body of Christ suffers, even as Paul wrote to the Corinthians, so all the members should "suffer with it."

D. L. Moody tells how he became accustomed to attending the funerals of a great many children because of his large Bible class. "I became hardened to it like a doctor," he said, "and could go to them without sympathy. One day one of my little Sunday school scholars was drowned, and the word was sent by the mother that she wanted to see me. I went. The father was a drunkard, and was then under the influence of liquor. I had my little girl with me. She was about four years old. When we got outside she asked, 'Suppose we were poor, Papa, and I had to go down to the river for sticks, and should fall in and get drowned, and you had no money to bury me, would you be sorry, Papa?' And then she looked up into my eyes with an expression that I had never before seen, and asked, 'Did you feel bad for that mother?' I clasped her to my heart," said Moody, "and kissed her; my true sympathy was aroused."

Do you in Christ-like kindness and affection sympathize with those who are passing through the "valley of weeping"? If in the desert of sorrow you can produce an oasis of heavenly comfort and consolation by your spiritual admonitions, the benediction of Psalm 84 will rest upon you: "Blessed is that man . . . Who passing through the valley of Baca (maketh) it a well"!

— H.G.B.

> Give me a heart sympathetic and tender,
> Jesus, like Thine; Jesus, like Thine;
> Touched by the needs that are surging around me,
> And filled with compassion divine.
>
> —Anon.

"We can measure our likeness to Christ by the range of our sensitiveness to the sorrow and pain of others."

GO TO THE SPRING YOURSELF

READ MATTHEW 10:34-42

. . . a cup of cold water . . . .   Matthew 10:42

This text is generally misquoted as a "cup of water"; but Jesus is talking about a "cup of *cold* water." The usual interpretation of this verse is that any little act of kindness done in Christ's name will be rewarded — even a mere cup of water. This of course is true, but that is not the meaning here. Rather it means that making a real "sacrifice" will be rewarded. People in Jesus' day could not just open the door of the refrigerator and take out a bottle of cold water or add some convenient ice cubes. Then a cup of *cold* water meant going to the spring — maybe far away up the side of a hill or among the rocks. Or it might mean going to a deep well, letting down a bucket, and laboriously pulling it back up. That was the only way to get fresh, cold water. It meant a sacrifice. Getting a cup of *cold* water probably involved going to the source of the spring; for the water in a stream a few hundred feet below the point of its origin was no longer cool in that hot climate but soon became tepid and nauseating.

The Word of God is compared to water (John 3:5; I Pet. 1:23). If you want it fresh — get it at the fountain. Too many are content to get it "piped in through the preacher" or even through these devotionals. But it has lost some of its freshness when brought by others from the spring. Take your cup and go to the spring *yourself*, and enjoy it to the full.

We occasionally meet folks who confess that they read our "devotional" for the day — but do not take time to read the Scripture assignment. How inconsistent to take our lukewarm articles and neglect the cold, fresh water of the Word! The excuse "I did not have time" is pretty lame, as we try to keep the Scripture assignments brief; but if you really don't have time, then please, please, *please* skip what I have written and read the *Scripture!* Get fresh water; go to the spring yourself!

— M.R.D.

Just a "cup of cold water" was given in His name,
But the soul of the giver was never the same!
For he found that when giving was done with a zest,
Both the heart of the GIVER and TAKER were blest!
—Anon.

"Some people are like what the schoolboy said about the mule, 'Awfully backward about going forward.' " — M.R.D.

SELF-EXAMINATION

READ I CORINTHIANS 11:17-30

But let a man examine himself, and so let him eat of that
bread, and drink of that cup.   I Corinthians 11:28

It was Monday morning. Two Christians were discussing
spiritual matters and the things which had transpired in their
individual churches on the Lord's Day. One of them, who tended
at times to be "separate" in the wrong sense of the word, was
unduly critical and over-pious in his condemnation of others.
Finally he commented, "My father says things are going from
bad to worse in our assembly. Why, yesterday as many as *twelve
people* partook of communion!" "Why," said the other, "would
you consider that unspiritual?" "Well," replied the first man,
"my father feels that many of them were too great sinners. Had
they properly examined themselves he thinks that only half
that number would have been present." "Was your father among
the twelve who remembered the Lord?" "Yes!" "Well," said the
second man, "I do not know about the other eleven, but there
is one thing of which I am certain; *your father should not have
been one of the twelve!*" "Why not?" replied the other one
angrily. "Because, instead of realizing his own sin and examin-
ing himself, he was sitting in pharisaical judgment upon other
Christians. The Lord is always eager to welcome the contrite,
but those who feel themselves 'good enough' to partake of the
Lord's Supper are just those who should refrain from doing so.
The Lord 'resisteth the proud, but giveth grace to the humble.'"

It is so easy to even unknowingly be pharisaical, like the dear
old lady who said to the preacher after a very searching sermon,
"That was a wonderful message today, Pastor, everything you
said applied to *somebody or other I know.*"

Self-examination is difficult but necessary. We should let the
Word and Spirit of God search our hearts daily. Especially, however, in regard to the Lord's Supper, should we first examine
ourselves to see if "we be in the faith," for only thus can we
partake with blessing.   — H.G.B.

Have Thine own way, Lord! Have Thine own way!
Search me and try me, Master, today!
Whiter than snow, Lord, wash me just now,
As in Thy presence humbly I bow.
—A. A. Pollard

**"The man who has a high opinion of himself may depend upon it that
he is a very poor judge of human nature."**

THE SEEING EYE

READ JOHN 16:7-15

. . . he will guide you into all truth.   John 16:13

I am sitting before an open window on the fourth floor of the
Yorketowne Hotel in York, Pennsylvania. It is the busy hour of
the day and the traffic is roaring on the street below, with horns
blowing and policemen whistling. I am impressed with the
dangers of city life. Every one of those people on the street is in
danger every moment. One thoughtless moment, one second
lapse in vigilance and—crash! A child dashing from behind a
car, a blowout, failing brakes, and a hundred other hazards put
the lives of men and women in jeopardy.

My attention is drawn to one man in particular—a pedestrian.
His eyes are shielded by dark glasses and his left hand firmly
grasps the harness on the shoulders of a beautiful dog. The man
is blind but he has two eyes and ears better than his own to aid
him. The dog is of the "seeing eye" variety—carefully trained to
take his master safely through the busiest traffic. I am amazed
at the calmness of the guide. With his tongue hanging, he is the
very picture of composure. He is not excited. He does not
wait for a chance to dash across between the cars. Without a sign of nervousness he leads his master to the curb
and STOPS. He waits with eyes and ears attent. When all is
clear he quietly and safely guides the man across. They pass
out of sight as I take my pen to write it up for you in the devotional, and I murmur to myself, "That man is safer than anyone
else in the street, for he walks *by faith in his guide.*" He trusts
the "seeing eye." Solomon says, "The hearing ear and the seeing
eye, the Lord hath made both of them." O God, help me to
calmly trust the Holy Spirit, the Faithful Guide and my "Seeing
Eye," as calmly, yea more calmly, than that blind man on the
street. For his dog may fail, but the Holy Spirit never! O teach
me to trust and to walk by faith amid the traffic of this life.
Thank You for the promise: "I will guide thee with mine eye."

—M.R.D.

Holy Spirit, faithful Guide,
    Ever near the Christian's side;
Gently lead me by the hand,
    Pilgrim in this desert land.
                    —M. M. Wells

"The task ahead of us is never greater than the Power behind us."

THE WONDROUS CROSS

READ JOHN 19:14-30

*And he bearing his cross went forth into a place called
the place of a skull, which is called in the Hebrew
Golgotha: Where they crucified Him . . . .* John 19:17, 18

Mahatma Ghandi asked some missionaries who visited him
during one of his numerous "fasts" to sing a hymn for him.
"Which hymn?" they inquired. "The one that expresses all that
is deepest in your faith," he replied. They thought for a moment
and then with full hearts sang:

"When I survey the wondrous cross
On which the Prince of Glory died,
My richest gain I count but loss
And pour contempt on all my pride."

Yes, there is always something wondrous about the cross
which stirs the heart and brings a love-tear to the believer's eye.
When with sanctified imagination we travel back to Calvary, our
souls are saddened and yet thrilled with the wonder of it all. For
there, "the just for the unjust," He suffered in our place, while
from His hands, feet, and wounded side the "love came tricklin'
down." With heartfelt gratitude we exclaim, "Thank You, Lord,
for saving my soul!"

When George Nixon Briggs was governor of Massachusetts,
three of his friends visited the Holy Land. While they were
there they climbed Golgotha's slope and cut from the summit
a small stick to be used as a cane. On their return they presented
it to the Governor, saying, "We want you to know that when
we stood on Calvary, we thought of you." He accepted the gift
with gratitude and courtesy but tenderly remarked: "I appreciate your consideration of me, gentlemen, but *I am still more
thankful for Another who thought of me there!*" Yes, He "thought
of you, He thought of me, when hanging there in agony!" Certainly a life of gratitude and praise is demanded by such a
sacrifice. "Love so amazing, so divine, demands my soul, my
life, *my all!*"   —H.G.B.

O Jesus Christ of Calvary, how deep Thy love to me!
When I survey on cruel cross Thy death of agony!
In blood and shame I see Thee now,
Pain-pierced on yonder tree;
And from this soul Thy love hast won,
I pledge my love to Thee!

—J. G. Ridley

"Calvary is the result of God's eternal heartache for perishing souls."

THE APPEARANCE OF EVIL

READ I CORINTHIANS 10:23-33

Abstain from all appearance of evil.

I Thessalonians 5:22

Suppose you, a Christian, saw a clerk put your purchase of groceries in a carton labeled: "Budweiser Beer," would you object? Is there anything wrong with carrying groceries in a beer carton? The answer to that could be "yes" or "no." In itself it makes no difference what it says on the *outside*, if there is nothing wrong inside. Still, there can be danger in this innocent incident. Suppose someone, who was looking for an opportunity of criticizing you (especially if you're a preacher), saw you leaving the store with your beer carton! He might conclude it was "beer" inside as well as on the outside. Result? Gossip! To avoid the very appearance of evil I'd rather have them put my groceries in a bag or an Ivory Soap carton. Is this an extreme position? Do you think this is narrow-minded? Do you say, "I don't care what anyone else thinks, my conscience is clear"? Yet it is not only your conscience but *your testimony* which counts. This illustration of the "beer carton" may be extreme, but if all of us were more careful about not giving occasion for the world to criticize, there would be less misunderstanding and gossip.

A Christian traveler ordered some ginger ale, which was served to him in a unique-shaped glass. The man opposite him ordered a highball, and it came in an identical glass. Outwardly the drinks looked exactly alike. The man thought, "Suppose someone whom I've been trying to win for Christ should pass by. What would he think?" His conscience was clear but his testimony was in danger. Calling the waiter, he asked him to exchange the ginger ale for a glass of milk. Do you think the man foolish? Not as foolish as the Christian who says, "It's none of anyone else's business. My conscience is clear." Today, brother, sister, watch for the little things which can give the wrong impression!   —M.R.D.

We can't afford to live our lives haphazard;
  We can't afford to grow lukewarm or cold,
For somewhere there is someone who is watching;
  Our smallest, single action they behold.
                                    —Georgia B. Adams

"Have you ever answered the question of Cain, 'Am I my brother's keeper?' " — M. R. D.

JUST A LITTLE LONGER

READ I THESSALONIANS 4:13-18

For yet a little while, and he that shall come will come,
and will not tarry.   Hebrews 10:37

We are told that in the Greek the words translated "For yet a little while," are more dramatic than the English indicates. They might well be rendered, *"How little, how little!"*

When the billows of trouble roll across the horizon, let this thought cheer you, Christian: the One for whom we are looking will soon put in His appearance to dispel the shadows and usher in the bliss of His "pleasures for evermore." Verily, "weeping may endure for a night, but joy cometh in the morning!" Let this truth purify your thought, energize your effort, rejoice your spirit, and comfort your heart. Just a few more tears, a few more disappointments, and the King of Love will come.

Dr. Guiness in speaking on the imminent return of our Lord once used the following illustration: He said that he had heard the singing of Handel's "Messiah" with great delight on the previous evening and he commented that if someone had asked him after the performance had proceeded a couple of hours, how much longer it would still continue, he would have answered, "Oh, about five minutes." "But," the individual might have objected, "how can that be? It is still in full swing and has been going on for two hours. I can see no reason why it should not continue for two hours longer. How do you know, sir, that it will be over in five minutes?" "Then," said Dr. Guiness, "I should have answered him, 'because *I have the score* . . . and I know it will soon be over for *they are singing the last chorus.*' "

Yes, it is wonderful to have the "score," as it is found in the Word of God, and recognize the unmistakable "signs of the times." Students of prophecy realize the lateness of the hour. We cannot, and should not, fix dates, but we can say with confidence, "The coming of the Lord draweth nigh" (James 5:8). "Wherefore comfort one another with these words (I Thess. 4:18).   —H.G.B.

Just a little longer and the trump of God will sound,
Just a little longer and we'll all be Glory-bound.
Look away to Heaven, your redemption draweth nigh,
Just a little longer and we'll meet Him in the sky!
—Anon.

"The truth of Christ's second coming, like a silver thread of hope, runs throughout the entire Bible."

SEPARATION OR INTEGRATION

READ ROMANS 6:1-11

> *. . . come out from among them, and be ye separate.*
> II Corinthians 6:17

This present age will undoubtedly go down in history as the "Age of Integration." The nations have finally realized that we are in an atomic age; we must either get together or perish together. So they have formed the organization known as the U.N.O. in an effort to unite for the abolishment of war. The slogan of the U.N.O. might well be: "Integration or Annihilation." However, the true believer follows an entirely different program. It is "separation" from the world and its evils—and "integration" with Christ and His people. Christians should be different because they serve a different Lord and Master. Can the world see a difference in you as you move among men? Can they detect that you belong to Christ and so cannot go along with the world in its evil program?

A certain prominent citizen was converted. He loved the Lord but knew nothing about separation and thought he could continue in his worldly associations. So when he received an invitation to a social meeting in a notoriously worldly club, he dressed and went as usual. Upon his arrival, several of the men standing at the club bar, drinking highballs and smoking cigarettes, looked up in surprise, and one of them grasped his hand saying, "Am I glad to see you here, Harry, and to find out it isn't true what I heard about you!" In surprise, Harry answered, "Well, what did you hear about me?" The answer cut deep. Said the man, "Why, I heard you were converted and got religion. I'm so glad to see you here and to know that the rumors were not true." "But it is true," Harry stammered, "and you are right—this is no place for a Christian. I am getting off the Devil's property."

The Christian has no business in the Devil's playground. "Be ye separate" and "come out from among them." Remember, the world knows you are out of place among them unless it is to witness for Christ.   —M.R.D.

> Living for Jesus a life that is true,
>   Striving to please Him in all that I do;
> Yielding allegiance, glad-hearted and free,
>   This is the pathway of blessing for me.
>   —T. O. Chisholm

"The only excuse for hobnobbing with sinners is that you do so to bring them to Christ." — M. R. D.

HONORING FATHER

READ PROVERBS 23:10-26

Honour thy father ....   Exodus 20:12

God tells us to reverence, obey, and honor our parents. This is not only an Old Testament command, but also a New Testament precept (see Eph. 6:1-3).

Some time ago in the Grand Rapids Press this letter appeared in the "Dear Abby" column: "I am the most broken-hearted person on earth. I always found time to go everywhere else but to see my dear, old, gray-haired parents. They sat home alone, loving me just the same. It is too late now to give them those few hours of happiness I was too selfish and too busy to give, and now when I go to visit their graves and look at the green grass above them I wonder if God will ever forgive me for the heartaches I must have caused them. I pray that you will print this, so that those who still have their parents will visit them and show their love and respect while there is still time."

In *Benedicte's Scrapbook* an unknown, friendly philosopher penned these appropriate comments: "Dad may wear last year's straw hat, his fingernails may need manicuring, his vest may hang a little loose, his pants may bag at the knees, his face may show signs of a second day's growth of beard, and the tin dinner-bucket he carries may be full of dents and doughnuts; but *don't call him 'the old man' — he's your father!* For years and years he has been rustling around to get things together. Never once has he failed to do the right thing by you. He thinks you are the greatest boy or girl on earth, bar none, even though you disappoint him in many ways . . . and fail to bring home a cent. He is *'some man'* and not *'the old man.'*"

Children should remember that they can expect the full blessing of God only if they heed the words of Solomon, who admonishes, "Hear thou, my son, and be wise . . . *Hearken unto thy father that begat thee*" (Prov. 23:19, 22)!   —H.G.B.

> Only a dad, but he gives his all
>   To smooth the way for his children small;
> These are the lines that for him I pen;
>   Only a dad, but the best of men!
>   —Anon.

"The command that speaks to the child and says, 'honor' — with equal force comes back upon the parent and says, 'Be honorable so that thy child may rightly show thee reverence.'" — W. SENIOR

"THE BREAD OF LIFE"

READ EXODUS 16:14-18; JOHN 6:49-51

I am the bread of life.   John 6:48

Jesus did not say, "I am the 'filet mignon' of life," or "I am the 'caviar' of life," for these delicate foods only the favored few can enjoy. How thankful we are that He is *bread*—the poor man's staff of life. There are many foods which are available only to a few, because of cost or because of their seasonable nature or scarcity. But bread is the universal food of mankind. It is found on every table—rich and poor—king and peasant. Whether it is made of wheat or corn or rye, oats or rice, it is *bread,* the cheapest and most nourishing food. The word "bread" is defined by Webster as "food made from ground grain; food in general." Bread represents all the elements of food needed to sustain life.

Jesus is the "bread of life." In Him are all the elements needed for a healthy, growing spiritual life. He is within reach of all, His blessings are free. The manna fell from heaven—all the Israelite needed to do was gather and eat it. It was good for young and old. It was a complete food.

Charles H. Spurgeon has aptly said, "I bless God that He gave us not a classical gospel, or a mathematical gospel, or a metaphysical gospel, or a gospel confined to scholars or men of genius, but a poor man's gospel, a ploughman's gospel, for that is the kind of Gospel we can live and die upon. It is to us not the luxury of refinement but the staple bread of life. We want no fine words when the heart is heavy, nor deep problems when facing eternity. Jesus manifest in the flesh is our bread of life, Jesus bleeding on the cross a substitute for sinners is our soul's drink. This is the Gospel for babes, and strong men want no more." Yes, we thank God, Jesus did not say, "I am the cake"— but rather, "*I am the bread of life.*" It is free to all—good for all—sufficient for all!   —M.R.D.

To feed the starving souls of men,
The Bread of Life was given;
And broken on the cross for us,
He gives us life and Heaven!
—G. W.

"Why eat the husks of sin and pay for it with your soul, when you can have the Bread of Life for the asking?"

WHITER THAN SNOW

READ PSALM 51:1-7

. . . wash me, and I shall be whiter than snow.

Psalm 51:7

In the fourteenth chapter of Leviticus the Lord gives instruction for the cleansing of the leper. Blood and water were to be applied for his purification. This all was typical of the sinner who must be purified from the *guilt* of sin (through the blood), and also from the *defilement* of sin (through the application of the water of the Word). This was fulfilled in Christ who "loved the church, and gave himself for it (redemption by blood); that He might sanctify and cleanse it with the washing of *water* by the word" (see Eph. 5:25, 26).

In this penitent prayer made by David in Psalm 51, after his terrible sin of adultery and murder, he shows his truly contrite heart and his understanding of the need of spiritual cleansing through the application of the "water and the blood." The expression—*whiter than snow*—is not a mere exaggeration, for though to our eyes snow is perhaps the whitest thing that one can look at, yet every snowflake has at its core a tiny speck of dirt around which its lacy pattern of ice has been formed. In other words, *every snowflake has a "dirty heart!"* The blood of Christ and the water of the Word cleanse us so that in God's sight we become "whiter than snow."

When King Edward VII was still Prince of Wales, he went visiting a country nobleman. The little girl of his host entered the room and climbed upon his knee. Being a sweet Christian she had determined to talk to the Prince about his soul. "Do you like to make guesses?" she asked in her childlike way. "Yes," he said, with a smile. "Is there something you would like me to answer?" "Please, sir, can you tell me what is whiter than snow?" The king looked confused and finally had to give up. The little maid with a sweet rebuke in her eyes said, "Oh, Prince, I'm sorry, but every soul washed in Jesus' blood should know that he is whiter than snow!"

Dear friend, have you experienced this wondrous cleansing?

—H.G.B.

Lord Jesus, I long to be perfectly whole;
I want Thee forever to live in my soul,
Break down every idol, cast out every foe;
Now wash me, and I shall be whiter than snow.

—J. Nicholson

"Men may 'whitewash' sin, but only Jesus' blood can wash it white."

ARE YOU A WASTER?

READ PSALM 90

. . . Gather up the fragments that remain, that nothing
be lost. John 6:12

Have you often wondered what was done with the twelve
huge baskets of fragments that were left after feeding the 5000
with the five barley loaves and the two small fishes? The Bible
does not tell us, but I suspect that they were probably dis-
tributed to the poor. Or they might have been fed to the
animals, or given to the birds. We don't know, but the lesson
Jesus would teach us is not to waste God's good gifts. He says,
"Gather the fragments that nothing be lost." After you are all
filled up yourself, don't forget about others around you. Many
are the lessons we may learn.

1. After we have been filled with the bread of life, we should
then gather some to give to others. It is not enough to read the
Word for our personal profit; we should also be able to give
some of it to others.

2. We are responsible for the little things as well as the
bigger things. No one would think of throwing a whole loaf of
bread away, but how many crumbs we waste.

3. We must realize that we are responsible for all that the
Lord gives us. The Lord Jesus is the Bread of Life prepared
at awful cost. If we realized how much it cost to provide this
Bread of Life we would be careful to prize it more highly.

The cheaper a thing is, the less we prize it. The more a thing
costs, the more careful we are to preserve it. A man who stuttered
badly and had great difficulty in talking, carried on a conversation on a telephone for six minutes without ever once hesitating
or stuttering. When his friend expressed surprise at his absence
of stuttering, he replied, "I can't afford to stutter through a
telephone, when it costs me seventy-five cents a minute." If we
knew the price of our redemption we would have no trouble
talking about it either.   —M.R.D.

After I have eaten, Lord,
  And on Thy grace have fed;
Help me to give to others
  Thy precious, living Bread!
                              —G.W.

**"Jesus came to seek and to save the lost, and no matter what good we
may be doing, if we are not winning folk to Christ, we are majoring
on minors." — F. WEBB**

NEEDED: SELF-EXAMINATION

READ PSALM 69:1-5

*O God, thou knowest my foolishness; and my sins are
not hid from thee.* Psalm 69:5

We are usually so busy mentally congratulating ourselves for
some supposed knowledge, achievement, or talent, that we seem
to have little time for true, humble self-examination. The criticism of others is often unkind; but if we are intelligent and study
what they say, it may be extremely revealing as to actual flaws in
our character and testimony. Not only should we examine ourselves, and listen to the comments of our critics, but we should
let the Word and Spirit of God search our hearts daily so that
we will know where the "old leaven" is, that must be "purged
out." If you think you are usually right about everything, and
are quite somebody, read God's stinging commentary on how
wrong you are as it is recorded in I Corinthians 8:2, "If any man
thinketh that he knoweth any thing, *he knoweth nothing yet as
he ought to know.*"

The *Ladies' Home Journal* printed this story one time as a
jest, but it really was quite revealing. "A rather pompous-looking
deacon was endeavoring to impress upon a class of boys the importance of living the Christian life. 'Why do people call me a
Christian?' the dignitary asked, standing very erect and beaming down upon his scholars with pride. There was a moment's
pause, and then one of the youngsters said, *'Maybe it's because
they don't know you.'*"

If you truly examine yourself in the light of God's Word, you
will come to the humbling conclusion that there is actually no
such person as you secretly (and pridefully) suppose yourself
to be. The only thing truly lovely in us as Christians is the
indwelling Holy Spirit. May our prayer therefore be, "O, thou
Spirit Divine, all my nature refine, till the beauty of Jesus be
seen in me." — H.G.B.

O God, my folly and my sin
　Thy holy eye can see;
Now, save from pride, blest Saviour dear,
　The saint that waits on thee.

—Anon.

**"Humility departs when we are secretly pleased that 'we are not
actually proud.'"**

"WERE YOU THERE, CHARLIE?"

READ JOB 38:4-13

In the beginning God created the heaven and the earth.
Genesis 1:1

Where wast thou when I laid the foundations of the earth?
Job 38:4

What a man does with the Bible depends on what he does with the first sentence in the Bible. The Bible opens with a simple statement, "In the beginning God created the heaven and the earth." If a man believes that, he can believe everything else which follows. If he rejects that statement, he will also deny every other cardinal truth in the Scriptures. Here in Genesis 1:1 infidelity begins, and here in Genesis 1:1 faith comes to rest. There is no better answer ever given for the universe. Compared to this simple assertion, all the theories of men are stupidly foolish.

In a court of law, the judge will accept only the testimony of actual eye witnesses. Hearsay testimony is immediately thrown out. Only those who know firsthand and were there can bear reliable testimony. The same is true of creation. God asks Job the question, "Where were you when I made the worlds?" Two men — Joe and Charlie — were arguing about Genesis 1:1. Joe said he believed the record of creation just as it was written. Charlie was an infidel, and went to great length in giving his own theory of how the world began and then developed from a primordial cell through reptiles, monkeys, and up to man. When he was all through, Joe looked at him and said, "*Were you there, Charlie?*" It was a good question. "Of course I was not there," said Charlie. Joe had the answer. He said, "Well, God was there. He was the only One there and I'll take the word of the 'eye witness' rather than the guesses of those who go only by '*they say.*'" "Were you there, Charlie?" What presumption for the creature to question the word of the Creator. — M.R.D.

I'll trust my all to Him alone,
Whose Word is truth and light;
I'd rather walk by faith with Christ
Than go alone by sight.

—Anon.

"Unless you believe you will not understand!" — AUGUSTINE

THE MARK OF CULTURE

READ ACTS 28:7-16

. . . be courteous. I Peter 3:8

Someone has said, "The mark of refinement and culture is *courtesy.*" Webster defines courtesy as "politeness combined with kindliness." The Greek word used in our text is *philanthropos,* from which our English word "philanthropy" comes. Webster again defines a "philanthropist" as "one who loves and seeks to benefit mankind." Every Christian should be a philanthropist, which means he should be courteous. Courtesy is a frame of heart and mind — not just an outward show of false refinement. Courtesy means having regard for others.

I came a bit late to a meeting and could not find a parking place within three blocks of the church. Yet in the church parking lot there would have been room for twenty-five more cars if the people of the church knew the meaning of courtesy. They just parked their cars in any old way — right angles, parallel, and with a space of four or five feet between cars (just close enough so no one else would get in). If I were not a Christian, I would hesitate to attend a church of such crude, discourteous members who did not consider anyone else.

Why will men remove their hats and step aside to admit a lady into the elevator, and then embarrass some bewildered woman driver at a red light by honking the horn and making some slurring remark about "women drivers"? Why will a husband, out in company, politely pull out the chair to seat his wife — while at home he doesn't give a thought to assist his wife by even wiping his feet when he comes in? Why does a big, fat woman plunk on the end of the pew and make everybody else stumble over her feet to get in? "End seat hogs," we call them.

Today drive like a Christian — park like a Christian — act like a Christian. Cultivate true Christian refinement, which thinks of others *first.* — M.R.D.

A bunch of golden keys are mine
  To make each day with gladness shine.
When friends give anything to me
  I use the little "Thank you" key;
"Excuse me," — "Beg your pardon," too,
  If by mistake some harm I do.
With golden ring these keys I bind;
  This is its motto, "Be ye kind!"
—Anon.

"A little of the oil of courtesy would save a lot of friction."

DELINQUENCY

READ II TIMOTHY 3:13-17

Train up a child in the way he should go: and when he is old, he will not depart from it.   Proverbs 22:6

Children do not go the "right way" by themselves. Naturally they are "children of wrath," having been conceived and born in sin (Ps. 51:5). Therefore, they tend toward delinquency, unless, by the grace of God and the prayers and guidance of their parents, they are directed in the "way everlasting."

Some years ago I ran across this "modern fable" in a little four-page magazine. It speaks so eloquently that I pass it on to you verbatim:

Once there was a little boy. When he was three weeks old his parents turned him over to a baby-sitter. When he was two, they dressed him up like a cowboy and gave him a gun. When he was three everybody said, "How cute," as he went about lisping a beer commercial jingle. When he was six, his father occasionally dropped him off at Sunday school on his way to the golf course. When he was eight they bought him a BB gun and taught him to shoot sparrows. *He learned to shoot windshields by himself!* When he was ten he spent his after-school time squatting at a drugstore newsstand reading comic books. His mother wasn't home and his father was busy. When he was thirteen, he told his parents other boys stayed out as late as they wanted to — so they said he could too. It was easier that way. When he was fourteen they gave him a deadly two-ton machine, wrangled a license for him to drive it, and told him to be careful. When he was fifteen, the police called his home one night and said, "We have your boy. He's in trouble." "In trouble?" screamed the father. "It can't be *my* boy!" But it was!

MORAL: As the twig is bent, *it is apt to snap back in your face!*
      — H.G.B.

Fathers and mothers, listen to me!
  Who is to blame for delinquency —
You or your untrained girl or boy
  Who turned to crime in search of joy?
Forsake the world and the social whirl,
  And go to church with your boy and girl,
O parents, pause and listen to me,
  For YOU are the cause of delinquency!
                —D. C. Ritchie

"Everything in the home today seems to be run by a switch, except children."

HOW TO BELIEVE

READ JOHN 3:14-19

He that believeth on him is not condemned. John 3:18

The story is told of a missionary who was translating the book of John into an African dialect. He had great difficulty in finding a word for the off-repeated expression "believe," so he had to leave it blank. He continued his work, but was constantly baffled by his inability to translate this key word. One day a native came from another community with a message of great importance. He had been running through the tangled underbrush for hours and so was completely exhausted. He blurted out his message and, being at the end of his endurance, threw himself upon a nearby hammock. As he went limp he breathed a sigh of relief and uttered a word in the African dialect which was new to the missionary. He asked the natives what the runner had said. One replied, "Master, it means '*I am resting all my weight here.*'" "Thank God," said the missionary, "that is just the word I need for 'believe' "; and he proceeded to complete his translation.

Many today are concerned about what God means with the word "believe." They wonder if they have the right "feeling," the right type of "faith." They fail to realize that it is *not faith but Christ who saves.* The Devil makes them concentrate on their poor, weak faith, rather than on the object of that faith. Look at the native again. At the end of himself, he does nothing but just rest his all upon the hammock. So, too, believing is just casting one's self unreservedly into the open arms of the Lord Jesus and saying, "Lord, I believe; help thou my unbelief. On Thee I rest my soul for eternity." Stop trying so hard and *just let Jesus do it all!* You want to come, don't you? Of course you do! Well, that shows that you have enough faith for "whosoever WILL *may come!*" Remember, Jesus said, "Whosoever cometh unto me *I will in no wise cast out.*" Don't let the Devil fool you any longer; turn everything over to Christ and rest in His love.

— H.G.B.

Though all unworthy, yet I will not doubt,
For him that cometh, He will not cast out;
"He that believeth," oh, the good news shout,
"Hath everlasting life!"

—G. M. J.

**"Someone has said the letters in the word FAITH explain its meaning:
Forsaking-All-I-Trust-Him!"**

A LESSON FROM A CHICKEN

READ PSALM 112

In every thing give thanks . . . .   I Thessalonians 5:18

When I was a boy my father kept a few chickens. I remember how mother would take me to feed the "chicks," and how they would come to the pan of fresh water and dip their beaks in the liquid and then lift their heads straight up and let the water run down their throats. One day I asked mother why the chickens lifted their heads when they drank and I shall never forget her answer. Said she, "They are lifting their heads in thanksgiving to God for their water." Of course, I know now that chickens don't know about God, but still the dumb creation praises God in its own way. The creation prays to God for deliverance (Rom. 8:19-21). The trees of the fields are said to clap their hands, and the hills dance and skip like little lambs. The heavens declare the glory of God and the firmament shows forth His handiwork. Even the day utters speech and the night showeth knowledge. Only man, of all God's creatures, forgets to thank Him for His blessings. If we were to write in a book all the blessings of the past week and then count the minutes we have spent to thank Him — it might awaken us to the need of "giving thanks."

A prominent church member and an old Indian whom he knew sat down opposite one another in a restaurant. The Indian bowed his head and waited for the professing church member to do likewise; but instead the man just began his meal, while the Indian paused to pray. A moment later the Indian said, "Do you know what you remind me of?" "Why no! What?" The Indian replied, "The man who sits down at a table and eats the food God gives him without thanking Him for it, reminds me of the hog under the oak tree eating acorns by the hour and never so much as looking up to see where the acorns come from." Remember, the wrath of God came upon the Gentiles for the sin of unthankfulness. Read Romans 1:21.   — M.R.D.

Praise the Lord! O all ye people,
Young and old, in glad accord,
Grateful hearts in song uplifting,
Swell the chorus — *PRAISE THE LORD!*
          —R. Walmsley

"Hem your blessings with praise lest they unravel."

LIVING PEACEABLY

READ DEUTERONOMY 32:29-35

*If it be possible, as much as lieth in you, live peaceably
with all men.* Romans 12:18

This Scripture speaks of Christian forbearance and understanding — the quiet willingness to suffer wrong rather than to foster or continue discord by quarreling and brawling.

Someone who had experienced great difficulty with an unreasonable neighbor, and who finally had to defend himself legally against the latter's unwarranted and dishonest actions, commented: "I have tried to follow Romans 12:18, but in a case like this I thank the Lord for the 'escape clause' He has put into this text. He does not say we have to live peaceably with all men *under every circumstance* — for even the Lord recognizes that with some people this cannot be done. Therefore, He says '*if it be possible*' we should refrain from taking violent issue with those who oppose us. — This is one of the rare cases in which I found it necessary to take other permissible measures."

"How do wars begin?" a boy once asked his father. Not wishing to admit that his son's question was beyond him, the father replied, "Well, take the first World War; that began because Germany invaded Belgium." At this point his wife interrupted him, "Tell the boy the truth. It began because somebody was murdered." The husband drew himself up with an air of superiority and retorted, "Are you answering the question, or am I?" Turning her back on her husband in a huff, the wife walked out of the room and slammed the door as hard as she could. When the room stopped vibrating, an uneasy silence followed, broken at length by the son, "Daddy, you needn't tell me how wars begin; *I know now!*"

Are you quick to retaliate, or have you cultivated a peaceable spirit? Jesus prayed for His enemies; do you? Live peaceably this day. — H.G.B.

I've found a little remedy
To ease the life we live,
And make each day a happier one
It is the word "FORGIVE."

—Anon.

"He who cannot forgive others breaks the bridge over which he himself must pass."

THAT WONDERFUL BOOK

> *. . . give me understanding, that I may know thy testi-*
> *monies.* Psalm 119:125

The Bible is the only eternal Book, and it shall never perish. How important then to *know* what it contains. David prayed, "Give me understanding, that I may *know* thy testimonies." But you cannot know it — unless you read it. Have you done so? In my notebook I came upon the following paragraph from an unknown author, which I pass on to you:

"The Bible is our greatest national asset, the masterpiece of God. It comes to us drenched in the tears of millions of contritions, worn with the fingers of the saints of the ages, expounded by the greatest intellects, and stained with the blood of the martyrs. It is the fountain in which dying believers cooled their hot faces, the pillow on which saints of all ages have rested their heads. It breaks the fetters of the slave, takes the heat out of life's fierce fever, the pain out of parting, the sting out of death, and the gloom out of the grave.

"The Bible is the old-time Book, the new-time Book, the all-time Book. It will demonstrate its own character and its own power. This is the Rock of all ages, and they who build upon it are as eternal as God. The Name of Jesus, the Supreme Personality, the center of the world's desire, is on every page in one form or another. Pierce the Book anywhere, and it bleeds with His priceless blood, shed for our redemption. The divine Book has all the answers to man's every need. To find them is our greatest privilege and opportunity."

In the Scripture for today (Ps. 119:33-40) David says that the Word teaches, gives understanding, directs, cleanses, establishes, turns us and quickens us. The importance of this Book outweighs all others! — M.R.D.

> Praise God for the Bible, Revealer of Light,
> This Sword of the Spirit puts error to flight,
> And still through life's journey until the last sigh,
> We'll travel together, my Bible and I.
> —Anon.

"The surest way to spoil your appetite for the 'good food' of the Word, is to eat the 'spoiled food' of the world!" — M. R. D.

PERSONAL SOUL WINNING

READ JOHN 1:35-42

. . . he that winneth souls is wise.   Proverbs 11:30

The church has lost most of its zeal for soul winning! Gibbon, the historian, says that the chief cause of the rapid spread of Christianity in the days of the Roman Empire was the tremendous amount of personal work carried on by the rank and file of Christ's followers. By the second century it is estimated that twenty per cent of the Roman world had been converted. St. Augustine was won to Christ by the prayers of his mother and the witnessing of Bishop Ambrose: Augustine in turn led Alypius and Nebridius to the Lord; Chrysostom was a trophy of grace personally converted by Bishop Meletius; and so we could continue on down the list.

Those who have tried "personal work" will tell you that few are immediately converted in "story book" fashion. The late Gypsy Smith summed it up well; he said, "It is easier to capture a city than to convert a soul. It is blood and tears, and anguish and sleepless nights and sacrifice and Gethsemane and Calvary — and yet, heaven in its all!"

A prominent evangelist was holding meetings in a church whose minister was a man of national prominence. The minister pointed out a man in the audience and said, "For twelve years I have tried to win that fellow to Christ. I have preached to him for so long that I sometimes find myself doing it almost unconsciously." "How many times have you gone to him with love in your heart and asked him to become a child of God?" asked the evangelist. "I must confess," said the minister, "that I have never personally contacted him." "Then," said the other, "perhaps he is not impregnable." That same evening the evangelist caught the man before he got out of the door. He spoke only a few words to him but they were earnest and loving. The next evening in the "after service" they found him on his knees with tears streaming down his cheeks. The Holy Spirit had used the personal touch to accomplish what appeared impossible.

Beginning today, make Paul's motto your prayer: "That I might by all means save some."   — H.G.B.

> How shall this passion for souls be mine?
> The answer I see is clear;
> Simply by throwing the old Life-Line
> To those who are struggling near.
> —H. G. Tovey

"The torch of Christianity may be lit in the church, but it does its best burning in the shop and in the street."

DIVIDING THE SPOIL

READ I CORINTHIANS 3:1-10

> *. . . as his part is that goeth down to the battle, so shall
> his part be that tarrieth by the stuff: they shall part
> [share] alike.*   I Samuel 30:24

In these words of David we have a great principle stated. David had gone forth into battle with four hundred soldiers to deliver Ziklag from the Amalekites. But there were two hundred of his army who "were so faint" that they could not follow David, and who were left behind to remain by the "stuff." They "kept the home fires burning." After David returns with a great deal of spoil, these 200 went to meet him. It was then that the 400 men who had fought in the battle objected to these 200, who remained behind, receiving any of the spoil. They said, "Because they went not with us, we will not give them ought of the spoil." But David steps in, and rebukes these selfish soldiers and says: "As his part is that goeth down to the battle, so shall his part be that tarrieth by the stuff."

This principle applies today. Some of you will have to meet the enemy today as you go forth into the world. Others of you, because of circumstances, will remain at home. Thousands of God's children must spend the day in bed, or a wheelchair, prevented from going forth into battle. Your business is to remain by the stuff. I doubt not for a moment but that these 200 spent much time in praying for the 400 soldiers and encouraging them, and providing their ammunition. Their work of "guarding the stuff" was just as important as the fighting. Some must keep the line of communication open, while others fight. Are you one of God's army who cannot go forth into the battle but must remain at home to pray? This is indispensably important, for without it others who fight would be "defeated." When the King returns, the reward of God's patient sufferers at home will be the same as others who went "down to battle."

Don't complain because you are laid aside — use it as an opportunity for this important part of Christian service. Keep the home fires burning!   — M.R.D.

Never a soldier in fierce conflict could a higher honor bring,
Than the shut-in who's performing secret service for the King!
                    —Anon.

**"The work an unknown saint has done is like a vein of water flowing
hidden underground, secretly making the ground green."**

ROMANS EIGHT TWENTY-EIGHT

> *. . . all things work together for good to them that love God.*   Romans 8:28

Fanny Crosby in her autobiography comments concerning the doctor who unwittingly caused her blindness as follows: "I have heard that this physician never ceased expressing his regret at the occurrence; and that it was one of the sorrows of his life. But if I could meet him now, I would say, 'Thank you, thank you, over and over again for making me blind.' . . . Although it may have been a blunder on the physician's part, it was no mistake on God's. I verily believe it was His intention that I should live my days in physical darkness, so as to be better prepared to sing His praises and incite others to do so." Thus by a doctor's apparent mistake, God gave to the Church the wonderful heritage of a blind Fanny Crosby who, with her increased spiritual insight, was able to write thousands of enduring hymns.

A visitor once went to see an old lady who had very few earthly possessions — just a bed, an old chair, a table, a stool, and a cupboard. After a little while the guest asked, "Do you never feel like murmuring at your difficult lot?" "Well, sometimes Satan does tempt me to complain, but then I just ask the Lord to put me into my easy chair, and to keep me quiet." The visitor looked around to see what she could mean, but all he saw was the hard stool and the broken armchair. "I don't see any easy place for you to sit," he said. "No, you misunderstand me," said the precious old saint. "*My easy chair is Romans 8:28.* It is always close by. When I need it the Lord just sets me into it, and I am at rest and say to Satan, 'Now, you be quiet!'"

Someone has said that in eternity we will probably thank God more for the difficulties of this earthly life than for some of the experiences that we now consider to be pleasant and desirable.

Stop sitting on the edge of the stool of worry; go and relax in the restful rocker of Romans 8:28.   — H.G.B.

> I sing because I'm in His care,
>   The Father's love is everywhere,
> I'm in His care — may this thought bring
>   A trustful peace through everything.
>   —C. Simpson

"God often empties our hands in order to fill our hearts; He gives us crosses here that we may wear crowns over there."

CARRYING BURDENS

READ GALATIANS 6:1-5

> *. . . my burden is light.*   Matthew 11:30

Every child of God is called to bear burdens in this life. We are to bear one another's burdens; and then there are burdens which we alone can bear (Gal. 6:2, 5). However, these burdens are given for a purpose (Rom. 8:28). They develop our Christian character and are a part of God's wise design to prevent tragedy in our lives. Are you bowed down under a heavy burden, sickness, sorrow, problems or care? Then remember, they all work together for good — and God will never give you greater trials than you are able to bear (I Cor. 10:13). If we had no burdens we would soon forget our need of Him and be swept away by the temptations of life.

Dr. Lambie, that greatly blessed medical missionary to Abyssinia, once told of a valuable lesson he learned from the natives. Lacking bridges, they were often compelled to wade across swollen streams to reach their destination. The current was swift and there was constant danger of being swept off their feet into deeper water or among treacherous rocks. The weight of the human body being only slightly heavier than water, it was difficult to maintain a foothold when waist deep in the stream. The natives therefore solved the problem by slinging a sack of stone over their shoulder for extra ballast to weigh them down so their feet would not slip. When they reached the other side, they emptied the sack on the bank. So, too, the Lord places upon us burdens which seem to weigh us down, but in reality keep us from slipping and falling. So trust Him and believe that He lays no burden upon you heavier than is necessary to keep you safe.

One of these days when we reach the other side we will lay all our burdens down and then we shall understand. Our Lord knows exactly how much we can bear, and how much we need to carry us through. May we with David say, "I have trusted also in the Lord; therefore I shall not slide" (Ps. 26:1).   — M.R.D.

> Are you struggling with your burden?
> 'Neath the chastening rod?
> God is working, wait upon Him,
> Wait, and pray, and plod.
> —A. B. Simpson

"To give us spiritual traction, God often keeps us DOWN so that He may keep us UP!"

THE WRONG SWORD

READ I SAMUEL 21:1-10

> *. . . The sword of Goliath the Philistine, whom thou*
> *slewest in the valley of Elah, behold, it is here wrapped*
> *in a cloth behind the ephod: if thou wilt take that, take*
> *it . . . And David said, THERE IS NONE LIKE THAT;*
> *give it me.*   I Samuel 21:9

David was in trouble, but instead of relying upon the Lord and His promises, and taking the "sword of the Spirit," he chose instead the unwieldy, literal weapon of the dead Goliath. He thus thought to meet King Saul in his own strength. We have here a defeated man of God with a lie in his mouth, instead of a testimony (I Sam. 21:2); and with fear in his heart, instead of faith (I Sam. 21:10)! This whole scene is the more remarkable because this is the same David who a short time before came up against the worst the world had to offer in the person of the giant Goliath, and with great assurance and spiritual discernment exclaimed: ". . . know that *the Lord saveth not with sword and spear: for the battle is the Lord's*" (I Sam. 17:47).

There are many lessons here. How often we too fight the "world" with great unction, power, and spiritual victory, only to become carnal, fleshly, and defeated when we find ourselves in difficulty with those of the Lord's own household! Like David we are tempted to twist the truth, obtain sacred favors (like the shewbread) under the pious guise of the haste required by the "king's business" (I Sam. 21:8), and in other innumerable ways destroy the sweetness of our fellowship. When a child of God becomes backslidden, fear enters the heart and is quickly followed by confusion and desperation. Like David our testimony may then become so blemished that the worldly "Achishes" laugh at our folly and madness (I Sam. 21:14).

Even the best Christian is weak and must constantly seek his strength from the Lord. May those of us who are now in sweet fellowship take heed lest we fall!   — H.G.B.

> I know not what may be the way
>   That I must take,
> But I can humbly trust and pray
>   That I may never from Him stray
> Nor Him forsake.
>   —Anon.

"Fear God . . . and your enemies will fear you!"

NEVER! NEVER! NEVER! NEVER!

READ DEUTERONOMY 31:1-8

. . . he will not fail thee.	Deuteronomy 31:6
. . . they shall never perish.	John 10:28
. . . I am with you . . . unto the end.	Matthew 28:20

Once the work of God's grace is begun in the heart, it must continue forever. A book might be filled with quotations like the three above assuring us that he that "hath begun a good work in you will perform it until the day of Jesus Christ" (Phil. 1:6).

Years ago a preacher addressed a great congregation on the security of the believer against the tempter of our souls. In a style vividly dramatic he pictured the Spirit of Evil traversing the earth to tempt the members of Christ's flock. To place after place he went seeking rest and finding none. Christian after Christian overcame his tempting suggestions by the power of faith and the energy of Scripture. At nightfall he entered the chamber of a dying saint. The shadow of death was on his face, the awful moment of the soul's transit had nearly come, attendants were waiting in the intensity of silence, for they thought that it was almost over. "I will cast a dart of doubt concerning Jesus into that saint's mind," said the Evil One, "and fill his last moments with fear." But just then the saint's lips parted and the words came forth, "Though I walk through the valley of the shadow of death, I will fear no evil: for thou art with me; thy rod and thy staff they comfort me. Thou preparest a table before me *in the presence of mine enemies:* thou anointest my head with oil; my cup runneth over. Surely goodness and mercy shall follow me all the days of my life: and I will dwell in the house of the Lord for ever." In a moment his spirit was glorified and Satan was foiled.

He has promised, "I will *never* leave thee." — M.R.D.

Look ye saints within the veil,
And raise your happy song,
Your joys can never, never fail,
For you to Christ belong!

—Anon.

"Adopted children can never be disowned — this is both a human and a divine law!" — H.G.B.

TWO BIRDS

READ LEVITICUS 14:1-7

> *. . . take for him that is to be cleansed two birds . . . and cedar wood, and scarlet, and hyssop: . . . one of the birds (shall) be killed (and) . . . the living bird (shall be let) loose into the open field.*   Leviticus 14:4, 5, 7

The law of Moses was full of highly symbolic types of Christ. The Scripture in Leviticus 14 has to do with the cleansing of leprosy, and is typical of the twofold aspect of man's deliverance from the scourge of sin. First a bird was killed in an earthen vessel over running water; then a cedar stick was bound to a bunch of hyssop by a scarlet ribbon, and a living bird attached to it. This second bird was then dipped into the water and the blood. While its tail was immersed, its wings were kept dry so that it might be ready for instant flight when released at the end of the ceremony. These two birds typified the one Christ in two states of His blessed work; namely, His death (Heb. 9:14), and His victorious resurrection and ascension (Rom. 6:6-11; II Cor. 5:21). Man needed both atonement and imputed righteousness. The first bird spoke of our canceled debt, the second of divine credit put to our account. We have not only been crucified and buried with Christ (Gal. 2:20), but we have also ascended to the heavenlies in Him (Eph. 2:6). What a glorious fellowship this affords! Having been pardoned from our sin, we have been incorporated into the mystical Body of our Lord and made partakers of the divine nature. We bask now in the fullness of God's love — the same love which the Father lavishes upon His only begotten Son. So organic is this union that all that touches us in grief, trial, and persecution, is also felt by Him. On the other hand, all the divine glory, blessing, and honor which belongs to Christ shall also be shared by us in the consummation.

Have you ever completely appreciated the fullness of His redemption? Thank God today that we have not only put off sin, but we have also put on Christ and eternal life with all its blessings and benefits.   — H.G.B.

> Saved to the uttermost; this I can say,
>   Once all was darkness, but now it is day;
> Beautiful visions of glory I see,
>   Jesus in fullness revealed unto me.
>   —W. J. Kirkpatrick

"Salvation is not only sin put out, but eternal life put in."

THE IMMIGRANT

READ GENESIS 12:1-9

*By faith Abraham . . . went out . . . For he looked for
a city which hath foundations, whose builder and maker
is God.* Hebrews 11:8, 10

Abram and Sarah were emigrants who left their native homeland to find a new home in a strange unknown land. They had
never seen it, but had heard about it.

There must be something appealing and romantic about immi-
gration. Man has ever been eager to pioneer in new fields, to explore the unknown "beyond." The urge to emigrate springs from
dissatisfaction with present conditions and a desire to find a
better place to live. By such folks this country was settled — by
people leaving their homeland to seek liberty and plenty as well
as adventure. Emigrants are people who are not satisfied just to
"get by," but feel the urge for better things.

This is the picture of the believer. He is an emigrant, born in
the world of sin, defeat, death, and want. But he has heard the
call from the land of promise to come out of the land lying under
the sentence of doom. He is an emigrant from the land of death
and darkness into the land of life and light. Henceforth we are
strangers and pilgrims here below (Heb. 11:13; I Pet. 2:11). We
are spiritual emigrants. The farther we go on the journey and
the older we become, the more we realize we are completely out
of step with this world. We realize we don't fit down here. Its
pleasures sicken us, its music disgusts us. Its empty conversation
bores us. But how sweet and refreshing the fellowship of the
few other emigrants who are traveling to the same new land of
glory with us. But best of all we have *His* fellowship. David
said, "I am a stranger with thee and a sojourner" (Ps. 39:12).
He does not say, "a stranger *to* thee (thank God) but *with* thee."
Can we wish for better company? Now we are "no more
strangers and foreigners" to the heavenly kingdom (Eph. 2:19).
— M.R.D.

I am a stranger here, within a foreign land;
  My home is far away, upon a golden strand;
Ambassador to be of realms beyond the sea —
  I'm here on business for my King.
—E. T. Cassel

**"The blessings of Christ and the pleasures of the world are at opposite
ends of the keyboard of life." — H. G. B.**

LOVE'S ROYAL WELCOME

READ LUKE 15:11-23

> *. . . But when he (the prodigal son) was yet a great way*
> *off, his father saw him, and had compassion, and ran,*
> *and fell on his neck, and kissed him.* Luke 15:20

There is a story in English history of a child of nobility who was stolen from his home and sold to a chimney-sweep. The frantic parents spared no expense or trouble in their search for their kidnapped child, but all their efforts were in vain. A few years later when the lad grew old enough to do some work, the evil man into whose hands he had fallen decided to use him in his dirty job of cleaning chimneys. One day the child was assigned to work in the very home from which he had been stolen while too young to remember. After sweeping the chimney of one of the bedrooms, he was greatly fatigued. In his exhaustion he forgot where he was, and hungry and tired he flung himself upon the clean bed and immediately dropped off to sleep. The lady of the house happened to enter the room. At first she looked in dismay and anger at the filthy black object which was soiling her beautiful bedspread. Suddenly, however, something in the expression of the pinched and dirty little face, some familiar pose of the weary limbs, drew her nearer for a closer inspection. A moment later with a cry of joy she threw her motherly arms around her long lost boy and pressed him to her heart. The filth and dirt of the street and the chimney meant nothing to her now. In her happiness, the soiled dress and the smudged bedspread were forgotten.

This is but a faint picture of the wondrous love of God for the returning prodigal, for in the story of Luke 15 the father was watching for his wayward son day and night. When he was yet a great way off, he saw him, loved him, ran to meet him, and embraced him while the smell and filth of the pigsty was still upon his ragged clothing. If you are tired of sin, remember the Heavenly Father is waiting to see your tears of repentance. Unlovely as you are, He will throw His arms of forgiveness about you, and give you a royal welcome! — H.G.B.

> I knew He'd receive me, so humbly I came
> A poor guilty sinner, His mercy to claim;
> And now I'm rejoicing through faith in His name,
> He never will turn me away.
>
> —E. E. Hewitt

"True repentance, like a magnet, always draws forth the pardoning grace, and paternal love of God."

FRAUDULENT ADVERTISING

READ PROVERBS 17:18-28

The wise man's eyes are in his head. Ecclesiastes 2:14
. . . the eyes of a fool are in the ends of the earth.
Proverbs 17:24

We have all heard the proverb, "A jack of all trades and master of none." A man who knows a little about everything is likely to know nothing about anything. "A little knowledge is a dangerous thing." It is better to concentrate on one thing and learn to do it well than to be a scatterbrain who bungles everything. Paul says in Philippians 3:13, "This one thing I do." This applies to preachers especially. His commission is "preach the Word," and don't become "entangled with the affairs of this life." What is true of preachers is true of preaching. A sermon which rambles over everything, hits nothing. A sermon without a point is like a blank cartridge without a bullet. Every time you shoot the gospel gun you should plan on hitting somebody.

How many times we have heard a preacher announce a text, and then immediately depart from it on an excursion over land and sea, and never come back to the text again. When the sermon is over we feel like saying what Mandy said to Sam after he had ridden the merry-go-round at the circus for one solid hour: "Sam, you've been gone an hour and spent a whole dollar, but you ain't been nowhere!"

My father used to tell of a deacon who slipped a note on the preacher's pulpit saying: "Stick to your text — and some of it will stick to us." *To advertise a text and then ignore it is fraudulent advertising!* So lest I be guilty of this same thing, I too must return to my text. "The wise man's eyes are in his head . . . The eyes of a fool are in the ends of the earth." The wise man's eyes are in one place — he has a purpose — a plan — an aim. He drives home the point. The fool's eyes are everywhere — rambling to the ends of the earth — without purpose, sense, or aim. Have your eyes on *one thing — one goal.* Stick to your text and it will stick fast in your listeners. — M.R.D.

> By the preacher perplexed,
>   How shall we determine?
> "Watch and pray" was the text;
>   "Go to sleep," said the sermon!
> —Anon.

"Remember truth is still truth even if it makes you mad!" — M. R. D.

TWO RIVERS CONVERGE

READ II CORINTHIANS 6:11-18

Can two walk together, except they be agreed?

Amos 3:3

The famous Brule River (boundary line between Northern Michigan and Wisconsin), scene of presidential trout fishing parties, flows for miles with clear, sparkling water, inhabited by an abundant population of speckled, rainbow, and brown trout. The water is clear and pure. Some miles before it joins the Menominee River, another stream enters its current. It is the Iron River, muddy and thick with sediment of ore and clay. Its water is brown and loaded with the washings of iron ore. Where it joins the famous Brule, the two streams flow separately for some distance, the waters of the Brule flowing clear in the right half of the river bed, while the muddy waters of the Iron flow in the left half of the bed. But this is only for a short distance. Deflected by rocks, logs, and bottom irregularities, the two currents begin to merge, and soon the waters are mixed into one stream. But now notice! The clear waters of the Brule did not cleanse the waters of the Iron, but vice versa. The muddy waters of the Iron polluted the whole stream. We never fish below the confluence of the two rivers.

Evil associations, too, cannot fail to corrupt those who indulge in them. To make alliances with evil or unconverted persons, either in business, social life, or marriage, and expect to reform them is as hopeless as keeping the waters of the Brule and Iron separate in the same channel. O Christian, shun the unequal yoke. Retain your separate position in every sphere of life, and especially in marriage. No Christian ever has a right to consider marriage with an unbeliever. How can "two walk together, except they be agreed?"

Keep thyself pure by avoiding integration with the impure.

— M.R.D.

Shun evil companions, bad language disdain,
  God's name hold in reverence, nor take it in vain;
Be thoughtful and earnest, kindhearted and true,
  Look ever to Jesus, He'll carry you through.

—H. R. Palmer

"An author is known by his writings, a mother by her daughters, a fool by his words, and all men by their companions."

FULL OBEDIENCE

READ ACTS 7:1-4

Now the Lord had said unto Abram, Get thee out of thy country, and from thy kindred, and from thy father's house. Genesis 12:1

Abram had received a call from God to leave his pagan country and seek Canaan, the homeland of promise. A careful reading of the seventh chapter of Acts, however, reveals that Abram allowed natural affection and ties of the flesh to hold him back from doing the will of the Lord completely. He just couldn't bring himself to the necessary separation from his father and his kinfolk. While he started out from Ur of the Chaldees, he bogged down in Haran and apparently dwelt there for some time. His old father Terah could go no further, and Abram couldn't bear the thought of parting with him; Abram fell short of God's perfect will for his life by failing to yield total obedience. God therefore had to remove Terah by the hand of death, for he was holding back Abram's spiritual progress.

How often we too are prone to forget that God demands total obedience and separation from the things of this world. Nothing must be allowed to retard our progress in sanctification. Often we tend to take lower ground and camp there for awhile rather than to press on immediately to the Canaan of complete surrender.

"Will you tell me in a word," said a Christian woman to a teacher, "what is your idea of consecration?" Pulling out a blank sheet of paper, the teacher replied, "It is to sign your name at the bottom of this blank sheet, let God fill it in as He wills, and then follow His orders."

Are you letting circumstances or loved ones stand in the way of your complete surrender to God's will? If you ever wish to reach the Canaan of victory, you will have to render full obedience! — H.G.B.

> Master, speak! and make me ready,
> When Thy voice is truly heard,
> With obedience glad and steady,
> Still to follow every word!
> —F. Havergal

"True obedience neither procrastinates nor questions." — QUARLES

YOUR MOTOR IS MISSING

READ I CORINTHIANS 12:12-27

The Lord gave the word: great was the company of those that published it. Psalm 68:11

Some years ago while riding happily in my car on a sparsely traveled road, it suddenly slowed down, sputtered a moment, and with a final gasp, gave up the ghost — *dead.* There I was, miles away from a garage with only a screwdriver and a pair of pliers. And what I know about the mechanics of a car you can put in your eye. I remembered seeing others lift the hood of the car, so that seemed the proper thing to do. I had heard people say that the motor was *missing.* So I looked to see if the motor was still there — it was! Everything looked in order but — no life. Then a friend came along. He jiggled the carburetor and said, "Plenty of gas." He placed the screwdriver across a wire and said, "Aha — no juice," and soon he came upon the culprit which caused all the trouble — a loose connection. One little bolt or screw or whatever it was had come loose and even the motor was dead. A twist with the pliers and zingo — off I went.

Now herein lies a great lesson. All the hundreds of parts in an auto have their place of importance. To stop the car you need not have a "missing motor," or take out the battery, or smash the radiator, or let all the air out of the tires. One tiny short circuit is enough.

We are members of the Body of Christ. Some are prominent members in the public eye, others are obscure, but all are important. (Did you read the Scripture — I Cor. 12:12-27?) Failure to do your part may hinder the whole body from its proper functioning. Your failure to pray will result in loss of power. Your failure to witness may cause some soul to be lost. Your failure to support the Gospel may cause the curtailment of the work of evangelism or missions. Your *little,* if neglected, may be the last straw in precipitating *much* harm.

Today, *do your part* — it is not the prominence of your part — but faithfulness which counts. — M.R.D.

Give me a faithful heart, likeness to Thee,
That each departing day henceforth may see
Some work of love begun, some deed of kindness done,
Some wand'rer sought and won, something for Thee!
—S. D. Phelps

"There is always something wrong with a man, as there is with a motor, when he knocks continually."

LIBERTY: POLITICAL AND SPIRITUAL

READ HEBREWS 10:1-17

> . . . *proclaim liberty throughout all the land unto all the*
> *inhabitants thereof* . . . .   Leviticus 25:10

It was in 1776 that the now famous Liberty Bell was rung for the first time. Fifty years later, July 4, 1826, it ushered in what was known as the "Jubilee Anniversary" of the American Republic. The bell, now cracked, no longer tolls, but it is still symbolic of our national and political freedom.

Our forefathers who founded this country were well acquainted with the Bible and therefore it is not surprising that they associated *liberty* and a *bell* with the blessings of our freedom. You may recall that in the Old Testament on the Day of Atonement the High Priest was required to go alone into the Holy of Holies to sprinkle the blood for the sins of the people. When he entered the Tabernacle he had on a beautiful robe on the bottom of which were woven pomegranates of blue, purple, and scarlet. Between these symbols of great fruitfulness there was attached a corresponding series of *tiny golden bells* (Ex. 28:33, 34)! As the priest walked into the holy place, the congregation could hear the bells tinkling. Just before he presented the blood, however, he had to remove this garment and could not put it on again until the atonement had been made and approved by God. The people, waiting outside in breathless silence, sent up a great shout when the bells rang once more; for they knew then that their sins had been forgiven and spiritual freedom had been obtained.

Christ, our great High Priest, also laid aside His garments of glory and made atonement for us. Then He went back to Heaven to present His blood. The coming of the Holy Spirit was evidence that His work had been accepted, but Christ Himself has not yet visibly returned. When He does, the "golden bells" will ring; and all creation will rejoice in the glorious "liberty of the sons of God" in a happy jubilee. *Has the Son made you free* (John 8:36)?
                                                        — H.G.B.

> That land is great which knows the Lord,
> Where freedom's guided by His Word.
>   —Anon.

"Freedom from sin is the greatest of all liberties!"

ARE YOU AFRAID? WHY?

READ PSALM 63

*What time I am afraid, I will trust in thee. In God have
I put my trust: I will not be afraid.*   Psalm 56:3, 11

The fifty-sixth Psalm is a hymn of progress, development, and growing in grace. It begins with a sore complaint. David says, "Be merciful unto me, O God: for man would swallow me up; he fighting daily oppresseth me. Mine enemies would daily swallow me up: for they be many that fight against me, O thou most High" (Ps. 56:1, 2).

David was afraid because he had his eyes on the enemy — and not on God. Finally he sees his need and cries out, "*What time I am afraid, I will trust in thee*" (verse 3). Now that is wonderful, but there is something much better. Why wait until you are afraid before you trust in Him? But David was not alone in this. We are often so much like him. When all goes well, and we have no great trials, we too often forget God, and only after the trouble comes, and we cannot see our way out, we flee to Him. And how gracious of Him to hear us then. But there is a better way. David began to realize this and so he arrives at a more excellent experience and says in verse 11, "In God have I put my trust; I will not be afraid."

This is quite different from trusting in God *because* you are afraid. Why wait until you are afraid? Trust the promises of God and be not afraid. Believe that nothing comes without God's permission and that "all things work together for good" and don't be afraid. In what class do you belong? Do you trust in God because you are afraid — or do you trust Him first and then say, "I will not be afraid"? When David could say that, then the Psalm which began on such a sad note could end with a shout of confidence: "For thou hast delivered my soul from death . . . my feet from falling, that I may walk before God in the land of the living."   — M.R.D.

In God I put my trust,
    I neither doubt nor fear,
For man can never harm
    With God my Helper near.
                                        —Anon.

"Why worry when you can trust?"

"LIVING WATER"

READ JOHN 7:28-39

. . . the water that I shall give him shall be in him a
well of water springing up into everlasting life.
John 4:14

As people travel about the world, they are impressed by the millions of acres of waste territory. Many nations constantly wrestle with starvation because their lands are arid and thirsty. Irrigation would cause these sections to be fruitful, but without water much of the land is reduced to unproductive desert. Spiritual life also requires water. Without it the garden of man's soul is a lifeless wasteland. Jesus alone provides the spiritual water from the fountain of eternal life that can quench the soul's thirst and give it lasting satisfaction.

A famous surgeon was seldom seen on the streets without a beautiful rose in his lapel. His friends wondered why these buds stayed fresh for so long a time. When they asked him his secret, he turned back the flap of his coat and revealed a little bottle of water into which the stem of the flower had been inserted to keep it from wilting. And so it is with Christians. If their lives draw from the great resources of the Lord Jesus Christ, who is in them the Water of Life, they will grow more fragrant and beautiful as the days and years go by.

A little girl who had been well instructed in Sunday school lived near a refreshing spring. The father, an unbeliever, noticed that his daughter often stayed longer than seemed necessary when she was sent to get water. One day he secretly followed her and observed that when she came to the spring she first read her Bible and knelt to pray before she filled her pitcher. He waited until she arose, and then said, "Well, was the water sweet?" "Yes, Father," she said with a shining face, "and if you would only taste one drop of what I have been enjoying, you would never partake of the things of this world again." She knew from experience that Christ's "living water" could make the desert of a sinful life blossom as the rose!   — H.G.B.

> I came to Jesus, and I drank
> Of His life giving stream;
> My thirst was quenched, my soul revived,
> And now I live in Him!
> —H. Bonar

"There is nothing that can satisfy the thirst of the soul except water from the well of divine grace." — G. W.

JUST A MINUTE TOO LATE

READ MATTHEW 25:1-13

And while they went to buy, the bridegroom came.
Matthew 25:10

Ten virgins knew the bridegroom was coming. Five of them were prepared, while the five foolish virgins were not ready; they had not expected him so soon. Great was their loss when the bridegroom suddenly came and left them outside. They had good intentions, but failed to act in time. They had no excuse. So many an opportunity is lost by not being ready.

It was the first week in June and I knew my bees would swarm on one of those warm days. I did not have a hive box ready for this eventuality. I sincerely intended to take a half-hour some day and nail together some brood frames with foundation, as the new home for the coming swarm. "I'll do it this evening," I said to myself. When I returned from the office I saw the swarm had emerged and was hanging on a branch in the apple tree. Frantically I ran to the barn to quickly assemble the parts of the new hive: nailing ten frames together and inserting the sheets of wax foundation. Just as I finished and was putting the cover on, I heard a telltale roar and saw the swarm disintegrating and flying away to parts unknown. Before I could place the hive, get a step-ladder to cut down the branch on which they had clustered, *they were gone — forever.* Frustrated I stood and murmured, "There goes fifty pounds of honey." It was too late! Immediately the Scripture came to mind, "And while they went to buy, the bridegroom came."

Jesus Christ is coming again — it may be at any moment. What remorse there will be for those who were warned again and again but stopped short of preparing themselves. I waited just a little too long, and lost my bees. That is trivial; but think of the loss for those who procrastinate and wait to prepare to meet God — *until — just a moment too late!* "Be ye ready" therefore!   — M.R.D.

> "A little while" to keep the oil from failing,
> "A little while" faith's flickering lamp to trim;
> And then the Bridegroom's coming footsteps hailing,
> We'll haste to meet Him with the bridal hymn.
> —Mrs. Jane Crewdson

"The constant expectancy of the Lord's return fosters a spirit of preparedness which is a most potent aid to sanctification."

HOLD YOUR TEMPER!

READ COLOSSIANS 3:1-10

But now ye also put off . . . anger, wrath . . . .
Colossians 3:8

Someone has said the only way that one can be "angry and sin not" (Eph. 4:26) is to be *angry only at sin!* Usually, however, our indignation is not that holy, but is rather a manifestation of our carnal nature. Very few Christians are so spiritual that they can be "righteously angry" while still maintaining their communion with God. Most of our wrath is associated with temper tantrums and haughty self-defense, which is sinful. Such unholy anger is as an ill-wind which blows out the lamp of the mind and grieves the Spirit of God. Therefore, Paul's pertinent admonition to *"put off . . . wrath!"*

Stephen Merritt one day gave a free dinner at his mission for homeless men. After sharing the good banquet with them, he took up his hat to go, and found that some of the "skid row" characters in a prankish mood had half-filled it with bacon rinds and other scraps from the table. He was furious for a moment, and in a towering rage stepped on a chair to deliver a scorching denunciation of their action. He stormed at the tramps and berated them for their ingratitude. Then suddenly there flashed into his mind the words of Scripture, "*Love* suffereth long, and is kind . . . *is not easily provoked* . . . beareth all things." He lived too near to God to be led astray for long. The Holy Spirit rebuked him within, and contrition filled his heart. He hung his head for a moment and then apologized in all humility, telling the men he knew he had grieved His Lord by becoming angry. To show his goodwill he invited them all back to another dinner the following night. His true humility and spirituality was rewarded — for that time nearly forty men accepted the Saviour.

If you let the love of Christ rule in your heart, you too will not be "easily provoked." — H.G.B.

> Lost your temper, did you say?
> Truth says, state it in this way:
> "When I count the tragic cost,
> WOULD TO GOD IT HAD BEEN LOST!"
> —Anon.

"Men, like steel, are useless when they lose their temper."

DON'T WASTE IT!

READ PROVERBS 12:24-28

The slothful man roasteth not that which he took in hunting.   Proverbs 12:27

The American Indian was a good conservationist. He took only as much game as he needed for food or clothing. He was not interested in trophies or wholesale slaughter. But "civilized" man hunts for the sport of killing or turning game into gold. As a result, our wildlife faced extinction till the government passed conservation laws and set limits and seasons on the kill. And even then it came too late to save the passenger pigeon, the grayling, and other forms of game. The buffalo, the moose, and the elk were barely saved. Buffalo were killed for their tongue only, while the rest of the carcass was left to rot.

We waste more than we use. It is estimated America throws enough food into the garbage can to feed all the starving of the world. We are too indolent, too lazy to prepare our own foods like mother and grandmother did, and instead we are a nation eating out of tin cans, glass jars, and frozen food lockers. Solomon already saw this evil and said in effect, "The slothful man throws away what he has killed."

Last summer, while cleaning a fish at a resort, I found a whole mess of beautiful fish in the waste can. They had been caught the day before and allowed to spoil because someone was too lazy to clean them. *Such waste is sin!* The Bible says, "He also that is slothful in his work is brother to him that is a great waster" (Prov. 18:9). If you have more than you need, give it to someone in need. *Don't waste it!*

Of the lazy man the Bible says, "He coveteth greedily all the day long: but the righteous giveth and spareth not" (Prov. 21:26). Make every moment count for Christ today. Don't waste time!   — M.R.D.

> Only one life, 'twill soon be past,
> Only what's done for Christ will last.
>   —Anon.

"Extravagance may be excusable, but waste, NEVER!" — E. R. C.

AFTER THE PRAYER — THE POWER!

READ ACTS 4:23-31

*And when they had prayed, the place was shaken . . .
and they were all filled with the Holy Ghost, and they
spake the word of God with boldness.*   Acts 4:31

In a magazine some months ago there appeared an account concerning the installation of a new organ in a New York City church. It was a rare and costly instrument. Its throat of many pipes was capable of pouring forth glorious melody in a multitude of different shades and tones. However, the first Sunday it was used, very early in the service, the electric current that was required to operate the console was cut off. The organist was helpless to do anything about it, and the great, majestic organ fell silent. A call for help was made and soon an electrician appeared on the scene to see if he could locate the short circuit. He made a quick investigation and saw that the difficulty could soon be remedied. A note was hurriedly scribbled and passed to the organist. It said, *"After the prayer, the power will be on!"* Of course, the electrician did not realize the hidden, spiritual truth expressed by his simple words, but the organist immediately recognized that he had written more wisely than he knew. Indeed, *"after the prayer — the power!"* A prayerless person is a powerless one. A church that works without prayer may have much activity, but it will exhibit little spirituality; there may be much program, but there will be little, if any, power.

Dr. A. C. Dixon of Spurgeon's Tabernacle once wrote, "When we rely on organization, we get what organization can do; when we rely on education, we get what education can do; when we rely on eloquence, we get what eloquence can do; and so on. I am not disposed to undervalue any of these things in their proper place—BUT *when we rely upon prayer, we get what God can do!"*

Apostasy and lack of power begins when the inner closet of prayer is neglected or forsaken!   —H.G.B.

Wrestling prayer can wonders do,
Bring relief in deepest straits;
Prayer can force a passage through
Iron bars and brazen gates.
—Anon.

"Prayer moves the Hand that moves the universe." — GURNALL

LIVING STONES

READ I PETER 2:1-8

To whom coming, as unto a living stone.   I Peter 2:4

A living stone is a paradox, a natural impossibility. Stones are mineral, and not organic, and we even have the expression, "as dead as a stone." Yet the Lord Jesus is called a living stone and we also are called living stones (I Pet. 2:5). Dead and yet alive! Life and death united in one. Christ indeed died on the cross, yet He lives forevermore. He is the living Cornerstone. Believers by their union with Him too are both dead and alive. The believer is dead to sin and alive to righteousness — dead to self and alive to Christ — dead to the law and alive to God! All this is because of our union with Him who said: "I am he that liveth, and was dead; and, behold, I am alive for evermore, Amen" (Rev. 1:18).

The Lord Jesus, the living Stone, is the eternal Rock on which the Christian builds and underneath which the sinner will be crushed. This Rock appears in the Scriptures in various ways.

1. He is the Rock foundation on which our saving faith is built (I Cor. 3:11).

2. He is the Rock on which the Church is founded (Matt. 16:18).

3. He is the smitten Rock of Calvary typified by the rock in the wilderness (Ex. 17:6; I Cor. 10:4).

4. He is the Stone of stumbling to the nation of Israel (Rom. 9:32, 33).

5. He is the "Stone" cut without hands from the mountain to demolish Gentile domination (Dan. 2:34).

6. He is the crushing Stone under which the sinner will perish forever (Matt. 21:44).

7. He is the growing Stone which shall ultimately fill the entire earth when "Christ shall have dominion over land and sea and earth's remotest regions shall His empire be" (see Dan. 2:35).

— M.R.D.

> O near to the Rock let me keep,
> If blessings or sorrows prevail;
> Or climbing the mountain way steep,
> Or walking the shadowy vale.
> O then to the Rock let me fly,
> To the Rock that is higher than I.
> —E. Johnson

"In a world full of change and decay, the living Stone (Christ) and the living Word (the Bible) are the only pillars of stability on which one can build for eternity!" — G. W.

LED BY A WOUNDED HAND

READ PSALM 22:11-16, 23-26

> *. . . he calleth his own sheep by name, and leadeth them out.* John 10:3

How precious it is that God thinks of each one of us *by name!* How assuring to know that the Good Shepherd Himself will ever lead us with His nail-scarred hand through the green pastures of spiritual blessing, up the blood-sprinkled way, until we reach the fold of God in the heights of Paradise.

Recently there came to my desk the excellent little booklet, "Hills of God," by Ruth Gibbs Zwall. With her permission we quote her beautiful *Parable of Tomorrow,* which poetically describes this precious leading:

"I looked at the mountain. 'It is too hard, Lord,' I said, 'I cannot climb.' 'Take My hand,' He whispered, 'I will be your strength.' I saw the road. 'It is too long, Lord,' I said: 'So rough and long.' 'Take my love,' He answered, 'I will guard your feet.' I looked at the sky. 'The sun is gone,' I said, 'Already it grows dark.' 'Take the lantern of My Word,' He whispered, 'That will be light enough.' We climbed. The road was narrow and steep, but the way was bright. And when the thorns reached out, *they found His hand before they touched my own.* And when my path grew rough, I knew it was His love that kept my feet from stumbling. Then I grew very tired. 'I can go no farther, Lord,' I said. He answered, 'Night is gone. Look up, my child.' I looked, and it was dawn. Green valleys stretched below. 'I can go on alone now,' I said . . . and then I saw the marks: 'Lord, Thou art wounded. Thy hands are bleeding, Thy feet bruised. Was it for me?' He whispered, 'I did it gladly.' Then I fell at His feet. 'Lord, lead me on,' I cried, 'No road too long, no valley too deep, if Thou art with me.' We walk together now, and shall forever!"   — H.G.B.

> But none of the ransomed ever knew
>   How deep were the waters crossed;
> Nor how dark was the night that the Lord passed through
>   Ere He found His sheep that was lost.
> "Lord, whence are these blood-drops all the way,
>   That mark out the mountain's track?"
> "They were shed for one who had gone astray
>   Ere the shepherd could bring him back."
>   —E. C. Clephane

"No man can follow Christ and go astray." — A. L. FAUNCE

THE HAMMER OF THE WORD

READ HEBREWS 4:12, 13

Is not my word . . . like a hammer that breaketh the rock in pieces?
Jeremiah 23:29

The prophet had evidently been visiting a quarry where the stone cutters were at work cleaving the rocks into their proper shape to be fitted into the building. He observed how the workman placed his heavy chisel on the rock, and then brought down the heavy hammer again and again upon it. The rock did not cleave at the first blow. One blow, two blows, three, a dozen and no (seeming) result. And then some more blows, twenty, thirty, forty, and then, at the forty-fifth blow, the rock yields and falls apart as though it had never been united. It was the forty-fifth blow that did it. Or was it? Ah no, it took forty-four other blows as well. It was the cumulative effect of each successive blow which caused the particles within to shift for the final cleavage. There could be no forty-fifth blow without the first blow and all the rest. There was no visible result till the last blow fell, but each blow caused some change. Had the workman become discouraged at the forty-fourth blow, the job would have failed, as if not a single blow had fallen.

Have you been praying for and dealing with a loved one, trying to win him to Christ? Have you given him Scripture after Scripture and prayed and prayed? Are you now tempted to give up, saying, "What's the use?" Remember, every blow does something, for His Word "shall not return void." Don't give up! Your prayers for that son or daughter, that unsaved wife of yours, will be answered if you just patiently apply the hammer of the Word. If you stop now, your past blows are ineffective and wasted. The next blow — it may be the forty-fifth — and the rock may split! Patience brother — patience sister — keep witnessing!
— M.R.D.

With hammer blows the Lord convicts
The sinner of his need;
The flinty heart must yield at last,
God's Word shall e'er succeed.
—G. W.

"Be assured that God's Word is certain and powerful and cannot fail, even though you cannot always see its secret workings."

ENJOYING THE SERMON

READ PSALM 85:6-13

I will hear what God the Lord will speak . . . .
Psalm 85:8

I have just recently learned how to enjoy even the poorest sermon, as long as it is delivered by one of God's servants. Having received quite a lot of training in speech, literature, and logic, I have frankly often been disturbed by some preachers. Though well-meaning, they seemed to lack certain qualifications, and often delivered sermons which indicated that they had spent little time in proper study and preparation. Then, by the grace of God, I chanced to run across a little item (the authorship of which I have not been able to ascertain) which has been of significant help to me in receiving a blessing from even the most "un-nourishing sermon." Seriously considered, I believe it will also revolutionize your listening habits. The article started out very pointedly by saying:

"At one time in every sermon God breaks through the words of the preacher and speaks directly to the people! It may be in a single phrase or in just one sentence. We can well afford to listen to the entire discourse with care, lest we miss that one illuminated and searching sentence in which God speaks to us — a sentence that brings conviction, penitence, hope, strength or renewed faith! So many of us miss that one word of God because we are comparing the preacher's manner with that of some other preacher we have recently heard. From now on *just listen intently for that one portion which God means should be especially applied to* YOUR *heart!"*

As you enter your place of worship this week, make the earnest cry of the psalmist your prayer: *"I will hear what God the Lord will speak"!*
— H.G.B.

> Open my ears, that I may hear
> Voices of truth Thou sendest clear;
> Echoed in love Thy words shall out-ring,
> Sweet as a note that angels sing.
> —C. H. Scott

"A poor listener seldom hears a good sermon."

BLESSED ARE THE DEAD!

READ II CORINTHIANS 9:6-15

> *. . . He which soweth sparingly shall reap also sparingly; and he which soweth bountifully shall reap also bountifully.*
> II Corinthians 9:6

The Apostle Paul informs us that Jesus once said, "It is more blessed to give than to receive" (Acts 20:35). He is speaking of material possessions, and Paul compares it to sowing in anticipation of a harvest. I wonder if we have looked upon "giving" as a matter of sowing in the hope of reaping. When we "give" to some needy cause, we do not expect a return, for we consider it a "gift." But not so with the Lord, for there is a blessing promised to those who cheerfully give to the need of others. Let me ask a pertinent question. Do you get as much joy out of giving as you do out of receiving?

Too often we forget that it is a blessing to be able to give, and are not on the other side with those who would like to give but who are unable. If we were as eager to do things for others as we are to receive favors we would better understand the words of Jesus, "It is more blessed to give than to receive."

A spring of water continually gives while a pool continually receives. That is why the spring is always fresh, while the pool becomes stagnant and filled with refuse. What a privilege to be able to give!

If we knew the blessing of giving, there would be no need for drives and schemes, rummage sales, entertainments, and circuses to support church work. The poor preacher would not need to plead and urge and beg to keep things going. A giving church cannot die, but when a people stop giving — the church dies — spiritually as well as materially.

After a minister had earnestly pleaded for the cause of missions, a penurious old deacon complained, "All this giving will kill the church." The pastor replied, "Take me to one church which died from 'giving' and I will leap upon its grave and shout to high heaven, 'Blessed are the dead which die in the Lord' "! (Rev. 14:13). — M.R.D.

> The luxury of doing good
> Surpasses all employment;
> Remember well the Saviour's word —
> Make giving your enjoyment!
> —G. W.

"What we retain we may lose, but what we give to Christ we are sure to keep." — T. L. CUYLER

"LICKIN'S AND LOVE"

READ PROVERBS 29:10-17

He that spareth his rod hateth his son: but he that loveth him chasteneth him betimes. Proverbs 13:24

All of us are probably familiar with the rather humorous story of the boy who had received a good thrashing from his father. When he protested, the father said, "Son, I only do this because I love you." The boy muttered, "I'll be glad, Dad, when I'm old enough to *return your love!*" Perhaps there was some reason for the boy's resentment, for parents do not always punish their children correctly. Admittedly, the Scriptural admonition, "Be ye angry, and sin not," is not always heeded in administering corporal punishment in the home. One thing, however, is certain: *children need a well-balanced diet of "lickin's and love" to develop into well-adjusted adults.* Love, to the exclusion of punishment, will spoil the child and cause him to lose respect for his parents. Over-pampered children become self-centered and unhappy. The result is an adult that is a social misfit. On the other hand, too much application of the rod results in frustrated, ugly youngsters. Such children grow up to be rebellious, nonconformists — always seeking to compensate in their adult life for the time spent in the "straight jacket of laws and restrictions" which was laced too tightly. God's Word prescribes the healthy formula: *love tempered by the rod* — discipline guided by kindness! The child's self-expression must not be stifled, but it must be directed. It must be bounded by moral principles, undergirded with spiritual understanding and perspectives, and directed toward proper goals of attainment.

I would like to see an artist draw a picture of a good parent. It should, I believe, include a friendly, *kneeling* figure with outstretched *arms of love extended toward a child.* In one hand would be an open *Bible,* and nearby the other — *a convenient rod* to be used in thoughtful discipline when the occasion demanded. Such parents, with the help of God, can raise lovely, well-behaved children — groomed for God's glory by "lickin's and love."

— H.G.B.

Ere a child has reached to seven
Teach him all the way to Heaven;
Better still the work will thrive
If he learns before he's five.
—C. H. Spurgeon

"Juvenile delinquency is the result of parents trying to raise their children without starting at the bottom."

RAIN ON THE GRASS

READ PSALM 72:1-15

He shall come down like rain upon the mown grass . . . .
Psalm 72:6

What a seeming misfortune to have it rain upon the mown hay! Ask the farmer whether he wants sunshine or rain upon the hay field which he has just cut, and he will answer, "Sunshine, of course." But this is not the meaning of the text, for the last phrase explains it, "As showers that water the earth." The meaning is clear. The expression, the "mown grass," does not refer to that part which was cut down and already brought into the barn, but to the grass stubble left behind, the bruised and bleeding stump left in the earth. The rain upon this field gives new strength and healing to begin all over again for another crop. It is not going to die but bring forth another, even more tender harvest. Farmers tell us that second cuttings of hay are the best, the most tender and sweet, and contain the most nourishment.

Are you grieving today because of God's pruning of your life? Have you been disappointed with the chastening of the Lord? Have you been deprived of things which you much desired? Has some precious thing been suddenly cut down and taken away? Then He promises to come as "fresh" rain upon your bleeding, bruised heart, and out of it will come a second harvest more tender, more sweet than all that went before. When the gentle showers of His grace and comfort fall upon your heart from His Word, it will mean fresh blessings. Do you have a lawn? How do you keep it lovely and green? The more you cut it and roll it, the more beautiful it becomes. To neglect the cutting will soon result in a wilderness. But after the cutting, God sends the showers. Without the cutting, the grass will only "go to seed," dry up, and die. The most mature and mellow Christians are those who have seen much sorrow, for they have been watered by His grace.　　　　　　　　　　　　　　　　　　　— M.R.D.

Sunshine and rain, refreshing, reviving rain,
Light of faith and love, showers from above!
Sunshine and rain to nourish the growing grain,
Send us, Lord, the sunshine and the rain!
—C. H. Gabriel

"On the clouds of our difficulty, God paints the rainbow of His promise!" — H. G. B.

CHOCOLATE CAKE

READ I CORINTHIANS 4:8-18

. . . all things work together for good . . . . Romans 8:28

It was my privilege for several years to work with Rev. Wendell P. Loveless when we were both at the Moody Bible Institute station, WMBI, Chicago. I recall how he used to tell about the delicious cake which Mrs. Loveless often baked for him. He said, "My wife can make the best chocolate cake of anyone I know. I thought one day that I would go into the kitchen to see what wonderful ingredients she put into the batter. First she sifted out some flour — this did not appeal to me at all, for it was dry and unappetizing. Then she put in some sour milk — I certainly would not have wanted to partake of that by itself, for it would have turned my stomach. Then to make matters worse, she threw into the whole untasty mess of ingredients *a raw egg!* By this time I was not too sure whether I liked chocolate cake or not. I left just as she was popping it into the oven. To my surprise — that evening her 'masterpiece' was as delicious as any I had ever had before! I saw in the whole thing a parable. In this life we often experience many dry stretches (like the flour) which are tasteless and uninviting; we also have sour experiences (like the milk); and even a few raw deals (like the egg), but after we have gone through the furnace of affliction (the oven), praise God — reverently speaking — it will all be *chocolate cake* over there!"

I have never forgotten that illustration, for it was certainly Scriptural. (See our text, and also Rom. 8:18.) Each thing as it comes may seem undesirable and uninviting, but when it is mixed together with the love and providence of God it works for our eternal good. In that assurance may we continue courageously onward with our eyes fixed on Jesus, and with our wills resigned to His precious leading. As Christians we may rest assured that the words of the old catechism are comfortingly true: "God in love averts all evil, or otherwise turns it to our profit!"   — H.G.B.

Thus calmly, Lord, on Thee we rest;
No fears our trust shall move;
Thou knowest what for each is best,
And Thou art perfect Love.
—Anon.

"For the Christian, the grief and gloom of time are refined by the divine alchemy of grace into the golden rewards of eternity."—G. W.

LOOKING FOR BUTTS

Read Psalm 49

But God.   Ephesians 2:4

While waiting for a traffic light to change I watched a poor skid row derelict slowly walking along the curb intently looking in the gutter for butts. I saw him eagerly stoop down and pick up a few cigar and cigarette butts and place them in the pocket of his filthy, torn, and ragged coat. Poor, poor fellow — looking for cast-off butts. If he only knew about the "buts" of Heaven instead of the "butts" in the gutter! The Bible is full of "buts," and each one is a gem. In our Scripture Paul tells us how we too once walked the gutter in search of the "butts" of this world. He says that " . . . in time past ye walked according to the course of this world . . . (and) we all had our conversation . . . in the lusts of our flesh . . . and of the mind; and were by nature the children of wrath, even as others" (Eph. 2:2, 3).

But God! "But God who is rich in mercy, for his great love wherewith he loved us . . . hath quickened us together with Christ" (Eph. 2:4, 5). *But God!* We were lost, *but God!* This is one of the greatest expressions in the Bible! In Romans 5:8 we have another great *But.* "*But God* commendeth his love toward us, in that, while we were yet sinners, Christ died for us."

The Bible is full of *buts.* Notice just a few of them:
The "but" of redemption (Ps. 49:15).
The "but" of sovereignty (Ps. 115:2).
The "but" of stability (Isa. 40:8).
The "but" of power (Luke 11:20).
The "but" of resurrection (Acts 13:30).
The "but" of God's love (Rom. 5:8).
The "but" of freedom (Rom. 6:22).
The "but" of eternal life (Rom. 6:23).
The "but" of mercy (Rom. 9:16).
All these, and many more are there for your blessing. Start looking today for Bible "buts."   — M.R.D.

I cannot, BUT God can; oh, balm for all my care!
The burden that I drop, His hand will lift and bear,
Though eagle pinions tire — I walk where once I ran —
This is my strength to know: I cannot, BUT God can!
—A. J. Flint

"The word 'BUT' is the 'Stop, Look, and Listen' sign of the Bible."

ANXIETY FORBIDDEN

READ MATTHEW 6:25-34

Take therefore no thought for the morrow . . . .
Matthew 6:34

Worry is not only a sin against God; it is a sin against ourselves. Worry is a slow form of suicide, for it poisons the system and shortens life.

Many years ago in the *Chicago Daily News* there appeared an article by the world-renowned physician, Dr. Osler, in which he made some wise observations concerning worry. He pointed out that ocean liners are built in such a fashion that the captain, by pressing a button, can lower steel doors in the hold of the ship to divide it into watertight compartments. Then, even if the hull is pierced in a disaster, only a small portion of the boat can be flooded. In this way the ship can be kept afloat even though it has a gaping hole in its side. "So," said Dr. Osler, "in the voyage of life we should learn how to make doors come down and shut out the yesterdays with all their errors and failures. We should learn also how to lower another door to shut out the unborn tomorrows so that we can live for this day alone. As each of us moves into the next bulkhead we should close the doors that will shut out both the past and the future."

The expression, "Take no thought," in Matthew 6, literally means "do not worry!" Jesus did not mean that we are to completely disregard the things that lie ahead in this life, but He did underscore that fact that we are not to be *overanxious* or *too deeply concerned about tomorrow.* We should not waste our time and energy in *needless worry,* for "sufficient unto the day is the evil thereof"! Jesus assures us that the primary necessities of life will always be provided for those who are in the center of God's will and who put *first things* FIRST!

Remember, anxiety does not empty tomorrow of its troubles, but *it does rob today of its strength!*   — H.G.B.

> Stop that worrying and fretting;
>   Help divine you are forgetting — shift the burden!
> From the Lord your thoughts been straying;
>   Learn to drop the load that's weighing,
> Lift your heart — and do some praying!
>   Shift the burden!
>
> —Anon.

"Worry is both unprofitable and ungodly — it is unbelief parading in disguise!"

PUMPKIN PIES AND SPICES

READ I KINGS 10:1-10

*. . . of spices great abundance . . . neither was there any
such spice as the queen of Sheba gave king Solomon.*
II Chronicles 9:9

Thank the Lord for spices and for condiments – for salt,
pepper, cinnamon, cloves, nutmeg, and paprika. What an unpleasant chore our eating would become if we had no seasonings.
Take pumpkin pie, for instance. It really is not pumpkin pie at
all but "spice pie." It is not the pumpkin which makes the pie
so delicious but the spices which have been added. Pumpkin
alone is flat, insipid, tasteless, disgusting. But disguise the pumpkin with cinnamon, cloves, ginger and salt, and it becomes fit for
a king. You don't taste the pumpkin at all and you can substitute carrots, squash, or yams for pumpkin and with the same
spices they all taste alike.

The Queen of Sheba brought to King Solomon the rarest and
best spices in all the world (II Chronicles 9:9). Solomon is
usually considered a type of Christ and the Queen of Sheba a
picture of the saints of God who came to admire his wisdom and
greatness.

We too must come with the spices of spiritual grace like she
did. Like pumpkin, we by ourselves are flat and useless. To us
must be added the spices of the Word and Spirit, if we are to
attract others to Him.

Does your life exhale the fragrance of Christ? Are you a
stimulating, refreshing, happy believer? I must confess that much
of Christian profession today is utterly flat and insipid. There is
nothing piquant, pungent, or stimulating about it. People shun
it and avoid it. You need to add some spices. Here is the recipe
from God's own "cook book"–"Add to your faith virtue; and to
virtue knowledge; and to knowledge temperance; – patience –
godliness – kindness – charity. For if these things be in you . . .
ye shall neither be barren nor unfruitful in the knowledge of
our Lord Jesus Christ" (II Peter 1:5-8). Good pumpkin pie!

–M.R.D.

Be like Jesus, this my song,
   In the home and in the throng;
Be like Jesus, all day long!
   I would be like Jesus!

–J. Rowe

**"Let your mind and heart dwell on the things of God and your actions
will naturally have the 'smell of Heaven' upon them." — I.H.**

SHINING FOR JESUS

READ EPHESIANS 5:1-8

Let your light . . . shine before men.   Matthew 5:16

It takes more power to generate light than it does sound. An amateur electrician recently rigged up an electric light for his room and found after a little time that it flickered and went out. A friend who examined his generating plant told him that although the light would never come on again, there was still sufficient power to run a call bell. He said "A battery which is not strong enough to make a light often is still sufficiently powerful to make a noise." H. D. Moore in commenting on this says, "That is what is the matter with some of our church members. They are not strong enough spiritually to make a light, but they are strong enough otherwise to make a noise! And the noise they make is so disquieting that they actually disturb the peace of Zion!" Jesus tells us to let our light shine before men. Paul in his letter to the Philippians reminds us that we are to "shine as lights in the world, holding forth the word of life." The *nature* of light itself is always the same, although all lights are not of the same *magnitude*. If we mirror Jesus, the "true Light," then no matter how small a reflector we are, the light which we give will have its good and illuminating effect. We cannot all be Martin Luthers or John Wesleys, but we can let our light shine in the home, in the store, in the factory, in the mines, and everywhere that we meet the multitudes in this world of darkness.

I recently heard of a dear Christian lady who did not "preach much" to her unconverted husband, but she lived such a sanctified life, witnessing to all who came to her door, that finally in tears he came to her asking to be led to the Lord Jesus. He said, "I thought I was happy and successful, until I saw the joy, and peace, and light that you have. Now I know I am miserable and lost and blind. I want to know Jesus too."

How well are you reflecting Christ in your everyday walk?

—H.G.B.

> Would you shine for Jesus 'mid the careless throng?
> Imitate His grace as you pass along;
> Make no weak surrender to the coarse and vile:
> Keep your tongue from evil, and your lips from guile!
> —Anon.

"A candle in a cottage may be a more blessed luminary than a star in the sky."

"LISTEN TO THE ECHOES"

READ I CORINTHIANS 3:10-15

> *. . . the sounding again of the mountains.*   Ezekiel 7:7

We considered it a wonderful discovery when Edison invented the "talking machine," as the phonograph was first called. Today we have "platters and tapes," on which we record any audible sound, and we can hear it come back to us again. But God's tape machine is much older. It is the echo. Do you remember when as a child you were entranced by certain places where the echo came back to you clear and loud? You stood on the porch and yelled: "Hello!" and the distant woods sent back the echo, "Hello!" Ezekiel too had been intrigued by the echoes of the hills and calls it "the sounding again of the mountains."

The echo always repeats only what it hears; it is the record which never dies, for we are told that sound waves continue forever, though our ears cannot hear them.

Paul tells us about another kind of echo, when he says, "Whatsoever a man soweth that shall he also reap" (Gal. 6:7). Or listen to the echo in II Corinthians 5:10: "For we must all appear before the judgment seat of Christ; that every one may receive the things done in his body, according to that he hath done, whether it be good or bad." All we do has an echo which will be played back at the end of the road, as an incontrovertible record of our past.

Even now, however, we hear the echo. Parents hear their echo in the conduct of their children. With few exceptions, children are like their parents. Echoes are hard to stop. Only God can stop them and unless He does, eternal echoes will become a veritable hell, for eternity will be the echo of time. The lost in Hell will suffer the torment of the eternal echoes of their wicked deeds, thoughts, and words. But God can stop the echoes, and will for all who put their trust in Christ. The promise is, "I will forgive their iniquity, and I will remember their sin no more" (Jer. 31:34).

—M.R.D.

> "The sounding again of the mountains"
> The harvest of life's fertile seeds,
> Is held in reserve for tomorrow —
> 'Twill echo the worth of our deeds.
>
> — H.G.B.

"Right or wrong doing . . . is sure in the end to meet its appropriate reward or punishment." — H. W. BEECHER

GOD ANSWERS PRAYER

READ PSALM 34:8-17

> *The eyes of the Lord are upon the righteous, and his*
> *ears are open unto their cry.*   Psalm 34:15

A Quaker, speaking in the open air, was opposed by a man who ridiculed the idea that there was a God who heard and answered prayer. The Quaker stopped and asked the trouble-maker, "Friend, dost thou pray?" "No, of course not!" was the reply. *"Then what dost thou know about it?"* said the Quaker shrewdly. The scoffer was put to silence.

There is rarely a Christian who cannot tell of some remark-able answer to his petitions. D. L. Moody, for instance, used to relate the following true story of an experience that happened to him in 1893. At that time he was holding his World's Fair campaign and needed a great sum of money very badly. He knelt by his desk in his room at the Bible Institute in Chicago and prayed, "Lord, You know I need $3000 today; I must have it, and I am too busy with Thy work to go out and get it. Please send it to me. I thank You that You will." He then arose and went back to his work. At the meeting that night, after the audience had gathered, a young woman came to an usher and said, "I wish to see Mr. Moody." She was told the service was about to begin and that she could not see him. She went to a second usher with the same result. Finally, working her way through the crowd she made her way to the platform where she managed to hand Mr. Moody an envelope. He hastily pushed it into his pocket and went on with the meeting. At dinner time he remembered the incident, opened the letter and found it contained a check addressed to him for $3000! It was the answer to his prayer. He afterwards learned that it first had been written for $1000, and later changed to $2000. Then, just before the generous donor had left for the meeting, the Holy Spirit had impressed her with the thought that the amount was still not sufficient. Tearing up the second check, she had then written a third and final one for $3000 — the exact amount that Mr. Moody needed. Impossible you say? You just don't know my Jesus!   —H.G.B.

> Do not travel on in darkness,
>   When you may walk in sunshine fair,
> You can find the light, and the pathway bright,
>   By the aid of a whispered prayer.
>   —Anon.

"Praying is to the soul what breathing is to the body."

THE FIFTH GOSPEL

READ I PETER 3:10-17

> *Ye are our epistle (letter) ... known and read of all men.* II Corinthians 3:2

A new convert testified that he had been saved by reading a copy of the fifth gospel. It was not Matthew, Mark, Luke, or John, but it was the gospel according to Mike the butcher. Mike was an earnest Christian whose godly life and testimony had been used of God to save this man. This is what Paul says in our Scripture. We are letters which men read every day. There are thousands who never read about Christ in the Bible but see Him only in the lives of men and women like Mike the butcher. Are you a walking letter for Christ?

Handwriting experts tell us that they can discern a person's character by his handwriting. Since we are His epistle, this becomes a solemn thing that the estimate of the character of the Lord Jesus is made known by us. Jesus is judged and estimated by the kind of lives we live. Then too, letters are written to be read, but if people are going to get the message, the writing must be legible and readable. If the writer has poor penmanship, no one will be able to read it. It is legibility, not ornamentation that people want. Some people's writing is just a "scrawl" which none can read. See then that your life is written in a legible, uncompromising, bold hand. Be clear in your testimony, pure in your conduct, steady in your walk, honest in business, consistent in all your dealings, and always ready to give a "reason for the hope that is in you."

The Bible is God's big letter but few read it. But the world does read you as a living epistle. "He himself cannot read," said some rough Navy men concerning a comrade, "but we can all read *HIM*, for he is a true Christian!"

There are at least five gospels: Matthew, Mark, Luke, John and the gospel according to YOU! — M.R.D.

> You are writing each day a letter to men,
> Take care that the writing is true,
> It's the only Gospel that some men will read,
> The gospel according to you!
> —Anon.

"Men who won't study the Bible will read 'living epistles'."

THE LONGEST DAY

And there shall be no night there . . . . Revelation 22:5

How long is a day? That depends upon where you live. In New York it is said that the longest day lasts approximately fifteen hours; at Montreal, Canada, it is sixteen hours; in London, England, it is sixteen and one-half hours; at Hamburg, Germany, it is seventeen hours; at Stockholm, Sweden, it is eighteen and one-half hours; and in certain spots in Russia it is nineteen hours. At Faroe, Finland, there have been days where the inhabitants enjoyed twenty-two hours of sunlight. Even farther north, however, in Warzburg, Norway, and at Spitzburgen, the days have been known to last *from two to three and one-half months!* These are long periods of sunlight indeed, yet they are relatively short and insignificant in comparison to the day predicted in Revelation 22:5. God tells us that in the capital city of the New Earth — in the final Heaven — day will last FOREVER, for "there is *no night there.*"

James H. McConkey tells of a ship caught in a fierce storm on the Great Lakes. All night long the passengers were tossed to and fro by the tempest, which jeopardized their lives. In the morning, however, they found a peaceful harbor. The captain testified later that during the long night, while they were being beaten and tossed, the one thing which kept them from sinking in despair was the *lights of home* shining brightly through the darkness and the storm! So too, the Christian is encouraged as he fixes his eye upon the "Pearly White City" just ahead. He realizes that earth's shadows will not always last. There is a terminus to our pilgrimage which is as bright as it is beautiful. After the fearful night of sin will come God's eternal morning! After the drab existence of earth, the rainbow glory of His presence! "Sunrise with Jesus for eternity!" — oh, what will it mean to be there!　　　　　　　　　　　　　—H.G.B.

> There is no night of things unknown, uncertain;
> 　Things which now try the heart to make it strong:
> There is no night — there is no veiling curtain;
> 　Just light; and bliss; and joy; and endless song!
> 　　　　　　　　　—J. Danson Smith

"Unless you WALK in the light HERE (Eph. 5:8; John 12:36), you will never DWELL in the light HEREAFTER (Col. 1:12)." — G.W.

CONCERNING MIRRORS

READ JAMES 1:22-27

> *But we all, with open face beholding as in a glass*
> *(mirror) the glory of the Lord, are changed into the*
> *same image from glory to glory, even as by the Spirit*
> *of the Lord.* II Corinthians 3:18

An African queen had never seen her own reflection and was made to believe she was a very beautiful woman. Then a trader came to the community to barter with the natives, and some of the articles of trade were mirrors. The queen, eager to see herself for the first time, was given one of the best and clearest. When she looked at her image, she saw how ugly she really was, instead of being beautiful as she had imagined. Enraged, she dashed the mirror in pieces and expelled the trader from her country.

How foolish we say, but it is no more foolish than that which thousands of educated, refined people do today. Because the Bible reveals their ugliness and sin, they seek to destroy the Bible. But for those who accept God's verdict and portrait of themselves, the mirror of the Word reflects the image of another Person. As we look at Him we are transformed and *WE BE-COME MIRRORS* reflecting His image. Notice our text. Beholding as in a mirror the glory of the Lord we are "changed into the same image." When God looks at us, He expects, if we are clean mirrors, to see the image of Jesus in us.

The world also expects to see Christ in us. They cannot see Him directly, but only indirectly as they behold Him in us.

You have all seen a mirror placed before a church organist so that he can see the director and the audience behind him. His back is turned to them, yet he can look at them in the mirror. In like manner the world cannot see Christ, for they have their backs turned on Him. The only way they can behold Jesus is by seeing His reflection in us.

A broken piece of glass can sparkle like a diamond if turned to the sun in the right position. The same is true of our broken lives. —M.R.D.

> May Christ be seen in me, O Lord;
> Hear Thou my humble plea.
> Oh, take me, fill me, use me, Lord;
> Till Christ be seen in me.
> —C. E. Baer

"To receive Christ is salvation, to reflect Him is consecration."
— H. G. B.

WHEN BROOKS RUN DRY

READ I KINGS 17:1-16

And it came to pass after a while, that the brook dried up . . . . I Kings 17:7

This wonderful story in I Kings 17 concerning Elijah and his experiences at the brook Cherith is rich in spiritual lessons. Not the least of these blessings for us is the comfort it can afford when the brooks of our cherished desires also dry up, even though we have done all to be in the center of God's will! In verse 5 of this chapter we are told that Elijah showed unquestioned obedience, for we read, "So he went and did according unto the word of the Lord: for he went and dwelt by the brook Cherith, that is before Jordan." Yet, though his daily supply was just bread and flesh brought by the ravens and a trickle of water from a little stream, still God tested him further, for suddenly *the brook dried up!* Elijah was severely tried! Would he rebel like Jonah when the going was unpleasant, or would he rely completely on God alone! Disappointing as the dried-up brook was, no word of complaint is recorded from the lips of God's consecrated prophet. He was speedily rewarded for his faithful trust by being given new directions from God; even as those who wait upon the Lord today may ever be sure of Divine guidance when their way becomes so dark that human reason sees not one step ahead. Yes, *we may experience difficulties even when we are in the center of the will of God* — as did Elijah — but if without murmuring we simply place our hand in His, God will reward our faithfulness with *new directions, new supplies, and much blessing!*

Have you any brooks that are drying up? Brooks of health, brooks of finance, brooks of precious loved ones and friends that have apparently vanished? Cheer up, do not despair, turn to the Word of God for fresh help and guidance. The strengthening "meal" and the comforting, invigorating "oil" of the Holy Spirit (I Kings 17:16) will soon refresh your soul and more than compensate for your "dried-up brooks!" —H.G.B.

> God will take care of you still to the end,
> Oh what a Father, Redeemer, and Friend;
> Guiding, protecting, and keeping His own,
> He will take care of you — trust Him alone!
> —Anon.

"Faith must be tested; therefore, the ships God builds are sent to sea!"

CONFESSING AND FORSAKING

READ PSALM 32

*He that covereth his sins shall not prosper: but whoso
confesseth and forsaketh them shall have mercy.*

Proverbs 28:13

The unconverted sinner lives in sin and loves it. The born-again believer hates sin and yet may often fall into it. The sinner looks for sin and pursues it; while the saint is often overtaken by it even though he tries to flee from it. Paul admonishes us in Galatians 6:1: " . . . if a man be overtaken in a fault, ye which are spiritual, restore such an one in the spirit of meekness."

This is quite a different thing than wilfully living in sin. The believer cannot "continue" in sin (Rom. 6:2). As long as we are in the body and our old nature is still with us, we live in constant danger of falling into sin. We should not sin (I John 2:1a), but provision has been made for us in case we do sin (I John 2:1b). We must be careful not to judge those who fall into sin, and conclude they are not saved. Think of Noah, Abraham, David, Solomon, and Peter. There is a simple test which we may apply to determine whether it is a Christian "falling," or a sinner "planning" his sin. How can we distinguish? Suppose a pig is so cleverly clothed with the wool of a sheep that we cannot tell the difference. Let both fall into the same mudhole and become besmeared with mire that you cannot tell the one from the other. The swine will be perfectly content, and put up a loud squeal when any attempt is made to extricate him. And when pulled out, he will go right back in. The sheep on the other hand will cry, struggle and bleat for help, and when delivered will never go near that slough again. The genuineness of a man's repentance and confession of his sins is proven by his forsaking of them.

—M.R.D.

While I kept guilty silence
My strength was spent with grief,
Thy hand was heavy on me,
My soul found no relief;
But when I owned my trespass,
My sin hid not from Thee,
When I confessed transgression,
Then Thou forgavest me.

—Anon.

**"The sin that now rises to memory is your bosom sin; confess and
forsake it."**

GOD'S PROMISED DIRECTION

. . . I will direct all his ways . . . .   Isaiah 45:13

When we acknowledge the Lord in all our ways, He perfectly and wisely directs our paths.

The story is told of a lone survivor of a shipwreck who was thrown upon an uninhabited island. After a while he built for himself a rude shelter in which he placed the few precious possessions he had managed to save from the ship. Being a Christian he prayed most earnestly for deliverance, and anxiously scanned the horizon to hail any ship that might come in that direction. One day, upon returning from a hunt for food, he was horrified to find his campsite in flames. All that he had salvaged was disappearing in the smoke! Disaster had struck, or so it appeared. However, that which seemed to have transpired for the worst was in reality for his gain. While to his limited vision such a cruel blow was inexplicable, to God's infinite wisdom his loss was for the best, and actually resulted in the very thing for which he had been praying most earnestly — for *the very next day a ship arrived!* *"We saw your smoke signal,"* the captain said! The Christian recognized then that even his seeming calamity had been God-directed.

Remember, Christian, there are no accidents with the Lord. Look with the discerning eyes of faith for His wise leading, and trace with sanctified understanding His hand of love even in your deepest trial. Be assured that "God's way *is the best way*," though at present the blessing of His direction may be hidden from your tear-dimmed eyes!   —H.G.B.

> Be not dismayed, for evermore
>   Thy God thy steps will guide;
> The desert-need will soon be o'er;
>   The Lord doth still provide.
> No, never thee the Lord will leave;
>   No, never thee forsake;
> No, He who "sinners" doth receive,
>   The saints His care doth make!
>   —Anon.

"The Lord may lead you AROUND, but He will lead you ARIGHT."

ONLY PRETTY PICTURES

READ COLOSSIANS 2:1-7

In whom are hid all the treasures of wisdom and knowl-edge.
Colossians 2:3

The Bible is a mine of spiritual wealth but its treasures do not lie merely on the surface. Most of them can be found only by "digging" for them, and the deeper we dig the more precious are the jewels which we discover. What a tragedy that men will build their houses over a mine of gold and never realize it is there, and continue to live in poverty and ignorance. There is not a need of the human heart which cannot be met in the Word, for therein "are hid all the treasures of wisdom and knowledge."

A poor old widow was living in poverty and want. A friend, hearing she was in need, went over to visit her and if possible help her. The old lady complained bitterly of her condition and remarked that her son in Australia was doing very well. Her friend inquired, "And doesn't he do anything to help you?" She replied, "No, nothing. He writes to me regularly once a month but he only sends me some little pictures with his letter." The friend asked to see the pictures she had received and to his surprise found each of them to be twenty-pound notes. The poor old lady did not realize the value of this foreign currency, but had only imagined them to be pretty pictures. She had lived in poverty and want, whereas she could have had all the bodily comforts she desired and needed so much.

We smile at the impossible story, but is it not like thousands of believers who go about as though they are paupers, instead of sons of the King? They doubt, and question, and fear, and halt, all because they do not realize the riches of the promises of the Lord. Our Heavenly Father has given us many exceeding great and precious promises. Like the old lady, we have seen the pictures, but have failed to realize they are for us. They must be cashed by faith and trust, for unless believed and appropriated, they are worthless to help us. —M.R.D.

Standing on the promises I cannot fall,
List'ning ev'ry moment to the Spirit's call,
Resting in my Saviour, as my all in all,
Standing on the promises of God.
—R. K. Carter

"The Bible is a window in this prison of hope, through which we look into eternity." — DWIGHT

GOD'S SECOND BOOK

READ ISAIAH 40:21-28

> *...I meditate on all thy works; I muse on the work of thy hands.*
> Psalm 143:5

Although it has been marred by sin, creation still testifies to the handiwork of the Master Artist who formed it. God is absolutely distinct from His creation, and yet He has left His indelible imprint upon it. The Father in Heaven has not left Himself without a witness even to those who will not read the Bible, for nature loudly declared His power, majesty, and glory.

> I stroll down a quiet country lane
> And God speaks to me.
> I gaze upward on a clear summer night,
> And I hear His voice.
> While winding down a rough mountain trail,
> I hear Him calling me.
> God speaks as the wind whispers
> Through a field of ripened grain;
> As a bird calls and echoes his mating song.
> That's God speaking as the water in a mountain stream
> Tumbles over its rocky bed.
> Yes, God speaks in all of creation;
> And listening, I hear Him!

Dr. Phil Marquart says: "In childhood, how our hearts thrilled in reading the story of *Robinson Crusoe!* He was stranded on an island which he thought to be without human inhabitant, except himself. One day he found footprints in the sand, and following these, he discovered a man, whom he called Friday! So too, throughout creation, God has left His footprints!"

Have you seen these marks of beauty and design that speak of the Creator? Have they called forth from your thrilled and awestruck soul praise and adoration? It is true that a man can only be saved through the operation of the Holy Spirit applying the Word — God's *Special Revelation* — to his heart; yet we must also not neglect God's second great book — the colorful volume of *nature!* Today, see the handiwork of God in bush and flower as you travel the wonder-world of life! —H.G.B.

> If God will use His utmost art
> On His small creatures of the wild,
> What intricate design of life
> Has He not planned for me, His child?
> —M. A. Anderson

"Nature is an outstretched finger pointing toward God."
— R. LUCHINGSER

WHAT DO YOU BELIEVE?

READ I JOHN 2:9-17

>*...This is the bread which the Lord hath given you to eat.*
>Exodus 16:15

The manna was a perfect food — good for babies, adults, and old people. The Bible is God's manna, and so is Christ. In them every Christian finds perfect nourishment.

There are three kinds of Christians: bottle-fed, spoon-fed, and fork-fed; those who are babes and must be fed by others; older children who can feed themselves; and mature Christians who can feed others. John in his first epistle calls them "little children" (I John 2:12); "young men" (I John 2:14); and "fathers" (I John 2:13).

The Bible offers three kinds of food for these classes — *milk* for babies, *bread* for young men, and solid *meat* for the fathers. To help you to become mature, so that you can not only study for yourself but become a teacher of others, these studies are given. Too many Christians are perpetual babies in a state of arrested development, always depending upon others rather than digging it out for themselves. It is the path of least resistance, the lazy man's religion.

The Christians at Berea were called "more noble" than those of Thessalonica because they received the Word with all readiness of mind, and searched the Scriptures (not just read — *searched*) daily (regularly) to see whether these things were so. Don't be like the old lady who was asked by a friend what she believed, and replied, "I believe what the church believes." "But what does your church believe?" Her reply was, "The church believes what I believe." The friend asked, "But what do you and your church believe?" She replied, "We both believe the same thing."

My friend, what do you believe? Did you find it in the Bible for yourself or did you just accept what someone else told you? You cannot be sure unless you find it in the Book. Believe rr, and reject all else.

How far have you advanced? How much are you able to help others in the things of the Word? Read carefully Hebrews 5:12-14.　\
　　　　　　　　　　　　　　　　　　　　　　—M.R.D.

"Infants," "young men," "fathers,"
Yet His children all;
Some, through growth, so helpful,
Others — still so small!
　　　　　　　　　　　—Anon.

"It is tragically possible to have a saved soul, but a lost life."

ONLY A SHADOW!

READ PSALM 23

*Yea, though I walk through the valley of the shadow
of death, I will fear no evil . . . .*   Psalm 23:4

In this verse David is not speaking of walking *to* the valley, or
even walking *in* the valley; rather he says, "Yea, though I walk
through the valley." For the child of God the tomb is not a ter-
minal, but a junction where he leaves behind the heavy freight
cars of sin, trouble, and mortality, and boards the heavenly
chariot to ride on into immortality!

Shadows are harmless. We may shrink in dread and fear from
them, yet they cannot hurt us. A shadow of a dog cannot bite,
nor can the silhouette of a sword wound us. Ivor Powell, in his
splendid book *Bible Pinnacles* says: "Shadows are not possible
unless a light is shining somewhere; and this shadow of death is
cast across the valley by the Light of the world Himself who
waits to welcome His Home-coming pilgrim."

Christ delivers us from the *sting* of death by His blood (I Cor.
15:56); from its *fear* by His grace (Heb. 2:15); from its *loneliness* by His presence (Psa. 23:4); from its *hopelessness* by His
resurrection (Prov. 14:32); from its *dread* by renaming it (John
11:11); and from its *unwelcome sight* by giving us a view of
Himself (John 8:51; Rev. 22:4).

An old man in his final moments called in much distress for his
minister. "Oh, pastor, I am dying!" he said. "For years I have
been feasting on the promises of God, but this morning when I
awoke I couldn't remember one of them! What shall I do?" The
preacher knew that Satan was disturbing him, so he said, "Father
Junkins, *do you think GOD will forget any of His promises?*"
Suddenly a sweet smile came over the face of the dying Christian
as he exclaimed joyfully, "Praise God, that is wonderful! *He'll
keep His promises,* won't He? I'll just fall asleep and trust Him
to remember them all, even though I cannot." Soon he was "beyond the shadows" in the bright sunlight of the Homeland. Don't
fear death; it's only a shadow!   —H.G.B.

> There's a light in the valley for me,
>   So no evil will I fear,
> While my Shepherd is so near,
>   There's a light in the valley for me.
>   —P. P. Bliss

**"It is blessed to know that the Light in the valley is real, and that
death is only a shadow!"**

'TWAS A SAD DAY!

READ I CORINTHIANS 5:1-7

> *...a little leaven leaveneth the whole lump. Purge out therefore the old leaven.* I Corinthians 5:6, 7

Yesterday was a sad day, for we were compelled to part with some very dear friends. The little friends were two colonies of honey bees. Hours I spent last summer studying their ways and praising God for the lessons they taught me. All summer long they labored faithfully and gathered many pounds of beautiful white clover honey, but yesterday (sniff, sniff) it all went up in smoke. The bee inspector came along and informed me that a disease (called foul brood) had infected the hive, and the bees were doomed. They would have to be destroyed immediately lest they spread the disease to other bees in the neighborhood. It was the law—no room for grace here. I stood sadly by as the inspector killed the bees with cyanide, carried the hives into the field and burned the frames and boxes, together with 75 pounds of honey, with which I had hoped to surprise my family and friends. It all went up in smoke! All that remained was the hive bodies, scorched and thoroughly sterilized with a blow torch.

My material loss, however, became a spiritual gain for me. I realized the need of frequent "inspection" of my own heart for the "foul brood" of the works of the flesh. Sin in our lives must be purged out or it will grow worse and even infect others. That is why Paul admonished the Corinthian church to "put away from among yourselves that wicked person" (I Cor. 5:13). Unless sin in the assembly is judged and disciplined it will "leaven the whole lump." This is also true personally. To harbor or condone known sin in our lives not only injures us but others as well. May we this day ask ourselves honestly, "What is there in my life which I know is contrary to God's Word and displeasing to Him?" And then apply the blow torch of repentance and confession and be clean before Him. —M.R.D.

> Search me, O God, and know my heart today;
> Try me, O Saviour, know my thoughts, I pray:
> See if there be some wicked way in me:
> Cleanse me from ev'ry sin, and set me free.
> —E. Orr

"The Devil's chloroform is the denial of sin, for the greatest of all faults is to be conscious of none."

NEEDED: MORE ANDREWS

[Andrew] first findeth his own brother Simon . . . and he brought him to Jesus.   John 1:41, 42

A pastor was met on the street one day by a parishioner who had missed church the day before. "What did you preach about on Sunday?" he asked. "I preached about Andrew," was the reply, "and do you know, I found him a most interesting person!" "Andrew?" replied the parishioner wonderingly. "Why I hardly remember him at all among the disciples. He didn't write any books in the Bible, did he? What was so remarkable about him?" "Well," replied the pastor, "I do not suppose many would call him a great man, but the significant thing about him was that every time he is mentioned in Scripture, *he was introducing someone to Jesus!* In John 1:42 we find him bringing his brother Simon to Christ; in John 6:8, 9 he brought a lad with a simple lunch to Jesus, that by it our Lord might miraculously feed a multitude; and finally in John 12:22 he directed the seeking Greeks to Jesus." The parishioner walked away with a thoughtful look. He had gotten a new glimpse of the importance of the often unnoticed, unpraised disciple — Andrew.

When we think about Andrew we recall that without his work we would not have the great preacher, Peter, at Pentecost. Tradition tells us that one of the Greeks he brought to our Saviour was Luke, the physician, who wrote one of the gospel accounts as well as the book of Acts. In Heaven, no doubt, Andrew's name will stand high as the man who knew how to bring souls to Christ.

You, too, can be a humble, helpful Andrew. You may not be able to write books, preach sermons, or direct a choir, but you can witness to others and seek to bring the needy souls all around you to Jesus. How much could be accomplished in the church today if we had a few more who would be willing to work and yet stay in the background and be just "little Andrews!"

—H.G.B.

There are lonely hearts to cherish,
  Weary souls who must not perish;
  Oh, so much for you to do.
Then for Jesus be a worker,
  'Tis not right to be a shirker,
  Consecration now renew.

—G. W.

"The biggest piece of work a Christian can do is to find his friend and introduce him to Jesus."

GERIATRICS

READ PSALM 71:7-18

With us are both the gray-headed and very aged men . . . .
Job 15:10

Geriatrics is the science or study of "old age." Today we have in medical practice a specialized branch of research which makes a study of the infirmities and peculiar maladies of the elderly, and seeks remedies for them. As the functions of the body slow down, science in its never-ending search for the "fountain of youth" seeks to stave off "aging" by stimulants, hormones, pep pills, and applied psychology. But in spite of it all — people still grow old.

Much better than rebelling against growing old is to adjust one's self to it — and then "act your age."

Since we cannot turn back the clock of time, we are to use the opportunities which age affords to the best advantage. For the trusting Christian, sunset should be a time of quietness and peace. There is nothing quite so depressing as a bitter old man or woman who has become sour with age instead of sweeter. There is nothing so refreshing, comforting, and reassuring as an aging Christian who becomes sweeter and more mellow as the days go by.

Dr. Wm. Pettingill said to me shortly before he went to be with the Lord at the age of 84, "I shall never grow old — only older, and I hope the Lord will let me die with my boots on." He did — and all who were acquainted with this aged saint of God knew the stimulus of his radiant sparkling testimony to the very end.

What makes the difference in people growing old — either bitter or sweet? *It is a matter of perspective!* It is all in the direction you look — back — or ahead. To mope over past joys, fading youth, will not change the picture — but to look ahead and see the glory — this is victory. (Read II Cor. 4:16-18.) Remember the Bible says, "They shall still bring forth fruit in old age. They shall be fat and flourishing." Take liberal, daily doses of the *Word* and you won't need any "Geritol."   — M.R.D.

Ere long my soul shall fly away,
And leave this tenement of clay.
I'll meet you on the Streets of Gold,
And PROVE that I'm not growing old!
— J. E. Roberts

"If you dread growing old, think of the many who never have that privilege." — M. R. D.

PRAYER MISSIONARIES

READ MATTHEW 9:35-38

. . . pray ye therefore the Lord of the harvest, that he would send forth labourers into his harvest. Luke 10:2

S. C. Todd, in his good tract, "The Intercessory Missionary," tells of a discovery he made while looking through the records of the work carried on in the past by the China Inland Mission. He was struck by the fact that in one of these stations the number and spiritual character of the converts had far exceeded anyone's expectation. It could not be accounted for by the consecration of the missionaries who were employed at that particular place, for equally consecrated men had been in charge of similar but less fruitful areas of service. The rich harvest of souls remained a mystery, he said, until Hudson Taylor on a visit to England discovered the secret power which had resulted in such astonishing accomplishments. At the close of one of his messages a gentleman from the audience came forward to make his acquaintance. In the conversation which followed, Hudson Taylor was surprised at the accurate knowledge the man possessed concerning this inland China station. "But how is it," Mr. Taylor asked, "that you are so conversant with the conditions of that work?" "Oh," he replied, "the missionary there and I are old college-mates, and for four years we have regularly corresponded; he has sent me the names of inquirers and converts, and these I have daily taken to God in prayer." Suddenly Hudson Taylor saw the reason for the abundant harvest which had been gleaned at this one outpost for Christ. *The spiritual intercession of a truly dedicated man at home, praying definitely and daily for specific needs, had abounded to the glory of God!*

If we would just be more specific in our prayers, we too could expect more specific answers. You and I may not be able to go to the foreign field for various reasons, but we can all be "prayer missionaries." Will you volunteer?   — H.G.B.

Somebody prayed, and across the sea
  The old, old story of Calvary,
With its new, sweet meaning of love untold,
  To the waiting millions' hearts was told.
Somebody prayed! Oh, gift divine!
  May e'er such service be yours and mine.
                —Anon.

"At every breath we draw, five souls perish, never having heard of Christ; therefore, breathe a prayer!"

THE POWER OF THE WORD

READ JOHN 17:1-17

*Now ye are clean through the word which I have spoken
unto you.* John 15:3

The Word of God is compared to water for three distinct purposes. When the Bible speaks of water for drinking purposes
it refers to regeneration through the Spirit (John 3:5). When
used as a figure of floods and torrents, it signifies the judgments
of God (II Pet. 3:6). Water used for cleansing and washing
points to the sanctifying power of the Word of God.

Jesus prayed, "Sanctify them through thy truth: thy word is
truth" (John 17:17). The Church is cleansed by the "washing
of water by the word." No believer can be clean without daily
"bathing" in the Word of God. Just reverently reading the Bible
daily will be a sanctifying experience, even though you may not
even remember much of what you have read. Some people have
very poor memories. A man once complained: "I might as well
stop reading the Bible for I get so little out of it and remember
so little afterwards." Is this your trouble? Then listen to the
little story of a simple Hindu convert. A missionary diligently
tried to teach her the Word of God daily, and became greatly
discouraged because her new convert was so slow in remembering what she had been taught. One day she complained, "I
guess it's no use trying to teach you the Word, you seem to forget
all I tell you about the Bible. Your mind seems like a sieve. As
fast as I pour the water in, it runs out again." The reply of the
poor woman reveals a great truth. Said she, "Yes, I realize my
mind is like a sieve. I do forget so much, but when you pour
water through a sieve it makes the sieve clean, even though it
seems to retain none of it. I am sorry I forget so much, but please
don't stop pouring the Word into me. It makes my heart and
mind feel so clean afterwards. The water is not wasted."

It is not how much Scripture you can memorize, but rather
how "much" it does to you. — M.R.D.

Who would not love the Bible,
So beautiful and wise?
It cleanses and refreshes,
And points us to the skies.
— E. Hood

**"The vigor of our spiritual life will be in proportion to the place held
by the Word in our life and thoughts."** — G. MUELLER

DRAWING NEAR TO GOD

READ PSALM 119:145-151

. . . it is good for me to draw near to God. Psalm 73:28

In justification God first stoops down to us and draws us with cords of love and the power of His irresistible grace; but in sanctification we must make the initial move and seek to have intimate fellowship with Him. Asaph in Psalm 73 had experienced the joy and true happiness that results from such nearness to God. James, in his epistle, tells us that if we want to feel God's presence we must first "draw nigh" to Him (James 4:8). Too many Christians wait passively for God to fill them with joy, victory, and spiritual zeal; they fail to recognize that such intimate blessings are impossible unless they — by Bible study, prayer, witnessing, and fellowship with other Christians — advance into the light and warmth of the Lord's most intimate presence. Because we as Christians often are so blind to this fact, God sometimes has to encourage us to come closer to Him through pressing trial and encumbering need. How much better if true gratitude and love inspires our hearts to seek His warming embrace! But whatever the reasons for our drawing near — our slightest movement Godward delights His heart and brings an instantaneous response and increased fellowship.

You perhaps may recall the story of the little fellow who through fear was prompted to nestle very close to his father as they were riding along on a strange and dark road. The indulgent father, thinking the child was about to ask for some favor, inquired, "Out with it, what do you wish now?" "Nothing, Father, I just want to be near you," said the child with a soulful look. The father's heart was gladdened, and the fellowship between the two was made more precious. So, too, the Father in Heaven rejoices when, because of our love, we seek to embrace Him in a warmer fellowship. Indeed, "The Lord is nigh unto all them that call upon him . . . in truth" (Ps. 145:18).   — H.G.B.

Nearer, still nearer, while life shall last,
Till safe in Glory my anchor is cast;
Through endless ages, ever to be
Nearer my Saviour, still nearer to Thee.
—C. H. Morris

"Fellowship with God is a sacred flower which is experienced here in the bud, but whose full bloom is reserved for Heaven."

CHEERFUL CHRISTIANS

READ PSALM 30

A merry heart maketh a cheerful countenance.
Proverbs 15:13

A gloomy Christian is an abnormal Christian. Cheerfulness should characterize the walk of every believer. By cheerfulness we do not mean frivolousness or silliness but a condition of peace, joy, and inner satisfaction. Cheerfulness stems from the inside, and is not affected by the outside circumstances alone. Our text tells us a cheerful countenance is the result of a "merry heart." A long face, be it ever so pious, is not a good advertisement for our Saviour. Johnny came home from Uncle Tom's farm with the amazing news that he had seen some "Christian cows" because they had such long faces. When we make some sacrifice today for others, and do it as if it were a painful task, it loses the blessing and testimony. Paul says we are to show "mercy, with cheerfulness" (Rom. 12:8).

Three times in the gospels Jesus said to His disciples, "Be of good cheer." The first time is in Matthew 9:2 where Jesus says to a lame man, "Be of good cheer; thy sins be forgiven thee." He did not say, "Cheer up, because I am going to heal your paralysis," but "your sins are forgiven." In Matthew 14:27 and Mark 6:50, the disciples are about to perish in a great storm and Jesus walking on the sea says, "Be of good cheer; it is I." In John 16:33 Jesus bids His followers good cheer because while "in the world ye shall have tribulation (but) . . . be of good cheer; I have overcome the world." Cheer up — your sins are gone! Cheer up, He is with you in the storm! Cheer up, the future holds victory! Past, present and future!

A deacon was delegated to meet the visiting preacher at the train. Never having seen him, he scanned every face till he saw an extra gloomy looking man and asked him, "Are you a minister?" The man replied, "No, it's my indigestion that makes me look like this!" Cheer up, brother!   — M.R.D.

Cheer up, ye saints of God, there's nothing to worry about;
   Nothing to make you feel afraid, nothing to make you doubt;
Remember Jesus never fails, so why not trust Him and shout?
   You'll be sorry you worried at all tomorrow morning!
—Anon.

"A smile is a light in the window of the face that shows a happy heart is at home."

STILL WATERS

. . . he leadeth me beside the still waters.   Psalm 23:2

Palestine is a semi-arid country and water is therefore scarce and precious. The picture that is drawn here in the Twenty-third Psalm is an interesting one. The streams during the rainy season are swift and treacherous so that it is not safe for a sheep to approach their raging current. Should they do so, they would probably be carried away and drowned. The sheep, however, in this rather dry and thirsty land are very eager for the sparkling refreshment when they see it pouring in an inviting torrent, but the shepherd, recognizing their danger, keeps them back until he has dug a ditch leading off from the main stream. Only when the water has collected in this special pool and distilled to a crystal clearness does he allow his sheep to satisfy their thirst. By these still waters they find their necessary refreshment without the dangers associated with the swiftly flowing streams of the rainy season. No wonder the sheep love the shepherd, for through his tender care and provision they can enjoy cooling mouthfuls of water in tranquility, and slake their thirst without fear.

So too the boisterous streams of the world, although they appear inviting, can never satisfy the Lord's sheep. The allurements of sin promise much, but their subtle threat to life and limb is apparent to the Good Shepherd. He knows our need and graciously supplies the sweet water of the Word and heavenly refreshment. The quiet beauty and crystal purity of the water of salvation ever invites His obedient sheep to peaceful repose and true contentment. Only as these "waters of stillness" (as the phrase may be literally translated) are imbibed can our souls be restored and our thirst for God be satisfied. How precious and delightful are His "still waters." "O taste and see that the Lord is good." He ever leads aright!   — H.G.B.

> The Lord is my Shepherd, no want shall I know;
> I feed in green pastures, safe-folded I rest;
> He leadeth my soul where the still waters flow,
> Restores me when wandering, redeems when oppressed.
> — J. Montgomery

"The Twenty-third Psalm has charmed more griefs to rest than all the philosophy of the world." — H. W. BEECHER

WITH ALL YOUR MIGHT!

READ I THESSALONIANS 5:14-28

Whatsoever thy hand findeth to do, do it with thy might . . . .
Ecclesiastes 9:10

If a thing is worth doing, it is worth doing right. If a job does not call for the best that is in you, there is something wrong with you or with the job. Yet how much of our time and effort is given over to things which are of no profit. I met a friend of mine sitting on a park bench with his hands folded, staring into the distance. When I questioned what he was doing, he replied, "Just killing time." What a cruel thing to do to such a valuable creature as *time*. Why kill it? Time is given to us to be cultivated, not murdered. Time should never be wasted but used to the best advantage. Of course, we know that there are times when we must relax and rest. Even Jesus said to His disciples, "Come apart and rest awhile." But this was not "killing time" — it was restoring time. After they had rested they would be able to use their time more fruitfully and profitably. If a fraction of the time Christians "waste" could be utilized in prayer, Bible reading, witnessing to others, visiting a friend in distress, or comforting some bereaved one, what a difference it would make! Today, when you have leisure time, ask yourself how you can best improve these extra hours. You think I am narrow-minded? Then the Bible is narrow-minded, for it tells us we shall give an account of every moment God has given us.

Thank God every morning when you get up that you have something to do that day which must be done — whether you like it or not! What you do today will determine in a large way your tomorrow. Today, see how much good you can do for Him and others — *not how little you can get by with*. It is *not* true that "a man can make up *lost time*." It is gone forever! — M.R.D.

> With every rising of the sun
>   Think of your life as just begun;
> You and today! A soul sublime
>   And the great pregnant hour of time,
> With God Himself to bind the twain!
>   Go forth, I say, attain! attain!
>
> —Anon.

"You don't make any footprints in the sands of time while you're sitting down."

PATIENT ENDURANCE

READ HEBREWS 6:10-15

And so, after he had patiently endured, he obtained the
promise. Hebrews 6:15

Trials can be turned into triumphs if we patiently endure
them! There was once a mission station in Japan, we are told,
which built a meeting place with the stones that were thrown
at the Christians who had witnessed there in years gone by.
When more peaceful times came the believers had picked up
these rocks and bricks and worked them into the foundation of a
new church. So too, our trials, if they are borne patiently, bring
blessing and lay the foundation for future reward. In Hebrews
6:15 the example of Abraham is cited in regard to such faithful
endurance.

Someone has written, "Abraham was long tried, but he was
richly rewarded. The Lord tried him by delaying to fulfill His
promise; Satan tried him by temptation; men tried him by
jealousy, distrust, and opposition; Sarah tried him by her peevish-
ness; but he patiently endured. He did not question God's
veracity, nor limit His power, nor doubt His faithfulness, nor
grieve His love; but he bowed to divine sovereignty, submitted
to infinite wisdom, and was silent under delays, waiting the
Lord's time. And so, having patiently endured, he obtained the
promise. God's promises can never fail of their accomplishment.
Patient waiters cannot be disappointed. Believing expectation
shall be realized. Beloved, Abraham's conduct condemns a hasty
spirit, reproves a murmuring one, commends a patient one, and
encourages quiet submission to God's will and way. Remember,
Abraham was tried; he patiently waited; he received the promise,
and was satisfied."

Let us imitate Abraham's example of patient endurance and
share the same blessing! —H.G.B.

> Be still, be still, and know that I am God,
> The Father speaks in pleading tones of love;
> Oh troubled soul, beneath the chast'ning rod,
> He seeks to mold thee for His Home above
> Be still, be still, when tempted to complain,
> And calmly bear the cross of grief or pain.
> —H. B. Elwell

"Endurance is a prime requisite for spiritual success. James wrote,
'Blessed is the man that endureth temptation, for when he is tried, he
shall receive the crown of life.'"

WHAT A WORLD!

READ ISAIAH 1:1-9

. . . God hath made man upright; but they have sought out many inventions.   Ecclesiastes 7:29

The whole world lieth in the Wicked One. Satan is the God of this age; and wickedness, violence, destruction, misery, and death are on every hand. But God did not make the world thus, for after He had finished His work He said, "Behold, it (is) . . . *very good*" (Gen. 1:31). Then sin came, and now *behold the awful mess!*

There is some truth in a statement made by Abe the tailor. A customer had ordered a pair of pants, but after two weeks the tailor had not started the pants, because, said he, he had not yet had an inspiration. Finally, after much pressure, the pants were ready in about ten weeks. The customer was satisfied and said, "Yes, Abe, it's a good job, but it took you too everlastingly long. It took you ten times as long to make a pair of pants as it took to make the world — six days." The tailor carefully eyed his creation (the pants) and then looked out the window and finally said, "Vell, maybe it took me longer to make them pants than it took to make the world — but I'm telling you, Jake, take a look at the world, and then take a look at deze pants." In a way Abe was right. The world is in an awful mess, but it was not so in the beginning. God made man upright but he has sought out many inventions. Someday all this will be changed when God destroys this present world and creates a new heaven and a new earth. And this new heaven and new earth will be inhabited by men and women who are "new creatures" by faith in Jesus Christ. Sin will be gone!

Only new furnishings will be allowed in the new earth. Are you a new creation (II Cor. 5:17)? If not — then accept the offer of Matthew 11:28.   — M.R.D.

> Oh what a joy to know,
>   Each sinner still can come,
> And through God's grace alone
>   Find peace, and heaven and home!
>   —M. A. Peters

"Christianity is not a cloak put on, but a new life put in!"

TESTING IN DEEP WATERS

READ PSALM 18:11-19

*Save me, O God; for the waters are come in unto my
soul.* Psalm 69:1

A flood of "overflowing waters" was a familiar Hebrew figure
for the calamities of life which often threaten to drown the soul
in misery and despair. David in Psalm 69 expresses the frantic
cry of one who is so beset by trial that he immediately recognizes that only God can possibly help and deliver him. Many of
us can echo David's petition of distress, for we too have experienced "sorrows like sea billows" that have ominously threatened to engulf our soul. Yet when He who is love dwells within,
we may be confident that the waters of distress will never completely overflow us. Indeed, we are assured in His Word that
"Many waters cannot quench (His) love, neither can the floods
drown it" (Song of Sol. 8:7).

A jeweler gives as one of his surest tests for diamonds, the
so-called *"trial by water"* experiment. He says, "An imitation
diamond is never so brilliant as a genuine stone. If your eye is
not experienced enough to detect the difference, a simple test is
to place the jewel in question under water. The light of an imitation stone when submerged will be practically extinguished,
while a genuine diamond will sparkle and remain distinctly
visible. The contrast is so marked that none can mistake the
counterfeit." So, too, many seem joyful and confident as long as
they have no trials in this life; but as soon as the waters of
sorrow begin to flow about them, their faith loses its brilliancy.
Those, however, who have been fortified in advance by laying up
in their heart the precious promises of the Word, and who have
appropriated more fully the sanctifying grace of the Holy Spirit,
will shine forth in the "deep water test" as genuine jewels of the
King! —H.C.B.

When through the deep waters I call thee to go,
The rivers of sorrow shall not overflow;
For I will be with thee thy trials to bless,
And sanctify to thee thy deepest distress.
—G. Keith

"Nothing will show more accurately what we are than the way in
which we meet trials and difficulties."

PROVE ANYTHING BY SCRIPTURE?

READ II PETER 1:15-21

> *. . . no prophecy of the scripture is of any private interpretation.*
> II Peter 1:20

"You can prove anything by the Bible," is an expression we hear all too often. It is not true — it is a lie! You cannot prove just anything by the Bible if you take the Bible as a *whole* and remember that no part of it can contradict any other part. There are several hundred so-called Christian sects, denominations, and organizations in America, all claiming to be based on the Bible and able to quote texts to prove it. But we cannot build a doctrine or system of faith on an isolated passage of the Bible. It must be viewed and interpreted in harmony with all the rest of Scripture. Yes, you can "prove" anything by an isolated text taken out of its context. For instance the Bible says, "There is no God." That statement is found in Psalm 14. But the rest of the verse is: "The *fool* hath said in his heart, There is no God." That makes quite a difference.

If you are confused by the many different sects, churches, and denominations, study the whole Bible. If a church builds its theology on isolated verses and pet doctrines instead of on the Book as a whole, beware of it.

A man asked his friend this riddle: "There was a donkey tied to a rope only four feet long. Eight feet away was a bale of hay which the donkey wanted because he was hungry. How did he get it?" His friend said, "I've heard that one before. You want me to say, 'I give up — and you'll say, that's what the other jackass did too.' " "Not at all," said the man. "It's really quite simple. You see the donkey just walked over to the hay and ate it." The friend, now confused, replied, "But you said the rope was only four feet long." "Very true," was the reply, "but the rope wasn't tied to anything. You mustn't jump at conclusions before you have *all* the facts."

Only as you study the Bible can you get all the facts and get the true message. *Study for yourself!* — M.R.D.

> Lamp of our feet, whereby we trace
> Our path, when wont to stray,
> Stream from the fount of heavenly grace
> Refresh us on our way!
> —B. Barton

"When you have studied the WHOLE Bible you will have found in it the key to your own heart, your own happiness, and to all truth!"

THE SIN OF SELFISHNESS

<small>READ I CORINTHIANS 13:1-5</small>

Look not every man on his own things, but every man also on the things of others   Philippians 2:4

Supreme regard for our own things at the expense of others violates God's principle of loving our neighbor as our self. Such selfishness not only harms the slighted brother, but it also injures the one who practices it.

There is a parable, oft repeated in India, concerning a selfish fool to whom a ricefield was bequeathed. The first season the irrigation water covered his property, making it abundantly fruitful, and then flowed on to his neighbor's fields, bringing equal fertility everywhere. The next season, however, the selfish fool said in his heart, "This water is wealth; it is liquid harvest. I was too generous in letting this treasure escape to others." He therefore stopped the water with a specially made dam and robbed his friends of the beneficial flood. In so doing he spoiled his own crop, for the irrigation water brought blessing while it flowed, but when it became stagnant it turned his rice-paddy into an unfruitful marsh. Love that stops at itself breeds trouble!

How much different the true spirit of Christianity manifested by a farmer in Denmark who, when his own house and the entire section surrounding him was threatened by fire, first rushed next door to take care of his sick neighbor because he knew the man relied upon him. At the hazard of his life he entered the flames, gathered the invalid into his arms, and rushed to a place of safety. While he did this his own possessions burned. He was, however, rewarded by his government with a special gift which made up for all of his losses. What is more, he saved a life and built a reputation. So, too, there is not a believer, who for Christ's sake has unselfishly given up things for others, who will not receive a special reward at the Judgment Seat.

Remember, friend, selfishness is a terrible tyrant. Wherever it reigns it blights and ruins.   — H.G.B.

> Not as we take, but as we give,
> Not as we pray, but as we live —
> These are the things that make for peace,
> Both now and after time shall cease.
> —Anon.

"Extreme self-love has often blinded even the wisest." — VILLEFRE

BREAKING GROUND

READ ISAIAH 28:24-29

> . . . *Break up your fallow ground, and sow not among thorns.*
> Jeremiah 4:3

My dictionary defines "fallow ground" as follows: "ground which is plowed but not seeded; untilled and neglected." The prophet likens Israel to a field freshly plowed and then left neglected and idle, not cultivated or tilled and consequently barren. In Hosea 10:12 Jehovah says, "Sow to yourselves in righteousness, reap in mercy, break up your fallow ground: for it is time to seek the *Lord*." We make the application to the Christian, who, after being saved and "plowed," goes no farther but allows the soil to grow up in weeds and thistles. How long have you been saved? How is the crop progressing? Is there growth and promise of a harvest? Or is your life at a standstill spiritually? The Lord expects fruit from your life. It may be that God is cutting deep into the soil of your soul but it is only because He wants fruit. And so He sends tribulation, testing, and chastening to break up the neglected clods and chunks in your life.

As the farmer breaks the hard clods in the spring, putting the points of the plow deep into the earth and then letting the sharp teeth of the harrow and the drag dig into the soil, the clay might well cry in pain and wonder at it all; but the farmer knows what he is doing, and so he keeps on digging and breaking. The deeper the plow works and the oftener the sharp harrow is pulled across the face of the land, the more precious the crop of fruit will be when the harvest time comes. God's plow goes deep, but only that the fruit may be more abundant, that in the end we may forget the plowing and rejoice in the blessing of bearing much fruit for Him.

If you have not already done so, will you take time to read the Scripture for today. Be a fruitful field and your reward is sure!
— M.R.D.

When my harvest days are past,
 Shall I hear Him say at last,
"Welcome, toiler, I've prepared for thee a place"?
 Shall I bring Him golden sheaves,
Ripened fruit, not faded leaves,
 When I see the blessed Saviour face to face?
 —N. A. McAulay

"The seed you nurture determines the crop; it is not enough for the gardener to love flowers: he must also hate weeds."

CONFESSING OUR FAULTS

READ JAMES 5:11-16

Confess your faults one to another.   James 5:16

The Bible is clear that we are to *confess our sins to God,* and *our faults to one another!* A mark of true spirituality and restored fellowship is always demonstrated by those who are willing to admit their offenses, acknowledge where they have slipped from the way, and ask other saints to pray for them in their struggle against the world, the flesh, and the Devil. Missteps in our spiritual walk which are known to other Christians may also have to be acknowledged before the church, for public sins are to be publicly confessed. On the other hand, our private sins are not to be aired before the world; for this would only bring undue reproach upon our testimony and the name of Christ. Therefore, secret sins are to be privately confessed to God alone.

Frederick the Great once humbly confessed, "I have just lost a great battle, and *it was entirely my own fault!*" Sir Roger Bacon, in more trying circumstances, said: "I do plainly and ingenuously confess that *I am guilty of corruption, and so renounce all defense;* I beseech you all to be merciful to me as a broken reed."

Oh, to be able to say, "I was wrong — I have sinned — pray for me," instead of trying to brazen out our mistakes and gloss over our failures. How much better husbands and wives would get along if they would just acknowledge their faults one to another! Honest confession is not only good for the soul, but it awakens Christian compassion in others and produces the fragrant flower of wholehearted forgiveness.   — H.G.B.

> 'Tis hard for anyone to say
>   That failure's due to him,
> That he has lost the fight or way
>   Because his light burned dim.
> It takes a man, aside to throw
>   The vanity that's strong,
> Confessing, " 'Twas my fault, I know,
>   I'm sorry; I was wrong!"
>   —Anon.

"It requires moral courage, Christian maturity, and spiritual strength to show others our weaknesses."

NOTHING IS FREE — EXCEPT

READ ECCLESIASTES 11:7-10

*For the wages of sin is death; but the [free] gift of God
is eternal life . . . .* Romans 6:23

It was an embarrassing moment. A young mother, in modern
slacks and painted up like a new barn, rolled her cart of
groceries up to the checker, while holding her baby in her arm.
After the checker had added up the load of "luxuries" she said,
"Fourteen dollars and thirty-eight cents, please." The young
shopper fumbled in her purse amid a maze of compacts, lip-
sticks, mirrors, combs and other nondescript articles, but was
able to produce only about $8.50. What should she do? Could
she have credit? Only if she could be identified. But they had
just moved into town and didn't know anyone. Sorry — those
groceries are not free. Only one thing to do — put some of those
unnecessaries back on the shelf.

You can get what you want, if you pay for it. There is a price
attached to everything we receive *except* the Gospel. That is
free! Sin costs something; everything temporal and material costs
something. There is a reckoning coming. It is like the woman
in the super market. She took her wire cart and filled it with
cans of fruit and meats, cheese, bread, pies, frozen foods, eggs,
hamburger, spaghetti, and beans. But wait a minute! She can't
take it out without paying for it. The "checker" is waiting for
the $14.38.

If you have not received Christ as Saviour, you owe an eternal
debt which you cannot pay. If you *have* taken Christ as Saviour,
you have a credit card for all past debt and enough to admit you
by free grace into Heaven. You may refuse God's gift and take
what you want in the "super market of the world," but remember, you will have to face the divine "Checker" at the end of the
line. Your own poor works will never pay the bill. Only Christ's
blood is sufficient for that! — M.R.D.

Grace there is my every debt to pay,
Blood to wash my every stain away,
Power to keep me spotless day by day,
Peace He gives, which shall forever stay.
—Anon.

**"Let 'Deserved' be written on the door of Hell, but on the door of
Heaven 'The Free Gift'!"**

HIDDEN WISDOM

READ PSALM 25:10-14

The secret of the Lord is with them that fear him.
Psalm 25:14

Although the Lord Jesus openly taught people so that He could truthfully say, *"In secret have I said nothing"* (John 18:20), yet He often did speak words in parables and utter deep spiritual truths which the unbelieving, due to their darkened understanding, could not properly comprehend. So today unbelievers may scan God's Word in vain with little or no perception of its meaning, for the things of God are "spiritually discerned." Divine truth is hidden from the wise and the prudent, and revealed to "babes in Christ" whose eyes have been opened by the Holy Spirit. Blessings temporal and spiritual are reserved for the pious who enjoy intimate communion with God. They alone can know the secret things of His will. This truth is evidently set forth in the Word. Proverbs 3:32 tells us ". . . his *secret* is with the righteous." In John 7:17 we read, "If any man will do his will, he shall know of the doctrine, whether it be of God." In I Corinthians 2:7 Paul tells us that our legacy is to know the *"hidden wisdom."* The deep things of God are reserved for the consecrated, for Hosea tells us, "Then shall we *know*, if we follow on to know the Lord" (Hosea 6:3).

"How do you know you are a Christian?" asked a workman of another. "Mate," he replied, "how do I know I have sugar in my tea? I have tasted it, and therefore I can tell you there is sweetness in it, even though it is not discernible to your eye. *So, too, I have tasted and seen that the Lord is good* (Ps. 34:8)!"

The more intimately you know the Lord and His Word, the more the "secret of His will" and the secret of "rightly dividing" His Word will be your joyous reward.   — H.G.B.

I've been drinking at His fountain,
There I ever would abide
For I've tasted life's pure river,
And my soul is satisfied.

—Anon.

"The hidden things of God are not revealed until we are treading the path of obedience."

THE WOLVES AND THE DOGS

READ GALATIANS 6:1-9

> *But if ye bite and devour one another, take heed that*
> *ye be not consumed one of another.* Galatians 5:15

John says, "If a man say, I love God, and hateth his brother, he is a liar" (I John 4:20). These are arresting and startling words indeed. Who are the "brethren" I am to love? Are they only those who belong to my little sect or church or communion? Ah, no! Every born-again child of God is a brother, no matter where or how he worships. Are you interested only in your own church, your own denomination, or does your love reach out to all of God's people? How dishonoring to God is all this bickering and fighting among those who claim to belong to Christ. We may be as orthodox as the Devil, but if it makes us narrow, bigoted, and exclusive, it is but a shallow profession.

Melanchthon the reformer, and contemporary with Luther, already mourned in his day over the many divisions among the reformers, and wrote a striking parable in an effort to bring the groups together. He said, "There was war between the wolves and the dogs. The wolves sent out a spy to see how best to defeat the dogs. Returning, the spy said, 'If we just leave them alone they will defeat themselves. There are so many different kinds of dogs, one can hardly count them, and as for the worst of them, they are mostly little dogs, who do a lot of barking but cannot bite. However, this I did observe and I could clearly see, that while they all hated us wolves, yet each dog suspected every other, and were constantly fighting each other.' The wolf was right. The dogs defeated themselves."

Remember, we are not commanded to always agree, but we *must love.* — M.R.D.

> Partakers all of that One Bread,
>   Of the One Body too;
> Yet, though by the One Spirit led,
>   WE CANNOT EAT WITH YOU! —
> God save from this "sectarian sin"
>   In all we say and do!
>
> —S. Levermore

"Too many Christians are snapping at other Christians, when they had better save their teeth for the wolves." — M. R. D.

THE MEEK

READ PSALM 149:1-4

The meek shall eat and be satisfied: they shall praise the Lord that seek him: your heart shall live for ever.
Psalm 22:26

A little boy was once asked, "Who are the meek?" He thought for a moment and then replied, "The meek are *those who give soft answers to rough questions!*" His definition was not complete, but he had caught the spirit of what constitutes true humility.

Perhaps we might more accurately define the "meek" as those who in conscientious humility and reverential fear turn to God, seeking only His mercy and grace.

The Scripture gives seven beautiful promises for those who are thus minded. We are told that the meek shall be:

1. Beautified with salvation (Ps. 149:4);
2. Guided by God (Ps. 25:9);
3. Taught of the Lord (Ps. 25:9);
4. Lifted up (Ps. 147:6);
5. Supremely satisfied (Ps. 22:26);
6. Inherit the earth (Ps. 37:11; Matt. 5:5); and
7. Greatly treasured by the Lord (I Pet. 3:4).

Some years ago *Moody Monthly* published an account of one who had heard "Lucky Baldwin" pray. "Lucky" — whose real name was Christopher Balfe — had been redeemed from a life of deep sin, and therefore recognized that God's grace was the only thing in him that was worthy. It was reported that he said in his prayer, "O Lord, I was nothin', and I am nothin'; and *nothin' from nothin' leaves nothin'*, so I know *Christ in me must be everything!*" Is this your attitude? Then you may expect the reward of the meek!　　　　　　　　　　　　　　 — H.G.B.

> Just and good the Lord abides,
> He His way will sinners show,
> He the meek and just doth guide,
> Making them His way to know.
> —Anon.

"Humility is the Christian's loveliest virtue and his crowning grace."

FIRST LOST – THEN FOUND

READ ROMANS 1:18-32

For the Son of man is come to seek and to save that which was lost. Luke 19:10

Until a man is lost he cannot be found. Christ died for sinners, and one must first be a sinner before he can be saved. One would suppose that Jesus would call unto Himself "good" people. But then he would not have come to this world, for when He came unto this world there were no "good" people in it. All were sinners, all were lost, all were under condemnation. David says about all of us, "They are *all* gone aside, they are *all* together become filthy: there is *none* that doeth good, *no, not one*" (Ps. 14:3). Have you ever seen yourself as a lost sinner?

The great George Whitefield had a wayward brother who one night heard the evangelist preach and came under deep conviction. Meeting with some friends for lunch after the service, he burst out in tears, and unable to eat or drink cried out, "I am a lost man." A Christian lady at the table replied, "What did you say, Mr. Whitefield?" "I said I am a lost man!" "I am so glad of that," replied the lady, "I am so glad you are lost!" Amazed and surprised, the miserable Whitefield cried, "How can you be so cruel, so heartless to say you are glad I'm lost?" But she replied, "Yes, I'm so happy you are lost, I'm happy about it for the Bible says, 'The Son of man is come to save that which was lost' " (Matt. 18:11). With tears streaming down his cheeks he saw the light and cried out, "Then He came to save me – for I am that lost one." And then and there he received Christ and was saved. An hour later he was dead – but not until after he had been *found.*

If you have never done so – then take your place as a sinner *now* – and trust Christ to save you. — M.R.D.

> I was lost, but Jesus found me,
>   Found the sheep that went astray,
> Threw His loving arms around me,
>   Drew me back into His way.
>
> —F. H. Rowley

"The password which alone can unlock the 'treasure house of grace' and make one a candidate for salvation is the heartfelt cry: I have sinned!" — G. W.

THINGS WHICH ARE LITTLE

READ: JAMES 3:1-5

> *. . . things which are little.*   Proverbs 30:24

A group of men were carrying on a friendly conversation. One of the men remarked that he had learned not to pay much attention to little things. "Little things," he said, "don't bother me." One of the other men smiled. "Are you sure?" he asked. "Would you believe that a little thing, just a pair of socks I wore once, changed the course of my entire life?" "I can hardly believe that," was the reply. "It is true though," continued the man. "It happened this way. One day I expected to take a trip with some of my friends on a canal boat. Two days before we intended to leave, I was chopping wood. The ax I was using slipped and injured my foot. The blue dye in the homemade socks I wore poisoned the wound, and I was compelled to stay at home, while my friends went on the trip. While they were on their journey, a powerful preacher came to our town to hold some meetings. Since I didn't have anything else to do, I decided to attend. The message the preacher brought touched me deeply. He spoke to my heart. As a result of it, I surrendered to the Lord. Truly converted, I saw that my life needed a real change. New desires and purposes took hold of me. I determined to seek an education that would enable me to live more usefully for my Lord." *The man who told the story was the former president of the United States — James A. Garfield!*

Little things often have far-reaching consequences. On the one hand, we should beware of coddling "little sins," for often they grow into great tragedies; on the other, we should not neglect little duties and small kindnesses that await our attention on the road of life, for by tending them with care we will find many jewels of true reward sparkling our future.

Big things are obvious; it is the little things that often cause us to stumble.   — H.G.B.

> God sees the little sparrow fall,
> It meets His tender view;
> If God so watches little things,
> I know He loves me too.
> — M. Staub

"Most of the critical things in life which become the turning points in human destiny are little things" — R. SMITH

SMOOTH PREACHING

READ: II TIMOTHY 4:1-8

> *. . . speak unto us smooth things . . . .*   Isaiah 30:10

The faithful preacher of the Gospel is never universally popular. While some will love him for his faithfulness, great numbers will hate him for his unwillingness to compromise. In the days of Isaiah, the Lord pronounced judgment because the people refused the warnings of doom, for they wanted the prophets to bring messages which would not condemn their sins. They said, ". . . speak unto us smooth things, prophesy deceits."

People often believe that a good sermon should make folk feel comfortable and at ease. On the contrary, however, a real good Bible sermon is one which first of all disturbs, irritates, awakens, causes dissatisfaction and unrest. Before anyone can find comfort in Christ, he must first of all be made to feel his failures and shortcomings. There are three steps in the process of conviction. First the sinner becomes mad, then he becomes sad, and, finally, he becomes glad when he confesses his sin and turns to Christ.

What kind of a sermon did your preacher give you last Sunday? Was it one that made you feel satisfied with yourself? If it did, you better hear someone else next Sunday. But if the sermon awakened in you a consciousness of your unworthiness, then thank God for him.

A man described under three heads a certain sermon he had heard. He said it was a moving, soothing, and satisfying message. It was very *moving* for half the audience left before it was one-half over. It was very *soothing* because most of those who remained fell fast asleep; and it was highly *satisfying* since everyone declared that they had had enough of that kind of preaching. The Word of God is a sword (Heb. 4:12); a knife (Acts 5:33); a fire (Jer. 23:29); a hammer (Jer. 23:29); and a lamp (Ps. 119:105). The Word is a *two-edged sword*. It wounds to heal, it kills to make alive.   — M.R.D.

No Book so abounding in wonderful truth,
  No Guide so unerring for age and for youth,
No counsel so needed by man in his bloom,
  No comfort so sweet on the verge of the tomb.
So taught by the Bible revealing God's plan,
  We live by the Bible — God's message to man!
                    — F. E. Belden

"The Bible is not merely a book — it is a living power . . . surpassing all others." — NAPOLEON

MINISTERING TO CHRIST

READ: COLOSSIANS 1:18-25

. . . for his body's sake, which is the church.
Colossians 1:24

Many of us have often wished that like Joanna, Susanna, Mary Magdalene, and others (see Matt. 27:55 and Mk. 15:41), we might have had the privilege of personally ministering to the Saviour. We imagine how we would have lavished our alabaster boxes of precious things upon Him in heartfelt gratitude for His self-sacrificing love. Yet has it ever occurred to you that still today we can minister to Christ? Yes, it is true; for Scripture makes it very clear that when we help and bless others who belong to His mystical body, our Lord regards the service as having been actually rendered unto Him! Our Lord is extremely tender and sensitive to all that touches His own — in all their afflictions, He is afflicted (Isa. 63:9). When Saul was persecuting the Christians, Jesus stopped him on the Damascus road and made it very clear that all that he had perpetrated against the saints had actually been directed against Him, for He said, "Saul, Saul, why persecutest thou *me?*"

There was once a quiet little man, a vendor of fruits and vegetables, who regularly passed the door of a Christian. One day he dropped a small notebook. The Christian retrieved it and was about to return it when his eye was caught by the words on the first page. The inscription read, "For His Body's Sake, Which Is the Church." Then came notations like these: "The following were absent from Bible school last Sunday; be sure to visit them." "Ask about the sick baby." "Leave fruit for the blind lady." "Speak a word of cheer to the old crippled man." The humble fruit peddler took the book modestly from the hand of the Christian. "You see," he said, "this is my book of reminders." Pointing to the first page he continued, "This is my motive, my reason for doing these things, *'For His body's sake, which is the church.'* It keeps my soul out of the dust; for *as I do these things for His children, I know I am ministering unto Him."* — H.G.B.

> The cry of the sad and the sorrowing hear,
>   Toil faithfully on.
> A woe you may lighten and banish a tear,
>   Or brighten a life that is lonely and drear,
> There is many a heart you may comfort and cheer,
>   For Jesus toil on! — E. A. Hoffman

"The way to do great things for Christ is to do little things for His children."

THE SILENT WINDMILL

READ: ACTS 2:1-21

The wind bloweth where it listeth.   John 3:8

This verse could also be translated, "The Spirit breatheth where He chooseth," for the same word is used in the original for both "wind" and "Spirit." The Hebrew word for both wind and Spirit is *ruach,* and its use is governed by the context. The same is true of the Greek word, *pneuma,* which is either translated wind or Spirit, as the setting might indicate.

There are, however, two kinds of wind: man-produced and Heaven-produced. In the same way we must distinguish between the spirit or soul of man and the Spirit of God. In our King James translation the difference is often indicated by the use of a small "s" when referring to man's spirit and a capital "S" when applied to the Spirit of God or Holy Spirit.

Only the Spirit of God can give power and it is given to the believer as a sovereign gift of grace. It cannot be produced by man's efforts, feelings, or emotions. Much of "spirit" manifestation is not of the Holy Spirit at all, but only an emotional, worked-up evidence of the flesh. The difference can be determined by the result. The Holy Spirit produces power; the flesh produces only confusion. The wind must turn the windmill, for the windmill cannot produce the wind.

"Dey jeeted me on der windmill," complained Adolf. "I buy der windmill and set it up on my farm and it don't work. I don't pay for it; it ain't goot. I sit by him one whole day and it make no wind at all." "Maybe there was no wind, Adolf," said a friend. "Of course there was no wind! Would I buy a windmill to make wind when there was wind?" Foolish, you say? Yes, indeed, but no more silly than to live a Christian life by our own efforts without the power of the Holy Spirit.

The power of the Spirit comes through the Word. Don't neglect it.   — M.R.D.

> Breathe on me breath of God,
> Until my heart is pure,
> Until with Thee I will one will,
> To do and to endure.
> — E. Hatch

"Like the Scriptures, 'living epistles' too must be God-breathed and energized."

A PERFECT WAY

READ: PSALM 18:25-32

It is God that . . . maketh my way perfect. Psalm 18:32

There is a familiar story of a man who went into a famous tapestry establishment in Paris to watch the skilled laborers perform their work of art. They had their hands filled with threads of almost every color, and were weaving them into what seemed to him a rather ugly fabric of patchwork. When an opportune moment came he said to one of the directors of the project, "I do not see any beauty in that piece of work at all." "No," said the other, "it is not very attractive now, but return in a month and see it after it is finished; then you will change your mind." At the time appointed the man went back to view the piece of tapestry, but once again he was sorely disappointed at the jumble of colors. He shook his head and said, "I am still unable to see any beauty in it." The chief weaver took his arm and directed him to the other side of the room — how wonderful the beauty which now met his eye! What skillful and artistic mingling of the colors — what an exquisite design. The visitor could find no words to express his admiration and delight. He understood then that the tapestry is woven from the wrong side, and one who does not know what the weaver is doing sees only the tangled, snarled ends and oftentimes no meaningful symmetry or line.

So, too, all of us are on the loom of life, but if we have given ourselves over into the hands of the Master Weaver, we may be sure that His pattern of grace will be marvelously contrived. Here we may see only the tangled strands of trial and the knotted ends of disappointment, seemingly arranged without proper skill or meaning. However, when the weaving of our life has ended, we shall be allowed to view it from the Glory Side; then with eternal perspective we shall discover that the fabric of our existence was full of design and purpose. Indeed, with the psalmist we will exclaim: He *"maketh my way perfect."* — H.G.B.

No matter if the way be sometimes dark,
No matter though the cost be ofttimes great,
He knoweth how I best shall reach the mark,
The way that leads to Him must needs be straight.
— Anon.

"Let God control the shuttle and your life will prove to be a divine tapestry."

THE HEAVENLY WITNESS

READ: PSALM 19:1-7

The heavens declare the glory of God . . . .   Psalm 19:1

What will God do with the heathen who die without ever hearing the Gospel? This is a question often asked by men, and it is a good question. We may be sure that, whatever God's dealing with them will be, it will be in absolute truth and righteousness. They will be judged on the basis of the light they have had and have rejected. God reveals Himself in three ways: 1) By the testimony of creation (Ps. 19:1); 2) Through man's conscience (Rom. 2:14, 15), and finally, 3) Through the revelation of the Son of God in the Bible. All men have the light of the first two of these — the witness of creation, and the witness of conscience. But millions have never heard the message of the "Word." God will judge these, *not* by their rejection of the Word, but by their rejection of the revelation of creation and conscience. They will be without excuse (Rom. 1:20). The degree of man's judgment will depend upon the degree of light which he has had. It will be infinitely more tolerable in the day of judgment for the pagan savage who has never heard the Gospel than for those who have been born and raised under the sound of the Gospel and then rejected it. If a person is to be lost, it were better to go to Hell without ever having heard the Gospel. Judgment will be on the basis of light received and rejected (Matt. 11:24).

All men have a degree of light, and it cannot be put out. An infidel was arguing with a simple Christian peasant. Said the infidel, "We are going to wipe Christianity from the earth, disprove every statement of the Bible, tear down every church, chapel, and mission hall, destroy the last copy of the Bible until there will be nothing left on earth to remind people of a God." The simple Christian had an answer. He pointed to the sky above with its countless stars, and said, "How are you going to get rid of those?" As long as there is a creature — it will witness to a Creator.   — M.R.D.

> The spacious heavens declare
> The glory of our God,
> The firmament displays
> His handiwork abroad.
> — Anon.

"I cannot conceive how a man could look up into the heavens and still say that there is no God." — A. LINCOLN

LOVE FOR CHRIST

READ: I PETER 1:1-8

Whom having not seen, ye love.   I Peter 1:8

Little Emily looked up into the face of her father who was an unbeliever and asked in her sweet childish way, "Papa, do you love Jesus?" "Jesus died, my dear, long, long ago. He was crucified, and that was the end of him." "But Jesus rose again, and did what no other man could do. If Jesus is not living now, we would not be living either, because He gives us life and everything else, doesn't He, papa?" said the child who had learned her Sunday school lessons well. "Perhaps that is true, but how can I love someone whom I have never seen? Tell me that, my dear!" Emily at first did not know what to say, and her father looked secretly pleased to know that he had finally silenced her. At length, however, she said, "Papa, how old was I when mama died?" "Only about six months, my child." "Then I can't say that I ever saw her, for I don't remember her at all. But you have always tried to make me love her by telling me how good and kind she was. I do love her, too, although I have never seen her that I can remember." By this time the hot tears were running down the father's cheeks. Kissing little Emily, he said, "God has spoken to me by you, my dear, and now you must pray for me, and ask God to give me a new heart with which I shall love Jesus as you do." The Holy Spirit having done His work, the father's prayer was soon answered.

If you love Christ, friend, your life and action will show it; for one cannot truly love without giving!

Jesus has placed His special benediction upon those who believe and love Him, even though they have never seen Him with their physical eyes. To every Christian of this dispensation Jesus directs these gracious words of His favor, *"Blessed are (ye) . . . that have not seen, and yet have believed!"* (John 20:29).

— H.G.B.

> I love Him, I love Him,
>   Because He first loved me,
> And purchased my salvation
>   On Calv'ry's tree.
> — Anon.

"Faith honors God, and God honors faith!" (See Rom. 4:3).

WINDBAGS

READ: MATTHEW 23:1-12

. . . their mouth speaketh great swelling words. Jude 16

Jude is talking about religious windbags who claim they are full of the Spirit, but really are only full of "hot air." Beware of the man who piously boasts about his own achievements and holiness. That man will bear close watching. The mark of true holiness is a deep consciousness of our own shortcomings and unworthiness. The nearer we draw to the Light, the more the defects in our own life will be revealed.

God said concerning the patriarch Job that "there is none like him in the earth, a perfect and an upright man, one that feareth God, and escheweth evil" (Job 1:8). Yet when Job stood before the holiness of God he declared, "I have heard of thee with the hearing of the ear but now mine eye seeth thee. Wherefore I abhor myself and repent in dust and ashes."

Are you discouraged with your own lack of spirituality and the slow progress in your Christian life? Then remember, this may be a very healthy sign of your growth in grace. There is nothing so displeasing to God as a self-satisfied and complacent person.

The Pharisee boasted of his own goodness and said, "I thank thee, O God, that I am not like other men." His bragging was a stench to God. But the poor publican, beating upon his breast, cried, "God be merciful to me a sinner." When a person is filled with the Spirit he will be humble, but when he is filled with "wind," he will be proud and "blow" about his own deeds.

Today let us talk about what Jesus did for us, and not what we have done for Him. You can tell whether a man is full of the Spirit or full of wind by the person he talks about — Jesus or himself! — M.R.D.

A careless word may kindle strife;
An evil work may wreck a life;
A bitter work may hate instill;
Oh, make thy words fulfill His will.
— Anon.

"Great swelling words, like bubbles, have little substance, being filled with the spiritual emptiness of the evil heart from which they proceed."
— G.W.

NEEDED: DILIGENT LABORERS

READ: I THESSALONIANS 4:9-12

Not slothful in business.   Romans 12:11

When I was young we lived next door to a kindly old gentleman who worked with but average speed, yet with skillful precision and earnest diligence. As a boy of twelve I stood watching him one day when he turned to me and said, "Perhaps you, like some of the other neighbors, think I am spending a great deal of time on this particular project; but I have learned long ago that speed should always be secondary to quality workmanship. Remember this, my boy: years from now when I am gone and people view what I am building today, no one will ask, *'How long did it take him?'* but many will probably inquire, *'Who did it?'* It is well to recognize early in life the value of doing your best at all times!" There is not much else I remember about this man, but I have never forgotten the lesson he taught. Christians especially are to be diligent in their labors, performing all their duties as "unto the Lord." There is never an excuse for any of us to be "slothful in business." Men now may little mark our deeds, and often we may go unappreciated despite our most earnest and consecrated efforts, yet we must constantly keep in mind the thought that our real Master is Christ who ever demands our best. He will certainly reward the diligent.

Someone has said, "There are those who patiently climb the hills of life doing their duty with only God knowing the heroic quality of their work, but God keeps a blessed 'Book of Remembrance' and will someday open it. Then every faithful workman who labored conscientiously to obtain the praise of Heaven will receive a crown!"

Even though you may not have accomplished great things, it is comforting to know that a life of simple consecration always leaves a trace of imperishable beauty and worth on everything it touches.   — H.G.B.

Grant me, O Lord, the strength today
For every task which comes my way.
Grant me to live this one day through
Up to the best that I can do,
Through Jesus Christ our Lord, Amen!
— Anon.

"Not great deeds alone, but the smallest, the most obscure, write their record in fadeless lines." — J. R. MILLER

September 3

THAT'S ME

READ: MATTHEW 18:1-10

> *. . . Except ye . . . become as little children, ye shall not enter into the kingdom of heaven.* Matthew 18:3

A little child is the Bible example of faith and trust in God. A child knows no fear while in mother's arms. It is frank and honest in its requests, knows no hypocrisy, and makes no pretenses. And Jesus says the sinner must come like a little child in absolute confidence and trust that God will keep His Word.

Spurgeon tells the following incident: "Sitting down in the orphanage grounds upon one of the seats, I was talking with one of our brother trustees, when a little fellow about eight years of age left the other boys who were playing around us, and came deliberately up to us. He opened fire upon us thus, 'Please, Mr. Spurgeon, I want to come and sit down on that seat between you two gentlemen.' 'Come along, Bob, and tell us what you want.' 'Please, Mr. Spurgeon, suppose there was a little boy who had no father, who lived in an orphanage with a lot of other little boys who had no fathers, and suppose those little boys had mothers and aunts who comed once a month and brought them apples and oranges and give them pennies, and suppose this little boy had no mother and no aunts and so nobody never came to bring him nice things; don't you think somebody ought to give him a penny? Cause, Mr. Spurgeon, that's me!'"

Bobbie got his penny, of course, for such a frank appeal could hardly be denied. His simple confession, "Nobody never comes to bring me nice things," brought the results. When he said, "That's me," it was sufficient.

Have you ever, as a poor lost sinner deserving to go to Hell, come to Him and told Him, "That's me"? Then you have experienced the truth of His own words, "Him that cometh unto me I will in no wise cast out." And then the wealth of Heaven became yours!

— M.R.D.

> Suffer a sinner whose heart overflows,
>   Loving his Saviour to tell what he knows;
> Once more to tell it would I embrace —
>   I'm only a sinner saved by grace!
> — James Gray

"Proud intellectualism is the Devil's most dignified detour to Hell."
I. HONCY

TEST YOUR LOVE!

READ: SONG OF SOLOMON 7:10-13

I am my beloved's and his desire is toward me.
Song of Solomon 7:10

Someone has called attention to the three stages of love, set forth in the Song of Solomon, as follows: "At first the ruling thought of the soul is 'My beloved is mine, and I am his' (Song of Sol. 2:16). At this stage we think chiefly of Christ as ours, and so in some way only for *our pleasure.* Next we come to 'I am my beloved's and my beloved is mine' (6:3). *His ownership and possession* take the first place in our thoughts. At last we come to 'I am my beloved's and his desire is toward me' (7:10). Here the word 'mine' is dropped altogether in the perfect assurance of love that *to be His involves all!*" To what stage has your love for Christ developed? Do you still love Him selfishly only for His gifts to you; or do you adore Him for Himself — for His sweet Person and presence?

After a mission meeting I remember taking home, in the company of several other people, a lady who had recently been converted. We found to our surprise that she lived in a shack at the edge of the county dump. She smiled as she saw our dismay. "This is where I lived before Christ found me, and I am too poor to move," she said. "I used to complain, but now I can eat my simple meal and think of the heavenly treasures that are mine. I do not find it difficult now to live here; in fact I often exclaim with joy and gratitude, *All this, and Jesus Christ too!*" We marveled that one so young in the faith was already so far along on the pathway of sanctification.

Test your spiritual temperature. Is your love fervent and vibrant, or is it of a lukewarm, sickly variety — actually only a "self-love" that makes you seek after God? How much time do you spend in prayer adoring the Saviour and praising Him? How much in just asking Him for added favors? Oh, how all of us need to pray with the hymnwriter, "Kindle a flame of sacred love in these cold hearts of ours!"
— H.G.B.

Once it was the blessing, now it is the Lord;
Once it was the feeling, now it is His Word;
Once His gifts I wanted, now the Giver own!
Once I sought for healing, now Himself alone!
— A. B. Simpson

"The greater our love for God, the louder will be our notes of praise and adoration."

GOD'S DEVELOPER

And not only so, but we glory in tribulations also.

Romans 5:3

It takes a telescopic faith to be able to say "we glory in tribulations." One must be able to look ahead and visualize the end purposes of trials and tribulations, and rest in the promise of Romans 8:28. Every one of our trials and testings is known to God, is permitted by God, and has a purpose in the development of our Christian character.

Many of you own a camera. They are made so simple today that one needs to know nothing about photography to take good pictures. Just snapping the picture is easy enough, but to *develop* the film takes a knowledge of photography. A film is a piece of material covered with chemicals which are exceedingly sensitive to light. When the light falls upon this film, there is no visible change, yet the picture is there. It only needs to be developed. It is taken into a darkroom and immersed in a liquid containing certain chemicals which dissolve parts of the coating of the film exposed to the light. The negative is placed in this solution and the dish tilted from side to side, washing and rewashing the face of the plate or film until gradually the image is revealed. This we call "developing the plate." The picture was there all the time but it needed to be developed.

Trials and testings are God's "developers" of Christian character. There are gifts and graces and virtues which are never developed except in the darkroom of God's school of affliction. Some of you today are in God's darkroom, while He passes you through test after test of developing solution, while bringing out a beauty in you, which will be its own explanation and God's answer to the question, "Why must I suffer so?" He wants to bring out in you the image of Him whose likeness you bear.

— M.R.D.

Then know He giveth strength to help us in our weakness;
    He doth not test beyond what we can bear;
But with the testing doth provide, beloved;
    A way that leads into His love and care.
— Mrs. W. H. Jones

"Little furnaces are for little faith. The greatest compliment God can pay us is to heat the furnace to the utmost."

EVERLASTING REMEMBRANCE

READ: MALACHI 3:16-18

> *. . . the righteous shall be in everlasting remembrance.*
>
> Psalm 112:6

All of us like to be remembered! Some men, like the Pharaohs of old, build pyramids to perpetuate their memory; others, like Nebuchadnezzar, design "Hanging Gardens"; while still others do exploits of historical renown or create things of exceptional beauty to call attention to their name. But all earthly glory will sooner or later fade into nothingness; for "the world passeth away, and the lust thereof." The Bible tells us that the wonders which men have created to perpetuate their name will someday be consumed in a great, end-time explosion when God obliterates the old creation and makes room for His new world-order (II Pet. 3:7-13)! Temporal fame, like the painted wings of a butterfly, may be lovely to look at today, but it will be gone tomorrow! By contrast, "He that doeth the will of God *abideth forever*" and shall *"shine as the stars"* (I John 2:17; Dan. 12:3). We are told that the "name of the wicked shall rot" (Prov. 10:7), but that the righteous shall be in *"everlasting remembrance!"*

Dr. Alexander Whyte asked a friend who had been subject to unusual persecution how he was able to endure it. "Oh," he replied, "I always live with the Judgment Seat of Christ and eternity in view and that makes it easier to bear!"

A veteran Methodist preacher on the way to church was hailed by a scoffer who sought to question his motives for serving the Lord. "Well, John," said the infidel, "I suppose you are going to minister because you will get *half a crown today for your sermon.*" *"Nay, nay,"* replied the other promptly, "I'm going because I want to *get a whole crown by-and-by!"*

Faithful servants of God may go unnoticed here, but someday they will receive a "crown of glory which fadeth not away!"

— H.G.B.

The world may not praise you or notice your walk,
Yea, few here may care when you die;
But Jesus will mark all your labors of love,
For you there'll be fame — by-and-by!
— H.G.B.

**"The world may little notice us, but the Word in Isaiah stands fast:
'Yet will I not forget thee' (Isa. 49:15)."**

TELL SOMEBODY TODAY

READ: PSALM 105:1-7

Let the redeemed of the Lord say so. . . .   Psalm 107:2

There are two ways one can sin with the tongue. The first is well known and recognized by all. It is by "speaking." The use of the tongue for gossip, slander, idle talk, cursing, smutty and suggestive talk is sin. No one will deny this. Our daily prayer should be with David in Psalm 39:1: "I will take heed to my ways, that I sin not with my tongue."

There is, however, another sin of the tongue which is ignored by too many of God's people. It is keeping silent when we ought to speak. It is not usually considered a sin, yet Ezekiel the prophet warns against this in no uncertain words (Ezekiel 3:18, 19). If your neighbor's house were afire and you failed to sound an alarm, it would be an inexcusable act. Then why keep silent when those about you are facing eternal fire?

Two businessmen lived side by side in a suburb. One was a professing Christian, the other an unbeliever. They both worked in the city and rode the same train to work each morning. Several years were thus spent in pleasant, neighborly association, talking about business, current events, sports, and social activities. And then the unbeliever took desperately ill. His wife, a professing Christian, became concerned and said, "John, you are very sick. Would you let me call a good Christian to talk to you about your soul?" He slowly shook his head and said, "No, there is nothing they can offer. My neighbor, Mr. So-and-So, is supposed to be a good Christian, and we have ridden many miles together, but he has never once recommended his possession to me. If his religion is not worth talking about, it cannot be worth dying by." And thus he died — lost because of a Christian's silence. Oh, that we might realize that unless we tell it, there is no way they will hear it. "Let the redeemed of the Lord say so."   — M.R.D.

> Say, why are you so silent
> About salvation's plan?
> Why don't you speak for Jesus,
> And speak out like a man?
> — Anon.

"Speak out for the Lord; remember silence isn't always GOLDEN; on occasions it may be just plain YELLOW!"

September 8

BURDENS OR WINGS?

READ: PSALM 55:16-23

For every man shall bear his own burden. Galatians 6:5

There is an ancient legend about the creation of the birds which is very interesting. It tells us that when God made these feathery creatures, He gave them sweet voices and colorful plumage, but did not provide them with equipment for flying. The story goes on that God then laid some beautiful wings on the ground and said to the birds, "Take these burdens and bear them." The birds replied, "Burdens? Oh, how dreadful! Still, Lord, at Thy word we will carry them as bravely and cheerfully as we can." So, although they dreaded to do so, they took them up courageously. Then something wonderful happened! The burdens began to grow and attach themselves to their bodies. The birds stretched them out and suddenly found that by them they were enabled to fly. What God had called burdens were really *wings,* without which they would never have been able to soar gracefully into the clear, blue heavens. The story is pure fiction, but it does teach a worthwhile lesson: *Our burdens, too, can be turned into wings that will bring us spiritual blessing!* If we take them to our hearts with liberal amounts of grace, they will always bear us nearer to God and Heaven.

In life there are burdens of physical pain — heart sorrows — and soul distresses, that others cannot bear for us, much as they may want to help us. There are trials and certain weights of woe that we alone must carry. Although these burdens at times may seem unbearable, we may be sure that the Lord will never give us more than we can carry. Surprisingly, they will become lighter as we ascend the heights of sanctification. In the end we will find His yoke "easy" and His burden "light" (Matt. 11:30).

While our personal burdens cannot be shifted to the shoulders of others, they can be *cast upon the Lord.* He does not promise that He will completely remove them, but He does assure us that He will "sustain" and give grace sufficient for our need! — H.G.B.

Have you taken it to Jesus?
'Tis the only place to go
If you want the burden lifted
And a solace for your woe.
— Mrs. E. L. Hennessay

"God tells us to burden Him with what burdens us." (See Ps. 55:22 and I Pet. 5:7.)

THE DEVIL'S FIRST QUESTION

READ: GENESIS 3:1-20

> *. . . Yea, hath God said?* Genesis 3:1

This is the first question mark in the Bible or in all history. It was asked by the Devil, and he has been asking it ever since. His favorite attack is always to cast doubt upon the Word of God. He insinuated that God was very unjust and cruel by denying to His creatures the blessings of the garden. Of course, the Devil "misquoted" the Word of God. He altered it just a little, but that little was fatal. He quoted God as saying, "Ye shall not eat of *every* tree of the garden." God had said nothing of the sort. God had said, "Of *every* tree of the garden thou mayest freely eat" (Gen. 2:16). This was exactly the opposite of Satan's statement. There was only one exception — the tree of the knowledge of good and evil.

Think of the foolishness of Satan's question. If Adam and Eve had been prohibited from eating of *EVERY* tree, how then could they live? They were not permitted to eat *FLESH*, only fruit and vegetables (Gen. 2:16).

If Satan were correct in his quotation of God's Word, it meant that Adam and Eve were doomed to die of starvation. What a cruel suggestion. What a diabolical twisting of the Word of God. The first attack of Satan is to create in man's heart "doubt" concerning the Word of God. Satan is the author of doubt — God is the author of faith. Therefore, doubt is of the Devil — faith is of God.

Are you troubled with doubts? Doubts about God, the Bible, and your salvation? You can only find the cure for those doubts in God's Word. God is true — the Devil is a liar (John 8:44). Peace of heart and mind depends upon the answer to one question: "Whom do you believe: the Devil's lie, or God's Word?" Meet your doubts today by using the weapon of our Saviour Himself, "It is written!" "The Lord redeemeth the soul of his servants: and none of them that trust in him shall be desolate" (Ps. 34:22). —M.R.D.

> If aught should tempt my soul to stray
> From heavenly wisdom's narrow way,
> Still He, who felt temptation's pow'r,
> Shall guard me in that dangerous hour.
> — R. Grant

"Implicit faith in the Word of God is the only anchor that will hold amid the storms of doubt." — G.W.

"THE TUNEFUL CITY"

READ: REVELATION 5:1-10

Sing, O heavens; and be joyful, O earth.   Isaiah 49:13

The Lord loves singing. Lucifer was made with built-in pipes and tabrets that he might fill the courts of heaven with his melodies. When God created the earth and the star-studded universe, He gave each one of these "revolving jewels of matter" a note, which they still sound in beautiful symphony, so that the poet speaks in truth and delight of the "singing spheres." When from time to time in the Bible the curtain is pulled back, and we get a glimpse of Glory, we see great companies of saints and angels praising and adoring God in song. Dear Fanny Crosby who from a singing heart wrote over five thousand devotional pieces of music including, "Praise Him! Praise Him!" "Jesus Is Tenderly Calling," "I Am Thine, O Lord," "Blessed Assurance," and "All the Way My Saviour Leads Me," always referred to Heaven as the "Tuneful City" — and how right she was!

When we are born again and the song of the Lord begins in our hearts, it is no wonder that our lips too desire to frame melodies of praise and adoration to Him who has "washed us from our sins in His own blood." One has but to listen to the doleful, unhappy chant of the benighted heathen to recognize that only God can tune the heart to joy and singing. Someone has well said, "Christianity came into the world on wings of song. Infidelity never sings. Unbelief has no comforting music, no anthems, no hymns, no oratorios, no symphonies. When Robert Ingersoll died, the printed notice of his funeral said, *'There will be no singing.'*" Only when one is a Christian can he say with his final breath, as did Susanna Wesley, "Children, when I am gone, sing a hymn of praise to God!"

With radio, television, and a hundred other things occupying so much of our attention, singing, even in the Christian home, seems to have become a lost art. Remedy that situation in your family circle by blending your voices now in a hymn of joy and adoration! Let the world know you are on the way to the *"Tuneful City."*   —H.G.B.

> I have a song that Jesus gave me
> It was sent from Heav'n above;
> There never was a sweeter melody
> 'Tis the melody of love.
> — E. M. Roth

"Praise is the dress of saints in Heaven; it is meet that they should fit it on below." — SPURGEON

WONDERS OF THE RADIO

READ: JOHN 5:19-27

*...the dead shall hear the voice of the Son of God:
and they that hear shall live.*   John 5:25

When Paul was saved on the road to Damascus he heard the voice of the Son of God, and believing it, he was saved (Acts 9:4). The men with Paul also heard the sound of the voice but did not understand it, hearing only "a" voice (Acts 9:7), but not *"the"* voice of *Him* (Acts 22:9). It is possible to hear the Word and yet not hear it as the voice of the Son of God. There are millions who have heard the Gospel, but never heard it in faith as the voice of God. Dr. Wm. Pettingill used to say, "For years and years I listened to the Word and then one day *I HEARD IT."* That is the force of *hearing* the Word. It is to recognize it as the voice of God and to obey it.

But hearing the voice of the Son of God also refers to His shout from the air at His second coming. When He comes He will "shout" (I Thess. 4:16). But only believers will *HEAR* it. The unsaved will hear nothing. Believers will at that shout be caught away to be with the Lord. How only believers can hear the shout is easy to understand in these days of radio. I sit in my home and listen to our program on the radio. The people next door don't hear a word of it, although they have their radio turned on. The same ether waves which carry the program into my room are also passing through their house, but they hear nothing of it. They are not tuned in on the right wave length. So will it be at the Rapture, when Jesus shouts from the air. Only those who are tuned in by the new birth to Station B-L-O-O-D will hear the call and rise to meet the Lord.

Are you tuned in on Heaven's wave length by faith in Jesus Christ? "They that hear shall live."   —M.R.D.

> Perhaps today shall sound the mystic summons,
>   The shout, the voice, the trump, not by all heard;
> And, from their scattered silent resting places,
>   The dead in Christ will rise to meet the Lord;
> While we, the ransomed living, in a moment
>   Shall be caught up — according to His Word!
>   — Anon.

"The worldly reformers look to the crowd; the believers — to the cloud!"

NO INTEREST

READ: II PETER 1:1-13

Yea, I think it meet ... to stir you up.   II Peter 1:13

An elderly lady was once leaving a missionary rally in the company of a young woman. One who was close enough to listen to their conversation was surprised to hear the young girl say rather flippantly, "I just can't get interested in missions!" "Well, dearie," said the sweet old lady, " 'tisn't to be expected you would — yet awhile. It's just like getting interest in a bank. You have to put in a little something first or you'll never have any! The more you put in, the more you'll get out of it. Try it, dearie, just *put in a little something and you're sure of the interest.*" The old lady's philosophy was simple, but true. If you lack interest in something, it is probably because you have put very little into it. You say you can find no pleasure in Bible study, but have you ever sat down with a concordance and the Scripture and cross-checked the proof text on a given subject? Have you ever read the book of Psalms until you came to some promise that comforted you, and then meditated and rested upon that choice blessing until your soul had drawn all the spiritual honey out of it and your heart overflowed with the sweet nectar of praise? Have you ever completely read a book of the Bible at one sitting so that you could get the entire sense of its message? If not, no wonder you have no interest!

You say you can stir up little enthusiasm for soul winning or personal work, but have you ever tried to speak to someone or really worked at handing out tracts? Have you ever volunteered to go to a jail service or spent time visiting the needy? If not, it's no wonder you have "no interest."   —H.G.B.

> "Lost interest," Oh Lord, can it be?
>   Lost interest in souls who are calling for Thee?
> Lost interest? Oh, where would I be,
>   Yes — hopeless, had someone lost interest in me.
> Open my eyes, Lord, help me to see,
>   Lost interest in souls, means lost interest in Thee!
>   — Anon.

"Christian, are you cold and indifferent? Get busy for Christ and your zeal will soon be fanned to flame and produce shining results for God."

VERILY! VERILY!

READ: JOHN 3:1-12

. . . Verily, verily! John 3:3

Jesus used the word "verily" 101 times as recorded in the four gospels. He uses the two words, "Verily, verily," together 24 times in John alone, for a total of forty-eight times. In the original the word is *AMEN!* It is also translated: "So be it." It is a word of finality — it is Jesus' "last word." No more can be said. Jesus said Amen to His promises and that settles it.

A poor Scotchwoman in Glasgow who had attended some evangelistic meetings, resolved that she would rest her salvation on the words of the Lord Jesus as found in John 5:24. "Verily, verily, I say unto you, he that heareth my word, and believeth on him that sent me, hath everlasting life, and shall not come into condemnation; but is passed from death unto life." Major Whittle, the evangelist, wrote the words on a card, and gave it to her. She became very happy, so much so, her little boy was attracted by the joy of his mother, and asked what had happened. She told him the best way she could; the consequence was that he too was led to trust in the Saviour. But the next morning she felt very different. Despondency and doubt had taken the place of peace and joy. Her son noticed it at once, and asked her what was the matter. She replied: "I thought I was saved, but my feelings are all gone." "But," said the little fellow, "Mither, has the verse changed?" Quick as a flash he got the little card and read it, and looking up radiantly, replied: "Why no, Mither; it's just the same." And then he turned to the Bible, and read it there with great joy, shouting almost as he cried: "It's a' here, Mither, the verse is just the same!"

The unalterable Word of the living God is the only ground for assurance. The Word is the anchor to keep us steady amidst the storms of life (Heb. 6:18). It is the harbor light which shows us where the port of the Lord's protecting presence is (Phil. 2:16). It is the foundation upon which the believer can rest in safety (I Peter 1:23). Do not insult the Saviour by asking for more than His "Amen!" —M.R.D.

"Verily, verily, I say unto you,"
"Verily, verily," message ever new;
"He that believeth on the Son," 'tis true,
"Hath everlasting life."
— G.M.J.

"Jesus said it — I believe it — That settles it!"

THE DARKNESS OF HELL

READ: MATTHEW 22:1-13

. . . they shall never see light!   Psalm 49:19

There is a certain horror about absolute darkness that throws a chill over the human soul; for man was made to live in the light! Heaven is always depicted as a place of eternal brightness where there is "no night." The psalmist, however, declares that the wicked shall "never see light"; and Jesus warns that they shall be cast into *"outer darkness"!* What a horror of blackness that will be when each doomed soul is curtained off from every other in an eternity of utter loneliness.

Recently I was in a cave in Kentucky. When we had gone deep into the bowels of the earth through many winding passageways, the guide suddenly turned off all the lights and said, "I alone know the way out. If I were to leave you in this dark chamber, you would probably never make your way to the surface. Those who have been lost in this cavern have become *insane inside of a week* from the oppressive loneliness and the maddening, incessant drip of the water from the roof. Be quiet for a moment and *feel the darkness!"* I remember my youngster clutching my arm. Soon terror began to edge its way into all of our hearts. After about thirty seconds, someone in the party could endure the ordeal no longer and whimpered piteously, "Turn on the light! *I'm going crazy NOW!"* The guide laughed, but none of us will ever forget that eerie experience. I thought of the "outer darkness" of an eternal Hell and shuddered!

An evangelist once encountered a skeptic who, when asked to receive Christ, said, "I'm not afraid of Hell — all the *Hell* we get is here on earth! The preacher's reply was quick and devastating, "I'll give you three reasons why this cannot be Hell. First, I am a Christian, and there are *no Christians in Hell!* Secondly, there is a place just around the corner where you can slake your thirst, but there is *no water in Hell!* Thirdly, I have been preaching Christ to you, and there is *no Gospel in Hell!"* Friend, would you escape the eternal darkness of Hell? Receive Christ who is the Light!   —H.G.B.

> O do not let the Word depart,
>   Nor close thine eyes against the Light,
> Poor sinner, harden not your heart;
>   Escape God's wrath — be saved tonight!
>   — E. Reed

"Unbelief is the door to Hell!" — G.W.

TWO DOORS

READ: REVELATION 3:7-13

. . . I stand at the door, and knock . . . .   Revelation 3:20

. . . a door was opened in heaven.   Revelation 4:1

The third chapter of Revelation ends with a "closed" door, and Jesus on the outside knocking for admittance. The fourth chapter of Revelation begins with an "open" door and an invitation to "come up hither." The closed door is on earth — the open door is in Heaven. The second and third chapters of Revelation are the pre-written history of this Church Age — from Pentecost to the Rapture. It begins with Ephesus, the Church of the first century, and ends with Laodicea, the lukewarm Church of the last days. Just before the return of Jesus, the doors on earth are closing to Him. He is not now walking "amidst" the candlesticks (Rev. 1:13), but in Laodicea He is pushed outside. In thousands upon thousands of churches, Jesus has been crowded out by a social gospel, worldly amusements, liberal theology, and modernistic preaching. The blood is denied, the virgin birth of Christ and His atoning death and bodily resurrection are no more believed. It is a "church" in name, but in reality it is only a social center. Jesus is outside inviting individuals to let Him in. No wonder so many born-again believers feel so out of place in many a modern church.

But the doors are also closed in great parts of the world to all gospel preaching. Think of the millions behind the Iron Curtain, the Bamboo Curtain, and the ecclesiastical curtains in Spain and South America. But as these doors are closing, we may be sure the door in Heaven is about to open. We, like John, shall hear the voice "Come up hither," and in the twinkling of an eye be "caught up — to meet the Lord in the air." On every hand the increasing apostasy and the degeneracy of organized Christendom cries in no uncertain voice: "The Lord is at hand." —M.R.D.

> Let us, then, with such a hope
> Live as children of the day;
> Till the dawn of heav'n shall break,
> And the shadows flee away.
> — A. B. Simpson

"When the Church ceases to be IN TOUCH with another world, she is no longer A TORCH in this world!"

SHINING PATHWAY

READ: PROVERBS 4:11-18

But the path of the just is as the shining light, that shineth more and more unto the perfect day.
Proverbs 4:18

The upward course of the righteous is not always smooth. Often there are difficulties, winding ways of perplexity, and annoying obstacles of hard trial; yet it leads eventually to the invigorating heights of final victory in Christ! Often the ascent is so gradual, the path so circuitous that its celestial destiny is not obvious to the unenlightened eye. The zig-zag course is designed by God to break the force of the hill lest the ascent be too steep, too breath-taking, too difficult. By faith, however, we are certain that the path He chooses for us is ever onward and upward toward the noonday splendor of full blessing. He has promised that it shall end in "perfect day." Our Saviour, as He did at the wedding at Cana, reserves the "best wine" until the last!

Recently someone sent me a bulletin in which Rev. Kenneth Cober points out that the worldly man's broadway of carnal desire is "a dead-end street that terminates in frustration and despair. Lord Byron gave himself wholeheartedly to the pursuit of pleasure, but at the age of 35 he was writing —

My days are in the yellow leaf,
The flowers and fruits of love are gone,
The worm, the canker, and the grief
Are mine alone.

Compare the words of Lord Byron with those of Adam Clarke, a Christian saint and Biblical expositor. At 85 we hear him saying — 'I have passed through the springtime of life. I have withstood the heat of its summer. I have culled the fruits of its fall. I am even now enduring the rigors of its winter, but at no great distance, *I see the approach of a new, eternal springtime. Hallelujah!'"

Yes, the worldly avenue of pleasure is a dead-end street; but those of us who are on the narrow "shining pathway" know that it progresses toward God and will eventually terminate in a blaze of glory in His presence! —H.G.B.

So on we travel, hand in hand,
Bound for the heavenly Promised Land.
Always through all eternity,
I'll praise His Name for leading me!
— Anon.

"The Devil has no truly happy old people."

LEEKS

READ: NUMBERS 11:1-17

We remember . . . the leeks.   Numbers 11:5

Leeks, like onions, are mentioned only once in the entire Bible, and then only in association with the fruits of Egypt as contrasted to the heavenly manna. Leeks, together with the onions, melons, and cucumbers of Numbers 11:5, are symbolic of the works of the flesh and the old nature. When Moses delivered Israel, they went out of Egypt, but Egypt was not yet *OUT* of them. Egypt was still *IN* them, though they were no longer in Egypt. This is a picture of our salvation. When we are saved, we do not immediately lose our "old" nature, but instead we receive a "new" nature, which must ultimately overcome the old. The Bible nowhere teaches eradication of the old man in this life. Instead it teaches that every believer has two natures: the old, received by natural birth from father Adam, and the new, received in the new birth by the Spirit of God.

Hence there is the struggle for mastery between the two. Paul tells us "the flesh lusteth against the Spirit, and the Spirit against the flesh: and these are contrary the one to the other" (Gal. 5:17). Every true born-again believer is conscious of this struggle between the flesh and the Spirit — between the appetite for "leeks" and learning to feed upon the manna.

Someone has said, "A man is what he eats." This is surely true of the believer, for his entire spiritual development depends on his diet, even more than his exercise. Will you take a careful inventory and seriously examine your spiritual menu for today? How much time for the *word*, for *prayer*, for *witnessing*? That's manna for the soul. And then add up the time you spend in frivolous pursuits, idle talk, questionable entertainment. Study the long list of "leeks" to be avoided in Colossians 3:5-9: Uncleanness, covetousness, anger, wrath, malice, filthy communications, and lying. The nature you feed is the nature which will be victorious.   —M.R.D.

My soul, be on thy guard,
Ten thousand foes arise,
The hosts of sin are pressing hard
To draw thee from the skies.
— G. Heath

"Living for God involves dying to the world."

"FOR THIS CHILD I PRAYED!"

READ: II TIMOTHY 3:10-15

Train up a child in the way he should go: and when he is old, he will not depart from it. Proverbs 22:6

One cannot stress enough the vital importance of directing children to the Lord when they are still very young and impressionable. Satan seeks his prey early, and our children are only safe from his snares when their feet have prayerfully been guided to Him who said, "I am *the way!*" (see John 14:6.) Many heartaches can be prevented and much good accomplished by those who are Spirit-directed when life is still in the bud of its freshness and promise.

Isaac Watts was saved at about the age of nine. Through the medium of his hymns and the devoted use of his pen, millions have been lifted Heavenward. Jonathan Edwards whose clear testimony and dynamic preaching stirred all of New England for God, was converted when only seven. Henry Ward Beecher received his first important impressions of spiritual things from a consecrated Negro Christian when he was only five years old. The colored servant, whose name has been forgotten by all except the Lord, dealt with him earnestly concerning God's love for poor sinners. The impress of that humble life left an indelible mark on the soul of Beecher, and he in turn upon the people of his times. Matthew Henry was brought to Christ at the age of eleven, and it is not surprising that basking as he did for a lifetime in the blessings of grace, he was able to give the world his well-known commentaries on the Holy Scriptures. Time would fail us to mention Millet, the famous painter, Richard Baxter who wrote: *A Call to the Unconverted,* and thousands of others who were brought to the foot of the cross when their feet had scarcely strayed from the cradle of their childhood!

Are your children being instructed in the things of the Lord? Have you earnestly and individually dealt with them concerning the salvation of their soul? God grant that all of us who are parents shall be able to truthfully say with Hannah of old, *"For this child I prayed!"* — H.G.B.

Someone cried, "Where must this Seed be sown
To bring the most fruit when it is grown?"
The Master heard as He said and smiled,
"Go plant it for Me in the heart of a child!"
— Anon.

"I saw tomorrow look at me from the little children's eyes, and I thought how carefully we'd teach, if we were really wise!"

SAVED BY A HAIRBREADTH

READ: GENESIS 19:15-17, 23-25

. . . I am escaped with the skin of my teeth. Job 19:20

Job had a hairbreadth escape, for Satan was permitted to afflict him in everything short of actual death. Stories of hairbreadth escapes are always exciting and thrilling. See a lad curled up in a chair completely absorbed in a book, with his eyes sparkling and an eager, excited look on his face, and you may be reasonably sure he is engrossed in some exciting story of a hero escaping by "the skin of his teeth." Or listen to Grandpa over there surrounded by the children, all eagerly drinking in every word. It is "nine to one" that he is regaling them with some story of a narrow escape, some exciting experience of danger in which of course Grandpa emerges as the hero. People enjoy narrow escapes. Such expressions as "saved by the bell" and "escaped by a hair" are popular. That is one reason why the Bible is such exciting reading, for it is full of hairbreadth escapes. Think of Lot's escape from Sodom, Isaac's escape from the altar, Joseph's escape from the pit, Israel's escape from Egypt, Moses' escape from Pharaoh, Elijah from Jezebel's threats, David's escape from Saul, Jonah's escape from the fish, Daniel from the lions, Peter from drowning, and so we might go on and on.

If you are a Christian you have had the narrowest escape of all! You were on the way to Hell, without hope, and then just in the "nick of time" God saved you! If you are born again, you are an exception and not the rule. You are just one of a little minority among the millions of unsaved in the world. You got in by a "hair," for Peter says, "If the righteous *scarcely* be saved, where shall the ungodly and the sinner appear?" (I Peter 4:18). Oh, Christian, don't forget to praise Him today for your wonderful salvation. — M.R.D.

> If the righteous "scarce be saved"
> By the mighty Saviour's grace,
> How can sinners hope to stand,
> And alone God's judgment face?
> — G.W.

**"Good resolutions and reformation cannot save a soul; the price is the
life-blood of a Sinless One."**

THE PLAIN PATH

READ PSALM 27:7-14

Teach me thy way, O Lord, and lead me in a plain path.
Psalm 27:11

A convert in Africa was once heard to remark, "The trail is hard and tangled, but I am not afraid, for *there is a Man up ahead!*" Yes, our Saviour always goes before us for He is the Good Shepherd. He is ever out in front, smoothing out the to-morrows, but it is our duty to follow in His way. The plain path is not always the easy one, but it is the right one if He is leading.

The story is told of an old Scotch woman who tramped about selling goods from house to house. She was in the habit of tossing a stick into the air when she came to a crossroad and then taking the direction in which it pointed. One day she was observed tossing the stick several times. On being questioned, she said the road to the right looked so very dreary that she continued to toss the stick until it pointed to the left, for that seemed to her to be a much nicer way. How often we go to God for guidance in the same fashion. If His way seems dull we want to choose a brighter one, forgetting that He sees the end as well as the beginning. Only as we seek to know *His will* and earnestly follow in *His way* will we find our steps plainly directed and our life's journey lying along the highway of peace and blessing.

It is well for us to remember the words of Moody when he said, "Every hard duty which lies in your path that you would rather not do, that will cost you pain, or struggle, or sore effort to do, has a hidden sweet in it. Not to do it, at whatever cost, is to miss God's blessing. Every heavy load that you are called to lift hides in itself some strange secret of strength."

Study His Word, follow the Holy Spirit's leading, and you will find the plain path to be a highway of joy, but also a narrow way of holiness and self-denial.   — H.G.B.

"The road is too rough," I said:
"It is uphill all the way;
No flowers, but thorns instead;
And the skies are dark and grey."
But One took my hand at the entrance dim,
And sweet is the road that I walk with Him.
—Anon.

"When God directs our steps: the uplook is grand, the outlook is bright, and the future is glorious."

THE POWER OF THE SUN

READ PSALM 84:5-12

. . . the Sun of righteousness [shall] arise.   Malachi 4:2

Have you ever seen the sun rise on a foggy morning? Thousands spend their time in bed, when one of the grandest spectacles in all nature occurs — a sunrise. I remember some months ago I arose early to work in my garden, but found a dense fog over the the entire landscape, limiting my vision to only a few feet. It was so wet that work was out of the question. But my early rising was not in vain. Taking my position on a potato crate in the doorway of the barn facing east, I was to behold one of the grandest of all heavenly spectacles, the "sunrise." First, there was a lightening of the mist and a brightening of the fog. As the sun shed its light and warmth, the mist began to move. It resolved itself into clouds which began to move upward and at last the sun burst through in all its glory. The trees dripped with moisture and a thousand dew drops on the grass and shrubbery sparkled and danced with scintillating iridescence like so many diamonds as they welcomed the sun with its reflected light. I sat transfixed, forgetting all about the beans I had planned to pick. I saw in the sunrise my own experience. Once too I walked in a fog, lost and confused, until the Sun of Righteousness arose in my heart. First, a glimmer of hope, and then one day in a moment the light burst through and I saw *Him* who scattered all my doubts and fears.

Oh, that we today like the happy, sparkling dew drops may reflect His light and glory, glittering like the stars of heaven. Will men and women see Christ in us, as today "we walk in the light" and reflect the graces of Him who has left "us an example, that ye should follow his steps" (I Peter 2:21)?   — M.R.D.

> Sun of my soul, Thou Saviour dear,
>   It is not night if Thou be near;
> O may no earth-born cloud arise
>   To hide Thee from Thy servant's eyes.
> —C. Wesley

"Keep your light shining and God will put it where it will be seen."

DOES YOUR ROOF LEAK?

READ PSALM 66:8-16

When thou passest through the waters, I will be with thee; . . . they shall not overflow thee.   Isaiah 43:2

In an old book by Dr. Watson, written in 1696, I found this paragraph: "Sharp afflictions are to the soul as a soaking rain to the house. We know not that there are such holes in the roof, till the shower comes, and then we see it drop down here and there. Perhaps we did not know that there were such unmortified cuts in our soul, till the storm of afflictions came, then we found unbelief, impatience, and carnal fear dropping down in many places." How true it is that affliction tests us and proves what sort of Christians we are. If there are defects in our spiritual armor, they will show up best under the strain and pressure of trouble.

When the flood-gates of distress are opened and the trails come thick and fast, it is then we echo with understanding the words of the psalmist who exclaimed in his anxiety, "Save me, O God; for the waters are come in unto my soul" (Ps. 69:1). Yet we need not fear, for it is our loving Heavenly Father who holds the "waters in the hollow of His hand" and who metes them out in sufficient quantities to cleanse us — to indicate where our "spiritual roof" needs repairing — but never enough to overflow us or drown us.

Have you been passing through deep waters? Have you been disturbed, irritated, faithless, fearful, or rebellious? Realize then that God no doubt put you through this difficulty to reveal to you your spiritual needs. By prayer, faith, and yielding to the Holy Spirit, repair the "leaky roof of your testimony."   — H.G.B.

> Saviour, when Thy poor wayward child
> Droops faithlessly, 'midst doubt or ill,
> Thy voice shall calm the inward strife,
> And bid the aching heart be still.
> —F. Hastings

"There is nothing like the deep waters of trial to test our spiritual stature." — G. W.

DO YOU WANT TO BE A STAR?

READ EPHESIANS 2:1-6

*And they that be wise shall shine as the brightness of
the firmament; and they that turn many to righteousness
as the stars for ever and ever.*   Daniel 12:3

Would you like to be a star? We hear a great deal about
"stars" in this modern age — movie stars, football stars, baseball
stars, etc., etc. The highest ambition of many young people is to
become a star of some kind. But these stars all "burn out" in a
little while and their glamor is lost in the rising light of other
stars. But the Bible speaks of "stars" that will never grow dim
but will shine forever. Daniel says that "soul winners" are stars,
for "they that turn many to righteousness (shall shine) as the
stars forever." There is a familiar hymn, "Will There Be Any
Stars in My Crown?" We question the theology of the song, for
we ourselves will be stars in *His* crown.

Stars are first mentioned in the book of Genesis. It is said of
the stars, together with sun and moon, that "God set them in the
firmament of the heaven to give light upon the earth" (Gen.
1:17). What a wonderful picture of the believer. They are set
(seated) in Heaven, but they shine upon the earth. Two things
are stated; first our position — in Heaven, and then our sphere of
service — to shine upon the earth. The believer is seated in the
heavenlies with Christ (Eph. 2:6), but we are to give light on
the earth (Matt. 5:16).

Do you want to be a star forever? Then let your light shine
— witness to someone today, hand out the Word to some neighbor or fellow workman; pray for your own unsaved loved ones,
and be a "star" for your Lord.   — M.R.D.

We shall shine as the stars of the morning,
   With Jesus the crucified one;
We shall rise to be like Him forever,
   Eternally shine as the sun.
                              —J. W. V.

**"Those who light others to Christ in this world, will find their small
candle here turned into a shining star over there!"** — H. G. B.

PAYING THE PRICE

READ GALATIANS 6:7-14

*But God forbid that I should glory, save in the cross of
our Lord Jesus Christ, by whom the world is crucified
unto me, and I unto the world.*   Galatians 6:14

One cannot win a victory without self-denial and expensive
preparation; nor can one attain spiritual maturity without paying
the exacting price of full consecration.

The story is told of a woman who rushed up to Fritz Kreisler
after a concert and cried, "Oh, Mr. Kreisler, I would *give my
life* to play as you do!" The great violinist answered soberly,
"That's exactly what I did." The sacrifice had to be made of
time, effort, and the setting aside of selfish desires to attain the
heights of such human accomplishment. So too, in the spiritual
realm, if we would drink deeply of the water of life and find the
high plateau of perfect peace and spiritual attainment, we must
be willing to endure self-crucifixion.

Three crucifixions are in view in our text. First, the crucifixion
of *Christ.* In this Paul gloried as in nothing else. Secondly, we
have the *world* crucified. Its pleasures, honors, treasures, and anything that hinders us from full blessing must be rejected and
executed like a felon upon a gibbet. Finally, we see the believer
crucified, with *self* nailed to the tree. The first cross speaks of
the *basis* of our salvation, the second deals with the *result,* and
the third points to the *acme* of that salvation.

"I would *give the world to have your experience,*" said a
wealthy man to a devoted Christian lady. "That's just what it
cost me," she replied; "*I gave the world for it.*"

Can you truthfully say with her and Paul, "By whom the world
is crucified unto me"?   — H.G.B.

> Take the world, but give me Jesus,
> All its joys are but a name;
> But His love abideth ever,
> Through eternal years the same.
> —F. J. Crosby

**"Self-will must die, and Jesus has prepared a place for it to breathe
its last — at the cross."**

LENDING TO THE LORD

READ PROVERBS 19:1-7

*He that hath pity upon the poor lendeth unto the Lord;
and that which he hath given will he pay him again.*
Proverbs 19:17
. . . ye have the poor always with you. Matthew 26:11

Every believer has a responsibility to the poor who, because of circumstances or conditions, have been reduced to poverty. Solomon says, "He that giveth unto the poor shall not lack: but he that hideth his eyes shall have many a curse" (Prov. 28:27). Now these "poor" are not poor because of their own slothfulness or laziness. Solomon is very severe on all such (Prov. 12:27; Prov. 24:30-34; Prov. 26:14). But those who are poor because of misfortune, tragedy, sickness and disaster are a responsibility of all of us, and helping them will be surely rewarded.

A godly minister was accosted by a poor, ragged, hungry mendicant who begged for five dollars that he might finish his journey. Five dollars was all the minister had, and so he hesitated to give all to this poor man, until suddenly Proverbs came to his mind: "He that giveth unto the poor shall not lack." He gave the poor man all his money. Soon afterward a creditor demanded the preacher to pay him a debt of $5.00. He would call for it in the morning. The preacher resorted to prayer and said, "Lord, yesterday I lent the $5.00 and now I need it back again. In Thy Word Thou hast promised to repay me. I need it by tomorrow. Thank you Lord. Amen." That afternoon the postman brought a letter from an anonymous friend who wrote, "I am sending you $10.00 for blessings received." The letter being unsigned could not be acknowledged and so he could only thank *Him* to whom he had lent the money and received payment with 100 per cent interest. God will never remain "in debt" to anyone.

Are you willing to distribute? (I Tim. 6:18). — M.R.D.

"Giving is living," the angel said.
"Go feed the hungry sweet charity's bread."
"And must I keep giving and giving again?"
My selfish and querulous answer ran.
"Oh no," said the angel, his eyes pierced me through.
"Just give till the Master stops giving to you!"
—Anon.

**"Beware of the Christian with the open mouth and the closed
pocketbook."**

GOD'S KIND WILL

For whosoever shall do the will of God, the same is my brother, and my sister, and mother. Mark 3:35

We need never fear to resign ourselves completely to God's will. It is not only our duty, but a precious privilege that can bring us nothing but the greatest good. In addition, those who do the will of God experience a warm, personal relationship with Christ that is deeper and dearer than any human tie could ever hope to be. Jesus said of such that they become in a special sense His brother or sister or mother!

Many years ago the *Sunday School Times* carried this story: A lady who had an only child said to Mrs. Pearsall Smith, "I do not dare to pray — 'Thy will be done' — because I am afraid God will take away my little boy or will send me some heavy trials as a result of my yieldedness." To which Mrs. Smith replied, "Suppose your child should come to you and say, 'I want to be and do just what you desire today,' would you say to yourself, 'Now is my opportunity to make this child do all the disagreeable duties I want done; I will take advantage of his willingness to please me by cutting off his pleasures today, and will keep him at hard discipline'?" "No, no!" said the mother, "I would give him the best day I could possibly plan." *"And can you think that God is less just and loving than you?"* The lady saw the point, resigned herself to the Father's will, found the joy of the Holy Spirit's blessing, and experienced the preciousness of the promised intimate communion with the Saviour.

Trust God when you cannot *trace* Him; you will find that His will is always kind! — H.G.B.

> I cannot always trace the onward course
>   My bark must take,
> But looking backward, I behold afar
>   Its shining wake
> Illumined with God's light of love;
>   And so I onward go
> In perfect trust that He who holds
>   The helm, the course must know.
> —Anon.

" 'Thy will be done' is the keynote to which every prayer, and every life should be tuned."

STUNG BY A BEE

READ JOHN 11:47-52

*. . . it is expedient for us, that one man should die for
the people, and that the whole nation perish not.*
John 11:50

These words were spoken concerning Christ by Caiaphas, the
high priest. Even though Caiaphas may not have realized it, he
was speaking prophetically (verse 51). Jesus gave His life
(though innocent) that we, the guilty ones, might be saved.
Herein lies a great lesson, a marvelous example of an all-but-
forgotten truth. Jesus counted not His own well-being above
the welfare of others. He did not try to spare Himself at the expense of others who would suffer if He stood only upon His own
rights. Oh, that we would learn this lesson in our church life and
consider that the Church is bigger than any individual, its ministry far more important than our personal wishes, rights, and
desires. If we would only ask, when confronted with a situation
in the assembly, "How will my action affect the Church and the
program of Christ?" Instead, we feel we are right, and we are
going to insist on our position, even though it splits the church,
ruins our testimony, and stops the train of progress. How many
churches have been ruined and the faithful ministers driven to
despair because of some member or members insisting on having
"their way" instead of submitting themselves and their personal
opinions to the others for the good of the testimony.

Last summer I was picking beans near one of my beehives.
Some of the bees "spotted" me, and supposing me to be an enemy,
attacked me and drove me away, but in so doing two bees stung
me in my retreat (a bad place to be stung). Of course the bees
died in their defense of their hive. They had one thought only —
the safety of the others in the hive, and gladly gave their lives
for the good of the many. Instead of being angry, I admired
those bees and thought, "Oh, that Christians were like that, not
seeking their own comfort and safety, but living for the good of
others in the "body of Christ!"   — M.R.D.

> Love thyself last; and thou shalt grow in spirit
> To see, to hear, to know and understand.
> The blessing of the Lord, thou shalt receive it
> And all God's joys shall be at thy command.
> —Anon.

**"That man is of most use to the world who gives himself most freely
to God for God's use."**

LIVING THE BOOK

READ JOHN 8:21-31

But be ye doers of the word, and not hearers only, deceiving your own selves.   James 1:22

The Word of God is the "seed of truth" which requires clean soil if it is to thrive and be productive. The Holy Spirit must be allowed to purify our lives, to clean out the debris of malice and lust — to weed out besetting sins; then, in the soil of humble modesty and true dedication to Christ, the Word will take firm root and bring forth the delightful clusters of the "fruit of the Spirit." God wants us to walk in obedience to the faith that has been worked into our hearts, and to reflect to those about us the truths of His Word. Many are ready to hear, discuss, argue, and place into mental pigeonholes the great doctrines of the Bible, but this is mere "religion." It is all in vain, unless the truth is spiritually digested and translated into vital action that is discernible and effective in our everyday walk and conduct. Mere theological knowledge is not enough. We can only be sure that the truth has been received when it brings forth fruit.

A Brahmin is said to have written to a missionary: "We are finding you out. *You are not as good as your Book!* If your people were only as good as your Bible, you would conquer India for Christ in five years."

Indeed, the grace of God in our hearts should cause us to live "soberly, righteously, and godly in this present world" (Titus 2:12). How true it is that often:

> We are the only Bible the careless world will read,
> We are the sinner's Gospel, we are the scoffer's creed,
> We are the Lord's last message, given in deed or word;
> What if the type is crooked? What if the print is blurred?

If we who are Christians were only as good as our Book, what startling things would happen! No doubt it would be said of us as it was of the disciples of old, "These . . . have turned the world upside down" (Acts 17:6).   — H.G.B.

> May every voice be hushed in me,
> Except Thy living Word;
> Let every move be crushed in me,
> That does not own Thee Lord.
> —A. R. Wells

"It's good to be saved and KNOW IT; but it's better to be saved and SHOW IT."

PAINTING THE PUMP

READ JAMES 3:11-18

*. . . cleanse first that which is within the cup and platter,
that the outside of them may be clean also.*

Matthew 23:26

Jesus paints some ludicrous portraits of the pious, legalistic, religious, but unregenerate Pharisees of His day. He portrays them as straining out a gnat, and swallowing a camel. He compares them to a housewife who washes her dishes only on the outside. He says they are whitewashed sepulchers full of dead men's bones. It was an unmerciful exposé of their empty religion. These over-pious zealots were sticklers for doctrine and orthodoxy, but villains at heart. They thought they could justify their crookedness by being outwardly sanctimonious and religious. "Look out for these overly religious, pious talkers," Jesus seems to say. More skulduggery and dishonesty is covered up with pious prayers and religious cant than anything else. Religion fixes up the outside, but true regeneration begins on the inside.

In a broadcast some time ago, my son, Richard, used an illustration by Dwight L. Moody which was new to me. It goes like this: "A man bought a farm on which was an old pump. When the neighbors saw the new tenant pumping water, they rushed over and warned him the water was poisonous and unsafe for use. The former occupants — father, mother, and all the children — had died from drinking that poisoned water. The man thanked them kindly and then proceeded to remedy the situation. He mended the wooden platform over the well, put a new handle on the pump, fixed a crack in the spout, and then painted the whole works."

You smile at the folly of the man. Painting the pump was useless; what the man needed was a *new well.* The lesson is apparent. Jesus said to one of the finest, religious, honest, respected men of His day, "Ye must be born again."

Your pump looks fine, but *do you need a new well?*   — M.R.D.

> Oh! precious is the flow
> That makes me white as snow;
> NO OTHER FOUNT I KNOW,
> NOTHING BUT THE BLOOD OF JESUS!
> —R. Lowry

**"Christianity is not a new leaf — it's a new life; Salvation is not a
new start — it's a new heart!"**

ALWAYS ABOUNDING

R<small>EAD</small> I C<small>ORINTHIANS</small> 15:51-58

> . . . *always abounding in the work of the Lord, forasmuch as ye know that your labour is not in vain in the Lord.* I Corinthians 15:58

To "abound" in the work of the Lord one must do *more than his share!* The word actually *means to "go beyond the mark set."* Such effort, such zealous, unstinting labor will receive God's special commendation and an abundant "recompense of reward." Christians are therefore admonished by Paul to never be satisfied with just being average. The importance of being faithfully diligent at all times in our labors for Christ cannot be exaggerated.

Stephen Grellett was once asked to speak to some lumbermen in the backwoods of America. When he arrived he found only empty shanties, for the cutters had gone into the forest. However, when the hour arrived for him to preach he felt it his duty to do as he had originally agreed. Therefore, he faithfully stood and gave the message, hoping that someone would come back to camp in time to hear at least part of it; however, no one appeared. He left discouraged, considering his time wasted. Many years later, as he was walking across London bridge, a man stopped him and said, "I have found you at last!" "Pardon me, but I think you are mistaken, for I do not believe I know you," said Stephen Grellett. "That is true, but I know you, sir," said the first gentleman. "Did you not speak on a certain day at a certain place in the backwoods of America?" "Yes," said Grellett, "but no one came to listen." "Well, I was there! I had to return to the encampment to get some tools. I saw you through the trees and stood there and listened. When you finished preaching I was convicted of my sin and received Christ. Since then I have been telling men the blessed news of salvation. Over one thousand have professed Christ and three of them are now missionaries!" Stephen Grellett wept. He realized as never before that our faithful labors for the Lord are not in vain! — H.G.B.

> One little hour for weary toils and trials,
> Eternal years for calm and peaceful rest.
> One little hour for patient self-denials,
> Eternal years of life — where life is blessed.
> —Anon.

"He who attempts great things FOR GOD can expect great things FROM GOD."

THE GOD OF THE BEAUTIFUL

READ ISAIAH 33:13-17

He hath made every thing beautiful in his time.
Ecclesiastes 3:11

"What a beautiful God," exclaimed a new convert, as he gazed upon a sunset for the first time after his spiritual eyes were opened. God is indeed a God of beauty! Breath-taking is the beauty of the sunrise, the rainbow, the majestic mountains, the fertile fields, the delicate clouds, the stately trees, and the many, multicolored flowers. Just outside my study window is a flower garden, each of the blossoms containing a sermon, each petal a song, and all together producing a symphony of praise to God. Some flowers blossom unseen by human eyes. As the poet says,

"Many a flower is born to blush unseen
And *waste* its fragrance on the desert air."

But such blossoms are not unwanted, for they attract the insects and thereby pollinate their neighbors, thus preventing extinction of the species. Neither is their fragrance lost upon the desert air, for the honey bee, attracted by the perfume — that mysterious means of communication — flies for miles to gather a bit of its nectar. Then it carries its load of sweetness to the hive to provide for us during the winter months the honey given by the little flower unseen by human eyes. There is no waste in God's economy. There is a place for beauty in life, and unhappy is the man who sees only that in nature which can be turned into gold. God gives us eyes, not only to search out material things, but to see the "beauty of the Lord," even in nature.

Christians should be more than producing persons; they should be beautiful, fragrant, and attractive. Beauty is not absolutely necessary, for life could go on without it. Yes, we could *exist,* but we cannot *live without beauty.* Learn to appreciate the God of beauty today.   — M.R.D.

For the wonder of each hour
Of the day and of the night,
Hill and vale, and tree and flower,
Sun and moon, and stars of light,
Lord of all, to Thee we raise
This our hymn of grateful praise.
—F. S. Pierpoint

"The beauty seen, is partly in him who sees it." — BOVEE

TRUST

READ PSALM 56

Behold, God is my salvation; I will trust, and not be afraid.
Isaiah 12:2

Two Christian women were once talking together. One said to the other, "I have a comforting Scripture passage which helps me very much: 'What time I am afraid, I will trust in thee' (Ps. 56:3)." The other replied, "Yes, that is good when you are first starting off in the Christian life, but by-and-by when you have more faith and have experienced an increase in your sanctification you will find even a better text." "A better text?" said the first woman. "Yes, it is found in Isaiah 12:2, 'Behold, God is my salvation; *I will trust,* and *not be afraid'!*" How blessed to rest upon the promises of God right from the start so that you will not be afraid, rather than to wait until in desperation, at the end of your rope, you must trust in God because there is simply nothing else left for you to do.

A visitor was walking along the shores of the Dead Sea when he lost his balance and fell into the water. At that point it was rather deep and he was afraid because he could not swim. In desperation, lest he should sink and be drowned, he began to flail about frantically. At last, completely exhausted, he felt he could do no more. What a surprise! The water bore him up. You see, the Dead Sea is so heavy with salt and other minerals that if anyone lies still he can float easily upon its surface. He will not drown as long as he resigns himself to the power of the deep. It is the same with us. There is a Power beneath us and round about us to bear us up. If we would just cease from our flounderings, fears, and fruitless efforts and let the strong Everlasting Arms of God undergird us, we would know the safety and serenity of perfect trust!
— H.G.B.

Simply trusting ev'ry day,
Trusting through a stormy way;
Even when my faith is small,
Trusting Jesus, that is all!
—E. Page

"When God puts a burden upon you, He also puts His own arm under you."

THE GOD OF THE SHADOWS

READ II KINGS 20:1-11

> *. . . he brought the shadow ten degrees backward in the*
> *dial of Ahaz.*   II Kings 20:11

King Ahaz had invented a primitive watch. This earliest time-piece consisted of an upright shaft, and when the shadow of that shaft reached a certain point it was 9:00 A.M., and when it reached another point, it would be 3:00 P.M. This sundial was visible from the king's bedroom. Hezekiah was sick unto death but because of his prayer the Prophet Isaiah promised that the Lord would heal him and give him 15 years. But Hezekiah asked for a sign to assure him. The Lord gave him his choice of two signs. Would he want the shadow on the dial to hasten forward, or stop and go backward? He reasoned it would not be so wonderful for the sun to hasten down for it always goes down sooner or later, so he requested that the shadow retreat and go back toward the sunrise instead of to the sunset. Sure enough, the sun stopped and went back 10 degrees. The clock of time moved back 40 minutes and the fig poultice began to draw — the boil came to a head, and the king was healed while the shadow fell on the sundial of Ahaz.

Many are the lessons in this story, but one stands out prominently: God controls the shadows as well as the sunshine. We have no trouble in attributing the sunshine to God — but the shadows — ah, do we realize God also controls the shadows? We praise Him in the sunshine — but grumble and question *"why"* in the shadows. Anyone can be happy in sunshine, but oh, the shadows: shadow of sickness — shadow of depression — shadow of persecution — shadow of bereavement — shadow of death. Let the sundial of Ahaz proclaim God is in the shadow, for instead of pointing to the sunset and the night, it points joyously to the sunrise and the morning. Thank God for the shadows. It was God's sign to Hezekiah and His sign to us that "whom the Lord loveth he chasteneth" (Heb. 12:6).   — M.R.D.

> Soon thou'lt learn the "why" and "wherefore,"
> Although now thou can'st not know
> Why the storm and cloud are sent thee,
> Just because He loves thee so.
> —Mrs. M. E. Rae

"Weeping may endure for a night, but joy cometh in the morning"
(PS. 30:5).

MAKE CHRIST KING!

READ PHILIPPIANS 3:7-10

*. . . Thou shalt love the Lord thy God with all thy heart,
and with all thy soul, and with all thy strength, and with
all thy mind; and thy neighbour as thyself.*   Luke 10:27

It is said that in the Berlin art gallery there hangs a picture by
Menzel, which is only partially finished. It artistically pictures
Frederick the Great talking to his generals; however, there is a
bare patch in the center of the painting where just a charcoal
outline indicates the artist's intentions. He had painstakingly
sketched in oils all the generals and the background material, but
the king he had left until the last. Alas, poor Menzel died before
he had a chance to finish the picture. What a parable this is on
the life of many. They spend their time putting in all the "generals of insignificance," and the background material of "things,"
and leave the King until the last. Yes, how many Christians die
without putting Christ into the very center of their life and activity. Indeed, how many of us have truly crowned Him Lord, and
love Him with all of our heart, soul, strength, and mind? The
painting of your life will ever be incomplete without Him as its
Center. Don't put Him off until a more convenient season. Let
Him dominate your entire being, work, and thought — *today!*

If you really wish to crown Him Lord you must give Him:

1. Your *hands* (I Tim. 2:8);
2. Your *feet* (Isa. 52:7);
3. Your *eyes* (John 4:35);
4. Your *ears* (Mark 4:2-9);
5. Your *mouth* (Psalm 51:15), and
6. Your *heart* (I Kings 8:61).   — H.G.B.

> Poor is my best, and small;
> How could I dare divide?
> Surely my Lord shall have my all,
> He shall not be denied!
>   —Anon.

**"God has some wonderful things to display if He can only get the
showcases."**

JUMPING AT CONCLUSIONS

READ I SAMUEL 1:9-17

> *. . . How long wilt thou be drunken? put away thy wine from thee.*
> I Samuel 1:14

Hannah, the mother of Samuel, had gone to the house of God to pour out her heart to God for a son, for she was childless. She had vowed a vow that she would give the child to the Lord, completely dedicated to God. Eli, the indulgent, lazy priest, was sitting at the gate and watched Hannah as she entered the temple. He saw her move her lips, but she did not pray audibly, and Eli jumped at the conclusion that she was drunk. He severely rebukes her in the words of our Scripture (I Sam. 1:14). How inconsistent! Eli had failed as a father completely, and he was blind to the wickedness of his own two sons (I Sam. 3:13); but he was quick to judge others. He mistook a brokenhearted, praying woman for a drunkard.

What a lesson this ought to be for us — not to jump at hasty conclusions and judge our fellow Christians unless we know all the circumstances. There may be some facts which, if we knew them, would change our attitude from censure to sympathy. We may be blind to the motive. Balaam beat his ass because he misunderstood the dumb animal who had good reason for balking, and when Balaam saw the angel blocking the way, he must have been greatly embarrassed. Several weeks ago, I placed some extra honey boxes on one of my beehives, because they were crowded for room. One bee misunderstood my good intentions and, supposing me an enemy, promptly attacked me and stung me above my eye for my good deed. It was all a misunderstanding of my motive, but it cost the bee's life. We can excuse the dumb insect's mistake, for its motive too was good — protecting its hive — but she was all wrong.

Today don't judge others, but wait until all the facts are known — and then leave the judgment to God.   — M.R.D.

Oh be kind and understanding when you judge another's acts,
  For you may not know his problems, or be sure of all the facts.
Let the law of love control you, do not hastily decide;
  Breathe a prayer for those who stumble, lift the fallen —
  don't deride!

—G. W.

"Guard against the loss of spiritual power that comes through hasty words and judgments."

GOD'S LOVE AND OUR COMFORT

READ I JOHN 4:5-10

> . . . *God is love.*   I John 4:8

God is the great eternal Source of all warmth, concern, pity, and affection. The fact that love forms the very core of His personality assures us that He must display benevolence and goodness in all His actions. Even when sin came to separate man from his Maker, the Creator's prevailing affection resulted in God laying Himself out to the fullest extent and giving of Himself in the Person of Christ, that He might still continue to love us without violating His other attributes of righteousness and holiness. Our deepest understanding of the heart of God, therefore, is only realized when we view the cross. How it thrills our heart to know that He wanted to continue to embrace us, undesirable as we had become in our sin, *even if He must do so with nail-pierced hands and a riven side!* Such self-sacrificing, redeeming love certainly will send us now only what is best. In this assurance we rest content even in the storms of life, knowing that all must be working for our good in that it comes to us direct from His Father-hand.

A wealthy English gentleman had a beautiful weather vane atop his barn on which were inscribed the words, "God is Love." A servant, who was asked what was implied, said, "My master means that *whichever way the wind blows — God is Love!* He says it is not for Christians to judge when the wind is at its best, but that they must rest completely in this thought that all is well when God is in it." Some time later, death and affliction came to the home of this English gentleman, and his friends called to offer their condolences. Although he was overwhelmed in his sorrow, he pointed to his weathercock and said, "I put that text on it in my prosperity, when the desires of my heart were all being realized, and now, even though the icy winds of death and sorrow are blowing, I am confident His love for me is still the same!" His faith gave him grace to face the future with confidence.

God's love for us should ever be a soothing balm of comfort.

— H.G.B.

> Love divine has seen and counted
> Every tear it caused to fall,
> And the storm which love appointed,
> Is the choicest gift of all!
>
> —Anon.

**"If God numbers our hairs, will He not also number our tears?
Trust Him for His love!"**

HOME, SWEET HOME

READ EPHESIANS 6:1-9

> *. . . Come home with me, and refresh thyself.*
>
> I Kings 13:7

This invitation from the wicked king Jeroboam of Israel to a prophet and servant of the Lord was refused because Jeroboam's home was not a "place of refreshing," but one of sin, wickedness, and fearful judgment and death. The prophet, although forbidden to tarry in anyone's house, finally consented to come, and was consequently punished, being slain by a lion. But leaving the unhappy context, we want to ask the question: "To what kind of a home can you invite others? Is it a place of refreshing or depression?" There are some homes I dread to visit, and I seek every excuse possible when I am invited. It leaves me with a sense of having wasted my time. For although the home is beautiful and the furnishings ornate and costly, there is a spirit of unrest and dissatisfaction apparent. The conversation is critical and faultfinding — a long recital of complaints and ailments.

But how different are other homes I know. The house is just ordinary, the furniture old, the fare simple, but oh, how refreshing the atmosphere. Maybe the occupant is an invalid upon a bed, but her face radiates the Spirit of Christ, her conversation is about her blessings, and praise and thanksgiving characterize her attitude. Truly such a one can say without hypocrisy, "Come home with me, and refresh thyself."

Is your home one which is stimulating and uplifting? Thousands of folks have only a house, a place of shelter but know nothing about the meaning of the word *home.* Home should be a place of rest, peace, and relief from the evils of the outside world. No wonder Heaven is called a home and a "Father's House." We shall never be fully at rest until we go *Home.* On a tombstone in a small village is inscribed over the grave of a little girl: "But the dove found no rest for the sole of her foot, and she returned unto him into the ark" (Gen. 8:9). — M.R.D.

Oh think of years in childhood fair, at home, sweet home,
  Of mother's love and father's care, at home sweet home,
But think what home in heav'n will be
  When all our loving friends we'll see,
A paradise from sorrow free, in a better Home, sweet Home!
—W. Thompson

"Home is the sweetest type of heaven."

WHEN THE BREAD COMES BACK

READ PSALM 126

> *Cast thy bread upon the waters: for thou shalt find it*
> *after many days.*   Ecclesiastes 11:1

It is said that Ecclesiastes 11:1 may well be translated, "Cast your *seed* upon the waters." The thought is of a farmer in the land of Egypt who sowed his crop in the rich valleys of the Nile river. In the spring of the year the land was always flooded by the overflowing stream. When he scattered his seed upon these waters they were carried out over the field. When the liquid tide finally returned to the confines of the river, the seed settled down in the black loam that was left behind. Many days later a bountiful crop was reaped.

We too are sowers, and the Word of God is the precious Seed which we should be scattering (I Pet. 1:23).

It is said that Captain Fuchida, who led the attack on Pearl Harbor, was once full of personal hatred for all Americans. He has now, however, been led to a saving knowledge of the Lord Jesus Christ. What made him change from a destroyer of life to a Christian minister seeking now to rescue other lost souls? The story goes that a Japanese friend of his, who had been imprisoned in America, had been attended by a Christian nurse. When he found that her missionary parents had been beheaded by his people, he realized for the first time that the grace of Christ was something very real to make this young girl truly "love her enemies." By her earnest witness and the truths of the Gospel which she presented to him, he was gloriously saved. Later this Japanese was to a great extent instrumental in helping to lead Captain Fuchida to Christ; yet it was the Christian nurse who made the fruitful harvest possible by sowing the original "good seed." She shall receive part of the rewards when the sheaves are counted.

What kind of seed are you sowing? "As ye sow, so shall ye reap!"
                                                          — H.G.B.

> Someone sowed a tiny seed, long ago!
>   Someone whispered, "Lord, I plead, let it grow!"
> No one saw this seed resting 'neath the sod,
>   No one heard the silent prayer, only God.
> Where the seed was — now a tree lives and grows!
>   But the power the Word of God may be — no one knows!
>   —F. M. N.

"Go on sowing! Thou mayest not reaper be; yet with the reapers shall rejoice throughout eternity." — L. WRIGHT

COME AND GET IT!

READ PSALM 119:33-40

> *. . . I have esteemed the words of his mouth more than my necessary food.* Job 23:12

Hold everything! Wait a minute! Not so fast, brother, or you'll burn out a bearing before the day is over. Have you read our Scripture for today? Only eight short verses. It will take you only *forty-five seconds!* If you read it in less than that, go back and read it again, for you read it too fast the first time. No, No! don't lay this book down and mumble to me, "I'm in a hurry and you're delaying me." It is not my fault you overslept. I didn't keep you up late last night. Slow down, brother, slow down! I see you're eating breakfast this morning even though you are late. You take time to feed your body, but you were going to starve your soul. Take 45 seconds and read Psalm 119:33-40. Don't bother to read the rest of this devotional, but instead read the Bible. These articles are not designed to substitute for the Bible, but are meant to stimulate your desire to read more of the Bible. If this book has made you neglect the Word, so you read it instead of some verses of Scripture, then please, please, throw this book in the waste basket!

Still eating breakfast are you? Listen! you might better skip breakfast than skip reading the Word. Job says, "I have esteemed the words of his mouth *more than my necessary food.*" Man shall not live by bread alone. Yes, I know you had a rough day yesterday and everything went wrong and you're way behind. But why be surprised that yesterday was such a bad day, when you started the day without the Word? Remember, don't make the same mistake today. Look at Psalm 119:33-40 and make it your prayer today as follows: Verse 33 — Teach me; verse 34 — Give me; verse 35 — Make me; verse 36 — Incline me; verse 37 — Turn me; verse 38 — Stablish me; verse 39 — Spare me; and verse 40 — Quicken me.   — M.R.D.

> Slow me down, Lawd, I's a-goin' too fast,
>   I can't see my brother when he's walkin' past
> I miss a lot o' good things day by day,
>   I don't know a blessin' when it comes my way.
> Slow me down, Lawd, I's a-goin' too fast.
> > —Old Negro Spiritual

"Speed does not always spell progress; haste is often akin to waste."

"CORNERED"

READ PHILIPPIANS 1:18-24

> . . . *in a strait betwixt two, having a desire to depart,*
> *and to be with Christ; which is far better: Nevertheless*
> *to abide . . . is more needful.*   Philippians 1:23, 24

The Apostle Paul had once enjoyed a unique experience. Being caught up into the third heaven, he had tasted the indescribable bliss of Paradise and knew that it was gain and far better. He longed to return to those "many mansions," yet the urgent need of his converts here below tempered his yearning to "depart and to be with Christ." The expression Paul uses is picturesque. Literally he says, "I am *pressed in a corner* between two strong desires." It is not difficult to understand his problem, for in this life he had a thorn in the flesh, was languishing in a prison, and had the tremendous burden of all the new missionary churches resting upon his shoulders. Bearing in his earthly tabernacle the "marks of the Lord Jesus," he knew he would find blessed relief in the sinless bowers of Paradise. Yet Paul recognized that he must not selfishly seek to desert the duties which God had given him.

We often hear of those who because of illness or discouragement earnestly wish to "depart, and to be with Christ." However, the Lord has work for them to do — even though it may be only a silent witness from a white cot of pain — therefore, He leaves them here. If you are among those who are pressed into such a corner, remember the Apostle Paul, who was willing to remain here if it was for God's glory and the benefit of others.

On the other hand, there may be some who are clinging to life though they know death is near. To you Paul says in effect, "There is something far better beyond the horizon of time. You may soon be granted the joy of eternal gain — the glory of Christ's presence. Do not fear, for when you leave your cramped corner of pain, you will suddenly find yourself in the broad palaces of His eternal pleasures!"

Whatever your lot, keep trusting, knowing that to those who leave the choice with Him, God ever sends the best.   —H.G.B.

> Our times are in Thy hand;
>   Why should we doubt or fear?
> Our Father's hand will never cause
>   His child a needless tear.
> —Anon.

"Some things may come to us with rough wrappings, but there is gold inside."

BODY AND SOUL

READ I CORINTHIANS 6:9-20

> *. . . I keep under my body.*   I Corinthians 9:27

The body of a man without life differs in no wise from the earth from which he is taken. In Genesis we are told that God formed man "of the dust of the ground and breathed into his nostrils the breath of life and man became a living soul." Before God breathed into Adam, he was merely a lump of clay. It may have been fashioned in the shape of a man and all the organs may have been in place, but it was only clay.

Someone has broken down the chemical composition of the body of a 150 pound man, which among other elements contains about enough sulphur to rid a small dog of fleas, enough phosphorous for one match, enough calcium to whitewash a dog-house, fat enough for six bars of soap, enough sugar to sweeten 5 cups of coffee, iron enough for a ten-penny nail, nitrogen enough to blow up a house, and sufficient hydrogen to fill a ten-gallon pail of water. Total value of all the elements (before inflation): 98 cents.

But what a valuable structure the body becomes when life is imparted to it. It becomes the most versatile machine in the world. It can walk, talk, laugh, cry, sing, see, hear, think, and invent. It repairs itself without stopping, the air conditioning plant breathes 30 times a minute, the heating system keeps beating at 70-80 beats a minute for 60-70-80 years.

But still more astoundingly wonderful is the body when the Spirit of God comes to dwell in that person. Our bodies then become "temples of the Holy Spirit" (I Cor. 6:19). When we are saved our bodies become the members of Christ (I Cor. 6:15). How careful we should be to keep those temples clean. Our bodies belong to Him — take care of your body — for it is God's house.

— M.R.D.

> Oh, we never can know what the Lord will bestow
>   Of the blessings for which we have prayed,
> Till our body and soul He doth fully control,
>   And our all on the altar is laid.
> —E. A. Hoffman

"God wants more than your soul; He wants your body too!"
(See Romans 12:1, 2).

WORK AND THE CHRISTIAN

READ EPHESIANS 6:1-19

Not with eyeservice, as menpleasers; but as the servants of Christ, doing the will of God from the heart.
                                                          Ephesians 6:6

Man was created by God to be a worker. Already in Paradise he was charged with the care of the garden. *God has given us minds and bodies which can only be healthy and happy if they are occupied with fruitful labor!* It is true that toil has become more difficult due to sin, yet it is noble, and if performed as unto the Lord, brings a rich legacy of joy and satisfaction. Even the lowest type of service can be done with the highest possible motive; namely, that of glorifying God from the heart. Work done in this fashion transforms even the meanest drudgery into a glorious opportunity.

Christians are always to do their duty fully and carefully. They are not to be industrious only when the boss or overseer is looking, but must be faithful at all times, realizing that they operate under the very eye of the Lord Himself. Our labor is not to be done for the applause of men or merely for the joy of accomplishment, but must be carried on for the glory of God and for the blessing of mankind.

Before the days of Christ a sculptor was employed to erect a statue in one of the Grecian temples. He spent much time and labor in making it beautiful and ornate, *even the part which was to be against the wall.* On being asked why he carved the back part with the same pains as he did the front, he replied, "That is the way I always labor. Though men may not see it, *I believe the gods do!*" Although he was a pagan, he had caught something of the spirit of true, conscientious service.

Let us meditate on Paul's admonition to perform our daily tasks faithfully — "not with eyeservice, as menpleasers; but in singleness of heart, fearing God" (Col. 3:22).   — H.G.B.

> No service in itself is small;
>   None great, though earth it fill;
> But that is small that seeks its own,
>   And great that seeks God's will.
>   —Anon.

"Your work is an excellent commentary on your character; for as you ARE, so you LABOR!" — G. W.

SOAP AND SALVATION

READ MATTHEW 7:15-23

> *And why call ye me, Lord, Lord, and do not the things*
> *which I say?*   Luke 6:46

A strange paradox is evident in our country today; for while statistics show a marked increase in church membership and there is unquestionably a religious awakening in the land, statistics show an even greater increase in crime and wickedness. If the Gospel is the power of God unto salvation, this religious resurgence should evidence itself in its impact upon people's lives. A great increase of interest in religion, without a corresponding decrease in sin and wickedness just doesn't add up. Can it be that this religious fervor is only a pretext, caused by fear in this atomic age? A man sneeringly said, "The Gospel has lost its power, for while thousands profess Christ, nothing much is happening as a result." But it is not the fault of the Gospel. It is because people make a profession but have no possession. Coming forward, signing a card, joining a church — this is not salvation, but mere religious gesture. It is not enough to say, "Lord, Lord"; the Gospel must be practically applied, and not merely mentally endorsed. We fear that too many who say, "Lord, Lord," have never had His blood applied. It is not the fault of the Gospel.

A preacher and an unconverted manufacturer of soaps met on the street. Sneeringly the soapmaker said, "The Gospel you preach can't be very good for there are still a lot of wicked people." The preacher was silent until they passed a child making mud pies. The tot was smeared with dirt all over. Pointing to the little tot, the preacher said to his friend, "Soapy, your soap can't be very good, for there is still a lot of dirt in the world." "Oh well," said Soapy, "it cleanses only when actually applied." "Exactly!" said the preacher. The man was caught in his own trap.

What is your faith *doing in you* and *to you?*   — M.R.D.

> I've reckoned myself to be dead unto sin,
>   And risen with Christ, and now He lives within;
> The "life more abundant" He gives unto me,
>   This overflow life gives me full victory!
> —J. M. Kirk

"Christianity isn't worth a snap of your finger if it doesn't straighten out your character." — D. L. MOODY

MAHANAIM – THE ANGEL BANDS!

READ PSALM 34:1-7

> . . . *and the angels of God met him. And when Jacob saw them, he said, This is God's host: and he called the name of that place Mahanaim [or "Bands"].*
>
> Genesis 32:1, 2

Jacob, after many trials and a long absence, was finally homeward bound to Canaan. Twenty years before, as he had passed that same way going in the opposite direction, he had seen a wondrous vision of angels ascending and descending upon a heavenly ladder, and had been given some exceedingly great and precious promises. Now as he journeys he receives a new pledge of God's protecting presence and blessing as the angels again meet him and gather in a guardian band around him. He realizes that they have been especially sent to aid and defend him in his hour of coming crisis. What a thrill it must have been to his heart to know that God was still leading and encamping round about him with His protecting angelic hosts.

Alexander McLaren makes a practical application concerning this beautiful event in the life of Jacob as follows: "It is in the path where God has bade us walk that we shall find the angels round us. We may meet them, indeed, on paths of our own choosing, but it will then be the sort of angel that Balaam met, with a sword in his hand, mighty and beautiful, but wrathful too; and we had better not oppose him! But, the friendly helpers, the emissaries of God's love, the apostles of His grace, do not haunt the roads that we make for ourselves." In God's way, however, we can expect angelic protection.

Not only do the angels do service for us in this life, as they did for Jacob (Heb. 1:14), but they also bear our souls to Glory when our earthly sojourn here comes to an end (Luke 16:22). Christians, therefore, may well call the time of their death, *"Mahanaim"–for it is then in a special way that the angels of God meet them!*   —H.G.B.

> Angels, sing on! Your faithful watches keeping;
> Sing us sweet fragments of the songs above,
> Till morning's joy shall end the night of weeping,
> And life's long shadows break in cloudless love.
> — F. W. Faber

"Angels, the believer's friends, are everywhere depicted in the Word of God; indeed, we can as easily think of summer without flowers, as of the Bible without angels!"

WHAT TIME DID YOU GET UP?

READ MARK 16:1-8

> *. . . in the morning, then ye shall see the glory of the*
> *Lord.*   Exodus 16:7

Will you please tell me what time it is. My, oh my, is it that late already and you are just eating your breakfast? What time did you get up this morning? Yes, yes, I know you are late but why are you so late? You have missed the very best part of the day—the morning, when all is still and fresh and sweet, when the dew bejewels the grass and the birds sing their sweetest. I know you were sleepy, and it was hard to get up early, but why didn't you go to bed earlier last night? You sat up to watch a television show and this morning you missed the greatest show of all—the sunrise. You sat up to listen to the "can-can" and the "boop da doop" of modern music (??), and you missed the greatest orchestra in nature — the birds singing their chorus at dawn.

Really it doesn't make sense to stay awake so late by artificial light, that you have to spend three hours of glorious sunshine and daylight lying in bed in the morning. The morning is the best time of the day, when nature awakens refreshed, when your faculties are at their peak. It is the best time for meditation, for prayer, for communion with God. If you begin the day late, all the rest of the day you will be late.

Remember, the manna fell upon the dew *in the morning.* After the sun grew hot it melted. Morning is the time to sing (Ps. 59:16). Morning is the time to praise (Ps. 92:2). Morning is the time to pray (Mark 1:35). Morning is the time of resurrection and life (Mark 16:2).

What a mixed up world! We have become a flock of bats and owls, instead of larks and canaries. Tomorrow morning, try it — splash cold water in your face, take a deep breath of morning air, behold the majesty of the sunrise and then read a chapter of the Bible, lift your heart in praise and prayer. You'll feel better all day. ". . . in the morning . . . see the glory" (Ex. 16:7). In the morning take time for meditation.   —M.R.D.

> When morning gilds the skies,
> My heart awaking cries:
>   May Jesus Christ be praised!
> Alike at work and prayer,
> To Jesus I repair:
>   May Jesus Christ be praised!
>
>   —Anon.

"The early morning hath gold in its mouth!" — B. FRANKLIN

SHINING LIVES

READ MATTHEW 5:1-16

*Let your light so shine before men, that they may . . .
glorify your Father.* Matthew 5:16

Christ's followers are to let their light shine by their holy
walk and example. We are to consider each step of our pilgrim
journey carefully, realizing that the world is watching us. If we
live carelessly they may be inclined to "blaspheme that worthy
name" by which we are called, rather than to glorify our Father
which is in Heaven. One truly devout Christian can, by his
chaste conduct and consecrated living, exert more influence
upon the world than ten nominal church members who seek only
to impress sinners through cold, theological argumentation and
"holier-than-thou" condemnations.

C. H. Mackintosh pointedly reminds us that "Christianity is
. . . a newborn man following a living Christ, walking as He
walked, doing as He did; imitating His example. . . . It is keeping the eye fixed upon Jesus and . . . having His character im-
printed . . . and reproduced in our life and ways." Yea, our
prayer ought daily to be:

> Oh, touch my life that it may be
> Renewed with strength to live for thee;
> Oh, touch my being with a flame
> Till others seek Thy saving name!

One day Dwight L. Moody was conducting a testimony meeting. A certain man arose and delivered a particularly exuberant
account of his experience. "Hallelujah!" he shouted. "I've been
on the *mountaintop* for fifteen years!" Moody interrupted with,
"Brother, that's wonderful, but do you exhibit this joy and testimony in your daily living? Have you ever won a soul to Christ?"
The man's countenance fell; he turned crimson and stammered
an embarrassed, "No, sir, I'm afraid I haven't!" Then said Moody,
"That isn't the kind of mountaintop blessing we want in this
church, dear brother. We want those who will live their life in
the world and *go down into the valleys and win the lost ones
there to Jesus!*"

How bright does your light shine for Christ *in public?* —H.G.B.

> Say, is your lamp burning, my brother?
> I pray you look quickly and see;
> For if it were burning, then surely
> Some beams would fall brightly on me.
> —Anon.

**"Whether you are on an iron, brass, or golden candlestick is not so
important; just see to it that you SHINE!"**

GOOD FISHING

READ MARK 1:14-20

> *. . . Come ye after me, and I will make you to become*
> *fishers of men.* Mark 1:17

If you are a follower of Jesus, I imagine you are getting your tackle ready to do some fishing today. It should be very good fishing weather for the lake is full and they are ready to bite. I am referring to "men-fishing." I hope you will find opportunity to make a few casts for souls today. As I write this, I have just come in from a couple of hours on the lake. I brought in a nice string of fish. Some of the fish are evidently smarter than I am, but I did fool a few. I learned the following things—to catch fish you must:

1. *Go where the fish are.* They do not come to you as you sit on the porch.

2. *Keep your bait in the water* because you never know when a fish will come along.

3. *Keep your hooks sharp* to avoid losing the fish.

4. *Be sure to set the hook,* for they seldom hook themselves.

5. *It is easier to catch the little ones* than the big ones. The reason some grow so big is because they were never caught.

Apply these five rules to your spiritual fishing for souls today. 1. Don't wait for some soul to come to you, but you *go* and find them. 2. Have your bait always in the water. Have your Bible or New Testament ready with you everywhere you go. 3. Keep the hook sharp by prayer and appropriate memorized Scripture passages. 4. Set the hook—press for an immediate decision for Christ. 5. The easiest to catch are the little ones. Childhood and youth is the time to win folk for Christ. The big ones become too smart. Some sinners know "too much" to be saved. Good fishing, brother!—sister! —M.R.D.

> O'er all the world, the "seas of men" inviting,
> "Fishers of men" go forth to bring them in.
> Christians, awake! Your prayers and words uniting,
> Go spread the net, and rescue souls from sin.
> —G. W.

"Those who would be good 'soul winners' must remember that Jesus prefaced His invitation to be 'fishers of men' with the words, 'Come ye AFTER ME!' " — H. G. B.

LAYING DOWN THE "OLD INDIAN"

READ MATTHEW 16:21-27

> . . . *Except a corn of wheat fall into the ground and die, it abideth alone: but if it die, it bringeth forth much fruit. He that loveth his life shall lose it; and he that hateth his life in this world shall keep it unto life eternal.*   John 12:24, 25

A Christian can only be fruitful in the degree that he dies to self. Discipleship means crucifying the ego and putting Christ and others first.

Many years ago a young Indian lived alone, hunting and trapping in the mountains. His family had all been killed by the white hunters, and so he grew up by himself—wild, uncouth, and dirty. However, one day a white trapper, who was a Christian, came to the mountains to live. By his kindness and patience he got the now elderly savage to trust and love him. Then he began to teach the Indian about God and the Bible. Finally the red man came to appreciate more fully the meaning of the love and grace of the Lord Jesus Christ. The Christian saw that he was under conviction, and prayed for him most earnestly. One night soon after, the Indian, dressed in all his heathen finery, came to his friend's house, knelt at his feet, and prayed silently. The trapper was quite amazed but waited to see what all this would mean. When the red man arose, the trapper saw the light of Christ's forgiveness flooding his face and the joy of full dedication gleaming in his eye. The "original American" confessed Christ as his Saviour, and then, suiting action to the word, he said in his broken English, "Indian lay down blanket—Indian lay down pipe — Indian lay down tomahawk — *Indian lay down Indian!*" The poor savage had caught the vision. What Christ requires of us is not only a yielding of our soul to Him for salvation, but the yielding of our complete ego that He may give to us the "more abundant life."

Yes, you may be a Christian but *have you laid down "the old Indian"?*   —H.G.B.

> Oh, the peace of full surrender!
> All my joy to do His will!
> Mine to trust His faithful promise;
> His the promise to fulfill.
>   —Anon.

"The more we bury the old ego, the more fruit we bear; the more we die to self, the more we live unto God."

STEER THIS WAY, FATHER!

READ ISAIAH 30:15-21

*And thine ears shall hear a word behind thee, saying,
this is the way, walk ye in it.* Isaiah 30:21

A family of three—a father, a mother, and a five-year-old son —were vacationing at a large lake. One morning soon after the father had set out in his boat for a distant island, a dense fog settled down upon the lake and the man was hopelessly confused, having lost all sense of direction. In vain he tried to find his way back to the cabin and home. After beating about for hours and almost despairing, he thought he heard the faint echoes of a childish voice in the distance. Ceasing to row for a moment he caught in the stillness the sound of a familiar voice calling loudly, "Steer this way, Father; steer this way!" Guided by the voice of his boy, the father soon found home, shelter, and safety.

Not long afterward the little boy fell ill. He had learned to love Jesus in the Sunday school and one morning he said, "I am going home to Jesus today." The father was frantic and said, "Oh, no, no, Jimmy, I can't lose you!" But the little lad was correct, for that evening he closed his eyes and went home to Heaven. The father, still an unbeliever, was rebellious and bitter and unable to understand this disaster. He was beset by a thousand questions. "Why, why, oh why!" he moaned in his despair. Finally, exhausted, he lay down in the bitterness of soul, groping for an answer as though floundering in a thick fog of dread and uncertainty. Then suddenly he remembered his experience, and again he seemed to hear the call of his boy, "Steer this way, Father; steer this way." It was a voice from his son in Heaven, "Home is here, the way out of the fog is *this way.* Steer this way, Father." That night peace came to his heart when he turned to Jesus, "The Way, the Truth, and the Life."

Have you found your way out of the fog? —M.R.D.

Beautiful hands of a little one, see!
Childish voice calling, oh, father for thee;
Rosy-cheeked darling, the light of the home,
Taken so early, is beckoning, "Come!"
—C. C. Luther

"Earth hath no sorrow that Heaven cannot heal." — MOORE

WAITING ON GOD

READ EXODUS 14:10-14

> *. . . Their strength is to sit still.*   Isaiah 30:7

Waiting on God is not stagnation, but the wisest and most productive of all occupations; for it is then that God charges our souls with a super-abundance of His grace to prepare us for greater service! God never places us in any position where we cannot grow in some way. When we are not sending *branches upward*, we may be sending *roots downward*. When everything seems to us to be characterized by the word "failure," we may be making the best and the most spiritual kind of progress! While we sit still and patiently wait on God, our souls are imbued with His strength and prepared for greater tasks ahead.

When the pursuing Egyptians trapped the helpless Israelites at the Red Sea, Moses said, "Fear ye not, *stand still,* and see the salvation of the Lord" (Ex. 14:13). When the hosts of the Moabites and Ammonites closed in on Judah, King Jehoshaphat said to the people, "*Stand ye still,* and see the salvation of the Lord" (II Chron. 20:17). Yes, there are times when waiting is more essential than working, and when trying must give place to trusting! If God has set you aside through sickness or trial, do not be rebellious; it is His way of imparting to you His strength for greater victories ahead.

Luther Burbank often startled the world by the apparent wonders he performed in the realm of fruits and vegetables. What people did not know was that it sometimes took twenty-five years of selection and cross-breeding to make a "spineless cactus" or a "seedless orange." In the light of this should we be surprised or impatient when God takes a little time to work on our immortal soul so that He may perform His wonders? Trustingly resign yourself to His will and "let patience have her perfect work" (James 1:4).   —H.G.B.

> Wait, patiently wait, God is never late;
>   The budding plans are in thy Father's holding,
> And only wait His sweet divine unfolding;
>   Then wait — patiently wait!
>
> —Anon.

"True patience means waiting without worrying."

DIGGING DEEP

READ PSALM 1

. . . like a tree planted by the rivers of water. Psalm 1:3

Never mind reading the rest of this devotional, if you have not read the Scripture (Psalm 1). God's Word is far more important than anything I can say or write. These devotionals are *NOT* a substitute for Bible study — but only an aid to interest you in the Word. Today we talk about trees. David compares the believer to a tree (verse 3). I do not know what kind of a tree it was but I suspect it was a *PEAR* tree, for it suits my story so well. In my orchard are two pear trees. Last summer was excessively dry and all the vegetation was seared and withered. One of the pear trees was unaffected and remained fresh and green and yielded some luscious Bartlett pears. But the other tree did not do so well. Its leaves turned yellow, the fruit shriveled, and both dropped to the ground, leaving the tree *DEAD* (as it seemed from appearances). Then came the rains, and the ground was soaked with moisture. And the tree sprang to life again and was soon covered with leaves and (believe it or not) burst into full bloom. In the latter part of August it was full of blossoms, and little pears came into view — and then the *FROST*, and no fruit. The other tree was loaded. What was the difference? The one tree had its roots *DEEP* in the soil where it found water. The other had shallow roots, and depended on the uncertain rains for its fruit. The one was like David's tree, "planted by rivers of water." The other — though covered with belated bloom — bore no fruit.

What kind of a tree are you? Are your roots dug deep into the underground streams of the Word of God or do you depend upon the showers of circumstances? How sad to awaken too late to bear fruit, and be saved "so as by fire." Blossoms are *PROMISES* of fruit — but you cannot eat *blossoms! DIG DEEP*, brother, *DEEP* into the Book, and the drought of disappointment will not affect you. —M.R.D.

> The just are nourished like a tree
>   Set by the river's side;
> Their leaf is green, THEIR FRUIT IS SURE,
>   And thus their works abide.
>
> —Anon.

"To stop growing is the first symptom of decay."

A CALL TO SERVICE

READ II THESSALONIANS 3:7-13

And I said, What shall I do, Lord?   Acts 22:10

Christians are saved to serve! We are "created in Christ Jesus *UNTO GOOD WORKS*" (Eph. 2:10). This means that God expects us to get busy for Him after we have believed. "But what can I do?" someone asked her preacher. "I do not know," he replied, "but I know a doctor who gives tracts to his patients, a barber who testifies at his work, a mother whose knee was a preparatory school for her preacher sons, a Sunday school teacher who failed to get to the lesson, but saw three scholars saved that Sunday, a farmer who dropped his seeding to drive miles to help a soul in distress, and an ordinary sort of fellow who became the Lord's chauffeur and brought more than a score of souls to a meeting. — I don't know what *you* can do, sister, but you can do something. Even a 'cup of cold water' given in the name of the Saviour is a worthy task which will not go unrewarded. Just get busy!"

It is said that the elder of two boys in a certain family determined that he would make a name for himself by entering politics and becoming well known in the British Parliament. The younger son, however, sought no earthly fame but with the love of Jesus burning in his soul turned his face toward the foreign field. Years passed, and today history has written the verdict of their lives. When you look in any biographical dictionary for the name of the eldest son you will find only the words, "*Brother of J. Hudson Taylor.*" The youngest boy had asked, "What shall I do, Lord?" and had made a better choice.

Robert Chapman speaks of a William Haig, who lived with him, as *a most provoking brother,* for, says Chapman, "He was always *provoking me to love and good works.*" In the same spirit we have written this devotional (see Heb. 10:24).   —H.G.B.

> If you have not gold or silver, ever ready to command;
>   If you cannot for the needy, reach an ever open hand;
> You can visit the afflicted, o'er the erring you can weep;
>   You can be a true disciple, kneeling, serving at His feet.
> —G. M. G.

"Spiritual triumphs are not won by men in easy chairs."

DECEIT

Read Job 15:20-35

They conceive mischief, and bring forth vanity, and their belly prepareth deceit. Job 15:35

During the first World War, I was practicing medicine. Many young men were volunteering for service in the Army. Among them was one fellow, the son of a preacher, who, lured by the prospects of the thrill of combat, tried to enlist. However, when examined for service he was rejected because he was ten pounds underweight. He sought my advice as to how he might gain ten pounds, but it was all to no avail. The best he could do was gain five pounds. A few weeks later I heard he had been accepted into service. When I first saw him I enquired how he had managed to put on extra pounds, and he slyly replied, "Just before I went in for my examination, I ate five pounds of BANANAS, and just made it." He was later killed in action.

Job describes those who by deceit seek to gain their ends, but later must eat the bitter fruits. Job says of such, "He wandereth abroad for bread, saying, Where is it?" (Job 15:23). Of all such Solomon said, "Bread of deceit is sweet to a man, but afterwards his mouth shall be filled with gravel" (Prov. 20:17).

One may fool men, even the army physicians, but no such tactics can fool God. He weighs with a scale having x-rays attached and immediately recognizes the fraud of a man trying to make himself fit for God by his own efforts. God says of every sinner, "Thou art weighed in the balances, and art found wanting" (Dan. 5:27). The bananas of morality, good works, religion, and human righteousness cannot avail. Only as a sinner accepts Christ into his heart can he (in Christ) meet the standards of God's holiness. You cannot deceive God — you are only deceiving yourself. —M.R.D.

Jesus, my Lord, to Thee I cry,
Unless Thou help me I must die;
O bring Thy free salvation nigh,
And take me as I am!
—E. H. Hamilton

"Sinners work harder to go to Hell than Saints do to get to Heaven."
— M. R. D.

ABLAZE FOR GOD!

READ I THESSALONIANS 5:14-23

Quench not the Spirit. . . .   I Thessalonians 5:19

Who maketh . . . his ministers a flaming fire.
                                        Psalm 104:4

There is nothing that the lukewarm church needs more today than believers who are so filled with the Holy Spirit that they are truly "on fire" for God!

Concerning the necessity of maintaining this spiritual glow and the zeal of sanctification, Samuel L. Bringle once wrote: "The old Founder called a few of us to him on the train one day and said, 'Young men, take heed to the fire in your own hearts, for *the tendency of fire is to go out.*' I thought about that, and I said to myself, 'Yes, fire will go out unless I do three things: (1) Keep the drafts open; (2) Keep the ashes and the clinkers shaken out; and (3) Put on more fuel.' Then I applied it to my own soul. I am not to run around and kindle my fire at the altar of someone else. I have a fire of my own. I am to keep the drafts open — keep testifying, keep the prayer windows open toward heaven. I am to keep the ashes out — I cannot depend upon past experiences; I must seek God afresh. Then I must add fuel — pile on new truth, search the Scriptures, feed my soul. The blasts of Hell will seek to quench the flame if I don't guard the fire in my own heart."

What sputtering little sparks we are, when actually as His witnesses, we should be *aflame with the love of God!*

Are you allowing sin and worldliness to "quench" the Spirit?

                                        —H.G.B.

> I saw a human life ablaze with God,
>   I saw a power divine
> As through an empty vessel of frail clay
>   I saw God's glory shine.
> Then woke I from a dream, and cried aloud:
>   "My Father, give to me
> The blessing of a life, consumed by God,
>   That I may live for Thee!"
>
>   —Anon.

"Touched by the Holy Spirit, the ordinary man is made to possess extraordinary qualities."

HERE'S TO THE "CHIGGER"

READ SONG OF SOLOMON 2:8-17

> *. . . the little foxes, that spoil the vines.*
> Song of Solomon 2:15

Many a man who can face great and mighty problems and can overcome them, has gone down before some insignificant detail of little or no consequence. It is much harder to be faithful in the small and seemingly insignificant tasks than to tackle some great problem. The same is true in the spiritual life. Many a Christian who can slay lions of temptation will go down before a handful of ants. A famous explorer in South America was driven back and forced to abandon his journey by an army of almost invisible foes. He was equipped to meet leopards and serpents and crocodiles. He had guns and ammunition for these. They were no threat — but they had failed to reckon with the LITTLE fellows. These were the millions of "chigoes," better known as "chiggers." They are so tiny as to be almost invisible. In this country we have the "no see 'ums," the North American counterpart of the chiggers. The explorers were unable to cope with these Lilliputian invaders and were driven back! Someone has composed the following ditty, quite apropos to our subject:

> Here's to the chigger, the bug that's no bigger
> Than the end of a very small pin;
> But the point that he raises itches like blazes,
> And that's where the rub comes in!

Today, watch the little things which may spoil your testimony. You are ready to face the big problems but be on guard against the little foxes — that evil thought, that hasty word, that burst of temper, that bit of gossip, that snap judgment. Solomon did not fear bears and lions but "LITTLE foxes." Watch the "NO SEE 'UM BUT BIG BITE UM." Keep your armor tight, for "He that is faithful in that which is least, is faithful also in much." — M.R.D.

> Little sins like "leaven,"
> Work their evil through,
> Soon pervade the "whole loaf"
> Touching all we do!
> —G. W.

"Danger can hide in a drop of water, or ride upon a breath of air; Our BIGGEST danger lies in hidden, LITTLE things."

CONTENT OR COVETOUS?

READ LUKE 12:6-15

. . . Take heed, and beware of covetousness. Luke 12:15

A man is either content or covetous — *he cannot be both!* One of the most prominent but least talked-about sins of Christians is that of *discontent!* Such dissatisfaction is accompanied by an inordinate desire for things which God in His wisdom and grace has not seen fit to grant. Many therefore feed on the husks of carnal desire, with a resulting lifetime of frustration, who could be happily feasting at the King's table of satisfaction.

In Luke 12 our Lord had been discussing some very important spiritual matters, yet one of the multitude was so greedy of gain and so desirous of worldly "things" that he interrupted Jesus' discourse on matters of eternal import so that he might ask Him to settle a dispute about money! This occasioned Jesus' stern rebuke which is still so much needed today: *"Beware of covetousness!"* Worldly goods can never satisfy the soul; in fact, they are often the Devil's snare by which he drags men down to destruction with their carnal cravings still ungratified. "A round world can never fill a triangular-shaped heart!"

A Quaker once put a sign up on a vacant piece of ground next to his house, which read, "I will give this lot to anyone who is really satisfied." A wealthy farmer riding by hastened to claim the property. He reasoned with himself, "I may as well have it as anyone else; and as I am rich and have all I need, I should be well able to qualify." When he asked for the lot the aged Quaker said, "And is thee really satisfied?" "I surely am!" was the reply. "I have all I need, and am well content." "Friend," said the other, *"if thee is satisfied, what does thee want with my lot?"* The question revealed the true covetousness that was hidden in the rich man's heart.

Let your walk be "without covetousness; and be content with such things as ye have" (Heb. 13:5).   —H.G.B.

> Kept in Christ, I'm satisfied,
>   When in Him my soul doth hide;
> Ev'ry need by Him supplied,
>   Kept in Christ, I'm satisfied.
>   —Mrs. W. G. Taylor

"People who set their hearts on THINGS are equally disappointed whether they get them or whether they don't!" — R. HORTON

ROAD SIGNS

READ DEUTERONOMY 30:15-20

> *. . . therefore hear the word at my mouth, and give them* WARNING *from me."*   Ezekiel 3:17

Wherever and whenever the word "warning" appears, it is a signal to take notice and take care. You are notified of a danger, and if you ignore the warning and evil befalls you, no one else but you is to blame. *Warning—air brakes* is written on the rear of heavy trucks. Stay far enough behind! *Warning—high tension wires* appears on the electric poles. Keep away! *Warning—this bridge not safe! Warning—this water unsafe for drinking!* And then there are the various road signs warning us of dangers which lie ahead. In many areas, before a driver's license is issued the applicant must be able to identify these various signs by their shape. We have all the various shapes and designs which warn us: SLOW, STEEP HILL AHEAD, SHARP CURVE, SPEED 25 MILES, DO NOT PASS, YIELD RIGHT OF WAY, and STOP. These signs are for our safety, and to ignore them is to invite disaster. Many cities issue a booklet on traffic laws and require drivers to become thoroughly familiar with its various provisions. All signs should be heeded even if some are less important than others. Some are so obviously TRUE that we smile. Touring along, we saw a sign —SLOW MEN WORKING. We saw the men and murmured—How true! We saw another—equally prophetic—SLOW REPAIRS AHEAD.

We are all travelers to eternity on the road of life. The Lord has given us in the Bible the road signs to warn us of dangers and show us the right way. One sign says—TO HEAVEN this way, another says—TO HELL this way. You are being fairly warned. Once having started on the way to Heaven by taking Jesus as Lord and Saviour, He will guide by His Word and counsel. Pay close attention to the signs in the Book and you will not only arrive safely but have a most enjoyable trip. Read the warnings in the Bible!   —M.R.D.

> Lamp to my feet wherever I stray;
> Guide never failing from day to day;
> Leading me Homeward unto my Lord,
> Counsel of wisdom, God's precious Word.
>   —C. H. Gabriel

"Keep your Bible OPEN if you do not wish to find the door of Heaven SHUT."

A SWEET REWARD

READ PROVERBS 11:11-18

Be ye strong therefore, and let not your hands be weak:
for your work shall be rewarded.   II Chronicles 15:7

The story is told of a woman who had a rare rosebush. She worked over it for weeks, but saw little or no results for her labor. One day she observed a crack in the wall and upon investigation found a small shoot of the rosebush running through the crevice. When she went to the other side of the wall she found roses blooming in splendid beauty and her labor rewarded. Some of us too work year after year seeing little if any result, but we are not to be discouraged, for our work is truly blooming. However, it may be we shall only see its luxuriant growth when we get on the other side of the wall!

Gipsy Smith at one time was conducting meetings in Aberdeen. At the close of the service he was working his way through the great crowd when he felt a tug at his coat. For a few seconds he did not pay much attention, thinking it was merely someone trying to get ahead of him down the aisle, but the tug became more insistent. Finally he stopped. Looking down, he saw a little Scotch lassie. Although she was dressed in rags, her face and eyes were shining. Gipsy Smith said, "In her uplifted hand was something wrapped in tissue paper. It was moist and grimy for she had been clutching it for some time. 'What is it, my dear?' I asked. And she replied, 'I want you to have my candy.' 'Why?' I asked. 'Oh, sir,' she exclaimed happily, 'we've got a new daddy. He's never been sober until Saturday. We've never known him to be anything but drunk. He was in your meeting on Saturday, and it's all so wonderful now.' And didn't I take her candy?" said Gipsy Smith, "I should say I did—it was worth living a lifetime for that minute."

Yes, there are rewards for the righteous at the Judgment Seat, but there are also many sweet compensations even in this life when one is engaged in the service of Christ!   —H.G.B.

> The service of Jesus true pleasure affords,
>   In Him there is joy without an alloy;
> 'Tis heaven to trust Him and rest on His words;
>   It pays to serve Jesus each day.
> —F. C. Huston

"Blessings ever reward virtuous deeds; therefore, he who sows precious seed may expect a joyful harvest."

HOW ARE YOUR ROOTS?

READ EPHESIANS 3:13-21

Rooted and built up in him . . . .   Colossians 2:7

The believer is compared in the Bible to a fruitbearing tree (Ps. 1:3) which continues to be productive even in old age (Ps. 92:14). The reason it is fruitful is because the root has access to moisture, the one prerequisite for organic life. The tree is planted by the "rivers of water" (Ps. 1:3). It is fruitful for it has its feet in the water. The water, in Scripture symbolism, is *The Word* of God. The *Word* is twofold — the Incarnate Word, Jesus, and the written Word, the Bible. To be a healthy, fruitbearing tree one must be rooted in the water of the Word. Paul speaks of being "rooted and built up in him." The deeper we are rooted in the knowledge of Christ, the more luxuriant our life will be. But we can only know *Him* as we know His *Word,* the Bible. We cannot know about Jesus, the Word incarnate, except from the Bible, for it is the only Book which tells us of Him as our Redeemer. However, it is equally true that we cannot know the Bible until we know *Him,* for the natural man cannot receive the things of the Spirit of God, for they are spiritually discerned. First, we must trust the Lord Jesus, the Word, but the only way we can find Him is through His Word, the Bible. Then, secondly, having been saved, we must become *rooted.* In the degree that we are rooted in Christ, in that degree we can be fruitful, steadfast, productive Christians. But once again we must go to the Bible to learn about Him, so to be rooted in Christ, is to be grounded in the *Word* — the Bible.

How deep are your roots? Are they deep enough to withstand the storm without despairing and going down — deep enough to overcome the temptations of today — deep enough to give testimony for Him and to answer the questions of a seeking soul? Don't go to work today without first "wetting your roots" in the "water of the Word"!   —M.R.D.

> Salvation's wells are full of truth
>   And water of the Word,
> There, sweet refreshment can be found,
>   And holy motives stirred.
>   —G. W.

"What's on the tree above ground — reveals what it secretly feeds upon underground." — M. R. D.

SUPPORT

READ ISAIAH 41:6-10

. . . the Lord upholdeth the righteous.   Psalm 37:17

We are told by botanists that certain plants which are too weak to support themselves by their own stocks must twine about other plants or objects to grow properly. Sometimes the stems of such climbers attach themselves by spiral turns to their hosts; sometimes they cling to sturdy objects by putting out special twining tendrils. Those who have watched such growing plants intently tell us that their tips move slowly in circles, successively turning to all points of the compass. The bean is such a plant. Its twining motion is said to greatly accelerate as the plant grows older. The tendrils at first may complete only one turn a day, but later they make as many as eight spirals in a twenty-four hour period.

The naturalist, Balm, who made a special study of climbing plants, recognized twenty-five different families of them in which the twining is done with a waving motion toward the left, and ten others in which the climbing is done toward the right. But all of them, to thrive, must *climb!* Those which have no support and trail on the ground are usually stunted, unlovely, and fruitless.

Nature, as well as Scripture, has its lessons. The climbing plant is an illustration of the human life. Every heart searches instinctively for its *divine support.* Those who do not find such a stay are stunted, spiritually useless, and bring "no fruit to perfection."

Has your life been entwined with that of the Saviour? Are you leaning on Him for eternal support? Can you say with the psalmist, "My soul followeth hard after thee: Thy right hand upholdeth me?" Are you climbing Heavenward? If you are, then it is your duty to help some other struggling brother along the way, and thus in turn *"support the weak"* (I Thess. 5:14).

—H.G.B.

Lean on His arms, trusting in His love;
    Lean on His arms, all His mercies prove;
Lean on His arms, looking Home above,
    Just lean on the Saviour's arm!
—E. Lewis

"You can only have an UPRIGHT life as you LEAN ON JESUS!"—H.G.B.

REMOVING THE RUBBISH

READ II CHRONICLES 34:14-21

> *. . . I have found the book of the law in the house of the Lord. . . .*   II Chronicles 34:15

While on the way to a meeting in Toronto, Canada, we stopped in a lunch room for a cup of coffee. Next to me sat a young man with a Bible on his lap. I remarked about it, and he told me the following story: "I am on my way to the People's Church to hear you preach, for I learned about you and your ministry years ago. I was a refugee from a concentration camp during the war and was befriended by an old woman in Germany who gave me asylum in her home. She listened to a certain preacher from Grand Rapids, Michigan, on the radio, and therefore bought a Bible. Each day she asked me to read it to her. While doing so, I came under conviction and was saved. Later I escaped to America, and now I carry my Bible with me whenever I can." How my heart was thrilled as I heard this Polish boy tell of the transforming power of the Word. How thankful we should be that we have free access to the Scriptures.

In the Middle Ages, the Bible was lost under a mass of religious tradition and papal rubbish, but, as in Josiah's day, there were workmen who again found the Book. Among those who took a leading part were Luther, Calvin, Zwingli, and many others. This rediscovery which began in Germany resulted in the Scriptures being given back to the people. The great revival and awakening of the sixteenth century followed.

On this Reformation Day let us thank God for the Scripture — and dedicate ourselves anew to the task of giving its message to a lost world.   —M.R.D.

> I'll trust in God's unchanging Word
> Till soul and body sever:
> For though all things shall pass away,
> His Word shall stand forever!
> —Martin Luther

"These two God hath joined and no man shall part — DUST on the BIBLE, and DROUGHT in the HEART!"

UNANSWERED PRAYER

READ PSALM 34:8-17

The eyes of the Lord are upon the righteous, and his ears are open unto their cry.   Psalm 34:15

How often we pray without waiting for, or actually even expecting, an answer. Norman H. Camp used to tell the story of a woman who dreamed that she died and went to Heaven. As one of the angels was showing her about the rooms of that glorious palace she was brought to a large corridor where many bundles were piled in a corner. Finding her name on several of these, she asked for an explanation, saying as she did so, "Say, I remember praying for these very things when I was down on earth." The angel replied, "Yes, you see when any of God's children make requests to Him, preparations are immediately made to give the answer. However, the angels are told to first watch and see if the petitioner actually expects to receive the blessing. If he does not, we are told to return it, and store it up in this room." Of course this was only a dream, but one wonders if this does not account for much of our failure to receive the answers to our prayers. *Too often we fail to ask in faith, "nothing doubting!"*
                                                                —H.G.B.

> Unanswered yet, the prayer your lips have pleaded,
>   In agony of heart these many years?
> Does faith begin to fail? Is hope departing,
>   And think you all in vain those falling tears
> Say not the Father hath not heard your prayer:
>   You shall have your desire sometime, somewhere.
> Unanswered yet? Nay, do not say ungranted;
>   Perhaps your part is not yet wholly done;
> The work began when first your prayer was uttered,
>   And God will finish what He has begun.
> If you will keep the incense burning there,
>   His glory you will see — sometime, somewhere!
>   —Anon.

"God cannot disappoint the desires that are of His own kindling, nor deny the hopes of His own raising."

SELF-SATISFIED

READ PHILIPPIANS 3:10-14

Not as though I had already attained, either were already perfect . . . Brethren, I count not myself to have apprehended. Philippians 3:12, 13

Beware of the self-satisfied individual who, gloating over his past successes, spends the rest of his time bragging about it. Self-satisfaction is the death of progress. Dissatisfaction with past accomplishments is the mother of invention.

Because man was dissatisfied with carrying and lifting loads upon his shoulders, he invented the wheel and the lever. Because he was dissatisfied with walking, he invented vehicles to ride in. Pity the man who is content with his own progress and feels he has "arrived." This is all the more true in the Christian life. Nothing here is as deadly as self-satisfaction. The most boring people I ever meet are the ones who take up my time telling me what they have *done,* when they ought to be *doing more.*

An officer rode up to the general, saluted and said proudly, "Sir, we have just taken two gun emplacements from the enemy." He waited for the compliment of the general, expecting him to say, "Very good, now you can take a rest." Instead, the general curtly ordered, "Go back and take two more."

If any man could boast of his achievements, the Apostle Paul certainly had a right to do so. But instead he cried out, "Forgetting those things which are behind, and reaching forth unto those things which are before, I PRESS toward the mark for the prize of the high calling of God in Christ Jesus." Until the last soul has been added to the Body of Christ, our work is never done. Keep your mouth *shut* about YOUR accomplishments and *open* with HIS commission.

A little turtle cried out "Look, mama, what a big fish I caught." But the moment he opened his mouth the fish slipped away. It is fine to be satisfied with Jesus, but the more He satisfies, the more dissatisfied you are with self! —M.R.D.

> Ne'er think the vict'ry won,
>   Nor lay thine armour down;
> The work of faith will not be done,
>   Till thou obtain the crown.
> —G. Heath

"If you do not intend to work for God — at least get out of the way and let others serve Him."

PERSONAL WORK

READ II CHRONICLES 15:1-12

. . . A true witness delivereth souls.   Proverbs 14:25

One form of personal work with which we are all familiar is speaking directly to souls about the Lord; but there is another witness which we bear which is equally important, and that is *the witness of our conduct!* Dr. Daniel Steele says: "All jurists will tell you that one bit of *authentic evidence* is worth more than ten thousand words of sophistical, professional pleading. A faithful witness is far more important than a clever advocate. A testimony can go to the jury without argument; but it will not do to send the argument without the testimony. Yet this sad blunder, I fear, the modern Christian church has been committing when through eloquent preachers she sends to the world the argument — *without the evidence! . . .* Jesus Christ, on trial before the jury of an unbelieving world has had too many lawyers and too few witnesses!"

Some years ago in Philadelphia a man who knew the Lord was passing a tavern. Looking in, he saw a professing Christian drinking and playing cards. He took a pencil, wrote on a card, and seeing a boy passing by stopped him, pressed a coin in his hand and said, "Take this, my boy; I want you to do an errand for me. You see that man on the side of the table where those three are playing cards?" "Yes, I do," said the lad. "Well," said the man, "take this message to him." The young fellow went in and delivered the card to the Christian whose life was not squaring with his profession. The backslidden one blushed when he read the inscription, for it said, *"Ye are my witnesses!"* He sprang to his feet and rushed out of the tavern, asking the boy where the card came from. The lad replied, "A man over there gave it to me." But the other Christian by this time had slipped away. The one who received the pointed rebuke was convicted by the Holy Spirit and it was a severe lesson to him. Christian, be sure your personal testimony is backed up by *living evidence!*   —H.G.B.

> Help me to walk so close to Thee
> That those who know me best can see
> I live as godly as I pray
> And Christ is real from day to day!
> —D. C. Ryberg

"It isn't so much what we TALK ABOUT and KNOW, but what we PRACTICE and SOW that does the good."

CHASTENING LOVE

READ PSALM 94:12-19

As many as I love, I rebuke and chasten. Revelation 3:19

There is an eternal purpose back of all that befalls a Christian. The chastening of the Lord may take different forms. Sometimes it is a stern visitation because of our sin; at other times it can be a tender pruning by the nail-scarred Hand especially laid upon us because we are a promising vine. In either case, chastening is a mark of God's divine love and concern for us. In other words, chastening does not necessarily mean that you are the worst sinner in town; rather it may mean that you are *the most promising saint;* for the Scripture says, "Every branch . . . that [already] beareth fruit, he purgeth it, *that it may bring forth more fruit"* (John 15:2). Lives that have been the most afflicted are usually the most effective. As the tender hand of the Divine Gardener trims away the excess foliage of earthly joys and contentment, the spiritual nourishment from the vine of God is channeled to the productive buds of the branches. With hindrances, weights, and carnality cut away, we bring forth "more fruit." God's purpose in regard to our suffering, therefore, is to refine in us the gold of holiness. The Divine Sculptor employs His chisel often upon the marble from which He seeks to create a masterpiece.

A Christian mother lay dying. Beside her a loving daughter stood weeping silently. Conscious of the agony that caused the great tears to fall, the mother looked Heavenward, and whispered, "Patience, darling; *it is only the chiseling."* Alas, the Master Sculptor sees many deformities in His children which must be chiseled off before they can find a place of honor in His divine gallery of Heaven. How good to know that the chisel of trial is held in the never erring, skillful hand of God's love.   —H.G.B.

> When through fiery trials thy pathway shall lie,
> My grace all sufficient shall be thy supply;
> The flames shall not hurt thee; I only design
> Thy dross to consume and thy gold to refine.
> —G. Keith

"If you stand high in life, like a great pine on a cliff, expect to be shaken by the storms." — DR. W. W. AYER

PUDDLIN' OR SWIMMIN'

READ ISAIAH 43:1-11

> *. . . waters to swim in.*   Ezekiel 47:5

The Prophet Ezekiel was transported in vision to that future day when the earth would be redeemed from the curse and Jerusalem be the praise of all the earth. He saw the Temple in all its glory, but the thing which most impressed him was the steam which issued from under the threshold and swelled to become a great river. At first the waters were up to the ankles (Ezek. 47:3). A little farther the waters were up to the knees (verse 4). Soon they deepened up to the hips (verse 4). Finally the deepness had increased till it was a river that could not be passed over, "for the waters were risen, waters to *SWIM IN.*" This is of course a picture of the transformation of the Land of Palestine in the future. (It also suggests the River of Life — see Revelation 22.) It originates in the House of God, begins as a shallow stream and increases gradually in its depth until at a distance of a little over a mile it is deep enough to swim in. It suggests that this River of Life is adapted to believers of all ages. To the babes in Christ, there are the shallows for wading. For others, the waters are knee deep — enough for splashing. Then there are waters up to the loins, for those learning to swim, and finally the deep waters for the well-trained. God wants us to be swimmers and not just "puddlers." We must grow up to full Christian manhood until we can live in the deep waters of the Word. This comes only by constant practice. We must not only be waders and puddlers but learn to rest our whole weight upon it and launch out into the deep.

How can you learn to swim if you avoid the water? It reminds us of the little ditty:

> "Mother, may I go out to swim?"
> "Yes my darling daughter.
> Hang your clothes on a hickory limb,
> But don't go near the water."

How much time do you spend in the Word of God?   —M.R.D.

> Water of Truth for Adam's race —
> River of God from Heavenly Steep —
> Flood thou our lives with new found grace,
> As here we plumb thy crystal deep.
>   —G. W.

"Who wants to paddle around in a duck pond all his life? Launch out into the deep!" — M. R. D.

CONSIDER THE LILIES

READ MATTHEW 6:25-34

> *. . . Consider the lilies of the field, how they grow; they*
> *toil not, neither do they spin.* Matthew 6:28

Jesus often warned against the extreme folly of those who were overanxious about material things. In the Sermon on the Mount our Saviour points to the lilies of the field which toil not, and which do not spin, and declares that the God who clothes them in beauty which outshines the ancient glory of the kingly raiment of a Solomon, will also certainly care for His trusting children. If the flowers of the field which quickly wither and die, and have no eternal quality, are so adequately cared for, we need never doubt that the Father in Heaven will also bestow upon us all things that are required to get along in this world. Jesus therefore admonishes us to set our affections above, to concentrate on eternal matters, and to "seek first the kingdom."

How true the words of the chorus our little children often sing:

> "The birds upon the treetops sing their song,
> The angels chant the chorus all day long,
> The flowers in the garden lend their hue,
> So why shouldn't I, why shouldn't you, trust Him too?"

Worry is dishonoring to God. Anxiety over temporal things is not only needless, but positively hurtful. Let the world worry; we have a Heavenly Father who has promised always to care for us and furnish all needful, temporal blessings.

In China, men have conceived of a sleeping deity. In one city there is a statue of Buddha lying on his side, with calm face, closed eyes, and his head resting upon his hand. A good thirty feet long, the image is impressive in itself, but Buddha is *sleeping* while the world goes on — *he does not pay attention to his worshippers!* How unlike the Christian who has a God who never slumbers nor sleeps! In His care we are both safe and secure. Shame on us if we worry! —H.G.B.

> When we see the lilies spinning in distress,
> Taking thought to manufacture loveliness;
> When we see the birds all building barns for store.
> 'Twill then be time for us to worry — not before!
> —Anon.

"I would no more permit myself to worry than to swear."
— JOHN WESLEY

MINIMUM — AVERAGE — MAXIMUM

READ MATTHEW 13:18-23

> *. . . bring forth fruit, some thirtyfold, some sixty, and
> some an hundred.* Mark 4:20

The good seed of the Word fell in good ground, yet it did
not all produce the same amount. Some produced only thirtyfold,
other sixtyfold, still others an hundredfold. Jesus is not endorsing
thirty or sixtyfold as most people suppose. Often we hear people
pray for God's blessing on the Word that "it may bring forth
thirty, sixty, and one hundredfold." Don't pray like that again.
Why ask for thirty or sixty when one hundred is possible? Jesus
did not endorse anything less than an hundredfold, but He also
knew that most Christians would be satisfied with only thirty or
sixty — something less than the best. He spoke prophetically.
There are three kinds of fruit-bearers among believers. First,
there are those who are content with doing a bare minimum for
Christ. They try to get by with just as little prayer, Bible reading, testimony giving, and soul winning as they possibly can.
They shirk every possible responsibility and do only as much
for Christ and the Church as they are compelled to do.

The second class are the "sixtyfolders"; those who are neither
minimum nor maximum but just average. They feel that as long
as they are doing as much as the average, it is enough. Consequently most Christians are just average. "I'm carrying as much
as the others and a little more than some" is their excuse.

The third class, the "hundredfolders," are the "all outers" for
God. They do not measure themselves by what others do but by
what God requires. These are the little group whom God will
use. Out of the 32,000 in Gideon's army, God used only 300.
They were "one hundred percenters." Of the thousands who
came to Christ, He used only seventy disciples and twelve
apostles. Look at your score card tonight and grade yourself for
the day. Were you content with anything less than *one hundredfold?* Your reward will be based on your grade. —M.R.D.

> Go then, work, the Master calleth;
>   Go, no longer idle be;
> Waste no more thy precious moments,
>   For the Lord hath need of thee.
> —F. Crosby

**"Good intentions are no substitute for action; failure usually follows
the path of least persistence!"**

THE COMMUNION OF SAINTS

READ I JOHN 1:1-7

> *. . . we have fellowship one with another . . . .* I John 1:7

The Apostles' Creed, although never seen nor written by the Apostles themselves, summarizes some of the cardinal truths of the Bible. Among other things it states, "I believe in the communion of saints." That there *is* such a unique fellowship which binds believers together cannot be denied. (See Eph. 4:4, I Cor. 10:17 and I Cor. 12:12-27). As members of Christ's mystical Body, we are united by His blood through the operation of the Holy Spirit. This unity goes much farther than merely standing next to one another in a formal service, or having our names placed side by side upon some church roll. There is a fundamental, organic relationship between all born-again people which, as one dear old lady used to say, "is better *felt* than *telt*."

I shall never forget the communion of saints I experienced at one time with a man *whom I never actually met and with whom I never had a word of conversation!* It happened while I was traveling on a train between Chicago and Grand Rapids. In the dining car after bowing my head as usual to silently ask a blessing before I ate, I opened my eyes to see several passengers smirking at me as though I were some oddity. This did not bother me, for I know that "this world is not a friend to grace." However, as I glanced across the car, I saw a young man with a beaming smile nodding his approval. He could not fight his way down the crowded aisle to shake my hand, but he reached into his pocket, took out a little Testament and waved it at me, while his lips moved in a silent "Amen." In that moment I enjoyed the fellowship of the saints in a real and intimate way! If you have experienced the love that bathes your heart at such precious moments of communion, then you have another Heavensent token of assurance concerning your own salvation, for John tells us, "We know that we have passed from death unto life, because we love the brethren" (I John 3:14)!   —H.G.B.

> Blest be the tie that binds
> Our hearts in Christian love;
> The fellowship of kindred minds
> Is like to that above.
> —J. Fawcett

"If God is your FATHER through Jesus Christ, then you will know and feel that all of His children are your BROTHERS."

MY SMALL POTATOES

*. . . reckon ye also yourselves to be dead indeed unto
sin . . . .*   Romans 6:11

*. . . Except a corn of wheat fall into the ground and die,
it abideth alone . . . .*   John 12:24

I've just come into the house after digging a mess of potatoes
in my garden. I dug up something besides potatoes — I dug up
a sermon as well! The first hill of potatoes was a pleasant surprise for there were seven, beautiful, large potatoes, representing a real increase. With enthusiasm I plunged the fork under
the next plant and — what a disappointment, for all I found was
three little scrawny ones as big (pardon me — as small) as mar-
bles. I soon saw the reason. From some cause or another the
original seed potato had failed to die. There it was, almost the
way it had been planted four months before. It didn't die and
there was no fruit. There can be no life without death — no fruit
without sacrifice.

Yes, I dug up a sermon in the potato patch. In fact there were
at least three sermons, one for each small potato. First, it speaks
of the Lord Jesus who said, "Except a corn of wheat die . . . it
abideth alone." Jesus was the grain of wheat which died, only
to be resurrected in a host of believers as His fruit.

There is a lesson for the sinner too. Until the sinner dies to
his own works and to his own efforts, merit, and righteousness,
he cannot know life and be saved. And finally, what a lesson for
believers. We too have been "planted in the likeness of His
death" (Rom. 6:5). This establishes our position and salvation.
But to become fruitful we must die to self. We must put to
death the works of the flesh (the flesh of our old nature), and
if we "through the Spirit do mortify (put to death) the deeds
of the body we shall live" (Rom. 8:13).

Have a good crop of potatoes! !   —M.R.D.

> Oh to learn the lesson — treasure it with care:
> Planted in His likeness, In His death we share;
> Dying then to "self-life" — precious riches rare;
> Raised up in His glory, much more fruit we bear.
> —I. H.

**"If you want to get up, step down; if you want to be seen, get out
of sight; if you want to live the 'more abundant life,' die to self."**

THE RESTORED SOUL

READ PSALM 51:1-12

He restoreth my soul ....　　　　　　　　　　Psalm 23:3

The God-directed life is not all serenity, not all lying down in "green pastures" by restful waters. No, there are times when we must move onward along the paths of righteousness. When sin comes between us and our Guide, when self-will blinds our eyes, and the din of earth's pleasures drown out His voice of direction, we become confused and often stray into dangerous ways. Then it is that He must graciously "restore" our souls. The Hebrew verb in verse three of Psalm 23 is *shuv*, which literally means "to turn about." When the sheep of His pasture go along their own wicked and willful way, unmindful of the danger of straying from their Protector's side into the ways of sin and death, then by the "Shepherd's crook of chastisement" He turns them about and brings them back to the paths of righteousness!

James McConkey tells how he was once crossing a great glacier while on a sight-seeing trip in Switzerland. The path was extremely narrow and winding and seemingly filled with unnecessary detours. At one place especially it appeared as if the guide should have proceeded straight ahead, but instead he turned sharply and began to take a roundabout course. One man, evidently annoyed, resolved to take a shortcut, so he went straight ahead instead of following the leader. Immediately the guide rushed back, grasped him by the collar, and with no gentle hand dragged him back. Then he pointed to a patch of snow upon which the man had intended to walk. Instead of being a sure foothold, it was a mere crust of ice covering a great crevasse opening into the deep recesses of the glacier. The shortcut would have ended in disaster. Says McConkey, "A similar peril besets the believer's walk. Sometimes our Guide seems too slow for us ... and indeed seems to lead us by devious paths; but it pays us far better to take the detours *with* Him, than to take the shortcuts *without Him!*"

Lord, if we have wandered, restore our souls!　　　—H.G.B.

> There are times, when tired of the toilsome road,
> 　That for ways of the world I pine;
> But He draws me back to the upward track
> 　By the touch of His hand on mine.
> 　　　　　　　—J. B. Pounds

"The FORBIDDEN FRUIT of the self-planned life makes for a BAD JAM!"

SPITTING INTO YOUR OWN FACE

READ PSALM 14

The heavens declare the glory of God; and the firmament sheweth his handywork.　　　　Psalm 19:1

No intelligent person can deny the existence of God, for the Lord says he is a "fool" (Ps. 14:1). To argue against God is to reveal your own tragic ignorance. You are demonstrating your own stupidity. Tom Paine, the self-styled atheist who wrote the "Age Of Reason," once asked Benjamin Franklin what he thought of his book. Franklin's reply was to the point. He said, "Tom, he who spits against the wind, spits in his own face." Until a man is born again he is a fool, ignorant of spiritual things. He may be ever so clever and educated and cultured, and a genius in the sciences, but he will be an ignoramus concerning spiritual things. The fact is that very few, if any, so-called atheists have ever read the whole Bible. They specialize in isolated portions and dwell to the point of nausea upon certain "supposed" contradictions. As an example of the stupidity of the so-called "intelligentsia," the following true story is related:

A skeptic sat next to a Bible teacher at a dinner and soon the subject turned to the Scriptures. The skeptic said he had once been interested in reading the Bible but gave it up when he found too many contradictions. The Christian requested him to give him an example. "Well," said the skeptic, "I read in Genesis the story of Noah's ark. I began to figure out the dimensions, and the amount of lumber it required, and its proportions. I was really impressed, but then a few days later I read somewhere in the Bible that the priest and Levites took up the "ark" and carried it upon their shoulders from place to place. That cured me of Bible study. Such foolishness was too much for me; I have never opened the Book again." Poor, poor ignorant fool. He didn't know the difference between the Ark of Noah, and the little Ark of the Covenant in the Tabernacle. Yes, the wisdom of the world is foolishness with God.　　　　— M.R.D.

Blind unbelief is sure to err,
And scan His work in vain;
God is His own Interpreter,
And He will make it plain.
—Wm. Cowper

"Ignorance of the Bible is the spawning place of most of the skepticism concerning it."

THE PEARLY GATES

READ REVELATION 21:10-21

And the twelve gates were twelve pearls; every several gate was of one pearl. Revelation 21:21

The gates of the New Jerusalem, also described in Ezekiel 48:30-35, are most interesting. On them are inscribed the names of the twelve tribes of Israel. This shows God's faithfulness to the promises which He made at the dawn of history to Abraham, Isaac, and Jacob concerning their seed. It was toward this heavenly country that the father of the faithful journeyed, for he "looked for a city which hath foundations, whose builder and maker is God" (Heb. 11:10).

Twelve in Scripture always speaks of "fulness of blessing." What a thrill it will be, therefore, when the redeemed finally sweep through those lustrous portals to find perfect satisfaction, and experience eternal joys! The heavenly surprises He there has in store for us cannot here be imagined (see I Cor. 2:9).

J . Wilbur Chapman felt that there was special meaning in the fact that the dozen entrances to the New Jerusalem were all of pearl. He said, "Do you know the history of pearls? Humanly speaking, it is the history of suffering. It is said that pearls are formed by the intrusion of some foreign substance between the mantel of the mollusk and its shell. This becomes a source of irritation, suffering, and pain; and consequently a protecting fluid is thrown around it — thus a pearl is formed." So too, the cross sanctifies all trial and covers it with a special glory so that in the heavenly kingdom it looms as a glistening jewel of delight. The shining gates of the New Jerusalem therefore seem to *suggest something about the conditions necessary for entering there.* It is as if God would have us recall that we must "through much tribulation enter into the kingdom of God (Acts 14:22). Each pearly portal emphasizes the truth that "if we suffer with him," we shall also "reign with him."   — H.G.B.

He the pearly gates will open
So that I may enter in;
For He purchased my redemption
And forgave me all my sin.

—F. Blom

"Christ is the only Door to Heaven; but its capital city has twelve gates that we may know that the redeemed come from all points of the compass and from all tribes and nations!"

FOR PARENTS ONLY

READ I SAMUEL 1:10-20

*For this child I prayed; and the Lord hath given me
my petition which I asked of him:
Therefore also I have lent him to the Lord; as long as
he liveth he shall be lent to the Lord.* I Samuel 1:27, 28

Parts of the following item appeared in the December '58
issue of *The Evangel,* edited by my dear friend and brother in
Christ, Louis A. Jacobsen, Largo, Florida. It is written sarcastically, so if you will reverse the advice and do exactly the
opposite, you will be right. To avoid delinquency:

1. Begin in infancy to give the child all he wants. In this way
he will grow up believing the world owes him a living.

2. When he picks up a bad or dirty word, laugh at him as
though it were cute. It will encourage him to pick up similar
words.

3. Avoid the word "wrong." It may develop in the child a
guilt complex.

4. Don't help him to decide between right and wrong, but let
him find out for himself.

5. Always take his part against the school teacher and the
police.

6. Pick up everything after him: shoes, books, clothes, etc.
Avoid "child labor."

7. Always quarrel in the presence of your children. It will
give them experience.

8. Let him read anything he wants and be sure he has plenty
of spending money.

9. Spend all the time you can away from the house, so he
can be alone and develop self-reliance.

10. And when they take him to prison, excuse yourself by
saying, "I did my best, but I couldn't do anything with him."

— M.R.D.

With heartaches and longings we pay a dear price
For the getting of gain that our lifetime employs;
If we fail to provide through training and prayer,
A good home for our girls, a good home for our boys.
—Anon.

**"In regard to a child: a disciplined body results in physical fitness, a
disciplined soul in spiritual usefulness."** — B. S. WRIGHT, ALT.

THE LORD HATH TAKEN

READ JOB 1:9-22

> *. . . the Lord gave, and the Lord hath taken away;*
> *blessed be the name of the Lord.*   Job 1:21

Has icy death ever suddenly snatched a loved one from your embrace? The shock and chill of such a moment seems to deaden the senses and open the floodgate of our tears; yet if we are Christians we may know that the event which shaped our sorrow was no accident. All was planned and executed by God's loving Hand of Providence.

A bereaved one wrote recently, "The darkest hour of my life was when someone knocked on my door and told me that my little daughter had been killed. As I stood there in speechless silence, I felt I could not face this tragedy, and I silently asked God to take me also. That, however, was not His will for my life. I had to face the hard fact, but thanks to God, I did not have to face it alone. I know that God's promises are true. He has said, 'I will never leave thee nor forsake thee.' I took Him at His Word and after a night of anguished prayer, I was able to say, 'Though He slay me, yet will I trust Him.' "

Isaac Watts in speaking of sudden death once commented, "Our blessed Jesus walks among the roses and the lilies in the garden of His Church, and when He sees a wintry storm coming upon some tender plant of righteousness, He hides them in the earth . . . that they may bloom with new glories when they shall be raised from that bed. The blessed God acts like a tender Father, (and with) . . . the hand of His mercy snatches them away before some powerful temptation comes which would have defiled, distressed, and almost destroyed them. . . . They are but gone to rest a little sooner than we. . . . Blessed be our Lord Jesus who has the keys of the grave, and never opens it for His favorites but in the wisest season."   — H.G.B.

> Let us be patient, we who mourn with weeping
>   Some vanished face,
> The Lord has taken but to add more beauty
>   And a diviner grace!

>   —Anon.

"Resignation is putting God between one's self and one's grief."
            — M. P. SWETCHINE

LESSONS FROM THE CLOUDS

READ I KINGS 8:1-11

*Then a cloud covered the tent of the congregation, and
the glory of the Lord filled the tabernacle.* Exodus 40:34

Why do we usually associate clouds with calamity, trial, and
disaster? When everything is tranquil and prosperous we say,
"Not a cloud in the sky." But we are all wrong in our estimation of the meaning of clouds. For the believer in Christ, the
message of the clouds is always a message of hope and promise.
For the unbeliever the same clouds are omens of judgment and
doom, but for the trusting child of God, a cloud means the
presence of God and the promise of blessing.

I lay stretched out flat on my back on a beautiful spring day,
peering into the sky as the multi-shaped fleecy clouds sailed
majestically over a sea of purest azure blue. On they moved,
always changing shape and hue. When the sun shone on them,
they were as white as fresh driven snow. When the sun was
obstructed they were a foreboding, dark slate-gray. What did the
clouds say as they raced on? When I turned to the Word of
God I found that clouds are the messengers of hope, of blessing,
and of promise. They are God's servants to keep the earth from
being seared and burned up with perpetual sunshine.

The first mention of a cloud is right after the flood — with
a rainbow as a frame. It was God's promise of mercy. There was
to be no more worldwide judgment of a flood. The clouds are
God's chariots to bring the blessing of refreshing rain, to bring
life and verdure and fruit to the earth.

Are you experiencing clouds in your life, and do the shadows
alarm you? Then read Exodus 13:21; Leviticus 16:2; I Kings
8:10; Job 37:16; Proverbs 16:15; and Isaiah 18:4. Thank God for
the promise of the clouds.   — M.R.D.

> Ye fearful saints, fresh courage take;
> The clouds ye so much dread
> Are big with mercy, and shall break
> In blessings on your head.
> —W. Cooper

"Lest the gloom should appall us, God braids the cloud with sunshine!"
— H. BONAR

IMITATORS OF GOD'S LOVE

READ I JOHN 2:5-11

Be ye therefore followers [imitators] of God, as dear children; and walk in love, as Christ also hath loved us . . .

Ephesians 5:1, 2

What a great responsibility is laid upon us as Christians, to be imitators of the love of God in Christ. What self-sacrifice, what compassion, what forbearance this entails. Christ gave *Himself for us.* How self-sacrificing is our love toward the brethren?

An ancient legend concerning the Apostle John tells us that when he became too old to preach and too feeble to walk to church, his friends carried him to the assembly on a litter. As he lay there on the floor looking up at the rest of them, he would say over and over to each one who passed by his stretcher, "Little children, *love one another!*" Finally, the early Christians grew weary of his ceaseless repetition and asked him why he always said the same thing. "Because," he replied, "it is the Lord's most urgent command, and if only this be done, it is enough."

Some years ago, when a bridge was being built, the workmen came to a crucial point where the two sides were supposed to meet, but the iron girders refused to contact each other by several inches. Therefore the bolts and rivets could not be driven through to secure the whole together. Every mechanical method to bring them into union was tried, but to no avail. Finally, in despair, all further effort was abandoned for the night. The following morning the sun came up bright and warm, and gradually the great mass of metal, expanding beneath its genial rays, came together in a perfect union. Quickly the workmen inserted the bolts and rivets and the great span was completed. Such, too, is the warming power of the Sun of Righteousness if it is shed abroad in our hearts toward others. Things that cannot be knit in artificial ways by ritual or "religion" are then blended into a perfect fellowship. How blessed is the communion when by love we "serve one another" (Gal. 5:13).   — H.G.B.

God, make me kind!
So many hearts are needing
The balm to stop the bleeding
That my kind words can bring.
God, make me kind!

—D. M. N.

"If you are not very kind, you are not very spiritual!"

MORE ABOUT CLOUDS

READ EXODUS 40:35-38

> *. . . I will appear in the cloud upon the mercy seat.*
> Leviticus 16:2

A cloud upon the mercy seat! Clouds speak of mercy and grace. Israel was under the curse of sin, the cloud of God's judgment. However, when the blood was applied to the ark, the dark cloud of God's judgment turned to a bright cloud of mercy. Are there clouds in your life? Then notice what they mean in the Bible.

1. Assurance — no more judgment — Genesis 9:13.
2. Guidance — Exodus 13:21.
3. Mercy and forgiveness — Leviticus 16:2.
4. Acceptance with God — I Kings 8:10.
5. God's wisdom — Job 37:15.
6. Refreshing — Proverbs 16:15.
7. Testimony — Matthew 17:5.
8. Promise — Luke 12:54.
9. Encouragement — Hebrews 12:1.
10. Victory — Acts 1:9.
11. Judgment for the wicked — Revelation 1:7.
12. Glory by and by — Revelation 14:14.

We need the clouds! Without them our lives would be barren and fruitless. Clouds bring rain. Uninterrupted sunshine can only produce a desert.

On a recent plane trip, we took off on a dark, gloomy, cloudy day and I wondered how the pilot would manage the plane in the murky darkness. But he pointed the plane upwards and suddenly the light broke through upon a scene of breathless, indescribable beauty. Beneath us were billow upon billow of rolling silver fleece, as the clouds, now below us, sparkled with dazzling colors in the sun. By faith rise above the clouds and live in the sunshine of their promise. — M.R.D.

> Back of the clouds the sun is always shining,
> After the storms your skies will all be blue;
> God has prepared a rosy-tinted lining,
> Back of the clouds it's waiting to shine through.
> —C. R. Freeman

"For the Christian, clouds are but the shadow of God's wing!"

BESETTING SINS

> *. . . let us lay aside every weight, and the sin which doth so easily beset us.*
>
> Hebrews 12:1

Everyone has certain sins which to him seem especially attractive, and into which by nature he is most prone to fall. These enticing allurements of Satan and the flesh are called "besetting sins." Your besetting sin is the one for which you do not wish to be reproved; to which your thoughts run the most; and for which you find the most excuse! It is the fault which you are trying to persuade yourself is just a "natural infirmity." That sin must be given up or it will slowly but surely sap your spiritual energy and destroy your witness.

A certain woman had often requested prayer for her husband's salvation, yet he remained unrepentant. Finally, it was discovered that the reason her husband was uninfluenced by the call of Christ was that his wife had an uncontrolled temper. The preacher finally told her, "Mary, you must ask the Lord to give you victory over this besetting sin, and then I think you can more rightly expect your husband's conversion." In shame and despair she took the matter to the Saviour and, resigning her will to the Holy Spirit, obtained the power she needed. Sometime later she hung a new lamp in the hall, wishing to surprise her husband. When he came home he brushed against it by mistake, sending it clattering to the floor where it broke in a hundred pieces. He waited apprehensively for the fight to begin, and was amazed when his wife just quietly looked at him. "Never mind, dear," she said. "It's all right; you couldn't help it. We can get another one." "Mary," said he, "what has come over you?" "Oh," she replied, "I've not only trusted Jesus to save me, but also to cure me of my terrible temper." "Well," said her husband, "if He can do that for you, you'd better remember to pray for me tonight, for that's the kind of genuine salvation I want." It is reported that he was soon converted.

Say, what is your "besetting sin"?

— H.G.B.

> You can't paint black and not get black,
> You can't fool around with sin;
> It will leave its trace on your heart and life,
> And its mark on your soul within.
>
> —D. N.

"Sins are like weeds; you must pull them out or they will take possession" (see Gal. 5:16, 17).

STICK OUT YOUR TONGUE!

READ MATTHEW 26:69-75

> *. . . thy speech bewrayeth [betrayeth] thee.*
> Matthew 26:73

It makes little difference how dumb you are, if you only keep your mouth shut, no one will find it out. Nothing reveals the character of a man like his tongue. The tongue reveals what is going on inside. One of the first things your doctor says when you go to him, is, "Let me see your tongue." It is often possible to make a diagnosis just on the condition of the tongue. A clean tongue means a good digestion and health. A coated tongue indicates some disturbance of health. Different diseases can be detected by the peculiar condition of the tongue. Measles, scarlet fever, diabetes, and many infections are characterized by changes in the tongue. A fuzzy coated tongue, a bright red inflamed tongue, a dry tongue, a cracked tongue, or a spotted tongue — these will often reveal some particular disease. Yes, the doctor can learn a great deal just by looking at your tongue.

This is even more true as a test of spiritual health. Let me see your tongue, for "out of the abundance of the heart the mouth speaketh" (Matt. 12:34). Peter in the judgment hall made the mistake of opening his mouth. He talked too much, and some of the folks recognized his dialect and said, "Thou also art one of them for thy speech be bewrayeth thee." This is true in at least four ways of our speech.

1. It tells the country from which we came.
2. It reveals education and refinement, or the lack of it.
3. It betrays our chief interest in life. We talk about the things we love the most.
4. Our speech also reveals to which country we are going, for travelers to Glory will speak "the language of Heaven," while travelers to Hell will speak "the language of the pit."

A filthy tongue reveals a filthy heart. "If a man offend not in word, the same is a perfect man, and able to bridle the whole body" (James 3:2). *Let me see your tongue!*   — M.R.D.

> Take my tongue, that bridled well,
> Words of truth it e'er may tell.
> Take my heart, its well-spring deep,
> Cleanse and purify and keep.
>
> —I. H.

"A 'bit of love' is the only bit that will bridle the tongue."—F. BECK

GOD'S GRACIOUS INVITATION

READ LUKE 14:16-24

Come; for all things are now ready.   Luke 14:17

The Bible is a book of invitations; in it the word "come" is used over thirty-five hundred times! One such passage is found in Luke 14 where Jesus tells of a great feast prepared by a generous host. It was free, and more than ample to feed the many who had been invited. The excuses that were made for not partaking were poor and insufficient. Especially is this true when one understands the oriental customs of that day. In the East, when a man planned to have a banquet, he first sent out invitations and when everyone had agreed to come, he prepared the feast accordingly. Then at the proper hour he would send forth a servant to say, "All things are now ready; come to the supper!" To refuse to attend at the last moment, therefore, was a real insult to the host, and worthy of the highest condemnation. Jesus was pointing out that Israel was guilty of this terrible sin.

There was once a man who was under deep conviction but who could not grasp the truth that the Gospel invitation was meant for him. His employer, an earnest Christian man, wrote him a note asking him to come to his office. He obeyed the summons but was met with the question, "Do you wish to see me, James?" The man held up the note saying, "But sir, *you sent for me!*" "Oh," said the other, "you believed that I wanted to see you just because I told you to come?" "Yes!" "You thought I expected you to accept my invitation *promptly?*" "Certainly, sir," answered the man. "Well," said the Christian, "God has bidden you to come and He too means for you to *do it at once!* Why then do you hesitate?" The man's lips quivered and the tears ran down his cheeks. He said brokenly, "Am I just to believe God's Word in the same way that I believed your note?" "Just in the same way," replied the employer. "For 'if ye receive the witness of men, the witness of God is greater.'"

Today the Gospel feast is still spread, and the gracious invitation is directed to *you — "Come; for all things are now ready."*

— H.G.B.

Come, for the feast is spread; hark to the call!
Come to the Living Bread, broken for all;
Come to His house and dine, there on His breast recline,
All that He has is thine; come, sinner, come.

—H. Burton

"Either hearken to the 'come' of salvation, or expect to hear at last the 'depart' of damnation!" — G. W.

WHO IS YOUR NEIGHBOR?

READ LUKE 10:25-37

. . . And who is my neighbour?   Luke 10:29

This was the question a certain lawyer put to Jesus when caught in his own trap. He had come to Jesus to tempt him, saying, "Master, what shall I do to inherit eternal life?" It was a fool's question. It showed how ignorant this educated lawyer really was. His inquiry was a contradiction. You cannot *do* anything to inherit something. An inheritance is a gift for which you have not worked. It is something for which someone else worked. The question, "What shall I do to inherit eternal life?" was a dumb question to ask. Jesus therefore says: If you want to be saved by *doing* something, then keep the law — including the commandment, "Love thy neighbor as thyself." The man was caught and tried to wiggle out of it for Luke says, "But he, willing to justify himself, said unto Jesus, And who is my neighbor?" Then follows the story of the good Samaritan.

Who is your neighbor? In a real sense everyone is your neighbor and mine, and we have a responsibility to witness to them both far and near. The command is to go into all the world.

A Christian, asked to contribute to foreign missions, refused, saying, "I only believe in helping my neighbors." "And whom do you consider your neighbors?" he was asked. "Why, those around me," he replied. "Do you consider the man who owns the land adjoining yours as a neighbor?" "Yes, of course I do," he said. The next question was, "How much land do you own?" and he replied, "640 acres." "And how far *down* do you own it?" "Why, I hadn't thought of it, but I suppose all the way down." "Yes," came the reply, "all the way till it touches your next-door neighbor's land on the other side of the world, a heathen Chinese. He is your next-door neighbor."

To the believer in Christ, all men are his neighbors. — M.R.D.

All the speeches you are making may be very fine and true,
    But I'd rather see your Saviour by observing what you do;
For I may not comprehend Him through the fine advice you
        give,
    But there's no misunderstanding when I see the way
        you live!   —N. B. Herrell

"That which makes a good Christian, makes a good neighbor."

SOMETIME WE'LL UNDERSTAND

READ MARK 8:14-26

> . . . *What I do thou knowest not now; but thou shalt know hereafter.*
> John 13:7

With their limited spiritual horizons the disciples did not always understand what Jesus said and did. Like the blind man of Bethsaida, their prophetic insight was as distorted as one who sees, "men as trees walking." Later, at Pentecost, they were to receive a second touch of blessing which would illumine their minds to the meaning of many things. Therefore in John 13:7 Jesus tells them not to become confused or bewildered by the perplexing events that were to transpire. They were to proceed by faith, resting on the precious promise that "hereafter" they would comprehend His wise purposes. So, today, Christ's acts of love to us are often misunderstood. Yet His apparent "dark dealings" with us will certainly be explained in Heaven, for God knows what He is about.

The late Dr. H. A. Ironside often told the story of a noted painter who had been commissioned to prepare a great, artistic mural. The artist erected a scaffold and proceeded to put the background of the picture on the wall. A friend, coming to the studio, stood quietly at the rear of the room, for he saw the artist was preoccupied in slapping on the dark gray and the deep blue tones. Wishing to view his background preparation from a better perspective, the artist descended the ladder and moved toward the door with his eye still on the mural. He was so intent that he backed right into his friend without even seeing him. Enthusiastically he exclaimed, "This is going to be the masterpiece of my life! What do you think of it? Isn't it grand?" His friend replied, "All that I see is a great, dull daub of paint." Then said the artist, "Oh, I forgot. When you look at the mural you see only what is there; but when I look at it, *I see what is going to be there* — and that makes a lot of difference!"

How wise the Christian who can smile through his tears — confident that he will joyously view the perfect design of his trials in God's tomorrow!

— H.G.B.

> I know not now why schemes were spoiled
>   And lofty aspirations foiled;
> Hereafter I shall know, shall see
>   These very things were best for me.
>
> —A. G.

"Every tomorrow has two handles. We can take hold of it with the handle of anxiety, or the handle of faith."

IN THE WORLD — NOT OF IT

READ COLOSSIANS 3:1-11

> *. . . seek those things which are above . . . Set your*
> *affection on things above . . . Mortify therefore your*
> *members which are upon the earth.* Colossians 3:1, 2, 5

A small girl was watching her mother working among the flowers. "Mother," she said, "I know why flowers grow; they want to get out of the dirt!" We Christians are *in* the world, but not *of* it (John 17). With our feet on the ground, we are admonished to set our affection "on *things above,* not on things on the earth"; we are risen with Christ and are to "seek those things which are above, where Christ sitteth on the right hand of God" (Col. 3:1-3).

What is the mysterious force which causes a sprouting seed to grow up instead of down? I plant a bulb upside down in the ground, but it always comes out "right side up." It is the sunlight above which attracts the plant to itself. Plants always seek the sunlight. Notice how your house plants turn and bend way over to reach the light from the window. Why is a sunflower called a *sun*flower? Because it turns with the sun in the morning to the east and follows it to the west. Why does a dandelion open only on sunny days but remain closed on dark days? It is the power of the sun. Obstruct the sunlight and life fades out. I threw an old rug to dry on the lawn and forgot to remove it, and all the grass turned a sickly yellow, from which it did not recover for weeks. As a plant seeks the sun above, so we are to "seek those things which are above."

The clouds of earth often obscure the sun, but by the wings of faith we can rise above the clouds and dwell in the eternal sunlight. The ladder of faith, made of two uprights, the Word of God, and prayer, supporting the nine rungs of Galatians 5:22, 23, is long enough to reach beyond the clouds of doubt, fear, and defeat. Walk in the light of His Word and rise above the things of earth. — M.R.D.

> I want to live above the world,
>   Though Satan's darts at me are hurled;
> For faith has caught the joyful sound,
>   The song of saints on higher ground!
>   —J. Oatman, Jr.

"The influence of a holy life is often the greatest contribution we can make to the salvation of men."

"THOU REMAINEST"

READ HABAKKUK 3:13-19

... thou remainest ....   Hebrews 1:11

The faithfulness of God is constantly highlighted in the Bible. Men falter and prove untrue, but God remains constant. What a comfort this is to His weak and doubting children! It is not always easy to see this divine control in our lives. It looks sometimes as if things have gotten out of hand, but this can never be for "God abideth faithful."

In the spring of the year a preaching missionary band in China asked a poor Christian farmer to join them in carrying on their work. "But I haven't planted my wheat yet," he protested. Even as he made the excuse, however, a voice within his heart said, "*Your wheat?* Nay it is your Heavenly Father's wheat." He recognized that this was true and decided to go. His heathen neighbors scoffed at him and said he was very foolish not to stay and first plant his crop. However, he filled his days with scattering the incorruptible seed of the Word upon the good soil of needy souls, and was very happy. After some weeks it was possible for him to return home. His heart sank when he saw his neighbor's fields already lovely and green with the sprouting grain. He hadn't even planted his yet; how would he ever overcome their lead? His crop would come in last and he would receive little for it. Then he thought of the comforting words, "Your Heavenly Father knoweth what things ye have need of," and his peace returned. He planted his wheat but for some time there was no rain. The ground was so dry that the seed refused to sprout. The green fields of his neighbors turned yellow and before the drought was over, a third of their crop had withered and died. Then came refreshing rains and his wheat took root and sprang up. When the harvest season arrived he had a most beautiful field of waving grain, while his neighbors complained bitterly of their poor yield. Thus God honored His faithful servant.

Though all may seem to slip from your grasp, do not despair. With trusting heart look up to your faithful God and quietly say, "I thank Thee, Lord, that '*Thou remainest*'!"   — H.C.B.

> When sorrows press and hope seems dim,
> Hold fast, look up, and trust in Him —
> He faileth not!
>
> —Anon.

"God sometimes sends His love letters to us in black-edged envelopes — yet He abideth faithful." — SPURGEON

DO IT TODAY!

READ PSALM 95

Boast not thyself of to morrow; for thou knowest not what a day may bring forth. Proverbs 27:1

All we can be sure of is *now*. Today's opportunities will be gone tomorrow. The soul you should contact today may be gone in another day. Some years ago on our afternoon broadcast, James Draper, our music director, gave a hymn story which illustrates the urgency of *now*.

D. L. Moody said one of the greatest mistakes he ever made occurred October 8, 1871. On that night he addressed the largest crowd he had ever spoken to in Chicago. His message dealt with the trial of Jesus in Pilate's hall, and was based on the text, "What then shall I do with Jesus?" He concluded his sermon by saying, "I wish you would take this text home with you and seriously consider it, and next Sunday we will speak on the cross, and we will decide what we should do with Jesus." Speaking of this incident later, Moody called it a tragic error and "one of the greatest mistakes of my life; for I never saw that congregation again." When the sermon was finished, he asked Mr. Sankey to sing, "Today the Saviour Calls." Almost prophetically the third verse ran:

"Today the Saviour calls; for refuge fly;
The storm of justice falls and death is nigh."

It was the last song sung in that hall, for even as Sankey sang, his voice was drowned out by the clanging of fire engine bells in the street. It was the night of the great Chicago fire, in which Mr. Moody's hall was left in ashes and in which one thousand perished, some of them undoubtedly from that audience. Moody said he learned the lesson, "When preaching Christ, press for an immediate and definite decision." He explained, "I would rather lose my right hand than ever again give an audience a week or a day to decide for Christ."

Don't put off till tomorrow what you should do today. —M.R.D.

Today the Saviour calls;
Ye wand'rers, come;
O ye benighted souls,
Why longer roam?
—S. F. Smith

"God has promised forgiveness to your repentance; but He has not promised tomorrow to your procrastination." — AUGUSTINE

JESUS AND HEAVEN

READ REVELATION 22:1-4

. . . but we know that . . . we shall see him . . . I John 3:2

Death ushers the believer instantly into the visible presence of the Saviour, for to be absent from the body is to be at Home with the Lord. Yet many dread that momentous step from earth to heaven because so little of what will exactly transpire is related to us. God cannot express in human language the preciousness of our passing from earth to Heaven. We do believe that Jesus indicates in the true story in Luke 15 that the blessed angels will guide us safely to our destination (see verse 22), and that He Himself, will walk with us through the "Valley of the Shadow" (Ps. 23:4); but beyond that, little more has been revealed.

A Christian who was very ill once said to his physician, "Doctor, I am afraid to die. What happens to a Christian in that mystic hour of death?" Very quietly the doctor said, "I do not believe anyone really knows exactly!" As he walked across the sickroom to the door, he wished desperately that he could say something more comforting. Suddenly, as he stood holding the doorknob, there came the sound of scratching and whining from the other side. As the doctor opened the door, his faithful dog sprang into the room and leaped on him with an eager show of gladness. Turning to the patient the physician said, "Did you notice that dog of mine? He had never been in this room before. He did not know what was inside. He knew nothing except *that his master was here,* and when the door was opened he sprang in *without fear.* As Christians we know little of what is on the other side of death except that it will be glory and blessing, but we do know one thing — that *our Master and Saviour is there, and that is enough!* When the door opens I shall pass through with no fear but with gladness, for I know I shall 'see His face.'" Yes, to be with Christ is "far better" — it can be nothing but glory!

—H.G.B.

> Oh that will be glory for me,
>   Glory for me, glory for me;
> When by His grace I shall look on His face,
>   That will be glory, be glory for me!
> — C. H. Gabriel

"Christ has made death but a starlit strip between the companionships of yesterday, and the reunions of tomorrow!"

THE FIRST SIN

READ ISAIAH 14:12-15
    EZEKIEL 28:12-15

*Pride goeth before destruction, and an haughty spirit
before a fall.* Proverbs 16:18

So you don't drink, steal, curse, or commit adultery, play
cards, gamble, smoke, or lie, or go to shows! Well, that is wonderful; but after all, isn't that what is to be expected of any
decent person? The fact you don't indulge in these things is no
more than your duty. Whenever I hear someone boast of his
morality, I know that he is guilty of one sin he has overlooked —
pride. Pride is as great a sin as these others, in fact is at the
very root of all of them. I was surprised to find that pride is
more frequently mentioned and condemned in the Word of God
than adultery. The words "pride," "proud," "proudly" occur 106
times in the Bible, while the words "adultery," "adulterous,"
"adulterer," "adulteress" occur only seventy times.

The word "pride" in the original is a combination of two
words, *huper,* and *phaino. Huper* means "above," and *phaino*
means "to shine." Pride then is the desire of a person to "shine
above" his fellow men. It is self-exaltation, in direct disregard of
God's Word. (See Rom. 12:3.)

Pride was the first sin of the universe. It was the sin which
caused Satan to fall from his high position (read the Scriptures
at the beginning of this article), and this sin Satan instilled in
the heart of Eve by the words, "Ye shall be as gods" (Gen. 3:5).
Pride is deification of self. It always wants to be in the limelight,
wants to attract attention, a conceit of one's superiority. But the
Bible says: "For if a man think himself to be something when
he is nothing, he deceiveth himself" (Gal. 6:3).

So you don't drink, steal, curse, or commit adultery, play cards,
gamble, smoke, or lie, or go to shows! Aren't you proud of being
such a fine fellow, so much better than others about you? Don't
strut, brother, for it is only God's grace in which you can glory.
Oh, God, forgive us for the subtle, fleshly sin of pride. Amen.
— M.R.D.

> When I survey the wondrous cross
>   On which the Prince of glory died,
> My richest gain I count but loss,
>   AND POUR CONTEMPT ON ALL MY PRIDE!
> —I. Watts

"None have more pride than those who dream that they have none!"
— SPURGEON

FORGET NOT ALL HIS BENEFITS

READ PSALMS 107:1-9

Bless the Lord, O my soul, and forget not all his benefits.

Psalm 103:2

Praise and thankgiving should not be confined to a formal celebration on one day of the year alone (good as that in itself may be); it should characterize our continuing attitude of heart throughout the entire year. If our deepest joy is found in knowing God Himself and in gratefully blessing Him from the depths of our heart for what He means to us, then it will not be difficult to also remember His individual "benefits" to us. To have God as our Father, Jesus Christ as our Saviour, and the Holy Spirit as our Comforter and Guide, is to experience a fellowship and to enjoy a satisfaction that the broken cisterns of this world can never begin to provide. To have this true gladness in the heart is to know the greatest blessing of all. If this is your happy portion, you, with the psalmist, will put the emphasis in the proper place today by first blessing God for Himself, and then praising Him for all His benefits toward you.

Ira D. Sankey used to tell this beautiful story of a little girl who went sightseeing with her father to the top of Mount Washington. Standing in the rarified air and bright sunshine, with the clear blue sky above them, they saw to their surprise that dark heavy clouds were gathering below. As they looked down, the lightning began to flash and with a roll of thunder a storm broke majestically over the valley below. The father, a very prosaic, unimaginative man, said apologetically, "Well, Lucy, with the clouds all around, there is nothing much to see, is there?" Unlike her parent, the child, who was deeply spiritual, was enthralled by the beauty and majesty of the scene. Grasping his hand she said, "Oh, papa, I think it is wonderful. *I see the doxology!* Everything seems to be saying, 'Praise Father, Son, and Holy Ghost!' "

Those who have been enlightened by grace see God's goodness and love both in storm and in sunshine and reverently echo the words, "Bless the Lord, O my soul"!

— H.G.B.

> I thank Thee that instead of wealth
> Instead of riches of the mart,
> Or any prize my hands can hold —
> "Thou hast put gladness in my heart!"
>
> —N. L. Upton

"God's goodness hath been great to thee — let never day nor night unhallowed pass but still remember what the Lord hath done."

BEWARE OF THE DOG!

READ EPHESIANS 5:22-33

*He that passeth by, and meddleth with strife belonging
not to him, is like one that taketh a dog by the ears.*
Proverbs 26:17

Never catch a dog by the ears, for it is the most sensitive part
of his body. Pull his tail if you must — but his ears — never,
unless you want to be bitten. Solomon compares this foolish,
dangerous act with persons who meddle in other people's affairs.
But sometimes you can't avoid it and you are unwillingly
involved.

Pity the poor preacher who is expected to patch up a quarrel
between husband and wife. He has "two strikes on him" before
he begins. If he takes the side of the wife — the husband is mad.
If he sides with the husband — the wife is angry, and if he refuses
to take sides at all — both of them are ready to snap at him — for
trying to take a dog by the ears. If the couple are unsaved, then
we can often help them a great deal, probably show them that
their troubles would be solved if they would only accept the
Lord. But when Christians who know the Lord and His Word
cannot patch up their squabbles, what chance has an outsider
who comes in to tackle the longeared dog?

Some time ago a lady called begging me to come over right
away because her husband threatened to leave her. "Please
come over, please, and straighten this out!" They had been feud-
ing for days. I asked her if she was a Christian and she said
"Yes." "Is your husband a Christian?" The reply was "Yes, and
he's listening on the extension phone." "Well," I said, "if you are
both Christians, you can settle your trouble immediately. I am
not coming over until after you have read together Ephesians
4:32. 'And be ye kind one to another, tenderhearted, forgiving
one another, even as God for Christ's sake hath forgiven you.'
That is God's solution — try it first, and if that doesn't work, call
me and I'll come over. But you must believe Ephesians 4:32 and
do it. If it fails, call me." I am still waiting for the call. Don't
bother others with your problems when you have the answer
right before you in the Bible.   — M.R.D.

> I've found a little remedy
> To ease the life we live
> And make each day a happier one;
> It is the word, FORGIVE!
> —Anon.

**"I can forgive but I cannot forget is another way of saying,
'I cannot forgive.' "** — BEECH

SEGREGATION AND INTEGRATION

READ NUMBERS 7:1-6

> .... *and he was a Samaritan.* Luke 17:16

Ten lepers stood afar off as Jesus passed by and cried to Him for mercy. Jesus healed them, but only one returned to give thanks, " . . . and he was a Samaritan." The other nine were evidently Jews, for this one man is called a stranger or alien (Luke 17:18). In this incident we have a picture of segregation and integration. Leprosy had segregated these men from the assembly of the people of God. They were thrust outside the camp as unclean. They were carefully segregated. But while they were segregated from some, they were also definitely integrated with others. A Jew despised a Samaritan, and would have nothing to do with him. In John 4:9 we read, " . . . for the Jews have no dealings with the Samaritans." But here are nine Jews with one Samaritan. They were integrated by the common curse of leprosy. These lepers were segregated from the healthy ones by the disease of leprosy, but they were integrated with all others who had the same disease.

Leprosy is a picture of sin. Sin has integrated all of Adam's race, and they are all alike in their common fate — under sentence of death, "for there is no difference, for all have sinned and come short of the glory of God" (Rom. 3:22, 23). There is no difference. But this same sin has segregated us from God. "Your iniquities have separated between you and your God" (Isa. 59:2). But the Lord cures the leprosy of sin by the blood of the Lamb when we are saved, and the whole thing is turned completely around, and now we are separated from the world and integrated into the Body of Christ. Yes, we believe in spiritual segregation (from sin and condemnation), and also in spiritual integration (with all other believers).

— M.R.D.

> Separate from sinners, now joined unto Him,
> Christ's blood has broken my friendship with sin.
> Once it was union with those in defeat,
> Now with believers I've fellowship sweet.
> —Anon.

"Sin segregates us from God and integrates us with evil, while grace does just the opposite."

"FEAR NOT" – GOD WILL SUPPLY!

READ LUKE 12:22-34

Fear not, little flock . . . .   Luke 12:32
But my God shall supply all your need . . . .
                      Philippians 4:19

Christians in Scripture are referred to as "sheep." This underscores their inherent weakness, for sheep are feeble compared to lions, horses, and oxen. Since sheep are without much natural equipment for fighting off their adversaries, they are quite helpless when attacked. They just huddle together and bleat piteously when an enemy assaults them. Their only hope for survival is to be found in the protection afforded by a faithful shepherd who will often guard and defend them at the risk of his own life. Fear, therefore, is characteristic of sheep.

Our Good Shepherd, the Lord Jesus Christ, knows the inherent weakness of His own against their arch adversary—the Devil. He knows the fears that naturally arise in our hearts, and yet He admonishes us to take courage, to put aside our nameless dread. He invites us to find comfort in His sure protection and kindly leading. The fact that He will guide and encamp round about us provides sweet comfort and assurance. He will not only protect us and supply our every need, but will do so with an overflowing abundance that will make our cup of blessing "run over." His assuring words are, "Fear not, little flock"!

A Johns Hopkins doctor says that people who worry die much sooner than non-worriers! To live by worry means ultimate destruction of the body and results as well in a sad withering of the soul. God wants us to have faith and not fear!

One of Spurgeon's quaint sayings was: "If there was an ant at the door of your granary begging for help, it would not ruin you to give him a grain of your wheat." Then he would say, "Remember, you are but a tiny insect at the door of God's all-sufficiency – *do not doubt His sure supply!"*   — H.G.B.

> 'Tis comforting for me to know
> That God is with me as I go;
> Though troubles come within my range,
> The loving Father does not change."
>   —Emily May Young

"Fear is like sand in the machinery of life — faith is like oil."

DISABLED HUNTERS

READ: II CORINTHIANS 12:1-10

> *. . . the lame take the prey.*   Isaiah 33:23

HUNTER BAGS DEER WHILE SITTING IN A WHEELCHAIR. Thus ran the heading in the newspaper. A man very fond of hunting, broke his leg just before the season opened. Knowing how badly he felt about missing the hunt, his friends arranged to take him along in a wheelchair, so he could at least enjoy the camp life. While the men left to take their stations he sat disconsolately in his chair before the window, when lo and behold! a big buck stepped into the clearing! He opened the window, wheeled to the corner for a rifle and shot the buck through the open window, while sitting in a wheelchair. His companions came home, tired, ragged and disappointed — emptyhanded.

As I read the article the above text immediately came to mind. ". . . the lame take the prey." What seemed like a misfortune had its compensation. How often we must get in a wheelchair to get the "buck." What seems like calamity and misfortune often carries the greatest blessing.

Are you laid aside? Have your dreams been shattered? Have you met with disappointment, sickness, reverses, even bereavement? It is not without a purpose (Rom. 8:28), and you will have its compensation. If you are a child of God, you may be sure that for every hard experience God has a reason and a compensation. Good sailors are made in storms. Heroes become such only by meeting crises. There is no fruit without clouds!

— M.R.D.

> From the exhaustion of our fretful life,
>   From the world's ceaseless stir of care and strife,
> Into the shade and stillness of our heavenly Guide
>   For a brief space we are sometimes called aside.
>
> Our knowledge deeper grows with Him alone;
>   In secret oft His deeper love is shown:
> We learn in many an hour of dark distress
>   Some rare, sweet lesson of His tenderness.
>
> — Anon.

"God can take the source of our distress and change it by His grace into a channel of delight."

THE ISSUES OF LIFE

READ: PROVERBS 4:18-27

Keep thy heart with all diligence; for out of it are the issues of life. Proverbs 4:23

A man passing by a small lake heard some frantic calls for help. Diving into the water fully clothed, he saved a youngster from drowning. The boy was grateful, and tried to stammer out his thanks. The rescuer patted him on the head and said, "That's all right, young fellow; *just make sure that you're worth it!*" In later years the boy often pondered those well-chosen words. He came to understand that life is much more than mere existence. To be worthwhile it must be filled with service, purpose, and praise to God! *This can issue only from a heart touched by grace!*

Someone has said, "Take a piece of wax, a piece of meat, some sand, some clay, and some shavings, and put them on the fire. Each is being acted upon by the same agent, yet the wax melts, the meat fries, the sand dries up, the clay hardens, and the shavings blaze. Just so, under the influence of identical circumstances and environment, one man becomes stronger while another, without Christ, becomes weaker and withers.

"One Ship goes East, another West,
    By the selfsame winds that blow;
'Tis the *set of the sail* and not the gale,
    That determines the way they go.
Like the winds of the sea are the ways of time,
    As we voyage along through life;
'Tis the *set of the soul* that determines the goal,
    And not the calm or the strife."

Has the course of your soul been set at Calvary so that *Christ is now the Pilot at the helm of your heart?* Is the "wind" of the Holy Spirit blowing your bark ever closer to the Celestial City? Then your life is meaningful and worth while! — H.G.B.

Had I but this one day to live,
    One day to love, one day to give,
One day to work and watch and raise
    My voice to God in joyous praise,
One day to succor those in need,
    Pour healing balm on hearts that bleed,
I'd spend, O God, much time with Thee
    That Thou might'st plan my day for me.
—A. H. Muir

"Only one life, 'twill soon be past; only what's done for Christ will last."

THE KISS OF DEATH

READ: ROMANS 5:1-11

Let him kiss me with the kisses of his mouth: for thy love is better than wine.   Song of Solomon 1:2

Where the world's favorite indoor sport — "kissing" — originated, I do not know. The earliest record of kissing is in Genesis 27:26. There it was a kiss of deception and betrayal. The last mention of kissing is in I Peter 5:14 and here is a pure kiss of devotion. Between these first- and last-mentioned kisses we have recorded many other kinds. Some of them are: The kiss of (1) Death (II Sam. 20:9); (2) Lust (Prov. 7:13); and (3) Betrayal (Mark 14:44). These were all evil kisses—kisses of sin. But there are also other kisses: The kiss of: (4) Devotion (Luke 7:45); (5) Greeting (Rom. 16:16, I Cor. 16:20); (6) Farewell (Ruth 1:9); and (7) Reconciliation (Luke 15:20).

The father kissed his repentant son before he was cleaned up. He kissed him with all the filth of the pigs' trough upon him. What matchless love! It is a picture of God's love. He gave His Son to die for us "while we were yet sinners" (Rom. 5:8).

A little girl lay desperately ill with diphtheria. The mother had been warned to avoid all possible contact with the child for fear of contagion. The child sank into a stupor and the anxious mother with a prayer laid her tender hand on her brow. This touch revived her, and seeing mother, she whispered, "Kiss me, Mother." Love overcame fear and she stooped down to kiss her. Mother's love conquered, but it cost her life. She kissed the one she loved with the kiss of death; but God kissed the ungodly, the unlovely. Christ by His love-kiss took our contagion upon Him and bore it to the cross. It was the kiss of death; but the kiss of death for Him became the kiss of salvation for us. This kiss is offered to all. "Kiss the Son" (Ps. 2:12). Yes, kiss the Son and accept His reconciliation. Blessed are all they that put their trust in Him.

— M.R.D.

> Kiss the Son, lest o'er your way
>   His consuming wrath should break;
> For supremely blest are they
>   Who in Christ their refuge take.
>   — Anon.

"The kiss of God's forgiveness can change a prodigal son into a profitable one!"

GOD EXALTS THE HUMBLE

READ: I PETER 5:1-6

Humble yourselves therefore under the mighty hand of God, that he may exalt you in due time.   I Peter 5:6

Pastor Arthur H. Giles of Duluth, Minnesota, once related a story that so well illustrates the truth of I Peter 5:6 that I have asked his permission to pass it on to you. In a letter Brother Giles wrote: "My immediate predecessor at my present church was a blind layman by the name of John Taylor, a true servant of the Lord. When he relinquished the work here, he became pastor of the little Congregational Church at Brule. When President Calvin Coolidge visited the town and made it his summer White House (I believe it was in the summer of 1926), it was decided that it would be wise to substitute a Doctor of Divinity for the humble, unlettered Mr. Taylor during the time that the President would be at the Wisconsin resort. Mr. Coolidge, however, heard of the proposition, and declared that if the regular, faithful pastor was not permitted to remain, he would not attend the Church.

"The first Sunday the President was in town the small meeting house was so crowded that many were not able to get in. After Mr. Taylor had preached and closed the meeting with the benediction, he sat in his chair waiting for the church to empty. After a while a man said to him, 'Pastor, don't you think we should leave now?' The blind Mr. Taylor replied in a whisper, 'We had better wait until the President and his party have left.' The voice replied, '*I am the President!*' Whereupon, Mr. Coolidge took Mr. Taylor by the arm and led him outside the building where press photographers took pictures of the two. The next day the public saw the President of the United States and the humble, blind preacher locked arm and arm."

Those who humbly serve the Lord may not always thus be given recognition immediately, but in due time their true worth will be revealed by the Lord to their eternal exaltation. — H.G.B.

> Humbly at Thy cross I'd stay,
>   Jesus, keep me there, I pray;
> Teach me more of Thee, each day,
>   Jesus, blessed Jesus.
> — H. P. Blanchard

"Humility is that strange possession which you lose the moment you think you have it."

GO TO THE DEVIL

*But the tongue can no man tame; it is an unruly evil,
full of deadly poison.*   James 3:8, 9

If you can watch only one thing today, to keep you from
sinning — watch your tongue! More people have been slain by
the tongue than by the sword. If you can control your tongue,
you can manage the rest of your body (James 3:2). How many
a godly person's testimony has been completely ruined by one
burst of temper, one bitter blast in an unguarded moment. How
many Christians endowed with wonderful gifts and ability have
lost their usefulness because of a sharp tongue and cutting remarks which wound and smart and burn. A whole day's blessing
can be ruined by one unkind word!

A certain Christian man had written a famous tract: "Come
to Jesus," which had promise of being greatly used of God in
winning men for Christ. Sometime afterward he entered into a
theological argument and became so exceedingly angry with his
opponent that he sat down and wrote a scorching, blistering,
devastating article against this man, intending to have this article,
bristling with sarcasm and invectives, published as an open letter
in the church paper. Before sending it in, he asked a friend to
suggest a title for the article. The friend read it carefully, hesitated, and then said, "I suggest you call it 'Go to the Devil,' by
the same author who wrote 'Come to Jesus.'" The article was
never published.

God help us to bridle our tongues today and we'll be able to
handle the rest of the horse. No matter how right you are, if you
cannot say it kindly — Don't say it! You can say the right thing
in two ways, the right way — and the wrong way. There is nothing men pay less attention to than their words. They imagine if
they do what is right, what they say doesn't matter. Yet once a
word is uttered it can never be recalled.   — M.R.D.

> Only a hasty, thoughtless word, sarcastic and unkind,
>   But it darkened the day before so bright
>   And left a sting behind.
> Only a word of gentle cheer flooded with radiant light
>   The pathway that seemed so dark before,
>   And it made the day more bright.
>
> —Anon.

"A short intellect usually has a long tongue."

LITTLE THINGS

READ: PROVERBS 30:18-28

There be . . . things which are little upon the earth,
BUT. . . .   Proverbs 30:24

Little things are much more important than we often imagine; they have been known to turn the course of events for hundreds of years. For instance, a great king once noticed that his soldiers were using their sleeves instead of handkerchiefs, and — *that's how we all got buttons on our cuffs!* Another monarch was bald and had his servants make him a fancy toupee; immediately judges and courtiers took up the style *and for hundreds of years men of importance shaved off their own locks, and wore flowing wigs of artificial curls!* So too, for good or evil, each of us has his own widening circle of influence.

Someone once complained, "What I say or do doesn't matter. *My influence is like a drop in the bucket!*" "Ah, but a drop can be very important," said another. "It all depends on what it is made of, and what's already in the bucket. One little drop of water falling into a container of acid may cause an explosion. One drop of germ culture introduced into a container of milk can make the liquid dangerous to drink; while one drop of cleansing disinfectant can neutralize a whole pailful of contaminated water." Yes, even a "drop in a bucket" can make a tremendous difference. Our influence is greater than we suspect. In fact, those whom the world considers "insignificant" are probably the ones whose lives are making the greatest impact for eternity!

Have you ever thought of it, that after all, it's only the *small birds* that sing? You never heard a note from the eagle in all your life, nor from the turkey, nor from the ostrich. But you have heard thrilling melody from the throat of a canary, and bright, happy trills of praise from the robin, and the lark. My how they can sing! So too, the sweetest music often comes from those Christians who are small in their own estimation but great in the eyes of the Lord. Indeed, "There be . . . things which are little upon the earth, BUT*!!*"   — H.G.B.

Little crosses bravely carried,
Little duties daily done,
To the heart of God are precious,
And He counts them one by one.
— Anon.

"He who is a Christian in small things, is not a small Christian!"

LOOK AT YOUR HAND

READ: I CORINTHIANS 12:12-21

> . . . *the eye cannot say unto the hand, I have no need*
> *of thee.*   I Corinthians 12:21

"Give me a hand with this, will you please?" This common expression is used to request help in some situation or job. But why do we say, "give me a hand," or "lend me a hand," and not give me an ear, or an eye, or a foot? Just because the hand is the most useful member of the body. It helps every other member. The hand is truly the "helping hand." Which member protects you when you fall? When some object threatens your eye, what member rushes to the rescue immediately? When your back itches, on which member do you call? When you want to put food in your mouth, which member is called upon? To button your coat, tie your shoes, comb your hair, brush your teeth, carry the groceries, etc., etc., etc., it is that helping hand! It is the most useful, indispensable member of the body. No wonder Paul says, " . . . the eye cannot say unto the hand, I have no need of thee."

The hand is mentioned 1433 times in the Bible. The wrist has eight bones in two rows so it can move backward and forward and over half-way around. No other joint like it! The palm has five bones to act as supports for the hand proper. Four fingers and with a nail on each end. And look at that thumb, so set that it meets the fingers from the opposite direction. Look at your fingers. They are all of different lengths. Is it a mistake by the Maker? It would look so much nicer if they were even. But wait! Close your hand — and now they are all even! Now close your hand over an orange and even the thumb is even with the fingers. Wonderful hand! Look at it! No wonder Solomon calls them "the keepers of the house" (Eccl. 12:3).

God, too, has hands in which He holds us securely, for no man can pluck us out of His hand (John 10:29). Look at your hand, and praise God for His hands!   — M.R.D.

> Oh, the touch of His hand on mine,
>   Oh, the touch of His hand on mine!
> There is grace and pow'r
>   In the trying hour,
> In the touch of His hand on mine.
>   — J. B. Pounds

"In redemption God shows to us His heart, in providence—His hand!"

A CONVENIENT SHIP

READ: JONAH 1:1-17

But Jonah rose up to flee unto Tarshish from the presence of the Lord, and went down to Joppa; and he found a ship going to Tarshish: so he paid the fare thereof.   Jonah 1:3

God commanded Jonah to go to Nineveh to preach a sermon of judgment, but the prophet preferred to do exactly the opposite. Therefore, instead of going east to the city of God's choosing, he determines to travel west to Tarshish. Fleeing from the presence of the Lord (or so he thought), he goes down to Joppa. Here he finds a *convenient ship* waiting to take him in just the direction he desires. Probably rejoicing in such apparent "good fortune," Jonah pays the fare, gets on board and — *sails away into a sea of trouble!*

How prone we are to seize upon that which is *convenient* as being that which is *correct!* When we get out of the will of God, it is surprising how many excuses we can find for going our own way. Deeply impressed with our carnal desires, we quickly interpret that which may be only coincidental as a significant indication of God's will for us. Actually it may be nothing of that kind. The trend of circumstances must always be in line with the Word of God if it is to be meaningful. Jonah's "convenient ship" was soon storm-tossed, and he had some very gruelling experiences before the Lord got him back to the path of His will.

Beware of misinterpreting convenient ships! Remember the so-called "opportunity" may actually be the Devil's snare, the world's allurement, or the pathway of self-will that will result in God's chastening. Surrender yourself completely to His Spirit, saturate your mind with the directives in the Word — you too may rationalize yourself into boarding a boat of human convenience that will at most land you in the port of God's "second best." This day make the prayer of the psalmist your own, "Show me Thy ways, O Lord; teach me Thy paths" (Ps. 25:4).

> Help me find my way, Lord, help me find my way,
> May I through each valley in Thy footsteps stay;
> If 'twere but my choosing, I'd soon go astray,
> Lest I faint and stumble, help me find THY way.
>   — A. B.

"Beware of mistaking your OWN WISHES for

RUNNING YOUR OWN SALOON

READ: PROVERBS 23:29-35

> *Who hath woe? who hath sorrow? who hath contentions? who hath babbling? who hath wounds without cause? who hath redness of eyes? They that tarry long at the wine; they that go to seek mixed wine.*
>
> Proverbs 23:29, 30

So you are just a social drinker? You are not a slave to it, but have it under perfect control, and you can quit it anytime? Then why don't you? It must be because you don't want to, because you can't.

Modern society presents one of the strangest contradictions. We are all excited about deaths from polio, cancer, tuberculosis, the increase in the prevalence of heart disease, dystrophy, and other diseases; and we are deluged with pleas from a hundred organizations to support the heart fund, cancer fund, muscular dystrophy fund, Christmas seal fund, and are embarrassed by stamps and stickers for which we never asked. But alcohol kills more, and brings more misery, and costs society more than the other diseases, or almost all of them together. But we legalize liquor, advertise it, urge people to use it. It would be less wicked to legalize cancer, advertise how to get polio, and urge people to be inoculated with TB germs. Alcohol is more dangerous than any of these. But you insist you can drink moderately? Why not start your own saloon? Without a license! Give your wife $55.00 to buy a case of whiskey. Then pay her 60 cents a drink. When the case is gone your wife will have $145.00. She puts $90.00 in the bank and buys another case for the $55.00. If you do this for ten years and buy all your drinks from your wife, you will die with hardening of the liver, but leave a drunkard's widow with plenty of money (over $25,000.00), enough to trap a decent non-drinking man and forget she was ever married to a bum like you!

So you can quit when you want to? I dare you to do it. Why not admit your failure and let Jesus give you victory? — M.R.D.

> See how the stagg'ring drunkard reels;
>   What shame and mis'ry he reveals!
> His hungry children cry for bread,
>   And from their cold, damp cellar bed,
> They watch for His return with dread —
>   Old alcohol is king of tears!
>
> — F. E. Belden

inking in moderation is not the solution of the drink problem; it is the main cause of it!" — A. C. IVY

THE WEDNESDAY WORRY BOX

READ: LUKE 12:22-31

Be careful for nothing. . . .   Philippians 4:6

One version of the Scriptures more accurately and understandably translates this phrase in Philippians as: "In nothing be anxious." For the Christian, all worry is forbidden. As someone has said, "Anxiety is a spiritual fever which works havoc with the character and service of the child of God; for as we brood over our worries in the secret hours of the night, the mind gets exhausted, the spirit discouraged and depressed, and the body unutterably weary, *and yet the cares remain exactly what they were!*"

When we are anxious we are trespassers on forbidden ground, for worry and fretting are not compatible with the yielded life. *The peace of God* — the strong, deep calmness of faith which is born of the conviction that a loving Lord who knows the best has given the pressing burden and the sore pain — this tranquility of soul, *is the only proper antidote for worry!*

The story is told of J. Arthur Rank who had a practical way of handling his anxieties. Being unable to put his troubles aside completely, he thought the next best thing to do would be to set apart a single day, Wednesday, to do all his worrying. When something came up that disturbed him during the week, he wrote it down and put it in what he called his "Wednesday Worry Box." When the time came to review the problems that were of so much concern, he found to his great surprise that most of them had already been settled and no longer induced anxiety. He discovered that most worry is unnecessary and a waste of precious energy.

Cares indeed may come; but when they do, we must cast them upon the Lord (I Pet. 5:7). Then we may rightly relax, knowing that He will care for us and provide all things needful (Matt. 6:32, 33).   — H.G.B.

Let us shift from Grumble Corner,
There is room on Victory Street,
And though testing times may try us
Let us trust His promise sweet.
                    — M. Stott

"Worry is interest paid on trouble before it falls due."

THE PERFECT SQUELCH

READ ROMANS 3:9-20

> *. . . that every mouth may be stopped, and all the world*
> *may become guilty before God.*   Romans 3:19

A popular magazine regularly runs articles under the heading, "The Perfect Squelch." It consists of clever answers to silence all boasting, bragging, and sarcasm. Another name for "The Perfect Squelch" is also "The Last Word." A woman is always supposed to have the last word. A husband and wife drove along silently mile after mile. They had quarreled, and now both refused to speak for two solid, silent hours. Finally, they passed a field in which two jackasses were grazing. The husband could not resist the temptation to take a "dig" at his spouse. He sarcastically said to her, "Are those some of your relatives?" Quick as a flash she replied, "Yes, by marriage." His mouth was stopped.

Paul tells us in Romans 3 that God too has the last word. He proves in a masterly argument that all of us, everyone of us, have come short of the glory of God. If man would claim any righteousness before God, let him measure himself by God's perfect law. If man imagines that he can be saved by his own works, God points to the law and its requirement of perfect obedience, and closes every mouth. The Holy Spirit, using the pen of Paul, asserts: ". . . what things soever the law saith, it saith to them who are under the law: that every mouth may be stopped" (Rom. 3:19).

Israel tried to keep the law for one thousand years under the most salutary conditions and failed, thereby stopping the mouths of all men everywhere. God has the last word!

Now the message of the Gospel is this: "By grace are ye saved through faith . . . Not of works, lest any man should boast" (Eph. 2:8, 9).

— M.R.D.

> Now are we free — there's no condemnation,
>   Jesus provides a perfect salvation;
> "Come unto Me," O hear His sweet call,
>   Come and He saves us once for all.
>
> —P. P. Bliss

"The only One who could measure up to the perfect law was Christ; unless we are in Him by faith, we 'come short' of God's requirements for salvation."

THE GREAT CREATOR OUR HELPER

READ JOB 5:6-11

*I would seek unto God, and unto God would I commit
my cause: Which doeth great things and unsearchable;
marvellous things without number.*   Job 5:8, 9

It is comforting to know that the all-powerful Creator, whose
hand of wonder is marvelously displayed in all of nature, is the
same loving Heavenly Father who is equally mighty to help His
children in their times of need. With confidence, therefore, we
can rest our cause in His great, all-knowing care, assured that
the same wonders we see in nature will be matched by the
gracious blessings of His kindly providences. An unknown author
underlines this thought as follows:

"Consider the little bee that organizes a city, that builds 10,000
cells for honey, 12,000 cells for larvae, and, finally, a very special
cell for the mother queen; a little bee that observes the increasing heat and, when the wax may melt and the honey be lost,
organizes the swarm into squads, puts sentinels at the entrances,
glues the feet down, and then, with flying wings, creates a system
of ventilation to cool the honey that makes an electric fan seem
tawdry — a little honey bee that will include 20 square miles in
the field over whose flowers it has oversight. If a tiny brain in
a bee performs such wonders, who are you that you should question the guidance of God? Lift up your eyes and behold the
hand that supports the stars without pillars, the God who guides
the planets without collision — *He it is who cares for you!*"

Yes, this all-knowing, gracious God will "guide you with His
eye" and uphold you with His everlasting arms. Rest confidently
today in the center of His will.   — H.G.B.

I love to think that God appoints
  My portion day by day:
Events of life are in His hand,
  And I would only say,
"Appoint them in Thine own good time,
  And in Thine own best way."
                                        —Anon.

"The man who walks with God always gets to his destination."

GOOD CHURCH MEMBERS

READ ROMANS 15:1-13

Let every one of us please his neighbour for his good to edification.
Romans 15:2

The story is told about Phillips Brooks, the great preacher, who once asked the operator of a local livery stable for the best horse he had. Said Dr. Brooks, "I am taking my wife for a ride and I want the very best for the occasion." The livery man hitched up the buggy and led the horse out, and said, "Dr. Brooks, this animal is as perfect as a horse could be. It is kind, gentle, intelligent, well-trained, obedient, willing, responds instantly to your every command, never kicks, balks, or bites, and lives only to please its driver." The good doctor listened to it all and then whispered to the owner, "Do you suppose you could get that horse to join my church?"

Yes, what a powerful church we could have if all the things which were said of this dumb horse could be said about the average church member!

How prone we naturally all are to think only of our own desires and wishes and forget the good of others. Paul says in Romans 15:1, "We then that are strong ought to bear the infirmities of the weak, and not to please ourselves." The natural tendency is for the "strong to take advantage of the weak." The more we grow in grace, the more we think of others. In our church life we should not think of our own wishes, but be willing always to be the least and yield our desires for the good of the "whole." The Body is bigger than any one member and the Head is over the Body. And so our example should be Jesus, for even He "pleased not himself" (Rom. 15:3).

When you have conquered self, you have conquered all!

— M.R.D.

Spirit of grace, O deign to dwell
Within Thy Church below;
Make her in holiness excel,
With pure devotion glow.
—H. Auber

"Does your consistent, spiritual application of Hebrews 10:25 edify others? Remember, FLOATING church members make for a SINKING church!"

WHAT OF THE HARVEST?

READ II CORINTHIANS 9:5-10

> . . . *for whatsoever a man soweth, that shall he also reap.*
> Galatians 6:7

Lifetime is sowing time! Each of us by thought, word, and deed is constantly planting for future reaping! Some of the basic rules of sowing and reaping are: (1) Though the *seed* may be sown in *secret,* the *harvest cannot be concealed* but will be open for all to see. Sometimes the fruitage may not be completely viewed in this world, but a time is coming when every hidden and secret thing shall be revealed in the judgment (Rom. 2:16; and Luke 8:17). (2) There is always a time of *waiting* between the sowing and the reaping, but the harvest *never fails!* (3) The time of fruition will reveal the nature of the seed sown, for it will be of the *same kind!* (4) Finally, bear in mind that the *harvest will always be greater* than that which is sown!

Many years ago a wealthy man deeded all his property to an only son, and went to live with him and his wife. After a few years the daughter-in-law got tired of having the elderly gentleman around, and told her husband he would have to leave. Not willing or able to give the money back, the son broke the news to his father, now enfeebled by old age. A few days later the son walked with the old man down the road, over the hill, toward the poorhouse. Tired, the father asked to sit down, and finally began to weep. The son, pricked in his conscience, tried to make excuses. Finally, the elderly one controlled himself enough to say, "Son, I am not crying so much because I am going to this lonely home for unfortunates; but *I am crying because of my own sins.* Forty years ago I walked down this same road with *my* father and led him to this *same poorhouse.* I am reaping what I sowed!"

The Scripture clearly sets forth the truth that the unsaved can only "sow to the flesh." One must be *"born* of the Spirit" (John 3:5) before he can "*sow* to the Spirit" (Gal. 6:8). In your life — what shall the harvest be?
— H.G.B.

> Sown in the darkness or sown in the light,
> Sown in our weakness or sown in our might,
> Gathered in time or eternity,
> Sure, ah sure, will the harvest be!
> — E. S. Oakey

"Everybody sooner or later sits down to a banquet of consequences!"
— ROBERT L. STEVENSON

COASTING CHRISTIANS

READ EPHESIANS 4:17-29

. . . take thine ease, eat, drink, and be merry. Luke 12:19

Take it easy now, take it easy! This is the desire and dream of the natural man — to reach a place where he can retire from work and "take it easy." Instead of thanking God for the blessing of labor, man does everything in his power to avoid work. Although God has said, six days shalt thou labor, we have already cut it down to only five days and now the goal is four days a week. Man wants to "take it easy." The rich man in Luke 12, after he had filled his barns, said to himself, "Soul, thou hast much goods laid up . . . take thine ease." But God said unto him, "Thou fool."

There is no retirement for the Christian, such as the world desires. We must labor while it is today. The shorter days and shorter work-week should be an opportunity for the believer to do more spiritual work for the Lord. The world uses the extra leisure for idle pleasure and sinful indulgences. The Christian, however, should welcome the freedom from secular work as an opportunity of work for the Lord. Too many of us just waste our valuable leisure time and do nothing of an enduring nature.

A colored man went to a recruiting station to enlist. The officer in charge said, "What branch of the service do you prefer — the Infantry or the Cavalry? In the Infantry you walk, in the Cavalry you ride." The colored man thought a moment and said, "Please sir, if I may, I'd prefer the Coast Guard where I can just coast!"

Are you a coaster? Or are you a rider, hitch-hiking your way? Or do you walk at His command?   — M.R.D.

> Work, for the night is coming,
>   Work through the sunny noon;
> Fill brightest hours with labor,
>   Rest comes sure and soon.
> Give every flying minute,
>   Something to keep in store;
> Work, for the night is coming,
>   When man works no more.
>   —A. L. Coghill

"Coasting in life is easy for it follows the downward slope; to reach 'higher ground' you have to climb."

KEPT FOR SAFEKEEPING

READ I PETER 1:1-8

Who are kept by the power of God.   I Peter 1:5

A dying saint many years ago said during his last day on earth, "I am just like a package which has been all prepared for shipment to its destination. I am all packed, tied securely, labeled, postage paid, and standing on the platform, waiting for the express to come by and take me to my destination in Glory." All this is contained in the words, " . . . kept by the power of God . . . to be revealed in the last time." It suggests our security in Christ.

1. The believer is all wrapped up in the beautiful wrappings of Christ (II Cor. 5:21).

2. He is tied with cords of divine love (Hosea 11:4).

3. He is plainly labeled with the seal of the Spirit, "and the Lord knoweth them that are his" (II Tim. 2:19).

4. The postage is all paid by the precious blood of the Son of God, bought with a price (I Cor. 6:20).

5. He is resting on the platform of God's wonderful grace (Eph. 2:8).

6. He is waiting for the express of His glorious coming (Phil. 3:20, 21).

7. He is guarded all the way by angels of God (Luke 16:22).

8. He is guaranteed a safe arrival (John 10:28), registered (II Tim. 2:19), special delivery (Ps. 91:11, 12), and insured (Eph. 4:30).

"Beloved, now are we the sons of God, and it doth not yet appear what we shall be: but we know that, when he shall appear, we shall be like him; for we shall see him as he is" (I John 3:2).

Rejoice, O Christian!   — M.R.D.

He's coming back with glory rare,
    It won't be long, it may be soon;
We'll rise to meet Him in the air,
    It won't be long, it may be soon;
When He shall call me this I know:
    I'm saved and ready now to go,
I'm waiting with my heart aglow;
    It won't be long, it may be soon.
                                    —L. E. Bridges

"A true saint should not be completely earthbound; his thoughts and desires, like high-flying larks, should ever soar upward to Paradise."

LITTLE ACTS OF LOVE

READ I THESSALONIANS 4:1-10

> *. . . ye yourselves are taught of God to love one another.*
>
> I Thessalonians 4:9

True love reveals itself not so much in a great outward show of emotion, but rather in a thousand small acts of devotion and consideration. It is by these that we manifest our true colors and display our real attitudes.

When I was a little boy about three and a half years of age, I knew that my father was extremely fond of black walnuts. We did not often get them, so when I found one upon the street I was delighted! My first thought was to have my mother crack it so that I could eat it myself, but then my great love for father took over. I saved it until he came home that evening. It was my custom to wait until I saw him come around the corner and then — rush to meet him. I would throw my small arms around his one leg and thus, standing on his foot, would be swung along with his powerful stride until we got home. All the way he would be patting my head and smiling and talking to me. This night I presented him with the walnut and said, "Here, Papa, I've been saving it all day — just for you!" I thought it very strange that he did not want to crack it and eat it, and it was not until 30 years later that I found it again after he had left us for the heavenly mansions. It was in a place by itself in his desk. Mother told me he considered it such a deep token of my affection for him that he wanted to keep it as a memento.

Don't delay performing even the smallest act of love today; believe me, it is sorely needed and will be much appreciated. What is more, it will be richly rewarded by the Lord. Do not keep the alabaster boxes of your love and tenderness sealed up until your friends are dead. Fill their lives with sweetness now. By the power of the Holy Spirit, let us exchange our self-centered attitudes for heartfelt words and deeds which will manifest that we love the brethren "with a pure heart fervently"! (I Peter 1:22).

— H.G.B.

> Our God is love; and all His saints
> His image bear below:
> The heart with love to God inspired,
> With love to man will glow.
>
> —Anon.

"When God measures a man, He puts the tape around the heart — not the head!"

QUACK REMEDIES

READ ISAIAH 1:4-20

To what purpose is the multitude of your sacrifices unto me? saith the Lord . . .   Isaiah 1:11

The Prophet Isaiah compares the spiritual condition of Israel to that of a sick man, a leper, full of wounds and putrifying sores. (Have you read the Scripture at the head of this article?) The reason they were not cleansed was because they had tried to heal themselves by quackery, patent medicines, and nostrums. They had observed all the outward remedies of religion — vain oblations, incense, and the observance of rituals and ceremonies — but had refused God's remedy (see Isa. 1:12-15). Man will turn to God only as a last resort; he will try everything else first before he calls a competent physician. Man is a most gullible creature.

When I began practicing medicine over 45 years ago, I was amazed at the credulity of the average intelligent person. They would try everything before they would call me — often when it was too late. I could write a book on all the strange concoctions people used as home remedies — just because someone recommended it. Today, with all our scientific advance, men are still just as gullible. They believe every remedy friends recommend (and every friend has his infallible favorite). They believe every advertisement on radio or television (many of them lies). Billions of dollars are spent annually on worthless nostrums, cure-alls, diets (thousands of them), vitamins, minerals, salves, greases, and vibrators. The average medicine cabinet looks like a miniature drug store. Just look at those pills (four different kinds) right there beside your plate — right *now*. If people would eat normal, balanced diets, quit worrying about their health, go to bed on time, and be more concerned with their spiritual health than the physical — and throw away 95 per cent of those pills and gadgets, they would live longer and happier! An application to the sinner — abandon all your homemade remedies to make you fit for Heaven — and call upon the Great Physician — and be saved, happy, and free!   — M.R.D.

Have you been to Jesus for the cleansing pow'r?
Are you washed in the blood of the Lamb?
Are you fully trusting in His grace this hour?
Are you washed in the blood of the Lamb?
—E. A. Hoffman

"Sin is a disease that only a spiritual 'blood transfusion' can cure!"
—G. W.

OF PEARLS AND HUMAN HEARTS

READ I SAMUEL 16:1-13

> . . . *man looketh on the outward appearance, but the*
> *Lord looketh on the heart.*　　　　　I Samuel 16:7

For thousands of years genuine pearls commanded high prices. Great quantities of oysters were annually examined for their hidden treasure, but only a few contained pearls of real value. Within recent times, however, the market suddenly became flooded with these sparkling orbs, and merchants began to wonder if they were being deceived by skillful imitations. Examination revealed, however, that all the pearls were actually made by oysters. Finally the mystery was explained. It seemed that the Japanese merchants had found a way to cause almost *every* oyster to produce a bauble of loveliness. Knowing that a sharp foreign substance lodging in the tender flesh of the lowly oyster causes it to secrete a protective fluid which hardens around the source of the irritation to form a glistening pearl, the Japanese decided to personally insert *artificial irritants,* such as beads and tiny bits of buckshot. Then, carefully replacing the oysters in the ocean by means of nets, they waited until they knew the pearls had been formed, at which time they simply lifted the shells to the surface again and extracted their treasures. Wealthy patrons, becoming suspicious, insisted that the pearls be subjected to special tests to see whether they were natural or "cultured." Outwardly all were equally beautiful, but when X-rayed, some were shown to have large, *false hearts* of lead or glass, and as such were not "genuine."

So it is, too, with men. Many seem to be normally and ethically sound and even attend church faithfully; yet they have within their bosoms "false hearts." They may fool men, but they will never deceive the X-ray keen eyes of the Great Judge when He comes to "make up His jewels." God does not judge by *outward* appearances, as do men, but rather "looketh on the *heart*"*!*

Are you a "cultured" hypocrite, or a genuine pearl? "Blessed are the *pure* in *heart,* for they shall see God" (Matt. 5:8)! — H.G.B.

> Is there no more condemnation for sin?
> Is thy heart right with God?
> Does Jesus rule in the temple within?
> Is thy heart right with God?
> 　　　　　　　—E. A. Hoffman

"Our deepest self and the true condition of our heart is revealed by our attitude to the cross of Jesus." — J. G. MANTLE

THE BEST ADVERTISEMENT

READ II CORINTHIANS 3:1-6

> . . . *for of the abundance of the heart his mouth speaketh.*
> Luke 6:45

A man always advertises his own product and depreciates that of his competitors. I had a friend who sold Ford cars, and had a long list of the things in which the Ford was superior to the Chevrolet. Then he changed jobs and became a salesman for the "opposition." The transition was easy. All the objections he had previously made to the "Chevy" now applied to the Ford. Whatever a man sells is the best. Everybody's own baby is the prettiest. "*Sniffle* cold tablets" are three ways better than "*Snuffle* cold tablets." "Bluff it in" works three times faster than "Blast it in." Fraudulent advertising is the order of the day. The most fantastic claims are made for the worthless trash.

In spiritual matters this thing becomes serious, for we are not dealing here with the bodies of men, but with their souls — not with time but with eternity.

Every false religion makes its own claim of superiority, and thousands are deceived thereby. How then can we tell the true from the false? There are two tests: (1) Is it Scriptural? (2) Does it work? Test it first by the Word of God; and second, see how it works in those who advertise it. Does your faith show evidence of being genuine? Does it show itself in love, kindness, godliness, tolerance, and spirituality — or does it promote bigotry, criticism, intolerance, and self-righteousness?

A boy applied for a job, and asked the well-rounded, corpulent boss how much the wages were. The reply was, "Fifty dollars and board." The boy asked, "What kind of board?" The fat man answered, "Well, I eat it." The boy took one look at the man and said, "I'll take the job." Does your life speak well of the One you recommend to others? Remember, you are an epistle known and read of all men (II Cor. 3:2).　　　　— M.R.D.

> You talk about your business, your bonds and stocks and gold;
> And in all worldly matters you are so brave and bold;
> But why are you so silent about salvation's plan?
> Why don't you live for Jesus, and speak out like a man?
> —Anon.

"There are two parts in the Gospel; the first part is BELIEVING it and the second part is BEHAVING it."

A SILVER DOLLAR

READ MATTHEW 28:8-20

Go ye. . . .

Matthew 28:19

A handsome young preacher arose to give a brief testimony at the close of a hymnsing. "I should like to tell you a true story," he said. "Over thirty years ago a young man desired to attend a college located far from the farming community where he had been raised. The depression was on and money was very scarce. However, an elderly friend, knowing of his desire, handed him a silver dollar saying it was not much, but that he wanted to encourage him to go on into Christian service. The young man hesitated about taking the gift for he knew the old farmer was extremely poor, had one son in a sanitarium — dying of tuberculosis, and another who was seriously ill at home. As the Christian insisted, however, the student yielded. Soon, having gathered additional funds, he went off across the country to school. As he was a singer, he often assisted at mission stations in and around the college town. At one of the meetings he heard a speaker say, 'The Lord Jesus has commissioned all of us to go and preach the Gospel. *Each of us has a definite call to full-time service!* Only if we cannot go, or do not have sufficient talents, are we allowed to let others go in our place.' The young man felt even a greater urge toward the ministry than he had experienced when the silver dollar was given to him; but again he resisted the Spirit's wooing. Some time later his money ran out. Unless a miracle happened, he would have to leave college. Then the Lord spoke to him for the third time. Falling to his knees, he prayed most earnestly that he might continue his education — promising that if the funds were forthcoming, he would yield to the Spirit's call and become a minister. Within thirty-six hours the Lord answered that prayer, and now for many years that man has been preaching the Gospel." The speaker paused — then, pulling a large coin from his pocket, he said, *"Do you wonder that I cherish this silver dollar? It was really the beginning of God's special invitation to* ME *to enter into His service!"* Friend, the Lord Jesus is still saying today, "Go YE!" What is your answer?

— H.G.B.

Call me forth to active service,
And my prompt response shall be,
"I am ready, Lord, to follow,
Here am I! Send me, SEND ME!"

—E. A. H.

"Have your tools ready, and God will find you work!"

QUALITY – NOT QUANTITY

READ JUDGES 7:1-6

. . . The people are yet too many . . . .   Judges 7:4

This is the age of numbers. Everything is measured by size. If a thing is big it must be good, and if it is small no one pays attention to it. When a thing is large everyone wants to get on the bandwagon, but if it is small everyone ignores it. If we can boast of the huge crowds and hundreds of conversions(?) we are successful; but if we have to labor in a small, obscure place – then, well, we just feel sorry for you. But there is no precedent for any such sentiment in the Bible. God is not nearly as interested in *quantity* as in *quality*. Gideon had 32,000 men ready for battle but God told him he had too many, that he would have to get rid of most of them. Gideon reduced the number to 10,000 and the Lord said, "The people are yet too many." I want *quality* not *quantity!* Gideon ended up with 300 and God gave the victory.

Now have you ever asked the question, "Why did God refuse to use the 32,000? Why did He turn thumbs down on the 10,000? Why did He pare the army down to 300?" The Bible gives the answer: "The people that are with thee are too many . . . *lest Israel vaunt themselves against me,* saying, *Mine own hand hath saved me*" (Judges 7:2). Notice the reason, *"lest Israel vaunt themselves."* If they had defeated the enemy with the 32,000 or even the 10,000 *they would have taken the credit.* But when only 300 overcame an army of tens of thousands, they had to admit it was the Lord. In the work of the Lord the flesh must have no reason to boast. How often we detect the "proud flesh" in the exaggerated reports of *numbers,* and forget that *one* that is *counted by God* is more important than the hundreds counted by men. Jesus did His work with only 70 disciples, and the early church with a small number of despised witnesses turned the world upside down. Today, religion is popular. More church members than ever before in history, but – *No victory! We need quality!* The church would be stronger in spirit if we were weaker in the flesh.   – M.R.D.

> The corn of wheat to multiply
>   Must fall into the earth and die;
> So death to "self" and "flesh" we see
>   Brings blessing, and vict'ry, and QUALITY!
>   –G. W.

"The fewer apples on a tree – the bigger they are. Ask any orchardist!" – M. R. D.

MEETING ON THE STAIRS!

READ SONG OF SOLOMON 2:8-17

O my dove, that are in the clefts of the rock, in the secret places of the stairs, let me see thy countenance, let me hear thy voice. . . .   Song of Solomon 2:14

The Song of Solomon is a love story which typifies Christ and His Church. The "dove" in verse 14 represents the saved soul made "blameless and harmless in Him" (Phil. 2:15). She is in a place of safety for she is hidden in Christ the Rock, "cleft" for her at Calvary. The "secret" of the stairs has reference to the access and fellowship she may enjoy with Him in intimate, spiritual communion. Standing face to face with her Beloved in prayer, she may tell Him all that is in her heart, knowing that He loves to hear her voice and will surely sympathize with her need! Yes, there is joy, blessing, and victory in the "secret place" of intercession.

Individuals who accomplish much for the Saviour are frequently found on their knees. John Wesley, Samuel Rutherford, Martin Luther, David Brainerd, and many others — all shining lights for God — were devout Christians who often found time to ascend the golden stairs of prayer!

A British soldier, caught creeping stealthily back to his quarters one night from a nearby woods, was taken before his commanding officer and charged with holding communications with the enemy. He pleaded innocent and said that he had just gone in the woods to pray. "Have you been in the habit of spending hours in private prayer?" the officer growled. "Yes, sir!" "Then get down on your knees and pray now!" his superior roared. "Believe me, you've never needed it so much!" Expecting court-martial and death, the soldier knelt and poured out his soul with an eloquence and a familiarity with the Saviour that showed the power of the Holy Spirit in his life. When he had finished, the officer said simply, "You may go, friend, I believe your story! If you hadn't been often at *drill,* you wouldn't have done so well at *review!"*

Beloved, do not disappoint Him who is waiting to meet *you* "in the secret places of the stairs."   — H.G.B.

> Praise His blessed Name forever!
> There is nought that can compare
> To the glories of a contact
> With the Prince of Peace—through prayer!
>   —Anon.

"We are never so high as when we are on our knees!"

WHAT'S IN A NAME?

READ MATTHEW 1:18-25

. . . a name which is above every name. Philippians 2:9

WHAT'S IN A NAME? By common proverb we have been made to believe that the names we give our children are unimportant; but many a child is handicapped throughout its life by some fantastic name it was given just to satisfy the whim of its parents to be different. There is no good reason to call your child Adoni-Bezek, or Tiglath-Pilezer. So to help you to give your child a good name, we turn to the great Bible example. Before Christ was born, the mother of Jesus was told exactly what to call him. The angel said, "Call his name Jesus." This should suggest a pattern for us. Notice some things about this lovely Name.

1. It is an *easy* Name. It is pronounced almost the same in every language. It has only two syllables and a child can be taught it as easily as the word "mama."

2. It is a *beautiful* Name. Beautiful because of its association with a beautiful person. Some names are repulsive and arouse disgust because of whom they suggest. Such names are Nero, Judas, and Hitler.

3. It is a *comforting* Name, for it means: "God is our Saviour." It is the only name under heaven whereby we can, and must, be saved.

4. It is a *mighty* Name. At that name the demons tremble. Some day every knee shall bow and every tongue confess that "Jesus is Lord."

5. It is an *enduring* Name. Born in obscurity 1900 years ago, dying like a criminal at the age of only 33 — He has the most well-known name in the world.

6. It is the *best* Name. Our Saviour has many, many names but the name of Jesus is above them all.

Whatever the name we may bear here upon the earth, when Jesus comes we shall forever have written upon our foreheads the name *Jesus.* For "they shall see his face; and his name shall be in their foreheads" (Rev. 22:4).   — M.R.D.

> Nor voice can sing, nor heart can frame,
>   Nor can the memory find
> A sweeter sound than Thy blest Name,
>   O Saviour of mankind!
>   —Bernard of Clairvaux

"Jesus was born to die, died to save, lives to bless, and will come to reign — what a wonderful Person; what a worthy Name!"

THE INCREASE OF FAITH

READ HEBREWS 11:1-10

And the apostles said unto the Lord, Increase our faith.
Luke 17:5

Years ago, when plans were being made to build a great suspension bridge over Niagara Falls, the problem arose of getting the huge iron cables across the roaring cataract. The engineers finally solved the problem by use of a kite. Attaching a slender thread to it they managed to fly it across to the other shore. By means of the thread they drew a cord, by the cord a rope, and by that rope a larger rope, and finally the immense cables necessary to sustain and bear across the rapids the heavy steel materials needed to form the bridge.

In the same manner we are to use our small faith as a means of gaining more, until the slender thread of our trust has become a veritable bridge of faith and conviction.

Moody said that for years he prayed for an increase in his faith *with a closed Bible.* Then one day God directed his hand to open his Testament to the words in Romans 10:17. He was startled to read, "So then faith cometh by hearing, and *hearing by the word of God.*" Moody thought to himself, "Here I have been praying for an increase in my faith with a closed Bible, but this Scripture tells me that I can only obtain such a growth in grace with an open one!" From that day forward he studied the Scriptures earnestly, at the same time asking God for an increase in his spiritual power and trust. "From then on," said Moody, *"my faith grew by leaps and bounds!"*
— H.G.B.

God, give me the faith of a little child!
Who trusts so implicitly.
Who simply and gladly believes Thy Word,
And never would question Thee.
—G. W. Showerman

"Feed your faith, and your doubts will starve to death."

GOSSIPS AND TALEBEARERS

READ JAMES 3:5-10

*Thou shalt not go up and down as a talebearer among
thy people.* Leviticus 19:16

Backbiting and talebearing were considered cardinal sins by
the early Methodists as put down in John Wesley's "Six Points of
Methodism" written in his own handwriting. They are:

1. That we will not listen to or inquire after any ill concerning
each other.

2. That, if we hear any ill concerning each other, we will not
be forward (not in a hurry) to believe it.

3. That as soon as possible we will communicate what we
hear, by speaking to or writing to the person concerned.

4. That until we have done this we will not write or speak a
syllable of it to any other person whatsoever.

5. That neither will we mention it, after we have done this,
to any other person whatsoever.

6. That we will make no exceptions to these rules, unless we
think ourselves absolutely obliged in conscience to do so.

This covenant was signed by John Wesley, Charles Wesley,
John Lunbeth, E. Perronet, Jonathan Reeves, and Joseph
Cownley.

Proverbs 16:27 says, "An ungodly man diggeth up evil: and
in his lips there is as a burning fire."

A woman who had earned her living for more than forty years
by going about the neighborhood doing the washing for people,
was asked how it was she was so well-liked by everyone for
whom she worked. She replied, "I make it a practice never to
say in one house what I hear in another." Long ago God had
said, "Thou shalt not go up and down as a talebearer among
thy people." — M.R.D.

Cover my eyes and make me blind
    To the petty faults I should not find;
Open my eyes and let me see
    The friend my neighbor tries to be.
Help me to guard my tongue with care,
    When prone to gossip — breathe a prayer.
Let me at even rest content
    That for the Lord my day was spent.
—Anon.

**"A bridle for the tongue is an excellent piece of harness, for silence
cannot be misquoted."**

December 28

THE LAST ENEMY

READ HEBREWS 2:9-15

The last enemy that shall be destroyed is death.

I Corinthians 15:26

Death is the last enemy that will be vanquished. Potentially, redemption in all its fullness already belongs to the Christian; but actually, experientially, it is not yet completely extended to his body. When faith is weak, therefore, even saints become disturbed when they think of the pain and distress associated with dying. They do not dread what lies beyond, but they do fear the grim visage of death itself.

To Christians who are troubled about death, I would give a word of comfort. Remember first, that *God does not usually give dying grace until the very moment when it is needed.* Secondly, *you may be among those who will be instantly glorified* at the Saviour's coming — therefore God may not now be giving you grace for that which you will never experience! Be sure of this, however, if you are trusting the Saviour and the mystic hour comes, you will most certainly know His comfort, for yielded souls find Home-going a time of triumph and calm blessedness!

I remember one young man who, although a fine Christian, greatly feared "dying." However, when he did leave this earthly scene it was in his sleep, and then so peacefully that those about him did not even realize that he had passed away. The terrible death struggle he had anticipated never came. His sister remarked very aptly, "I believe that the Saviour, knowing how much George feared physical death, took him quietly in his sleep. No doubt while he was lying there so restfully, he suddenly heard the Lord say to him, 'Come on Home, George, there is nothing to fear, death is only a shadow — I will go with you through the valley.' And so, I believe he walked calmly, hand-in-hand with Jesus, until he came to the Father's many mansions!"

How comforting and true the words of the old hymn which exults, "Best of all, best of all, *He'll go with me when I'm dying; that to me is best of all!*"

— H.G.B.

Lord, when I shall take my final breath
And see Thee face to face in death;
Then shall my heart forever sing
The heavenly praises of my King.
—F. O. Raniville

"If the way to Heaven is narrow, it is not long; and if the gate be straight, it opens into endless life."

SELLING THE GOSPEL

READ JOHN 4:6-14, 29, 30

> *And many of the Samaritans of that city believed on him for the saying of the woman, which testified, He told me all that ever I did.* John 4:39

The woman of Samaria was a good saleswoman. So enthusiastically had been her recommendation of Jesus that many came to see Him and believed because of her convincing testimony. Every Christian should likewise be a salesman. Men do not naturally want salvation — they must be sold by others who themselves are "sold on it." We must present Christ in an appealing, attractive way, with an enthusiasm which will result in others wanting it. It is no different from selling produce.

Two farm wagons stood in a public market, both loaded with potatoes. A housewife stopped beside the first wagon and asked, "How much are your potatoes today?" "A dollar and a quarter a bag," replied the farmer. "Oh, my!" protested the woman. "That's pretty high, isn't it? I gave only a dollar last time." "Taters have gone up," grunted the farmer, and turned aside. At the next wagon, the housewife asked the same question, but Ma McGuire "knew her potatoes," as the saying goes. She spoke with enthusiasm. "These are especially fine white potatoes, ma'am. We raise only the kind with small eyes so there will be no waste in peeling. Then we sort 'em by sizes. In each bag you'll find a large size for boiling and cutting up, and a smaller size for baking. The baking size cooks quickly and uniformly, which means a big saving in gas. These potatoes are clean, too," the woman continued, "you could put a bag in the parlor without soiling your carpet — you don't pay for a lot of dirt! They're a good buy at a dollar and sixty-five cents. Shall I have them put in your car?" The woman who thought the first farmer's potatoes were too expensive bought two bags from Ma McGuire at a higher price. All of which proves that it is more important to establish a value than to quote a price. Go thou and do likewise — be a good salesman for the Lord. — M.R.D.

It was not the truth you taught,
  To you so clear, to me so dim,
But, when you came to me, you brought
  A deeper sense of Him!
—Anon.

"Be sure the goods on display in your window — represent exactly the product on the counter." — M. R. D.

EAT THE WORDS

READ JOSHUA 1:1-9

*Thy words were found, and I did eat them; and thy
word was unto me the joy and rejoicing of mine heart.*
Jeremiah 15:16

Have you ever been forced to "eat your own words"? It is a
very humiliating experience to admit we were all wrong and
have to "eat crow."

There are other words, however, which have exactly the opposite effect when they are eaten. It is the Word of God which
when eaten and appropriated becomes "unto me the joy and rejoicing of my heart." Do you ever pray for a greater love for
this Word? for a better understanding of the Bible? for a greater
knowledge of the Scriptures? Before reading or studying the
Bible, take time to ask God to illumine your understanding and
see how much more you will get out of it. James says, "Ye have
not, because ye ask not." To get the most out of your Bible
reading — eat it with plenty of prayer.

Jeremiah said, "Thy words were found, and I did eat them."
But if you really want to get the maximum benefit, then in addi-
tion to studying it — and praying about it — begin to practice it.
If you first learn it — then practice it — you will never forget it.

In our chemistry class in college we were taught that a piece
of metallic sodium when placed in water would generate hydrogen so fast that the heat produced caused it to burst into flame.
We read this in a book and probably would have forgotten all
about it, except for one thing. We were told to go to the labora-
tory and try it. A small piece of sodium was dropped in a dish
of water. It sizzled, popped, danced and spiraled — and then —
poof, it burst into flame. It worked — I never forgot it. Put your
knowledge of the Word to work. Practice it and you'll never
forget it.

— M.R.D.

Our watchword in life's battle,
    Our chart on life's dark sea,
The precious Holy Bible,
    Shall e'er our teacher be.
— E. P. Hood

**"The man who only samples the Word of God occasionally never
acquires a keen taste for it."**

WISE DISCERNERS OF TIME

READ ECCLESIASTES 8:1-7

> . . . *a wise man's heart discerneth both time and judgment.*
> Ecclesiastes 8:5

It is said that the great cathedral of Milan has a beautiful triple-doored entrance. All three doorways are crowned by splendid arches, artistically carved with thought-provoking inscriptions. Over one is a wreath of roses etched in stone with the legend: "All that which pleases is but for a moment." Over another is sculptured a cross accompanied by the words: "All that which troubles is but for a moment." On the largest doorway of all, however — the great central entrance to the main circle — there is this most telling of all the inscriptions: "That only is important which is *eternal!*" Indeed, as life moves inexorably onward there will come both passing pleasures and bruising sorrows. Only the spiritually wise recognize that all these experiences must be trustfully woven together so that the texture of life which results is well pleasing to God and worthy of being exhibited in His eternal "Gallery of Rewards."

Harleigh M. Rosenberger has written most poetically, "Life is like a fine piece of Oriental tapestry, put together with many exquisite strands. It has the gold of success, the crimson of suffering, and the somber hues of sorrow. Through the grace of God, all of these are made into a pattern of beauty. Through every experience, God can help the person weave a fabric of loveliness and wisdom."

The year ahead is untried — it is a beckoning tomorrow fraught with new experiences and possibilities. The wise in heart will enter it with faith, hope, and Scriptural optimism, determine to take advantage of every God-given opportunity. — H.G.B.

> But once I pass this way, and then — and then,
>   The silent door swings on its hinges — opens — closes —
> And no more I pass this way.
>   So while I may, with all my might,
> I will assay sweet comfort and delight
>   To all I meet upon the Pilgrim Way,
> For no man travels twice the Great Highway
>   That climbs through darkness up to light,
> Through night — to day!
> —John Oxenham

"It is comforting to know that the God who guides us, sees tomorrow more clearly than we see yesterday!"

TOPICAL INDEX

SCRIPTURAL INDEX